Additional Science

FOR **AQA**

David Glover **Jean Martin** Helen Norris

CAMBRIDGE
UNIVERSITY PRESS

CAMBRIDGE UNIVERSITY PRESS
Cambridge, New York, Melbourne, Madrid, Cape Town, Singapore, São Paulo

Cambridge University Press
The Edinburgh Building, Cambridge CB2 2RU, UK

www.cambridge.org
Information on this title: www.cambridge.org/9780521686747
© Cambridge University Press 1997, 2001, 2006

First published 1997
Second edition 2001
Third edition 2006

Printed in Dubai by Oriental Press
Cover and text design by Blue Pig Design Ltd
Page layout by Kamae Design, Oxford

A catalogue record for this publication is available from the British Library

ISBN-13   978-0-521-68674-7 paperback
ISBN-10   0-521-68674-1 paperback

Chemistry

Physics

■ An introduction for students and their teachers

This book is divided into Biology, Chemistry and Physics.
Within each subject, you will find three different types of material

- ■ boxes containing ideas from your studies of Science at Key Stage 3
- ■ scientific ideas that all Key Stage 4 students need to know
- ■ information to help you understand How Science Works.

■ Ideas from your studies at Key Stage 3

You need to understand these ideas before you start on the new science for Key Stage 4.
But you will <u>not</u> be assessed <u>directly</u> on these Key Stage 3 ideas in GCSE examinations.

Some ideas will take a whole page like this.

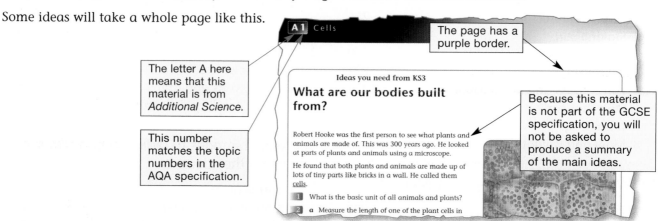

The page has a purple border.

The letter A here means that this material is from *Additional Science.*

This number matches the topic numbers in the AQA specification.

Because this material is not part of the GCSE specification, you will not be asked to produce a summary of the main ideas.

A1 Cells

Ideas you need from KS3

What are our bodies built from?

Robert Hooke was the first person to see what plants and animals are made of. This was 300 years ago. He looked at parts of plants and animals using a microscope.

He found that both plants and animals are made up of lots of tiny parts like bricks in a wall. He called them <u>cells</u>.

1 What is the basic unit of all animals and plants?

2 a Measure the length of one of the plant cells in

Some ideas will not take up a whole page. They are shown in a purple box like this. In such cases, the Key Stage 3 material is included in a box, usually at the start of the Key Stage 4 topic.

> **REMEMBER FROM KS3**
>
> - ■ Plants make glucose.
> - ■ Then they change some of this glucose into starch.

■ Scientific ideas that Key Stage 4 students need to know

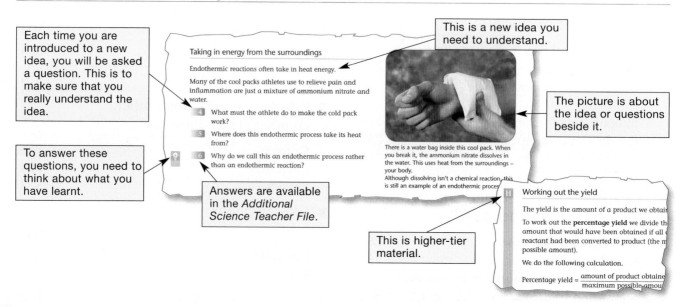

Each time you are introduced to a new idea, you will be asked a question. This is to make sure that you really understand the idea.

To answer these questions, you need to think about what you have learnt.

Taking in energy from the surroundings

Endothermic reactions often take in heat energy.

Many of the cool packs athletes use to relieve pain and inflammation are just a mixture of ammonium nitrate and water.

4 What must the athlete do to make the cold pack work?

5 Where does this endothermic process take its heat from?

6 Why do we call this an endothermic process rather than an endothermic reaction?

Answers are available in the *Additional Science Teacher File.*

This is a new idea you need to understand.

There is a water bag inside this cool pack. When you break it, the ammonium nitrate dissolves in the water. This uses heat from the surroundings – your body.
Although dissolving isn't a chemical reaction, this is still an example of an endothermic proces

The picture is about the idea or questions beside it.

This is higher-tier material.

H Working out the yield

The yield is the amount of a product we obtain

To work out the **percentage yield** we divide th amount that would have been obtained if all reactant had been converted to product (the m possible amount).

We do the following calculation.

Percentage yield = $\dfrac{\text{amount of product obtaine}}{\text{maximum possible amou}}$

You should keep answers to <u>What you need to remember</u> sections in a separate place.
They contain all the ideas you are expected to remember and understand in examinations.
So they are very useful for revision.

It is very important that these summaries are correct.
You should always check your summaries against those provided on pages 316–332 of this book.

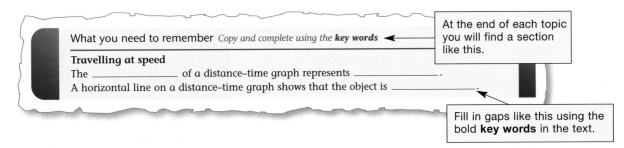

What you need to remember *Copy and complete using the* **key words**

Travelling at speed
The _____ of a distance–time graph represents _____.
A horizontal line on a distance–time graph shows that the object is _____.

At the end of each topic you will find a section like this.

Fill in gaps like this using the bold **key words** in the text.

■ Helping you to understand How Science Works

Some pages have information about how science works as well as the ideas that you need to learn.
They end with <u>What you need to remember</u> boxes like the one above.

Others are about how science and scientists work or let you practise scientific skills by answering different types of questions. They end with a different <u>What you need to remember</u> section.

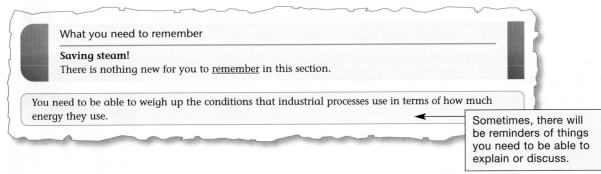

What you need to remember

Saving steam!
There is nothing new for you to <u>remember</u> in this section.

You need to be able to weigh up the conditions that industrial processes use in terms of how much energy they use.

Sometimes, there will be reminders of things you need to be able to explain or discuss.

Pages 294–305 also help you with How Science Works.

■ The back of this book

In the back of this book, you will find

- a section about How Science Works and handling data
- a section on revising for exams and answering exam questions
- a chemical data sheet
- a page about writing balanced symbol equations
- a page about working out the formula of an ionic compound
- a page about the mole
- a periodic table
- two pages of important physics formulae
- completed <u>What you need to remember</u> boxes
- a glossary of important scientific words.

■ CDs in the Science Foundations series

This book is accompanied by an *Additional Science Teacher File CD* containing adaptable planning and activity sheet resources. There are also accompanying Additional Science CDs of interactive e-learning resources including animations and activities for whole class teaching or independent learning, depending on your needs. The Science specification is supported in a similar way.

Ideas you need from KS3

What are our bodies built from?

Robert Hooke was the first person to see what plants and animals are made of. This was 300 years ago. He looked at parts of plants and animals using a microscope.

He found that both plants and animals are made up of lots of tiny parts like bricks in a wall. He called them <u>cells</u>.

1 What is the basic unit of all animals and plants?

2 **a** Measure the length of one of the plant cells in the picture.
b How long is the plant cell in real life?

3 Why do we need a microscope to see cells?

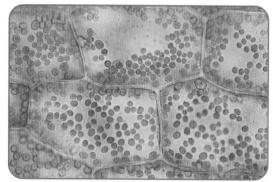

Photograph of plant leaf cells taken through a microscope. They are magnified 350 times.

Tissues

A tissue is a group of cells with the same shape and job. Different tissues do different jobs.

Muscle cells group together to form muscular tissue.

4 What does muscular tissue do?

5 What type of cells make up muscular tissue?

Muscle cells can contract, or get shorter. As a muscle gets shorter, it causes movement or a change of shape.

6 How does muscular tissue move food down the gullet to the stomach?

This athlete is using muscular tissue to move her body.

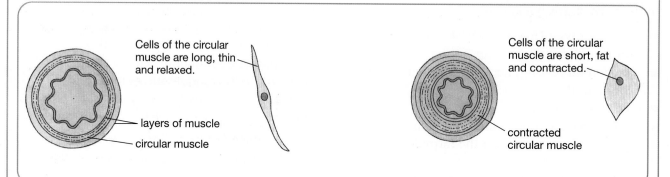

Cells of the circular muscle are long, thin and relaxed.

layers of muscle
circular muscle

Cells of the circular muscle are short, fat and contracted.

contracted circular muscle

When the circular muscles contract, they move the food along the gullet.

Other tissues have different jobs

Muscle cells are shaped so that the tissue can do its job. Other tissues in the body have different jobs, so their cells are different shapes.

7 Look at the picture.
Draw the shapes of a muscle cell and a gland cell from the stomach. Remember to label them.

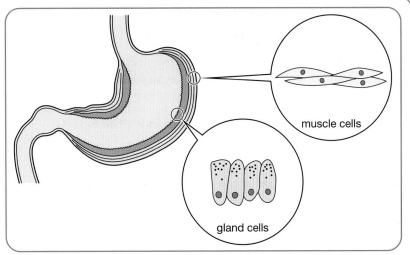

The stomach is one of the organs of the digestive system. It contains glandular and muscular tissue.

Some of the organs in the digestive system contain glandular tissue. This makes digestive juices, which help to break down food. Other glandular tissues in the body make other useful juices. For example, sweat glands make sweat.

8 Copy and complete the sentence.

In the stomach, _____ tissue churns the food and mixes it with _____ juices made by the _____ tissue.

Organs and organ systems

Different tissues join together to make an organ. Several organs work together in an organ system. Each organ system in the body does particular jobs.

9 List <u>six</u> organs in the digestive system.

10 What are the jobs of the digestive system?

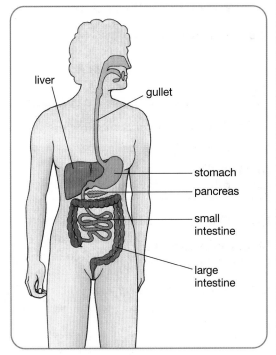

The human digestive system breaks down and absorbs food.

REMEMBER

You need to be able to relate the structure of <u>more</u> types of cells to their jobs in a tissue or an organ in the way that you did on these pages.

1 What are cells like?

Your body is made of billions of cells. Larger organisms like humans have more cells than smaller organisms like ants. Some organisms have only one cell.

Most animal cells, including human cells, have these parts

- a **nucleus** which controls everything that happens in the cell
- **cytoplasm** where most of the cell's chemical reactions happen
- a cell **membrane** to control which substances pass in and out of the cell, and also holds the cell together
- **mitochondria** that release energy in respiration
- **ribosomes** for making proteins (protein synthesis), including the **enzymes** that make chemical reactions happen in cells.

1 Draw a table with these headings.

Cell part	What it does

Complete the table to show the <u>five</u> cell parts shown.

A human white blood cell.

Some cells look different

Cells may be different shapes and sizes but they still have a nucleus, cytoplasm and cell membrane. They may also have other parts that are needed to do their jobs.
We say that the cells are specialised to do their jobs.

2 How is a red blood cell specialised to do its job?

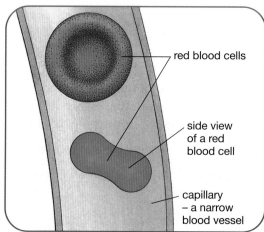

Red blood cells are unusual because their nuclei disappear when they are fully formed. These cells are full of a substance called haemoglobin that can join with oxygen. This means they can carry oxygen around the body. They release it in parts of the body that have a low oxygen concentration.

Some cells are very long

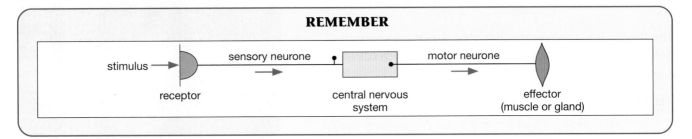
Nerve cells have to carry impulses between the central nervous system and other parts of the body.

3 How is a nerve cell specialised to do its job?

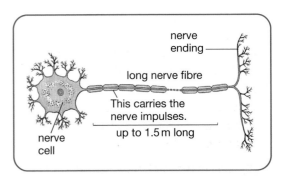

Cells that line the oviducts have hairs

Egg cells are released from an ovary and travel down an oviduct to the womb. Each oviduct is lined with special cells.

These cells have tiny hairs which move forwards and backwards.

4 Make a large copy of cell X. Label the nucleus, cytoplasm and cell membrane.

5 Why do the cells lining an oviduct have tiny hairs on their surface?

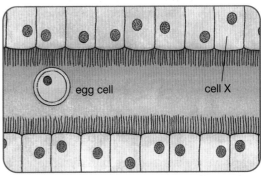

Inside an oviduct.

What you need to remember *Copy and complete using the* **key words**

What are cells like?
Most human cells are made up of the same basic parts.
Cells have a _____ which controls everything that happens in the cell.
It is the cell _____ that controls the passage of substances in and out of the cell.
Most of the chemical reactions in a cell take place in the _____.
For example, most energy release in respiration happens in _____ and protein synthesis happens in _____ in the cytoplasm.
These and other chemical reactions in cells are controlled by _____.

You need to be able to use your skills and knowledge to match specialised cells to the jobs that they do in tissues and organs or the whole organism.

2 How are plants built?

The first cells ever seen are shown in the drawing on the right. Robert Hooke drew them more than 300 years ago.

1 Why do you think he called them cells?

2 Draw a line 1 centimetre (cm) long. About 400 plant cells will fit along this line. Now use a sharp pencil to mark off each millimetre along your line. How many cells will fit into a space of 1 mm?

We know now that all plants are made up of cells.

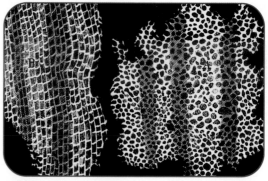

Cells from a cork oak tree.

These little spaces that bees make for their young and for storing honey are called cells.

Do all cells look the same?

Some things are the same in all cells, but other things are different. Look at the plant cells and the animal cell.

3 Write down <u>three</u> parts you can see in both types of cell.

4 Which part can you see in all three of the plant cells but not in the animal cell?

5 Write down the <u>two</u> parts you can see in some, but not all, of the plant cells.

All plant cells have cell walls made of cellulose.
This makes the cells **stronger** and more rigid.
The permanent spaces in plant cells, called **vacuoles**, are filled with a watery fluid called cell **sap**.

6 Make a large, labelled copy of the plant cell with chloroplasts. Draw some mitochondria and ribosomes in the cytoplasm. Remember to label them.

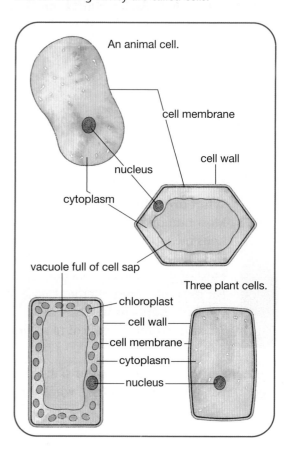

An animal cell.

cell membrane

cell wall

nucleus

cytoplasm

vacuole full of cell sap

Three plant cells.

chloroplast

cell wall

cell membrane

cytoplasm

nucleus

Why don't all plant cells have chloroplasts?

Chloroplasts contain chlorophyll. This is what gives plants their green colour. Chlorophyll absorbs light energy so that plants can make food. Chlorophyll is made only in the light. After a few weeks in the dark, it disappears from the cells.

Look at the pictures of the lawn.

7   **a**   What happens to the grass under the tent?
      b   Why does this happen?

8   Root cells do not have chloroplasts. Why not?

before

after

9   Look at the picture of a section cut through a stem of a plant. Only the outer layer is green.
Why isn't it green in the middle?

Potatoes are the underground stems of potato plants. They grow under the ground so they are not green, but they go green in the light.

- The bad news: the green parts of potatoes are poisonous.
- The good news: you would have to eat a lot to make you ill.

10   How should you store potatoes so they don't go green?

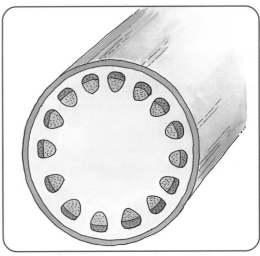

A slice across a stem.

What you need to remember *Copy and complete using the **key words***

How are plants built?
Plant cells have cell walls to make them _____.
They often have permanent spaces called _____. These are filled with a liquid called cell _____.
Some plant cells have _____ to absorb the light energy that plants use to make food.

3 The cell for the job!

All plants are made from tiny parts called cells. But not all plant cells are the same. You can see this if you cut a slice through part of a plant.

1 You would need to look at the slice under a microscope. Why is this?

Different jobs in a plant are done by different kinds of cells. A group of cells with the same shape and job is called a tissue.

2 Write down <u>three</u> kinds of tissue shown in the leaf section.

3 What job does a leaf do?

4 Which of the tissues can make food?
Give a reason for your answer.

5 In which part of a leaf is most of the food made?

The leaves, stems and roots of plants are called organs. Organs are made of more than one kind of tissue.

> **REMEMBER**
> Only plant cells which have chloroplasts can use light energy to make food.

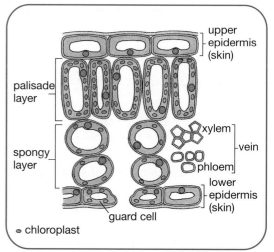

A slice across a leaf.

Why do leaves have veins?

Plants use veins to transport substances. Veins are made of two main kinds of tissue. The first is called xylem tissue. (You say this word 'zy-lem'.)

In xylem tissue, there are rows of dead cells with the ends missing. They form a long tube like a drinking straw. Water travels up xylem tissue from the roots.

Look at the drawing of xylem tissue.

6 What else besides water travels from the roots to the stems and leaves through the xylem tissue?

7 Xylem tissue also does another job.
What do you think this job is?

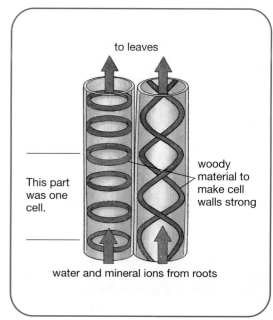

Xylem vessels are made of dead cells.
The pattern of woody material varies.

The second kind of tissue is called phloem.
(You say this word 'flo-em'.)

Look at the drawing of phloem tissue.

8 Write down <u>two</u> differences between xylem and phloem tissue.

Phloem carries sugar from where it is made to other parts of the plant.

9 **a** Which part of a plant does phloem carry sugar from?

b Where does phloem carry sugar to?

sugar from leaves

cytoplasm
end wall like a sieve
nucleus

sugar to storage organs and growing regions

Phloem tissue is made of living cells.

Where are the transport tissues?

10 Copy the drawings of slices of a root and a stem.
Then colour in the tissue which transports water.
Use a different colour for the tissue which carries sugar.
Add a key to show what your colours mean.

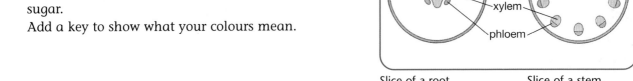

epidermis (skin)

xylem

phloem

Slice of a root.   Slice of a stem.

What other kinds of plant cells are there?

Other plant cells do other jobs. We say that they are specialised to do particular jobs.

11 What do you think each of the cells on the right is specialised to do?
Choose from:

■ support
■ storage
■ making new cells
■ photosynthesis (making food).

Give a reason for each answer.

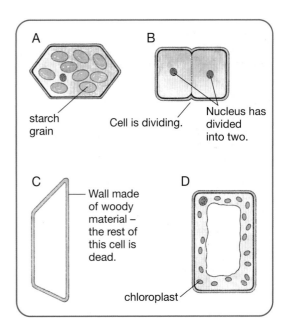

A   B

starch grain   Cell is dividing.

Nucleus has divided into two.

C   D

Wall made of woody material – the rest of this cell is dead.

chloroplast

You need to be able to look at a cell and work out its job like you did in question 11.

1 How substances get into and out of cells

To grow and to do their jobs, all living cells need water and other materials. Gases and nutrients pass into and out of cells in solution.

1 Which gas do all cells need for respiration?

2 Write down <u>one</u> gas that all cells have to get rid of at times.

Exchanges happen between

- cells
- cells and body fluids
- cells and the environment.

To get in and out of cells, water and dissolved substances have to cross **cell membranes**.

> **REMEMBER**
> Cells need to exchange water, nutrients, **oxygen** and carbon dioxide with the cells next to them and with the surroundings.

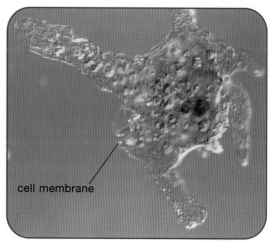

cell membrane

Oxygen passes into this single-celled organism from the water through the cell membrane. Carbon dioxide passes out of the cell.

Movement of molecules

Molecules in liquids and gases move in all directions. So they spread out.

Suppose that the concentration of a substance such as oxygen is higher in the water than inside a cell. More molecules of oxygen will be moving towards the cell than away from it.

3 Copy and complete.

Oxygen gets into the cell because there is:

⎯⎯⎯⎯⎯⎯ ⟶ ⎯⎯⎯⎯⎯⎯

concentration of   ⎯⎯⎯⎯⎯⎯   concentration of

oxygen in   oxygen in

⎯⎯⎯⎯⎯⎯   ⎯⎯⎯⎯⎯⎯

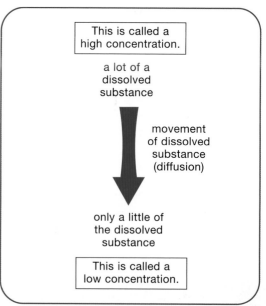

This is called a high concentration.

a lot of a dissolved substance

movement of dissolved substance (diffusion)

only a little of the dissolved substance

This is called a low concentration.

A big difference in **concentration** means faster **diffusion**.

More about diffusion

Like all animals, you exchange oxygen and carbon dioxide with the environment. This happens in the air sacs in your lungs.

You also exchange these gases between your body cells and your blood.

Look at the diagram.

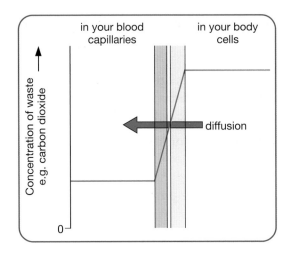

4   a Is the concentration of carbon dioxide higher in your body cells or in your blood?

b In which direction does carbon dioxide diffuse?

Remember that **dissolved** particles move in all directions. Look at the diagram. There are more particles of carbon dioxide in the more concentrated solution. So more move from the cells into the blood than from the blood into the cells. We say that there is a net movement from the **higher** concentration in the cells to the **lower** concentration in the blood.

Low concentration of carbon dioxide	High concentration of carbon dioxide
Fewer carbon dioxide molecules	More carbon dioxide molecules
More molecules of other substances	Fewer molecules of other substances

Key
⊙ carbon dioxide
· other particles (mainly water)

⟵ net movement of carbon dioxide in this direction (diffusion)

5   Copy and complete the diagram below.

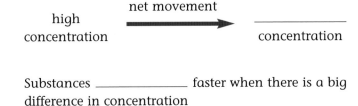

high concentration ⟶ net movement _____ concentration

Substances _____ faster when there is a big difference in concentration

---

What you need to remember *Copy and complete using the **key words***

How substances get into and out of cells
To get into or out of cells, dissolved substances have to cross _____ _____ .

Particles of a gas or a _____ substance move in all directions. So there is a net movement from a region of _____ concentration to one of _____ concentration. We call this _____ . The greater the difference in _____ , the higher the rate of diffusion.

This is how _____ for respiration gets through cell membranes into cells.

2 Losing and gaining water

Cell membranes are permeable to water. So, water can **diffuse** through them from where it is in high concentration to where it is in low concentration.

But cell membranes control the passage of dissolved substances (**solutes**) such as mineral ions. That's why minerals don't diffuse in and out of cells. We say that cell membranes are **partially permeable**.

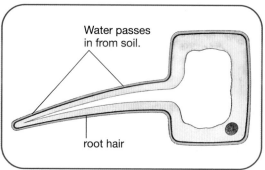

Plant roots take in water from the soil through root hair cells. The cell membrane lets water go in and out. It controls the passage of solutes.

How do plants take in water?

Soil water is a very dilute solution of mineral ions. So, water diffuses from the soil into root cells.

Look at the diagram.

> **1** Explain why the water concentration is higher in a dilute solution of mineral ions than in a concentrated solution of mineral ions.

The diffusion of water through a partially permeable membrane is called **osmosis**.

> **2** Copy and complete the sentence.
>
> A dissolved substance is called a _____ .

> **3** Copy and complete the diagram.
> Use the drawing of the cell to help you.

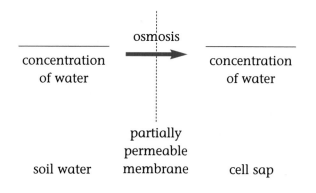

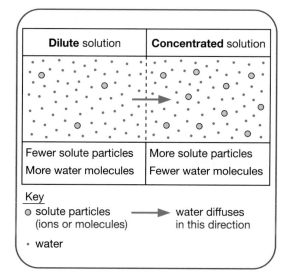

Dilute solution	**Concentrated** solution
Fewer solute particles	More solute particles
More water molecules	Fewer water molecules

Key
○ solute particles (ions or molecules)
· water
→ water diffuses in this direction

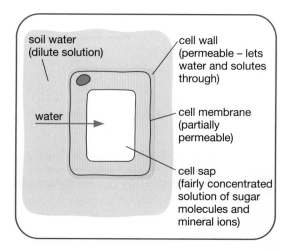

soil water (dilute solution)
cell wall (permeable – lets water and solutes through)
water
cell membrane (partially permeable)
cell sap (fairly concentrated solution of sugar molecules and mineral ions)

What happens in plant roots?

Most of the water and minerals that plant roots absorb go in through the root hair cells. Root hairs increase the surface area for absorption.

4 How big do you think root hairs are?
Give a reason for your answer.

5 Put the following sentences in the right order to describe where water goes in a plant. The first one has been done for you.

■ Water passes through the cell membrane into a root hair cell by osmosis.

■ Water goes into the xylem.

■ Water passes into the cell sap.

■ Water passes to the stem and leaves.

■ Water passes from cell to cell by osmosis.

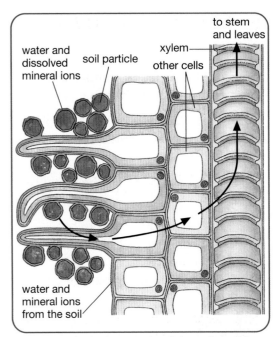

Soil water covers the outside of the soil particles and the root.

Osmosis and other cells

Water moves in and out of all cells by osmosis.
Any difference in **concentration** between the solutions inside and outside the cell causes this.

Because plant cells have a strong wall, they can't absorb too much water and burst. When they lose water, they become less firm.

6 Look at the pictures of cross-sections of red blood cells.

a Which one was put in a more-concentrated solution than the cell contents?

b Which one was put in a less-concentrated solution than the cell contents?
Explain your answers.

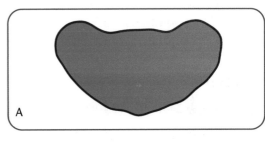

A

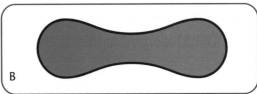

B

C

What you need to remember *Copy and complete using the **key words***

Losing and gaining water
Water can _____ into or out of a cell when there is a difference in the _____ of the solution inside and outside the cell. Water diffuses from a _____ solution into a more _____ solution through a partially permeable membrane. We call this process _____.
A _____ _____ membrane is one that freely lets water molecules through but controls the passage of dissolved substances (_____).

1 Food factories – leaves

Plants use **light** energy to make food.
This is called **photosynthesis**.

You can't see this happening, but you can prove that leaves
make food. The diagrams show you how you can test for
starch.

> **1** Copy and complete the sentences.
>
> You can remove the _____ colour from
> a leaf by putting it into hot _____.
> You can then test the leaf with _____
> solution.
> A black colour shows where there is
>
> _____.

> **2** Plants use light energy to make food.
> What do we call this process?

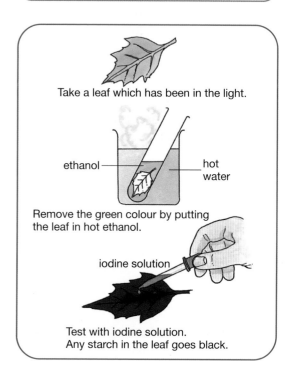

Take a leaf which has been in the light.

ethanol — hot water

Remove the green colour by putting
the leaf in hot ethanol.

iodine solution

Test with iodine solution.
Any starch in the leaf goes black.

Do all plant cells make food?

Carol tested a variegated (green and white) leaf for starch.
These are her results.

> **3** Which parts of the leaf had starch in them?

leaf which has
been in the light

remove
colour

add iodine
solution

> **4** What is the difference between the cells in
> the two parts of the leaf?

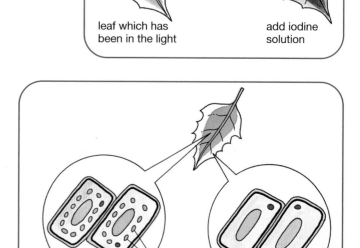

chloroplasts

REMEMBER FROM KS3

■ Plants make glucose.
■ Then they change some of this
glucose into starch.

Where do plants make their food?

The cells in the green parts of a plant contain **chloroplasts**. These are filled with a green substance called **chlorophyll**. Chlorophyll takes in light energy. The cells use this energy for photosynthesis.

5 Why are the leaves of the potato plant green?

6 Which parts of the potato plant can't photosynthesise?
Suggest why.

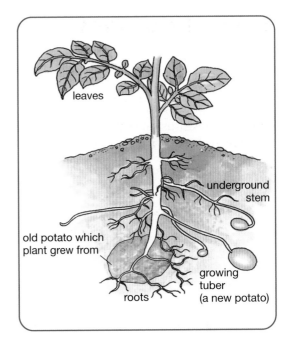

Why are leaves good at photosynthesis?

Most of a plant's chloroplasts are in its **leaves**.
Leaves are usually broad and flat.

7 How does the shape of a leaf help it to photosynthesise?

8 There are more chloroplasts in the palisade cells than in the cells in the spongy layer.
Suggest why.

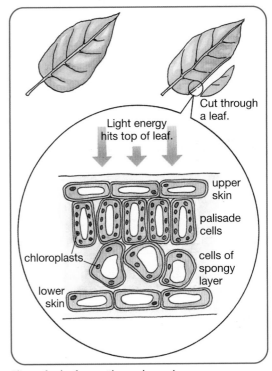

Slice of a leaf seen through a microscope.

What you need to remember *Copy and complete using the **key words***

Food factories – leaves
Green plants use _____ energy to make food. This process is called _____ .

A green substance called _____ absorbs the light energy.
Chlorophyll is found in the parts of cells called _____ .
These are mainly in the _____ of plants.

2 What do plants make sugar from?

Plants make their own food in a process called **photosynthesis**, using the energy from sunlight. The diagram shows the raw materials and the products.

1 Which <u>two</u> substances do plants use to make sugar (glucose)?

2 Where does each substance come from?

3 What else does the plant produce as it makes sugar?

4 Where does this other substance go?

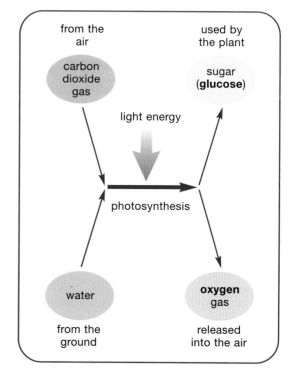

We can write down what happens during photosynthesis as a word equation.

5 Copy the equation below, then use the information in the diagram to complete it.

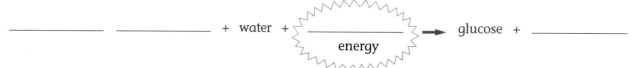

_____ _____ + water + _____ energy ⟶ glucose + _____

Why do plants need light to make sugar?

You may have used a Bunsen burner to give you the energy needed to join chemicals together. Plants need energy to convert carbon dioxide and water to glucose.

Plants get the energy they need for photosynthesis from light.

6 Where do plants usually get this light energy from?

7 Copy the graph. Then copy these labels onto the right place on the graph:

sunset   sunrise

8 No photosynthesis takes place at night. Explain why.

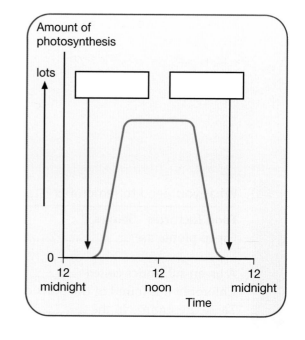

Investigating photosynthesis

A group of students learned that plants need light and carbon dioxide for photosynthesis. They decided to find out if this is true.

They set up four plants in different conditions.
After 24 hours, the students tested a leaf from each plant to see if it had starch in it.

9   Copy the table. Fill in the results you think the students got.

Plant	How it was kept	Was starch found?
A	In the light with plenty of carbon dioxide.	
B	In the light with no carbon dioxide.	
C	In the dark with plenty of carbon dioxide.	
D	In the dark with no carbon dioxide.	

10   In the UK, tomato plants are usually grown in glasshouses. Extra carbon dioxide is sometimes added to the air.
Why do you think this is?

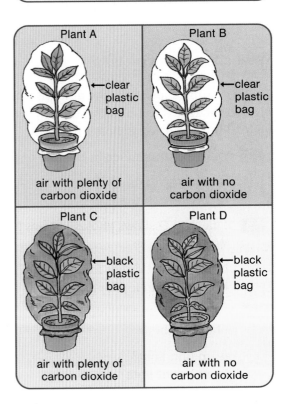

Plant A — ←clear plastic bag — air with plenty of carbon dioxide

Plant B — ←clear plastic bag — air with no carbon dioxide

Plant C — ←black plastic bag — air with plenty of carbon dioxide

Plant D — ←black plastic bag — air with no carbon dioxide

What you need to remember *Copy and complete using the **key words***

What do plants make sugar from?
Plants make their own food by _____. They use the energy from sunlight to convert carbon dioxide and water into sugar (_____). They release _____ as a by-product.

3 Limits to plant growth

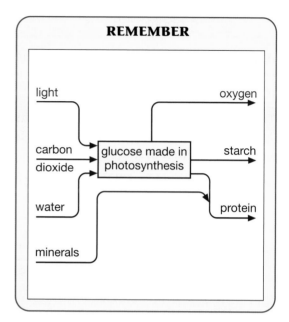

Even in the UK, wheat crops grow faster when farmers give them extra water.

1 To grow faster, a plant needs to make food faster. Write down <u>three</u> things that a plant needs to do this.

What affects plant growth?

The first graph shows how the amounts of **light** and **carbon dioxide** affect how fast a plant makes food. We call this the **rate** of photosynthesis.

2 Describe the change in the rate of photosynthesis

    a between A and B

    b between B and C.

3 Line A to D shows photosynthesis in the same plant. Write down

    a <u>one</u> way it differs from line ABC

    b <u>one</u> reason for the difference.

4 Look at the second graph. What limits the rate of photosynthesis

    a in dim light?

    b in bright light?

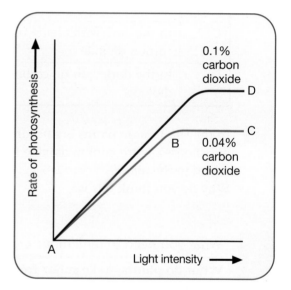

Temperature also affects the rate of photosynthesis. So the temperature was kept constant in the experiments that produced the data for both graphs.

The table shows the results of a different investigation. This was to compare the rates of photosynthesis at different temperatures.

Temperature (°C)	Light intensity	Percentage of carbon dioxide	Rate of photosynthesis
20	3	0.04	15
25	3	0.04	18

5 Copy and complete the sentence.

As you increase the _____, the rate of photosynthesis _____.

6 Why were light intensity and carbon dioxide concentration kept the same in this investigation?

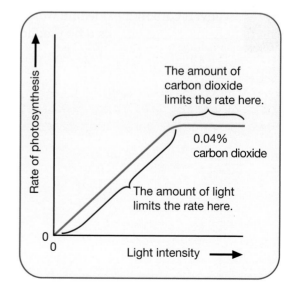

Growing plants faster

Farmers and market gardeners want to get their crops ready to harvest and send to market as quickly as they can. They get paid for their crops only when they sell them. There may also be time to get an extra crop in a glasshouse in a season if their plants grow quickly.

In theory, they can make their plants grow faster by

- giving them more light, water, fertiliser (to supply minerals) or carbon dioxide
- keeping them warmer.

7 Explain why it may be worth putting extra heating or lighting in a glasshouse.

But if plants haven't got enough of just <u>one</u> of the things they need, it's a waste of <u>time</u> and <u>money</u> giving them the others.

8 If the temperature is too low, providing extra light won't make plants grow faster.
Explain why.

9 Look at the picture. Unless it is very cold, the gardener doesn't use the burner on a dull day. Explain this as fully as you can.

10 Which of the factors light, temperature, water, minerals and carbon dioxide can be changed <u>only</u> in an artificial environment such as a glasshouse?

In this glasshouse, the gardener uses a gas burner
- to increase the temperature and the carbon dioxide concentration
- to protect his plants from frost.

What you need to remember *Copy and complete using the **key words***

Limits to plant growth

The _____ of photosynthesis can be limited by

- shortage of _____ or _____ _____
- low _____.

These factors interact and it takes a shortage of only one of them to _____ the rate of photosynthesis.

You need to be able to interpret data on factors affecting the rate of photosynthesis and to consider the advantages and disadvantages of changing the environment in which plants grow.

4 What else affects plant growth?

As well as absorbing water, **roots** absorb the mineral ions that provide plants with the elements they need.

If a plant can't get enough mineral ions, its growth may be stunted. Lack of a particular ion will have a particular effect. This is because different mineral ions do different jobs.

1 Which element in mineral salts do plants need in the largest amount?

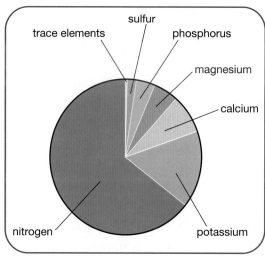

The elements that a plant takes in as mineral ions for healthy growth.

More about mineral salts

Tai grew the plants in the pictures from cuttings taken from one plant. He wanted to find out how mineral salts in the soil affected their growth.

2 Why did Tai take all the cuttings from one plant?

3 Tai grew all the cuttings under exactly the same conditions of light and temperature. Why?

The soil that plant Q is growing in hasn't got enough nitrates in it. Plants need nitrates to make **amino acids**. They use these to make **proteins** and, like you, they need proteins for growing.

4 Write down <u>two</u> differences between plants P and Q.

5 Copy and complete the sentence.

Plant P had more _____ than plant Q, so plant P could make more _____ and grow _____ than plant Q.

Plant R is short of a different mineral ion.
This mineral ion is the one needed to make **chlorophyll**.

6 Write down the name of a mineral ion that plants need for making chlorophyll.

7 Why do you think that the leaves of plant R aren't as green as those of plant P?

8 When a plant can't make much chlorophyll, it can't grow well.
Explain why.

Plant P is in soil with plenty of mineral salts.

Plant Q is short of nitrates, so its growth is **stunted**.

Plant R is short of magnesium so its leaves are yellow instead of green with chlorophyll.

Improving crop yields

When farmers and gardeners harvest their crops, they are removing the mineral ions that plants took in from the soil. To grow more crops well, they have to replace those lost mineral ions.

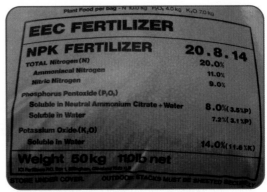

We use artificial fertilisers to add particular mineral ions to soil.

9 Copy and complete the sentences.

Some farmers replace mineral ions in _____ by adding chemicals called _____ fertilisers. Others use _____ fertilisers such as manure, which breaks down to release _____ ions.

Some crops take large amounts of one particular mineral ion out of the soil. If a farmer grows the same crop in a field year after year, the soil then lacks that mineral ion. We say that the crop is **deficient** in that mineral ion. The crop yield gets smaller.

10 Explain why the shortage of just one mineral affects the yield of a crop.

11 The yield of wheat in a farmer's best field was less than usual. He thought that the soil <u>might</u> be short of nitrate so he decided to add some next year. His wife suggested that he should have analysed the soil first.
Why was this good advice?

This farmer is spreading manure on his fields. Many minerals are released when microorganisms break down natural fertilisers such as manure and compost.

However, the farmer decided that he'd solve the problem in a different way. He added manure to the soil instead of an artificial nitrate fertiliser.

12 Why is natural fertiliser likely to solve the problem?

What you need to remember *Copy and complete using the **key words***

What else affects plant growth?

Plant _____ absorb the mineral ions that plants need for healthy growth including

- nitrates for making _____ _____. Amino acids are important for growth because they are used to make _____. Shortage causes _____ growth.
- magnesium for making _____. Leaves are yellow if magnesium ions are _____.

5 How plants use the food they make

> **REMEMBER**
>
> ■ Plants make food in a chemical reaction called photosynthesis.
> ■ We can describe this using a word equation:
>
> carbon dioxide + water $\xrightarrow{\text{light energy}}$ glucose + oxygen
>
> ■ Plants need mineral ions to make amino acids and chlorophyll.
> ■ Lack of light or lack of only one nutrient can limit the growth of a crop (and its yield).

Plants make **glucose**. Then they use it in different ways.

Look at the diagram.

1 Plants use glucose for respiration.
What does this mean?

2 Write down <u>one</u> storage substance in plants.

Starch is a good way of storing food because it's insoluble (it doesn't dissolve).

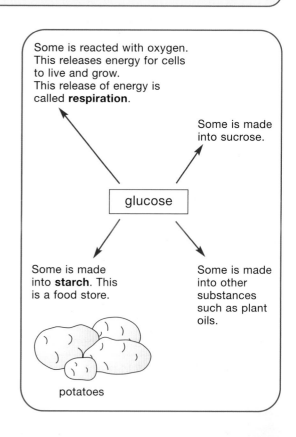

Some is reacted with oxygen. This releases energy for cells to live and grow. This release of energy is called **respiration**.

Some is made into sucrose.

glucose

Some is made into **starch**. This is a food store.

Some is made into other substances such as plant oils.

potatoes

How plants make starch

Plants join together lots of glucose molecules to make long starch molecules.

3 Copy and complete the diagram.

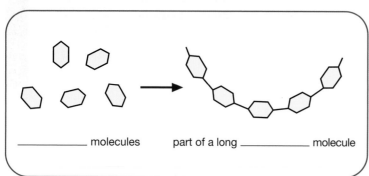

_____ molecules   part of a long _____ molecule

What do plants use the energy for?

Plants release energy from glucose in respiration.

They use the energy released to build other sugar molecules into larger molecules such as

- starch
- cellulose
- lipids (fats or oils)
- amino acids.

They need nitrates and other minerals, as well as glucose, to make amino acids.

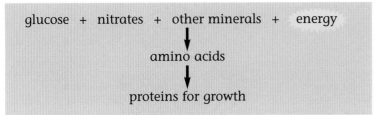

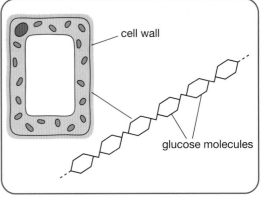

The cellulose in plant cell walls is made from lots of glucose molecules.

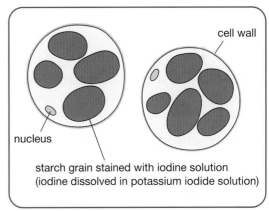

starch grain stained with iodine solution
(iodine dissolved in potassium iodide solution)

These cells from a potato tuber change glucose into starch for storage.

4 Copy and complete the diagram below to show what plant cells can do with the energy they release.

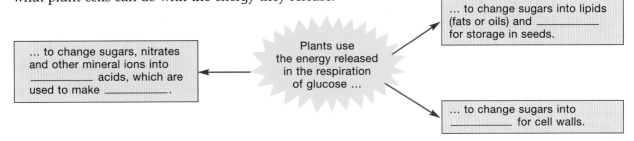

... to change sugars into lipids (fats or oils) and _____ for storage in seeds.

... to change sugars, nitrates and other mineral ions into _____ acids, which are used to make _____.

Plants use the energy released in the respiration of glucose ...

... to change sugars into _____ for cell walls.

What you need to remember *Copy and complete using the **key words***

How plants use the food they make

Plant cells use the _____ produced in photosynthesis

- for _____
- for making insoluble _____ for storage.

Food chains, webs and pyramids

Food chains

Food chains are a way of showing what animals eat. They always begin with green plants.

animal
↑
animal
↑
plant

Each arrow in a food chain means 'is eaten by'.
The food chain on the right tells you that the grass is eaten by the rabbit and the rabbit is eaten by the fox.

1 What does this food chain tell you?

barley ⟶ mouse ⟶ owl

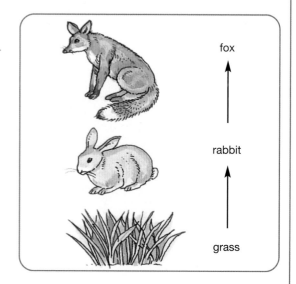

fox

rabbit

grass

Producers and consumers

We call plants <u>producers</u> because they produce or make food. This is why food chains begin with green plants.

Animals consume food made by plants, or they eat animals which have eaten plants. So they are called <u>consumers</u>.

The diagram shows what the words mean in a food chain.

The food produced by green plants is where all of the minerals and energy in a food chain come from.

So the arrows in a food chain show the transfer of materials and energy from one organism to another.

2 Copy the diagram. Complete the arrow to show the direction of transfer of energy and materials.

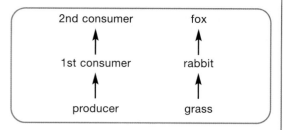

2nd consumer   fox
↑   ↑
1st consumer   rabbit
↑   ↑
producer   grass

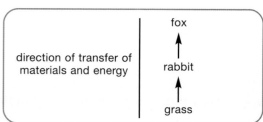

fox
↑
direction of transfer of   rabbit
materials and energy
↑
grass

Food webs

Most animals don't eat just one thing.
So they belong to more than one food chain.

When different food chains contain the same animals, we can join them together. We then get a <u>food web</u>.

3 Copy the food web on the right.
The missing animals are an earthworm and a fox.
Write their names in the correct boxes.

4 Blackbirds eat earthworms. Falcons eat rabbits and blackbirds. Add falcons and blackbirds to your food web to show this.

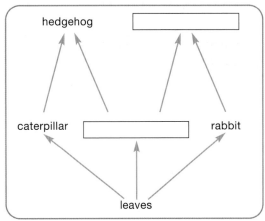

A food web.

Pyramids in food chains

5 Copy and complete the following sentences.

To stay alive, the owl eats _____.
So there must be lots of mice for each

_____.

The mice stay alive by eating _____.
So there must be lots of wheat plants for each

_____.

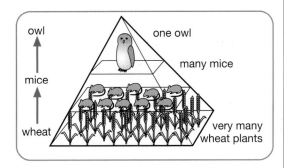

The numbers of plants and animals in this food chain make a pyramid. We call this a <u>pyramid of numbers</u>.

The diagram below shows a simple way of drawing the pyramid.

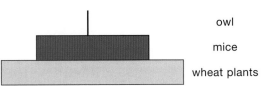

owl

mice

wheat plants

The diagram on the right shows this food chain in a field.

daisy ➝ caterpillar ➝ blackbird

6 **a** Count the number of each of daisies, caterpillars and blackbirds. Set out your results in a table.
b Draw a pyramid of numbers for this food chain. Use a scale of 1 mm to represent one plant or animal.

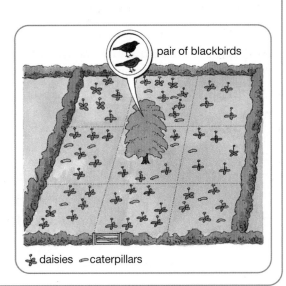

1 Energy for life

Radiation from the Sun is the energy source for most communities. To stay alive, plants and animals need a constant supply of energy.

> **1** How do plants get the energy they need?

> **2** What do plants do with the energy once they have got it?

Plants only use a small amount of the **energy** that reaches them. The **materials** in plant cells, such as glucose, starch and amino acids, are stores of this energy. When animals eat plants, some of this energy then passes along the food chain.

> **3** How do animals get the energy they need?

> **4** What else do plants and animals use food for besides providing energy?

This is the food chain shown in the pictures:

lettuce ➞ snail ➞ thrush

Food, or stored energy, passes along the chain:

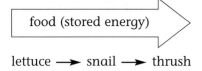

food (stored energy)

lettuce ➞ snail ➞ thrush

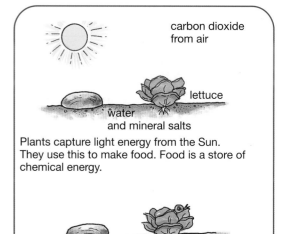

carbon dioxide from air

lettuce

water and mineral salts

Plants capture light energy from the Sun. They use this to make food. Food is a store of chemical energy.

Animals eat plants. They use some of the energy from food to move. They use some of the food to grow. Energy is then stored in the animals' bodies.

thrush

Animals may be eaten by other animals. Part of the energy stored in the food is used to move or to keep warm. Some food is used to grow so the energy is stored in the animals' bodies.

Less and less energy

Animals use a lot of the energy from their food to move about. Some animals also use energy from food to keep warm. All of this energy ends up in the surroundings as heat (thermal energy).

Animals use some of their food to grow. This means that they store some of the energy in their bodies.

The diagram shows what happens to the energy stored in the bodies of plants and animals as you move up a food chain. The higher you go, the less energy there is.

> **5** Draw, and label, a similar diagram for this food chain.
>
> cereals ➞ chickens ➞ humans

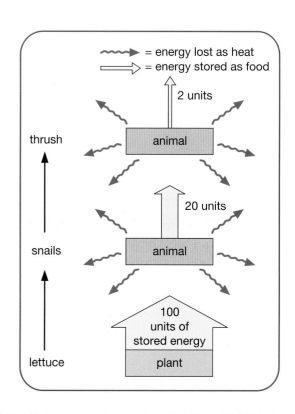

$\rightsquigarrow$ = energy lost as heat
$\Longrightarrow$ = energy stored as food

thrush

2 units

animal

snails

20 units

animal

lettuce

100 units of stored energy

plant

More pyramids

Energy is stored in the materials that animals and plants are made of. We call these materials **biomass**.

At each stage in a food **chain**, there is less and less energy. So there is also less biomass. We can show this by drawing a **pyramid** of biomass.

6   One thrush has a bigger mass than one snail. But the pyramid of biomass shows a bigger mass for the snails.
     Why is this?

REMEMBER

A pyramid of numbers shows how many plants and animals there are at different stages in a food chain.

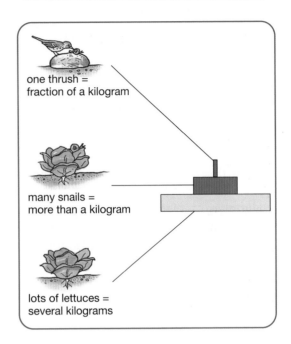

one thrush = fraction of a kilogram

many snails = more than a kilogram

lots of lettuces = several kilograms

The diagram below shows the pyramid of numbers and the pyramid of biomass for another food chain.

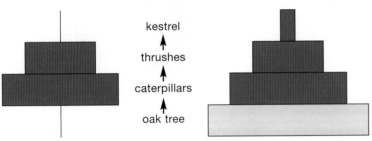

kestrel
↑
thrushes
↑
caterpillars
↑
oak tree

Pyramid of numbers.

Pyramid of biomass.

7   What is the main difference between the pyramids?
     Explain the reason for the difference.

What you need to remember *Copy and complete using the **key words***

Energy for life
The source of energy for most communities is _____ from the Sun. Green plants trap a small amount of this _____ and store some of it in the form of the _____ that make up their cells.
The higher in the food _____, the lower the mass of living material (_____). You can draw this to scale as a _____ of biomass.

You need to be able to draw and to interpret pyramids of biomass.

2 Less biomass, less energy

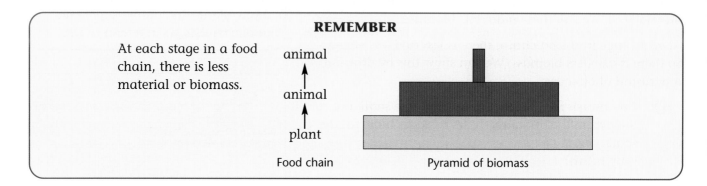

REMEMBER

At each stage in a food chain, there is less material or biomass.

animal
↑
animal
↑
plant

Food chain

Pyramid of biomass

Why is there less energy at each stage of a food chain?

The materials in plants are energy stores. A plant uses the stored energy for its life processes. When an animal eats a plant, it is taking over the plant's stores. In other words, the materials and energy pass along the food chain to the animal.

But the food that an animal eats doesn't all become part of its body.

Look at the diagram.

1   Why can't an animal's cells take in all the materials and energy in its food?

2   Cells break down food to release energy. What is this process called?

So, when a chicken eats plant seeds, only part of the material and energy in the seeds ends up in the chicken. Then the chicken uses a lot of the food in respiration.

This means that even less material or **biomass** passes to the next animal in the food chain. So there is also less energy to pass on.

3   Draw a food chain and a pyramid of biomass for the blackbird in the picture.

4   Copy and complete the sentence.

At each stage in the _____ chain, there is less _____ and less _____ in the biomass of organisms.

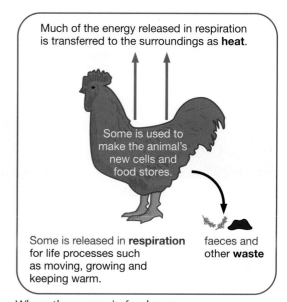

Much of the energy released in respiration is transferred to the surroundings as **heat**.

Some is used to make the animal's new cells and food stores.

Some is released in **respiration** for life processes such as moving, growing and keeping warm.

faeces and other **waste**

Where the energy in food goes.

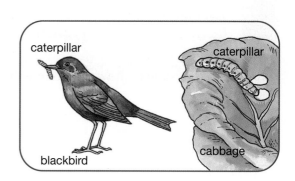

caterpillar

caterpillar

blackbird

cabbage

Reducing energy loss

The diagram shows what happens to the energy in the food that a chicken eats.

5 Copy the Sankey diagram and add figures to show what happens to each 100 J of energy stored in grain.

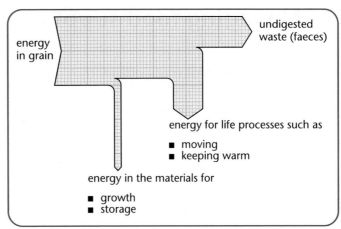

This Sankey diagram shows what happens to the energy in a chicken's food.

Chickens, like other birds (and also like mammals), have **constant** body temperatures.
In the UK, this body **temperature** is usually higher than the temperature of their surroundings.

6 Why do chickens use a lot of the energy from their food for keeping warm?

The chicken stores the rest of the food in its cells or uses it for growing. Only these parts of its food pass on to the next animal in the food chain.

7 How much of each 100 J of energy from the chicken in this example can pass to humans?

What you need to remember *Copy and complete using the* **key words**

Less biomass, less energy
At each stage in a food chain the amount of _____ and energy falls because

- materials and energy are lost in _____
- energy for life processes is released in _____. Much of this is transferred to the surroundings as _____.

Heat loss from birds and mammals is particularly high because they keep their bodies at a _____ temperature.
This _____ is usually higher than that of their surroundings.

3 Managing food supplies

Can we produce meat more efficiently?

Most farm animals are mammals or birds. These animals use a lot of the energy in their food for moving and keeping warm.

They use less **energy** if we

- keep them in **warm** conditions
- stop them moving about very much.

Then they use a bigger proportion of their food for growing.

1   **a**   Explain how farmers benefit when they keep chickens crowded together in barns or in cages.
      b   Explain why some people object to keeping chickens like this.

2   A farmer insulated the floor, roof and walls of her chicken huts.
     Explain the advantages of

     a   keeping farm animals in warm conditions
     b   insulating huts to prevent heat loss rather than heating them with electricity.

Fish don't keep their body temperature constant.
For fish, the conversion rate (amount of growth) for each 100 g of food is 25 g. For chickens, it is only 10 g.

3   **a**   What is the difference between the conversion rates of food for fish and chickens?
      b   Explain the reason for this difference.

4   Large mammals such as cattle have a conversion rate of about 4 g per 100 g of food.
     Explain this as fully as you can.

These chickens haven't much room to **move** about. They keep each other warm.

The fish on this fish farm are salmon.

Sheep and cattle keep their temperature constant and they take a long time to grow.

Feed the world

If we produced meat and fish more efficiently, we could feed more people. We could feed even more if we reduced the number of stages in human **food chains**. We call it <u>eating lower in the food chain</u>. It means, if possible, eating plants instead of meat.

5 Look at the pyramids of biomass.

    a How many times more food do humans get if they eat grain instead of feeding it to chickens?

    b So how many times more people can be fed?

6 Explain why more people can be fed if we all 'eat lower in the food chain'.

REMEMBER

At each stage in a food chain, there is less material or biomass.

humans
↑
chickens
↑
grain

humans
↑
grain

It's not as simple as managing food production

Farmers in India produce enough food for everyone there. The problem is its distribution. Like everywhere else, some people have too much, some enough and others too little.

7 Write down <u>three</u> reasons why some people in India don't have enough to eat.

People and governments have to decide how to use their resources, including food and money. They may decide that medicines are more important than food. We say that they give medicines <u>priority</u>.

8 **a** Suggest <u>two</u> possible ways of making sure that everyone gets enough food.

    b Suggest reasons why these don't happen.

I can't afford to buy much food.

I sold enough food to Europe to buy a new car.

My plot of land is too small to grow enough food.

I sell most of what I grow to pay the rent.

My priority is to make sure that my family eats well.

What you need to remember *Copy and complete using the* **key words**

Managing food supplies

We can improve human food supplies by reducing the _____ loss from food animals by controlling the amount they can _____ and by keeping them in _____ surroundings. Another way is to reduce the number of stages in human

_____ _____ .

You need to be able to weigh up the problems of managing food production and distribution. To solve the problems of competing priorities, we may need to compromise.

1 Recycling mineral ions

It isn't only people who produce waste.
Waste is produced all the time in nature.

Look at the picture of the wood. The woodland floor is covered in dead leaves. This is called leaf litter.

1 What sort of things do we usually call litter?

2 Write down <u>four</u> things in leaf litter.

animal droppings   acorn   woodlice   twigs   leaves

What happens to fallen leaves?

Leaves fall from trees and then **decay**, or rot. If they didn't, leaf litter would get deeper and deeper every year.
Animal droppings and the dead bodies of plants and animals in the leaf litter also decay.

All these things break down into simpler **materials**.

3 Write down the names of <u>three</u> substances that are made when dead plants and animals decay.

4 Leaves disappear as they rot. But the chemicals they break down into can't just disappear.
Where do they go to?

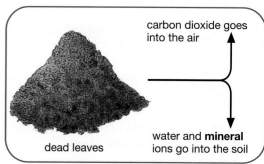

carbon dioxide goes into the air

dead leaves

water and **mineral** ions go into the soil

Dead leaves decay into simple substances.

What causes decay?

Tiny living things called microorganisms make plant and animal waste decay. Microorganisms digest the waste and take it into their cells. It is their food.

Like you, they need food for energy and **growth**. These microorganisms include bacteria and fungi.

5 The microorganisms that break down waste are often called decomposers.
Why do you think this is?

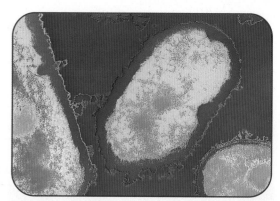

Bacteria which decompose waste (magnified 85 000 times).

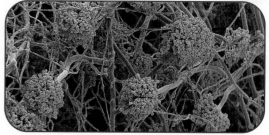

Fungi which decompose waste (magnified 300 times).

Does all waste decay?

Waste from living things that microorganisms can break down is called <u>biodegradable</u> waste. Unfortunately, microorganisms can't break down some of the litter we drop. It is <u>non-biodegradable</u>.

6 Copy and complete this table to show things that people drop as litter.
(Try to add at least <u>three</u> things to each column.)

These rot or decay (biodegradable)	These don't rot (non-biodegradable)
orange peel	cola can

6 months later

Why is decay important?

All living things depend on plants for food. So new plants must grow all the time. To do this, they take minerals from the soil. Soil doesn't run out of mineral ions because the same ones are used over and over again. We say that they are **recycled**.

7 Copy and complete the sentences.

To grow, plants need _____ ions from the soil. Plants may be eaten by _____.
Dead plants and animals and their waste _____ and release mineral ions back into the soil.

In a stable **community** such as natural woodland, there is a balance between processes that

- remove materials from the **environment**
- replace materials into the environment.

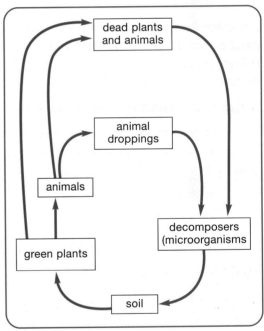

How mineral ions are recycled.

What you need to remember *Copy and complete using the* **key words**

Recycling mineral ions
Living things remove materials such as _____ ions from the _____.
They use them for _____ and other life processes. These _____ are returned to the environment when dead organisms and their waste _____.
They are then _____. In a stable _____ there is a balance between the materials taken out and those put back into the system.

2 Microorganisms – little rotters!

Microorganisms in gardens

Microorganisms do a very useful job in gardens. They recycle waste so that plants can use the materials to grow.

Just one teaspoonful of soil may contain a billion bacteria and 100 metres (100 m) of fine threads of fungi.

Look at the diagrams.

1 How many rod-shaped bacteria will fit end to end in 1 millimetre (1 mm)?

2 How can you get so many bacteria in a teaspoonful of soil?

These bacteria and fungi feed on **waste** such as dead plants and animal droppings. We call this organic waste.
The diagram shows what the **microorganisms** do to this waste.

3 Copy and complete the sentences.

The organic waste is first broken down into _____. Then it is broken down into carbon dioxide, water and _____ ions. Plants use these substances to grow.

Recycling waste in the garden

Many gardeners use compost heaps to recycle plant waste from kitchens and gardens.

4 Copy and complete the flow diagram.

Gardeners put dead parts of plants on to a compost heap.

↓

Microorganisms break these down into _____.

↓

Gardeners put the compost into the soil

↓

Plants use _____ ions from the soil to help them to _____.

5 List <u>ten</u> things you could put in a compost heap. (Remember, they must be biodegradable.)

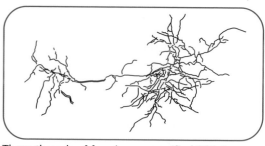

These threads of fungi are magnified 125 times.

This bacterium is magnified 2000 times.

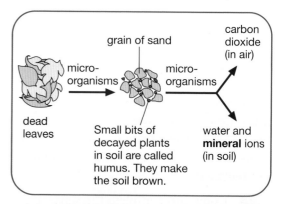

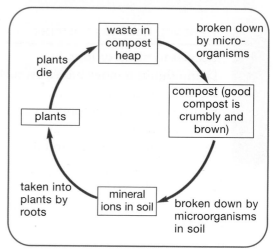

How to make a good compost heap

Microorganisms digest waste in a compost heap faster in **warm** conditions. They produce heat as they do this.

6 Look at the pictures.
Which heap, A or B, is best for keeping this heat in? Explain why.

7 Mice sometimes make their nests in the middle of compost heaps. Why do you think this is?

Most microorganisms digest waste faster when they have plenty of **oxygen**. They also need moisture. But no air gets in if a heap gets too wet.

8 Look at heap B. How does air get in?

9 What could the gardener do to stop the heap getting too wet in winter?

10 Compost is dark and crumbly when the microorganisms have done their work.
You can't see what it was made from. Why not?

A

1 m

wooden slats
(with spaces)

B

Why do gardeners need to add fertiliser to soil?

Gardeners often pick flowers, fruit and vegetables.
So the minerals from these things don't naturally go back into the soil. Plants can't grow without minerals, so gardeners have to replace them.

11 Write down <u>two</u> ways that gardeners can put mineral ions back into their soil.

12 Manure is animal droppings, often mixed with straw.
What happens to manure in soil?

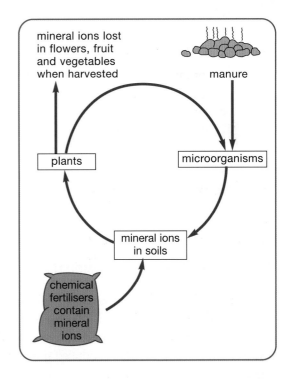

mineral ions lost in flowers, fruit and vegetables when harvested

manure

plants

microorganisms

mineral ions in soils

chemical fertilisers contain mineral ions

What you need to remember *Copy and complete using the **key words***

Microorganisms – little rotters!
Dead organisms and ＿＿＿＿＿＿ materials decay because ＿＿＿＿＿＿ digest them, or break them down. The decay releases ＿＿＿＿＿＿ ions and carbon dioxide, which plants need to grow. Microorganisms digest materials faster in ＿＿＿＿＿＿, moist conditions. Many work better when there is also plenty of ＿＿＿＿＿＿.

3 The carbon cycle

Carbon compounds in living things

All living things are made from substances called carbohydrates, fats and proteins. These substances all contain carbon so we call them **carbon** compounds. Carbon, like mineral ions, is constantly being recycled.

Green **plants** take carbon dioxide from the air. They use it to make glucose in photosynthesis.

Next, plants use the glucose to make other carbohydrates, as well as fats and proteins.
Plants use these carbon compounds to grow.

1 Write down <u>three</u> carbohydrates plants make.

2 **a** Write down <u>two</u> substances that plants use to make glucose.

b Which of these substances contains carbon?

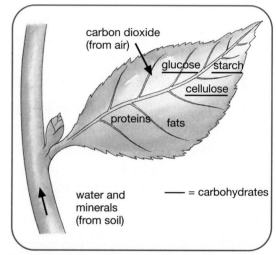

Foods made in a leaf. All the living things in almost all ecosystems depend on the food that green plants make.

3 The diagram shows just one part of the carbon cycle. You can make your own diagram. It is easier to do this one step at a time. Start by copying the diagram on the right near the top of a clean page.

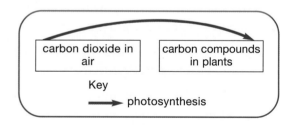

Why isn't all the carbon dioxide used up?

There is only a very small amount of carbon dioxide in the air. But it doesn't all get used up because animals feed on plants. They use some of the carbon **compounds** when they **respire**. The carbon dioxide produced goes back into the air.

4 Add the extra box and arrows to your diagram.

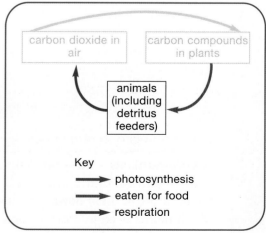

What happens to carbon.

Plants also respire. So, when there isn't enough light for photosynthesis, they put **carbon dioxide** into the air.

Detritus feeders such as earthworms are animals that feed on dead organisms and waste. Microorganisms called **decomposers** also use animal wastes and dead animals for food. They release carbon dioxide in respiration too.

5 Add the extra box and arrows to your diagram.

6 Copy and complete the sentences.

Microorganisms release carbon _____ into the air and mineral nutrients into the _____. By breaking down all the _____ compounds, they are also transferring the energy trapped by green _____ to the surroundings.

Detritus feeders and microorganisms are important for keeping **ecosystems** going. Dead and waste materials must be broken down and recycled as plant nutrients for the systems to stay balanced.

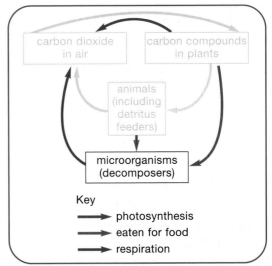

Key
→ photosynthesis
→ eaten for food
→ respiration

The **energy** captured by green plants in the carbon compounds is **transferred** from one living thing to another. Eventually it is all transferred to the surroundings.

Nature's balanced carbon cycle

In nature the same carbon is used over and over again. So we have a **carbon cycle**.

7 Look at the diagram.
Why should the amount of carbon dioxide in nature stay about the same?

Sadly, humans are now upsetting this balance by burning so much fossil fuel.

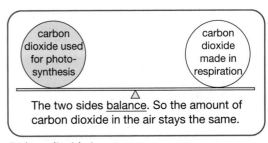

The two sides <u>balance</u>. So the amount of carbon dioxide in the air stays the same.

Carbon dioxide in nature.

What you need to remember *Copy and complete using the **key words***

The carbon cycle
Green _____ take _____ _____ from the air for photosynthesis. They use the _____ to make carbohydrates, fats and proteins. When animals eat plants, some of these _____ become part of the animals' bodies. Animals called _____ feeders and microorganisms called _____ feed on dead organisms and waste materials in _____.
All these organisms return carbon dioxide to the atmosphere when they _____.
In the _____ _____, all the carbon is constantly recycled. At the same time, all the _____ captured by green plants is _____.

1 Why are living things good chemists?

In science lessons, you have probably used both heat and catalysts to speed up chemical reactions.

Living cells produce their own catalysts to speed up reactions. We call them biological catalysts or **enzymes**. Because of enzymes, reactions in cells are quite fast, even though the cells aren't very hot.

1   What do we call substances (like enzymes) that speed up chemical reactions?

Cells use enzymes in reactions to join molecules together and to break them down. Without enzymes, these reactions would take place very slowly – too slowly for our life processes.

2   Copy and complete the sentences.

Because of _____, reactions in living cells are quite fast, even though the temperature isn't very _____. The same enzyme _____ can catalyse a particular reaction _____ of times.

Shape matters

Enzymes are proteins – large molecules made up of long chains of **amino acids**. Different amino acids are arranged in a different order in each enzyme so that each enzyme folds up into its own special **shape**.

Thousands of different chemical reactions happen in living things. Each enzyme speeds up only one particular reaction. So, there are thousands of different enzymes.

3   Copy and complete the sentences.

Cells need a different _____ for each kind of chemical reaction. For a reaction to happen, the _____ or substrate must fit into the enzyme.

4   The enzyme amylase in your saliva breaks down starch to a sugar called maltose but doesn't break down maltose to glucose.
Explain why this is.

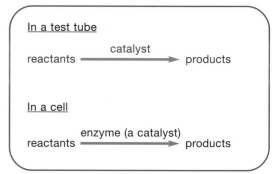

We call the reactant in an enzyme reaction the substrate.

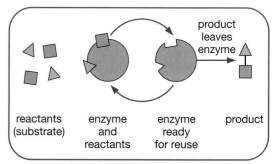

An enzyme molecule works over and over again. Some enzymes can catalyse thousands of reactions in a second.

For an enzyme to work, the **reactant** must fit exactly into the enzyme.
It's a bit like having the right key for a lock.

Temperature matters

Eggs contain proteins. If you put an egg in hot water, the shapes of the proteins in it change. You can't change them back again.

5 Suggest why high temperatures stop enzymes working.

6 Make a copy of the graph. On your copy, mark

a the part that shows the rate of reaction increasing

b the optimum or best temperature for this reaction.

7 In an experiment, a student heated a sample of the same enzyme to 55 °C. Then she cooled it to 35 °C and mixed it with some starch. It didn't digest the starch. Explain this as fully as you can.

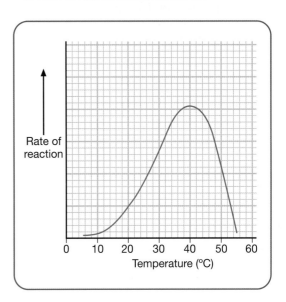

pH matters

The **pH** also affects how well enzymes work.
Different enzymes work best under different conditions.

8 The diagram shows some enzymes in your digestive system.
Write down the name of an enzyme that works best under

a acid conditions

b alkaline conditions.

increasingly acidic ⟵   neutral   ⟶ increasingly alkaline

Colour	red		orange		yellow		green	blue		navy blue		purple	
pH	0	1	2	3	4	5	6	7	8	9	10	11	12	13	14

protease (stomach) 2

protease (intestine) 7

carbohydrase (saliva) 6.5 to 7.5

carbohydrase (intestine) 8.5

What you need to remember *Copy and complete using the **key words***

Why are living things good chemists?
Catalysts increase the rate of chemical reactions. We call biological catalysts _____. An enzyme is a protein made of long chains of _____ _____ folded up into a special shape. It works only because its shape allows molecules of a particular _____ to fit into it exactly. High temperatures destroy this special _____.
Different enzymes work best at different _____ values.

2 Energy for life

Ideas you need from KS3

Food is the fuel for cells

Petrol is the fuel in a car. It burns to release energy. Glucose is the main fuel for cells. They release energy from it when they respire.

Cells normally use **oxygen** in respiration. Oxygen is a gas in the air so we call this aerobic respiration.

Look at the diagram.

1 Copy and complete the table.

In _____ respiration, our _____ …	
… use	… release
glucose and _____	_____, _____ and energy

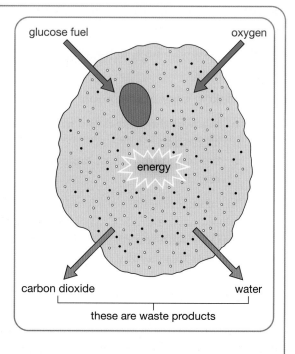

these are waste products

The reactions that release energy

Respiration isn't just one chemical reaction but a series of them. Different **enzymes** catalyse each reaction in the series.

So the **equation** for respiration is really only a summary of the reaction. It just shows the reactants and the products.

2 Where does aerobic respiration happen?

3 In what part of a cell are the mitochondria?

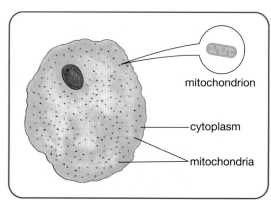

Most energy is released in structures called **mitochondria**.

4 Copy and complete the word equation that summarises aerobic respiration.

_____ + oxygen →^respiration _____ _____ + water + energy

Reactions that produce glucose

Green plants trap energy from sunlight to make glucose.
Like respiration, photosynthesis is a series of reactions.
So the equation is only a summary.

carbon dioxide + water $\xrightarrow{\text{light energy}}$ glucose + oxygen

> 5 Copy and complete the sentences.
>
> In the process of photosynthesis, the reactants are
> _____ _____ and
> _____. The products are
> _____ and _____.

> 6 Many enzymes are involved in photosynthesis.
> Explain why.

Reactions that make enzymes

Cells make lots of different proteins by joining up amino
acids into chains. They use energy to do this. The process is
called protein synthesis.

> 7 To make enzymes, cells need other enzymes, amino
> acids and energy.
> Explain this as fully as you can.

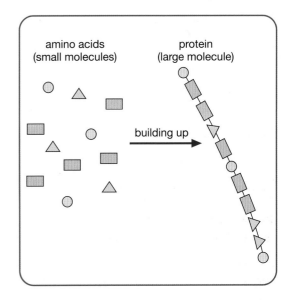

amino acids
(small molecules)

protein
(large molecule)

building up

What you need to remember *Copy and complete using the **key words***

Energy for life

_____ in cells catalyse many processes, including _____,
photosynthesis and protein synthesis.
Aerobic respiration uses _____. It is a series of reactions that release energy from
glucose (a sugar). Most of these reactions happen inside _____.
We can summarise these reactions in the _____

glucose + oxygen → carbon dioxide + water (+ energy)

3 Why do cells need energy?

All living cells need a supply of **energy**. The more active a cell is, the more energy it needs. One clue to how active cells normally are is the number of mitochondria they have.

> **1** Look at the picture. What can you say about the activity of liver cells and single-celled algae?

Energy for growth and repair

Different cells need different raw materials for growth and repair. They all need lipids (fats) and amino acids. They also need

- energy to join small **molecules** together
- enzymes to **catalyse** the reactions.

Plants use energy for these reactions:

glucose (sugar) + **nitrates** ═══ energy ═══➤ amino acids

amino acids (lots) ═══ energy ═══➤ proteins

Plants make **amino acids**. There are about 20 different kinds, so the equation just gives the general idea. Some amino acids contain other mineral ions (**nutrients**) as well as nitrates.

> **2** Write down the raw materials for making amino acids.

> **3** Copy and complete the sentences.
>
> Plants make proteins for _____ and _____ from _____ _____. The energy needed comes from _____.

Humans and other animals get their proteins from food. They break proteins down into amino acids. Then they build them back up again into different proteins. The proteins are different because different cells join amino acids together in different orders. Cells need energy to do this.

> **4** The diagram shows the breakdown of part of a protein.
> Draw a diagram to show the same amino acids built up into a different protein.

REMEMBER

Cells in living things release energy from substances such as glucose in respiration. Most of this energy release takes place in mitochondria.

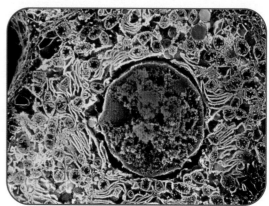

This liver cell has over 1000 mitochondria (here coloured blue–green). Some single-celled algae have only a single mitochondrion.

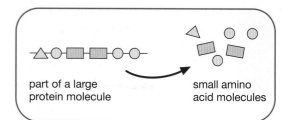

part of a large protein molecule   small amino acid molecules

Energy for movement

When animals move, their muscles **contract**. The diagram shows what happens when you bend and straighten your arm.

5 Copy and complete the sentences.

Your _____ muscle contracts to bend your arm. To straighten your arm again, the _____ muscle contracts and the _____ relaxes.

6 Why do you get hot when you run?

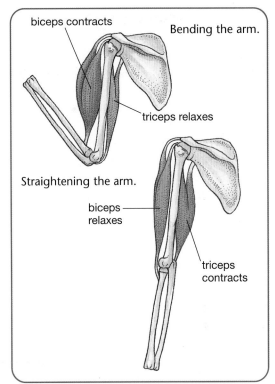

When a muscle contracts it gets shorter and fatter. Muscle cells need energy to contract. Some of the energy is released as heat.

Energy for warmth

Birds and mammals maintain a steady body **temperature**. The normal body temperature for humans is 37 °C. In the UK, the air is usually colder than this. So the heat energy released in your cells is important for keeping you warm. If your temperature falls too low, enzymes work slowly and the chemical reactions in your body happen too slowly to keep you alive.

Body temperature (°C)	How does the body behave?
37	normal behaviour
35	shivering, body movements and speech become slow, drowsiness, start of hypothermia
30	goes into coma
28	breathing stops

7 a What happens if your body temperature drops by 2 °C?

b What do we call this condition?

8 Shivering is rapid muscle contraction.
Suggest why we shiver when we are cold.

What you need to remember *Copy and complete using the key words*

Why do cells need energy?
All living things use the _____ released in respiration to build up large _____ from smaller ones. Plants build up sugar, _____ and other _____ into amino acids. All living things build _____ into proteins. Enzymes in cells _____ all these reactions.
Animals use energy to enable muscles to _____. In colder surroundings, mammals and _____ also need energy to maintain a steady body _____.

4 Enzymes digest our food

Ideas you need from KS3

Why do we need to digest our food?

Food substances such as starch, protein and fat are all made up of large molecules. These molecules are insoluble. We have to break them down into smaller, soluble molecules that can pass into the blood.

1 Write down <u>two</u> foods that contain starch molecules.

2 What sort of large molecules does butter contain?

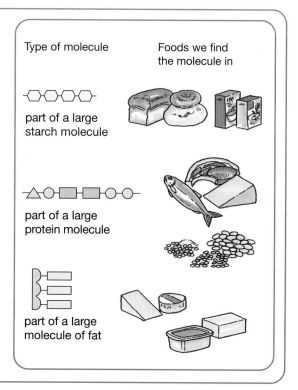

How do we break down large molecules?

We call the reactions that break down large food molecules digestion. Enzymes **catalyse** all these reactions. They work outside cells in the gut.

3 Copy and complete the table. Use the diagrams to help you.

Before digestion	After digestion
starch	sugar (glucose)
protein	_____ _____
fat	_____ _____ and _____
these molecules are large and insoluble	these molecules are _____ and _____

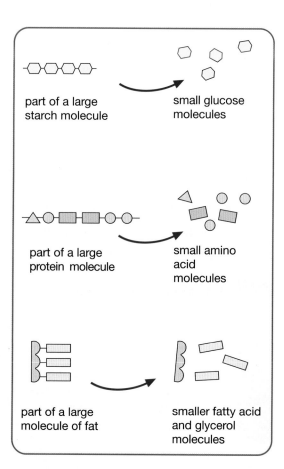

Why is your gut so long?

Think of your **gut** as a tube passing through your body. Food moves through this tube but it doesn't really enter your body until it is absorbed.

4 About how long is the human gut from the mouth to the anus?

5 Suggest why the gut has to be this long.

Digestive enzymes

We make **digestive** enzymes in **specialised** cells in the salivary glands and the pancreas. These are called digestive glands. Gland cells in the **lining** of the stomach and small intestine also make digestive enzymes.

As food passes along the gut, most enzymes pass out of the **glands** into the gut, where they mix with the food. So these enzymes are made in cells, but they do their work **outside** cells. Some enzymes remain in the cell membranes and do their work there.

Some glands produce only one enzyme. Others produce several different ones.

6 Suggest why your digestive glands need to produce several different enzymes.

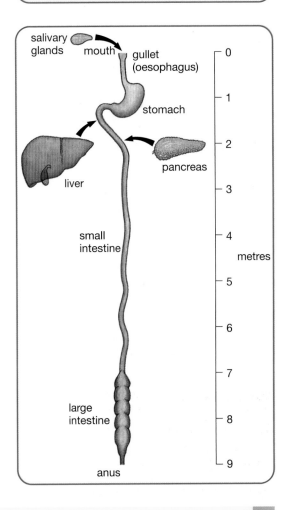

What you need to remember *Copy and complete using the **key words***

Enzymes digest our food

Some enzymes work _____ cells. Examples are our _____ enzymes. We make them in _____ cells in _____ and in the _____ of the gut. Most pass into the _____, where they meet the large food molecules. They _____ the breakdown of these molecules into smaller molecules.

5 Different enzymes digest different foods

Like other enzymes, a digestive enzyme catalyses only <u>one</u> reaction.

- Enzymes that break down lipids (fats and oils) are called **lipases**.
- Enzymes that break down **starch** are called amylases.
- Enzymes that break down **proteins** are called proteases.

Our bodies make several different enzymes in each of these groups.

1   Copy the table.
Put the words amylases, proteases and lipases above the correct arrows.
The first one has been done for you.

Large food molecule		Smaller food molecule
	amylases	
starch	⟶	sugars
protein	⟶	amino acids
fat	⟶	fatty acids and glycerol

2   Make a copy of the diagram of starch digestion. Add more stages to show the part of the starch molecule being completely digested.

3   Copy and complete the sentences to show how an enzyme called lipase digests fat.

First the enzyme snips off a _____ _____ molecule.
Then it does this _____ more times.
The fat molecule has now been digested into three _____ _____ molecules and a _____ molecule.

4   A small amount of enzyme can break down a large amount of food.
Explain why.

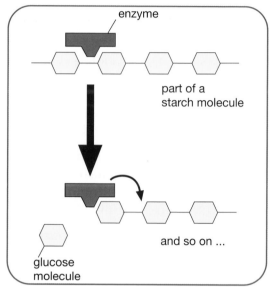

How a starch molecule is digested.

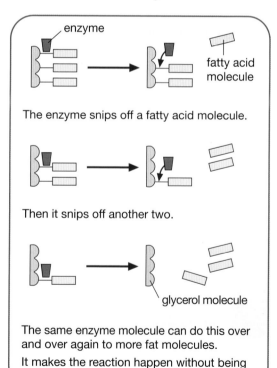

The enzyme snips off a fatty acid molecule.

Then it snips off another two.

The same enzyme molecule can do this over and over again to more fat molecules.
It makes the reaction happen without being used up. We say it is a catalyst.

How you digest fat.

More about starch digestion

You start to digest your food as soon as you put it into your mouth. Your **salivary** glands produce saliva. Saliva contains an amylase.

5 What sort of food does saliva digest?

6 How else does saliva help you to digest food? (Hint: think of eating a dry cracker!)

7 Suggest how chewing food helps digestion.

When you swallow, the food goes down your gullet (or oesophagus) to your stomach. Acid in the stomach stops the amylase working.

More amylase passes into the intestine from the pancreas.

8 In which part of the gut does this amylase do its job?

9 What happens to the glucose produced?

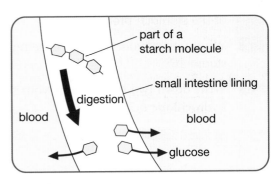

What you need to remember *Copy and complete using the **key words***

Different enzymes digest different foods

Amylase catalyses the breakdown (digestion) of _____ into sugars in the mouth and small intestine. It is made in the _____ glands and the pancreas.

Gland cells in the lining of the small intestine make a carbohydrase that completes the breakdown of starch to glucose.

Proteases catalyse the breakdown of _____ into amino acids.

_____ digest lipids (fats and oils) into fatty acids and glycerol.

6 Digesting proteins and fats

Breaking down proteins

Protein digestion starts in your stomach.

- Your **stomach** has a wall made of muscle tissue that churns up food for several hours.
- It also has a lining of glandular tissue. This makes **hydrochloric acid**, which kills most of the bacteria in food. It also produces proteases that work best in acid conditions.

1 Write down <u>two</u> substances that the glandular tissue of the stomach produces.

2 What part of your food starts being digested in the stomach?

3 Write down <u>two</u> reasons why your stomach produces hydrochloric acid.

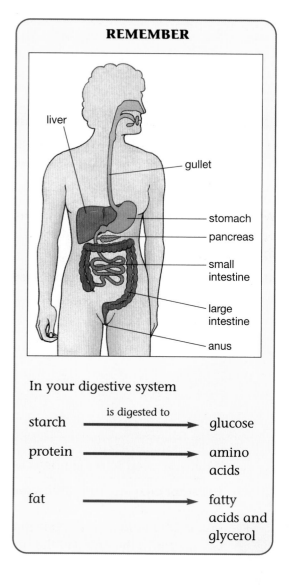

REMEMBER

In your digestive system

starch ⟶ glucose (is digested to)

protein ⟶ amino acids

fat ⟶ fatty acids and glycerol

Partly digested food leaves your stomach a little at a time. It goes into the small intestine. Your **pancreas** and **small intestine** lining make the proteases that complete the breakdown of proteins.

4 What are the products of protein digestion?

When food from your stomach passes into the small intestine, it is still acidic. The enzymes in your small intestine need **alkaline** conditions. Salts in bile neutralise the acid so these enzymes can work properly.

5 Where is bile

    a made?
    b stored?

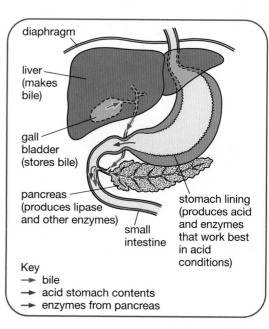

Key
⟶ bile
⟶ acid stomach contents
⟶ enzymes from pancreas

Breaking down fats

Bile also has another job. It breaks fat down into tiny droplets of oil. We say that it emulsifies them. It increases the surface area for lipase to act on.

6 What does the word 'emulsifies' mean?

Your pancreas and small intestine make the digestive juices that contain lipases.

7 Where are fats and oils digested?

8 Why is bile important for fat digestion?

9 The diagram summarises what happens in your digestive system. Make a large copy and then write these sentences into the correct boxes.

- Small, soluble molecules pass into the blood.
- Undigested waste leaves the anus.
- Food goes into your mouth.
- Large molecules are digested.

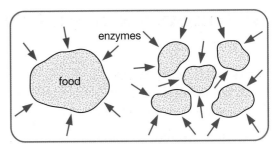

Enzymes break down food faster when the surface area of the food is large.

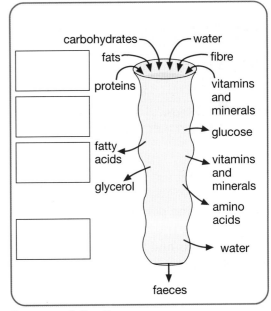

Summary of digestion.

What you need to remember *Copy and complete using the **key words***

Digesting proteins and fats

Type of food	Where it is digested	What makes the enzymes
protein	_____ and small intestine	stomach, _____ and small intestine
lipid (fats and oils)	_____ _____	pancreas

Your stomach makes _____ _____ to provide acid conditions for stomach protease. Your liver makes _____ and stores it in your gall bladder. In your small intestine, bile neutralises acidity to provide the _____ conditions in which the enzymes there work best.

7 Enzymes from microorganisms

Enzymes made in the cells of microorganisms such as bacteria and fungi do some of our chemistry for us. We use them to catalyse reactions in our homes and in industry.

For some jobs, such as making yogurt, we use whole **microorganisms**. In this case, we need two kinds of bacteria. For other jobs, we extract the enzymes and use them outside the microorganisms.

Enzymes work both inside and **outside** the cells that make them.

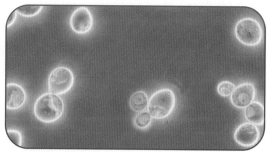

We use yeast cells for making bread and alcohol.

> **1** Copy and complete the table.

Microorganism	Used to make
_____	bread and alcohol
bacteria	_____

Enzymes that we use at home

Lots of washing powders contain enzymes that come from bacteria. They are the enzymes that the bacteria use to digest proteins and fats. So we can use them to digest stains like egg, blood and gravy, because these things contain proteins and fats.

The enzymes break down the large molecules into much smaller ones that will rinse out.

> **2** We call washing powders that contain enzymes 'biological' washing powders. Why is this?

> **3** Copy and complete the sentences.
>
> Biological washing powders contain _____ for breaking down the proteins in stains. They also contain _____ for breaking down the fats.

REMEMBER

- Temperatures above 45 °C damage most enzymes.
- **Proteases** digest proteins.
- **Lipases** digest fats (lipids).

Biological powders work at lower temperatures than ordinary powders. So less energy is used to heat water.

Using biological washing powders

Biological washing powders aren't suitable for everything. Sam tried one in washes at different temperatures.

Look at the table.

 4 **a** At which temperature is 'Cleeno' best at removing blood stains?
Why is this?
b 'Cleeno' can't remove blood stains at all at 55 °C.
Why not?

Temperature (°C)	What happened to blood stain
15	
25	
35	
45	
55	

Sam used 'Cleeno' to wash clothes with blood stains. Washing at different temperature gave different results.

Using enzymes safely

Biological powders are good at removing certain stains. But they can cause problems.

- Your skin is made of protein.
- Some people get rashes because they are allergic to the enzymes.

So you shouldn't use biological powders for washing clothes by hand.

5 The enzymes in biological washing powders work best at fairly low temperatures.
Write down **two** benefits and **two** problems of using biological washing powders.

> **What you need to remember** *Copy and complete using the **key words***
>
> **Enzymes from microorganisms**
> We use enzymes from _____ at home and in industry. We use many of them _____ the cells that make them.
> At home, we use _____ washing powders to remove biological stains because they contain _____ (protein-digesting enzymes) and _____ (fat-digesting enzymes).

> You may be given similar information about using an enzyme to bring about a chemical reaction. You need to be able to explain the advantages and disadvantages of using the enzyme.

8 Enzymes in the food industry

Our food comes from plants and animals. The food industry has processed a lot of the food we buy now. We call the people who work in food processing 'food technologists'.

Often, food technologists change cheap raw materials into expensive products. We say that they 'add value' to the raw materials.

Making sugar syrups

One example of added value is the sugar syrup in sweets, cakes and many other foods. Food technologists make these syrups by digesting cheap starch.
They used to digest the starch using acid. Then they found that it was cheaper to use enzymes.

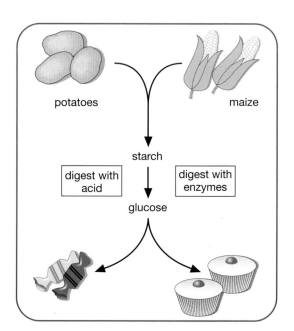

1   Look at the label.
    Write down the names of <u>two</u> sugar syrups.

2   a   Copy and complete the word equations to show <u>two</u> ways of digesting starch to make glucose syrup.

$$\text{starch} \xrightarrow{\qquad\qquad} \text{glucose}$$

$$\text{starch} \xrightarrow{\qquad\qquad} \text{glucose}$$

    b   Which of these ways is used most? Explain why.
    c   Write down <u>two</u> plants that we get cheap starch from.

Starch is a carbohydrate. The food industry uses several enzymes that break down carbohydrates. We call them **carbohydrases**. Food technologists get them from microorganisms.

The fungi and bacteria that they use have to be the kinds that don't cause disease.

3   Write down the name of the group of enzymes that we can use to change starch to glucose.

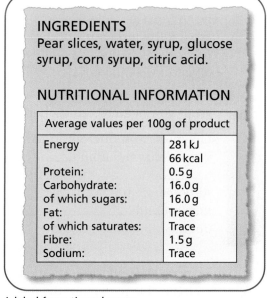

INGREDIENTS
Pear slices, water, syrup, glucose syrup, corn syrup, citric acid.

NUTRITIONAL INFORMATION

Average values per 100g of product	
Energy	281 kJ
	66 kcal
Protein:	0.5 g
Carbohydrate:	16.0 g
of which sugars:	16.0 g
Fat:	Trace
of which saturates:	Trace
Fibre:	1.5 g
Sodium:	Trace

A label from tinned pears.

Making an even sweeter syrup

Food technologists often use fructose syrup in slimming foods. It's more expensive than glucose but it's sweeter, too. So they use only small amounts and the foods contain less energy.

They make fructose syrup using enzymes too.

$$\text{glucose} \xrightarrow{\text{isomerase}} \text{fructose}$$

4 Write down the name of an enzyme that we use to change glucose to fructose.

5 We use fructose to sweeten foods for slimmers. Explain why.

Enzymes for tenderising meat

We can also use enzymes as meat tenderisers. They contain proteases that digest some of the protein. This makes the meat softer. South American Indians have used a protease called papain to tenderise meat for centuries. This enzyme is in papaya fruits and in the papaya leaves that they wrap their meat in before they cook it.

6 Is papain a carbohydrase, an isomerase or a protease? Explain your answer.

Babies don't digest some protein foods very easily. So **proteases** are used to 'pre-digest' the proteins in some baby foods too.

7 Why is the protein in baby foods sometimes pre-digested?

INGREDIENTS
Fructose syrup, cocoa mass, maltitol, sorbitol, cocoa butter, glycerine, flavouring, emulsifer (soya lecithin)

NUTRITIONAL INFORMATION
Typical values (grams per 100 g)

Energy value:	1432 kJ (344 kcal)
Protein:	2.3 g
Carbohydrate:	66.8 g
of which sugars:	1.1 g
Fructose:	15.6 g
of which Polyols:	50.1 g
of which Starch:	1.0 g
Total fat:	16.3 g
of which saturates:	9.9 g
Fibre:	4.4 g
Sodium:	0 g

People with diabetes have to limit the amount of sugars and other carbohydrates that they eat. This is a label from a food for diabetics.

Ingredients
Rice, Vegetables (4%) in variable proportion (Red Pepper, Green Pepper, Mushrooms), Mushroom Extract, Flavourings, Hydrogenated Vegetable Oil, Salt, Hydrolysed Vegetable Protein, Vegetable Bouillon, Parsley, Garlic.

You can find out whether a food contains pre-digested proteins by looking at the label. It will say 'extract of protein' or 'hydrolysed protein'. Both of these mean digested protein. This savoury rice contains hydrolysed protein.

What you need to remember *Copy and complete using the **key words***

Enzymes in the food industry

Job	Enzyme
to break down starch into sugar syrup	_____
to change glucose syrup to a sweeter fructose syrup for use in slimming foods	_____
to 'pre-digest' the proteins in some baby foods	_____

You may be given similar information about using an enzyme to bring about a chemical reaction. You need to be able to explain the advantages and disadvantages of using the enzyme.

1 Getting rid of waste

Your cells make poisons!

Your cells produce poisons such as **carbon dioxide** and urea. They aren't a problem in small concentrations. However, as the concentrations increase, so do the problems.

1 Normally the carbon dioxide concentration in your blood doesn't vary very much. Explain why.

When you are more active, the carbon dioxide concentration in your **blood** starts to increase. Then you breathe faster and more deeply. In other words, you pant. Normally, this brings the concentration of carbon dioxide back down.

2 When might your cells produce more carbon dioxide than usual?

3 Suggest why panting lowers the carbon dioxide concentration of your blood more quickly.

4 Look at the diagram.
Write down, in order, the parts of the breathing system the air goes through as you breathe out.

The concentration of carbon dioxide in the air you breathe out is about 4%.

If the concentration in the air rises, you have problems. As the concentration increases, you get rid of less and less carbon dioxide from your blood. Then it starts diffusing into the blood instead of out. The table shows some of the effects. If the concentration of oxygen is low, the effects are even worse. For example, it takes only a 10% concentration of carbon dioxide to kill you.

5 At 6% carbon dioxide in the air, will carbon dioxide diffuse into or out of your blood?
Explain your answer.

6 When divers use closed circuit breathing systems, they re-breathe the same air.
Why is it important to have a chemical in the system to absorb carbon dioxide?

REMEMBER

Your cells release energy in respiration. Carbon dioxide is a waste product.

↓

Carbon dioxide diffuses from your cells into your blood.

↓

Your blood carries it to your **lungs**.

↓

Most of it diffuses into your alveoli.

↓

You breathe it out.

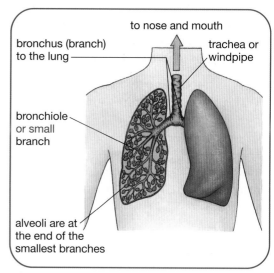

What your lungs are like.

% of carbon dioxide in air	Effects on humans
3	breathing more difficult
6	panting, headache
10	severe difficulties
15	drift in and out of consciousness
18	suffocation and death

More poisonous waste

Your body often absorbs more amino acids than it can use. It can't store these excess amino acids. The diagram shows what then happens to them.

7 What does your body use amino acids for?

8 Which part of your body breaks down excess amino acids?

Enzymes break amino acids down into sugars and a nitrogen compound called **urea**. Urea is poisonous, but it is less poisonous than many other nitrogen compounds. You have to get rid of it.
Getting rid of waste is called excretion.

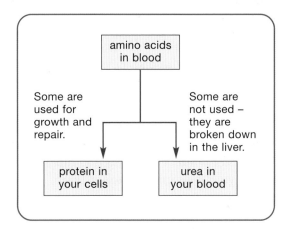

Getting rid of urea

Urea passes from your liver cells into your blood.
Your kidneys take it out of your blood. They also remove water and excess salts (ions). The liquid is called **urine**.

The diagram shows what happens to the urine.

9 Copy and complete the sentence.

Urine runs down tubes called _____ into your _____, where it is _____ .

You empty your **bladder** a few times each day.

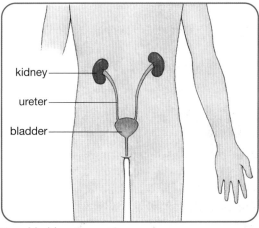

Your bladder stores urine.

What you need to remember *Copy and complete using the key words*

Getting rid of waste
You have to remove waste products from your _____ .
Your cells make _____ _____ waste in respiration.
You remove it via your _____ when you breathe out.
Your liver cells make _____ when they break down excess _____
_____ . Your kidneys remove this from your blood. They make _____
that is stored temporarily in your _____ .

2 Balancing acts

The blood in your body is constantly passing through your kidneys. Your kidneys remove the poisonous urea that your liver cells make. If your blood isn't cleaned in this way, you will soon die.

1 Write down <u>two</u> ways doctors can save the life of a person whose kidneys have stopped working.

To work properly, all the **internal** environment of your body must be controlled. Your body **temperature** must be right. Your **blood** must contain just the right amounts of water, salts (ions), **sugar** and other substances. If the water–salt balance is wrong, too much water moves in or out of your cells and **damages** them.

2 Copy and complete the sentence.

Water passes out of cells by _____ when the concentration of _____ in the blood is _____ than in the cells.

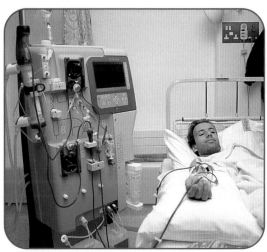

This man's kidneys have stopped working. His blood is cleaned by a kidney machine. He may be lucky enough to get a kidney transplant. Then he won't need the machine.

> **REMEMBER**
> Water passes in and out of cells by osmosis. It diffuses from where it is in a high concentration to where the concentration is lower.

Water balance

Your body is about two-thirds water.

3 If you weigh 45 kg, how much of this is water?

The amount of water you lose must balance the amount you take in each day. The diagram shows the different ways you gain and lose water.

4 Copy and complete the table.

	Water lost by body (cm³)	Water gained by body (cm³)
drink		
food		
respiration		400
sweat		
faeces	300	
urine		
breathed out		
total		

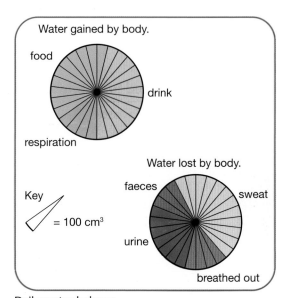

Daily water balance.

Salt balance

Too much or too little salt (ions) in your blood is also a problem. Most of us have a diet that is too high in salt. But people who live in hot deserts or who exercise a lot have to eat extra salt to replace the ions they lose in sweat. Some athletes eat salt tablets when they get cramp.

5   Marathon runners must drink plenty of water. They also have special drinks with extra salts in them. Explain why.

Marathon runners breathe hard and sweat a lot for a few hours. They need food and drink to replace lost **ions**.

Your kidneys and water control

Your kidneys control the amount of water and salts in your body. They get rid of the excess.

6   Look at the diagrams, then copy the table.
Choose the correct answer from each box and put a ring round it.

	A lot of water in body	A little water in body
water in urine	a lot / a little	a lot / a little
urine colour	yellow / colourless	yellow / colourless

How much urine you make in one day …

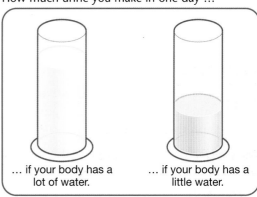

… if your body has a lot of water.

… if your body has a little water.

What you need to remember *Copy and complete using the **key words***

Balancing acts

Humans need to keep their _____ environment fairly constant. That includes the body _____ and the water, _____ and ion content of the _____ .

If the water or ion content of the blood is wrong, too much water passes in or out of cells and _____ them.

Water and _____ get into your body in food and drink.

3 Temperature control

Core body temperature

We call the temperature deep inside your body your **core** body temperature. It should be about 37 °C. It's safe for your skin and some other parts to get hotter or colder than this. But a core temperature of over 37.2 °C is a fever and 35 °C is the start of hypothermia.

> **1** What should the temperature of your body be?

> **2** Suggest why we measure body temperature under the tongue, inside the ear or in the rectum rather than on the surface skin.

In very hot or very cold weather, you can make it easier for your body to stay at 37 °C.

> **3** Explain how you can do this.

Your skin and your muscles help to control your temperature too. They work without your having to think about them.

> **REMEMBER**
>
> For your body to work properly, its internal environment must stay the same.
> That includes your body temperature.

How your skin helps to cool you

Try wetting the back of your hand and blowing on it. As the water evaporates, the wet part of your hand feels colder than the dry part.

Look at the diagram to see how body heat makes the water in **sweat** evaporate and cool you down.

> **4** What happens in your skin when you are hot?

> **5** Why does this cool you down?

> **6** Do you think you sweat much when you are cold? Give a reason for your answer.

> **7** You need to drink more when the weather is hot. Why is this?

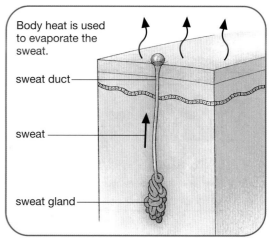

Body heat is used to evaporate the sweat.

sweat duct

sweat

sweat gland

When you are hot, sweat **glands** in your **skin** produce sweat.

Blood vessels help you to keep in and to lose heat

You have probably noticed that you flush when you are too hot. This is because more blood is flowing through the blood **capillaries** in your skin.

When your core temperature starts to rise above normal, the **blood** vessels that take blood to your skin capillaries widen. We say that they **dilate**. With more blood flowing through the skin, more heat is transferred to the surroundings.

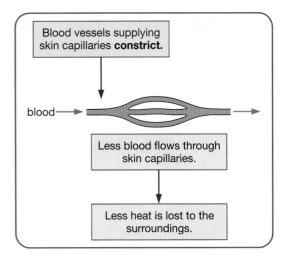

8   The diagram shows what happens when you are too cold. Draw a similar diagram to show what happens when you are too hot.

9   Explain why you lose less heat when the blood vessels to your skin constrict.

How your muscles can help to warm you up

Shivering muscles are **muscles** that are rapidly contracting and relaxing. To contract, they use the energy from **respiration**. Some of this energy is released as **heat** (thermal energy).

10   What is shivering?

11   How does shivering help to warm you?

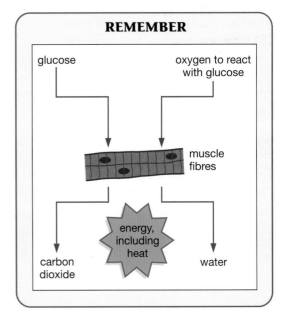

What you need to remember *Copy and complete using the key words*

Temperature control

If your _____ body temperature is too high, the blood vessels to the _____ capillaries _____. More blood flows through the _____ so more heat is lost. Sweat _____ release more sweat. Evaporation of _____ cools your body.

If your body temperature is too low, the _____ vessels to the capillaries in the skin _____ so that less blood flows through them and less heat is lost. You may shiver. The contraction and relaxation of _____ needs energy released in _____. Some of the energy is released as _____.

4 Your body's thermostat

Thermostatic control

The cooling system in your refrigerator and the heating system in your oven both have a thermostat. This includes a sensor to detect a change in temperature and a switch to turn a heater on or off.

> **REMEMBER**
>
> Your body keeps your core temperature constant by controlling
>
> - the amount you sweat
> - the amount of blood flowing through the capillaries in your skin
> - shivering.

Your body's control system

Your body also has a control system. Part of your **brain** acts like a thermostat. It contains **receptors** to sense the temperature of the **blood** flowing through your brain. So it can monitor and control your core body **temperature**.

It also receives nerve **impulses** from temperature receptors in your **skin**.

We call it your **thermoregulatory centre**.

1 Where is your thermoregulatory centre?

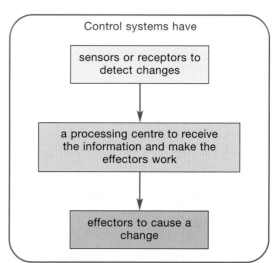

Look at the control system chart.

2 In your body's control system, write down

   a <u>two</u> places where there are receptors
   b the name of the processing centre
   c the name of <u>two</u> effectors that help you to control your body temperature.

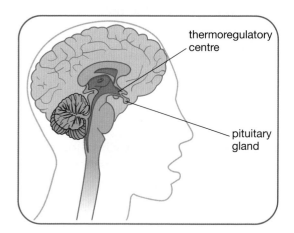

How the thermoregulatory centre works

If your core temperature is too high or too low, your thermoregulatory centre detects this and sends out nerve impulses. These affect

- your muscles
- your sweat glands
- the blood vessels to your skin.

3 Look at the diagram.
   Then copy and complete the table.

When your core body temperature is …	
… too high	… too low
no shivering	
	no sweat
blood vessels supplying your capillaries dilate (widen)	

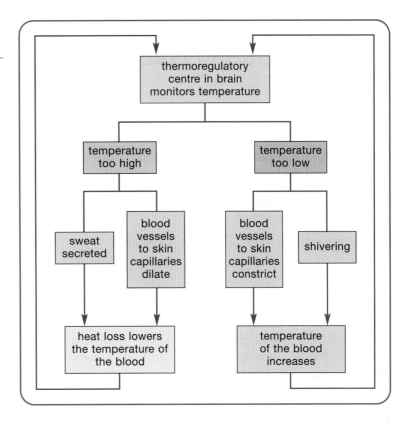

Why must your body be at 37 °C?

Chemical reactions happen all the time in your body. Enzymes are substances that make these chemical reactions happen. Your enzymes work best at several degrees above body temperature. At still higher temperatures, they are damaged. However, keeping your body above 37 °C

- takes too much energy
- makes it too hot for some other body proteins.

4 Copy the graph.
   Mark where you think the temperature 37 °C should be.

5 Why don't enzymes work as well

   a at higher temperatures?   b below 37 °C?

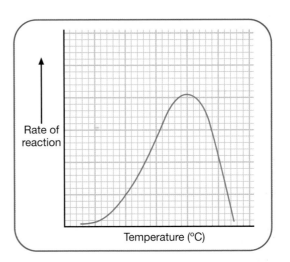

What you need to remember *Copy and complete using the **key words***

Your body's thermostat
The thermoregulatory centre in your _____ monitors and controls your core body _____. This centre has _____ that sense the temperature of the _____ flowing through your brain.
The _____ _____ receives information about skin temperature in the form of nerve _____ from temperature receptors in your _____.

5 Keeping your blood glucose concentration constant

It's important that the amount of glucose (a sugar) in your blood is kept constant.

Read the newspaper article. It tells you what happened to Barbara when the **concentration** of glucose in her blood fell.

1 What effect did a low blood glucose concentration have on Barbara?

2 What did Ben do to solve this problem?

Ben, 4, saves life of coma mother

Barbara, 25, told how 4-year-old Ben kept her alive.

He knew exactly what to do when he found her unconscious.

He poured a bottle of his strawberry drink with extra sugar into her mouth, then some glucose jelly, kept in the fridge for emergencies, and finally some sugar-rich cough mixture.

Making the first telephone call of his life, he dialled 999.

When the police arrived, Ben told them his mother was diabetic.

The amount of glucose in your blood goes up after a meal. It falls when you exercise. Usually, your body detects these changes and returns the amount of sugar to normal. Look at the graph.

3 What is normal blood glucose concentration?

4 At what time of day did this person have a meal? How do you know?

5 How long did it take for their blood glucose concentration to return to normal?

6 At what time of day did this person take exercise? How do you know?

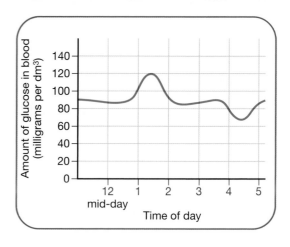

A control system for blood glucose

Your **pancreas** monitors and controls changes in blood glucose concentration. It releases special chemicals called hormones to bring your blood glucose concentration back to normal.

7 Copy and complete the table. Use the diagram to help you.

Blood glucose concentration	Hormone released by pancreas	What then happens
higher than normal		
lower than normal		

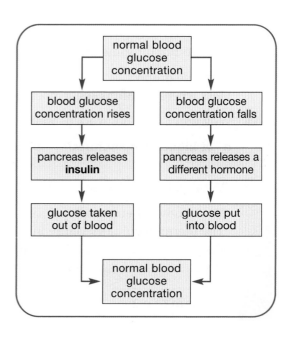

How do the hormones work?

Hormones are chemical messengers. Each **hormone** is produced by one organ in your body but travels through your blood and affects a different organ.

The diagram shows some organs affected by hormones.

> **8** Which organ does the hormone insulin affect?

> **9** How does the hormone reach this organ?

We say that the liver is the target organ for insulin.

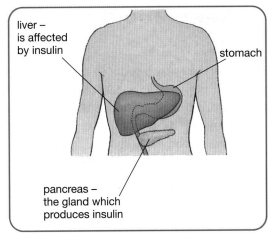

Blood carries insulin from the pancreas to the liver. The insulin allows **liver** cells to take up glucose from the blood.

What happens if your pancreas isn't working properly?

Barbara's pancreas doesn't make enough insulin.

> **10** Without insulin, what happens to Barbara's blood glucose concentration?

Barbara's disease is called **diabetes**. She must have regular **injections** of insulin. This lowers the amount of sugar in her blood. She must also be careful about how much carbohydrate (sugar and starch) she eats.

When Barbara's blood glucose concentration fell too low, she could have died.

> **11** How can you help someone in a diabetic (low blood sugar) coma? (Remember what Ben did.)

Many diabetics have to inject themselves with insulin. All diabetics have to control the amount of carbohydrates in their **diet**.

What you need to remember *Copy and complete using the **key words***

Keeping your blood glucose concentration constant
Your blood glucose _____ must be kept constant. Your _____ monitors and controls this.
If there is too much glucose, your pancreas releases the _____ insulin.
Insulin allows _____ cells to take in glucose from the blood. People with _____ cannot make enough _____ so the concentration of glucose in their blood can rise too high. Some diabetics need _____ of insulin and they all have to control their _____ .

6 More about insulin

Diabetes isn't just a modern disease. It is described in an Egyptian papyrus from 1500 BC. Its name comes from a Greek word meaning 'to run through'. This is because its symptoms are thirst and passing lots of urine. Water goes through the body quickly and in large amounts.

> **1** Lots of people have diabetes and don't know it. What symptoms should people look out for?

In 17th-century Britain, doctors recognised two kinds of diabetes. In one, the kidneys excreted excess blood glucose. So the urine of these patients contained glucose. The test was to taste the urine. Both kinds of diabetes caused death within a year or two.

> **2** Look at the picture. How do we test for diabetes now?

A clue about the cause of diabetes came in 1889. Baron Joseph von Mering and Oskar Minkowski removed a dog's pancreas. The dog's blood glucose concentration went up and it died of diabetes about a month later.

> **3** What does this suggest about the cause of diabetes?

Scientists searched for another 30 years to find the cause and a treatment for diabetes. They knew that the pancreas must produce something that prevented diabetes.

They removed dogs' pancreases and tried injecting them with pancreas extract. The dogs could still digest their food, but all of them died.

> **4** Look at the picture. Suggest why the scientist thought each of these ideas worth investigating.

> **5** We now know that insulin is a protein. Why can't diabetics take it as a pill?

REMEMBER

- Having too little or too much glucose in your blood is dangerous. Either of these can cause a coma or death.
- Your pancreas monitors your blood glucose concentration. If this is too high, your pancreas releases insulin.
- Without insulin, cells can't take glucose out of your blood.

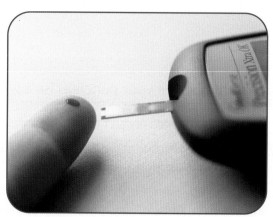

There are chemical tests for glucose in urine. Blood tests are even more accurate.

REMEMBER

The pancreas also makes digestive enzymes.

Perhaps enzymes from the pancreas digest whatever prevents diabetes.

Perhaps the pancreas extract is too strong.

Scientists were puzzled about why pancreas extract didn't cure the dogs.

An important discovery

Scientists discovered that tying the tube to the dog's pancreas didn't cause diabetes.

> **6** Look at the picture.
> What can you conclude?

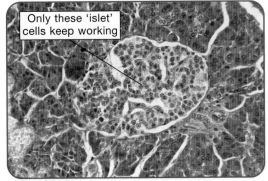

Only these 'islet' cells keep working

There are two kinds of cells in the pancreas. When the tube from a dog's pancreas is tied, one of the kinds of cells stops working.

Banting and Best succeed

In 1922, Frederick Banting and Charles Best thought about trying to make an extract from the cells that remained alive after the tube between a dog's pancreas and its small intestine was tied off.

They made an extract of these cells alone.
Then they removed the pancreas from another dog and injected their new extract. It worked!

> **7** Look at the graph.
> Then describe the results.

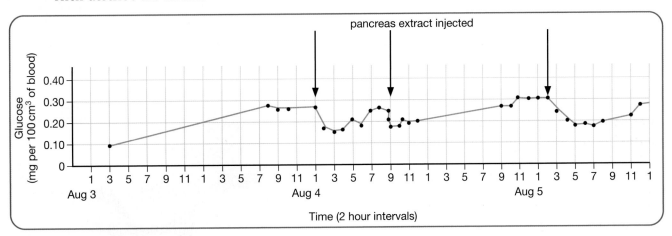

pancreas extract injected

Glucose (mg per 100 cm³ of blood)

Time (2 hour intervals)

> **8** What can you conclude from this experiment?

> **9** Suggest why the dogs weren't cured.

> **10** Suggest some further work scientists would have to do before humans could be treated for diabetes.

What you need to remember *Copy and complete using the* **key words**

More about insulin
Without treatment, _____ is fatal.

You need to be able to evaluate data from experiments by Banting and Best which led to the discovery of insulin.

7 Diabetes now

An increasing problem

There is another kind of diabetes. Doctors are worried because it's becoming more and more common. People who are overweight seem to be most at risk.

1 Look at the Box.
Suggest which type of diabetes people always have to control with insulin injections.
Explain your answer.

Estimates suggest that, in the UK, about

- 1 million people have diabetes but don't know it
- 1.8 million people know they have diabetes
- 0.25 million of these have type 1 diabetes.

Most people with type 2 diabetes control it with diet and exercise. Some need insulin. People with type 1 diabetes always inject insulin as well as watching their diet. About half a million people in the UK use insulin.

2 Suggest how many type 2 diabetics control their blood glucose level by diet and exercise.

The original treatment

At first, people used purified insulin from farm animals.

3 Look at the photograph.
Write down <u>three</u> things that Clare had to learn to do when she was 8 years old.

Diabetics who use insulin have to be very careful. Forgetting an insulin injection causes an increase in blood glucose. Being late with a meal after an insulin injection can make blood glucose fall too low. Either can cause coma and death.

When she was 10 years old, Clare went into a coma. She recovered when her mother gave her an insulin injection.

4 Was Clare's coma caused by too much or too little glucose in her blood?
Explain your answer.

Types of diabetes

There are two types of diabetes:

- type 1 – the cells that make insulin have been destroyed.
- type 2 – either the cells don't produce enough insulin or a person's body doesn't respond normally to its own insulin.

Diabetics are at increased risk of heart disease.

'I'm Clare. I developed diabetes when I was 8 years old. In hospital, the doctor worked out how much insulin I needed and when.
The nurses taught me how to test my urine for glucose and to inject insulin.
I also had to learn how much carbohydrate I could safely eat. For example, if I ate 100 g of chips, I couldn't have an ice cream too.'

Human insulin

Now Clare injects human instead of animal insulin.

It is extracted from genetically engineered bacteria. It's less likely to cause allergies and side-effects than animal insulin but it does cause some problems.

5 Suggest some advantages and disadvantages of using human insulin.

As well as human insulin, there are

- altered forms of insulin which are fast acting
- new drugs to stimulate the pancreas.

'When I used animal insulin, I knew when my blood glucose was getting low. My lips tingled and I'd sweat. With human insulin, there are no warning signs. It's worrying.'

Other developments

Clare now tests her blood for glucose. This gives more up-to-the-minute information than a urine test.

She also has a new way of injecting her insulin.

She has a special 'insulin pen' to give her measured doses of insulin. When she was in hospital for an operation, her nurse used an insulin pump. This gave her, automatically, the insulin she needed when she needed it. Pumps are expensive and people need training to use them.

6 Suggest some advantages and disadvantages of using

a an 'insulin pen'
b an insulin pump.

A very small number of people have had pancreas transplants or transplants of the islet cells that make insulin.

7 Write down <u>two</u> developments that may offer hope of a cure rather than a treatment for diabetes.

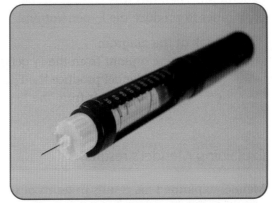

It's a bit more expensive, but many people find it easier to use an 'insulin pen' than a needle.

Newsflash!

A team at Toronto University has found immature cells in the pancreases of adult mice. These cells were able to develop into cells that produced insulin.

This gives hope that, one day, it might be possible to cure type 1 diabetes!

What you need to remember

Diabetes now
There is nothing new for you to <u>remember</u> in this section.

You need to be able to evaluate modern methods of treating diabetes.

1 How are characteristics inherited?

This question was answered in the middle of the 19th century. Gregor Mendel worked out the inheritance pattern of several characteristics of peas. Peas are easy to grow and to cross-pollinate. Also, the inheritance pattern for many features of peas is fairly simple. So, it was lucky that he chose peas.

Gregor Mendel (1822–1884). Mendel was a monk in a monastery in Brno in what is now the Czech Republic.

In one experiment, Mendel cross-pollinated flowers of lots of tall pea plants with those of lots of dwarf plants. He grew more pea plants from the seeds. He called these the F_1 generation. Then he cross-pollinated the F_1 plants with each other to produce the F_2 generation.

1 Look at the diagram.
   a Describe a plant from the F_1 generation.
   b How did Mendel produce the F_2 generation?
   c Describe the plants from the F_2 generation.

Explaining Mendel's results

Mendel explained his results in terms of what he called inheritance factors. He realised that these factors must come in pairs.

Look at the diagram.

The F_1 plants show that the tallness factor is more powerful than the dwarfness factor. A pea plant only needs one tallness factor to make it tall. So we say that the tallness factor is dominant. A pea plant needs two dwarfness factors to make it dwarf. So we say that the dwarfness factor is recessive. Mendel called tallness T and dwarfness t.

2 Copy and complete the table.

Inheritance factors	What the plant is like
TT	tall
Tt	
	dwarf

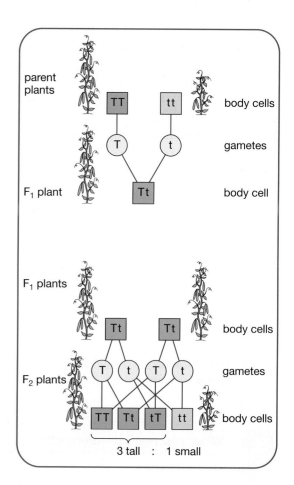

parent plants — TT — tt — body cells

T — t — gametes

F_1 plant — Tt — body cell

F_1 plants — Tt — Tt — body cells

T t T t — gametes

F_2 plants — TT Tt tT tt — body cells

3 tall : 1 small

Publishing scientific results

Mendel wrote up his work. Like other scientific papers, it was published in a scientific journal. The journal was the *Archives of the Brno Natural History Society*. Mendel's work was published in papers in 1865 and 1869, but the journal was little known outside Brno.

It was 1900 before scientists rediscovered his papers and recognised the importance of Mendel's work. Three different biologists worked out the **inheritance** patterns for themselves. Scientists always search science journals for similar work. They all found Mendel's earlier work. In 1901, they each credited him with the discovery in their papers.

3 When did Mendel die?

4 Explain why the importance of Mendel's work was not recognised until after his death.

Mendel discovered some of the patterns of inheritance in peas. Other scientists did experiments using other plants and animals. They found similar patterns.

They found out about human patterns of inheritance. They did this by looking at **family trees**. These show inheritance patterns in families.

We now call Mendel's 'inheritance factors' genes. Different forms of a gene can produce differences in a characteristic.

5 How do scientists investigate inheritance patterns in humans?

Rediscovering Mendel

The biologists who rediscovered Mendel's work were

- Hugo de Vries in the Netherlands
- Carl Correns in Germany
- Erich von Tschermak-Seysenegg in Austria.

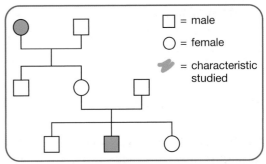

Family trees show how characteristics are passed on in humans.

What you need to remember *Copy and complete using the **key words***

How are characteristics inherited?

We find out about _____ patterns from breeding experiments and, in the case of humans, from _____ _____.

You need to be able to explain

- why Mendel suggested that factors were inherited separately
- why the importance of Mendel's discoveries was not recognised until after his death.

You don't need to remember the details of Mendel's work.

2 Body cells and sex cells

In any individual animal or plant

- the chromosomes in body cell nuclei are in pairs. So there are two sets of **genetic** information.
- all the body cell nuclei are genetically identical.

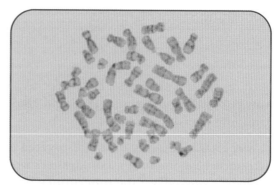

Chromosomes from a human body cell coloured to show the banding.

What's special about sex cells?

In **sex** cells or gametes, the chromosomes are **single**. They contain one chromosome from each pair. Look at the diagram.

1. How many pairs of chromosomes are there in all human body cell nuclei?

2. How many chromosomes must there be in each gamete cell nucleus?

3. How many sets of genetic information are there in gametes?

Just one cell starts a new human life. It forms by the fusion of two sex cells or **gametes**. We call this fertilisation.

One of the gametes comes from the mother. This is the ovum or egg cell. The other, the sperm, comes from the father.

4. Copy and complete the sentences.

Half of the chromosomes in a sex cell or _____ come from each parent.
So _____ the genetic information of a baby comes from the mother and _____ from the father.

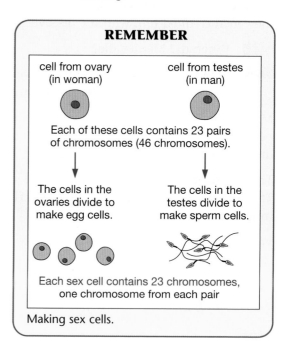

REMEMBER

cell from ovary (in woman)   cell from testes (in man)

Each of these cells contains 23 pairs of chromosomes (46 chromosomes).

The cells in the ovaries divide to make egg cells.

The cells in the testes divide to make sperm cells.

Each sex cell contains 23 chromosomes, one chromosome from each pair

Making sex cells.

Making gametes

The types of division used to make gametes and body cells are different.

■ To make gametes, the chromosome number is halved.
■ To make body cells, the chromosome number is kept the same.

Look at the diagram.

5 What do we call the kind of division that produces gametes?

6 After each chromosome copies itself, how many copies of the genetic material are there in the nucleus?

7 Why does this nucleus then have to divide twice?

8 How many gametes are made from each original cell?

The four sets of chromosomes sort at random into the new cells.

So lots of different combinations of chromosomes are possible.

The diagram shows the chromosomes in a sperm-producing cell.

9 Draw diagrams to show the chromosomes in <u>three</u> different sperm nuclei that can be made from a cell like this. The example shows how to do it.

Sperm and ova also fuse at random. So babies of the same parents can vary a lot.

10 Write down <u>two</u> reasons why the offspring produced by sexual reproduction vary.

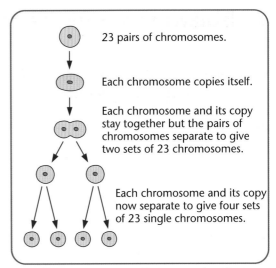

23 pairs of chromosomes.

Each chromosome copies itself.

Each chromosome and its copy stay together but the pairs of chromosomes separate to give two sets of 23 chromosomes.

Each chromosome and its copy now separate to give four sets of 23 single chromosomes.

Meiosis produces new cells (gametes) with a single set of chromosomes.

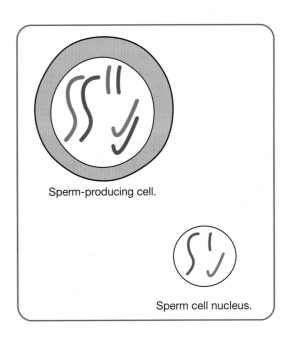

Sperm-producing cell.

Sperm cell nucleus.

What you need to remember *Copy and complete using the **key words***

Body cells and sex cells
Testes and ovaries contain cells that divide by _____ to form _____ cells or gametes.
These cells make copies of their _____ then divide twice to make four _____.

Each gamete has a _____ set of chromosomes. So it has a single set of _____ information.

3 Making new body cells

You start your life when two gametes join at **fertilisation**. You have one cell with 23 **pairs** of **chromosomes** in its nucleus. This cell divides, takes in materials, grows and divides over and over again.

1 How many chromosomes are there in the nucleus of each new cell?

By the time you are grown up, you could have 60 million million cells. This is not the number of cells you'll have made. You don't make cells for **growth** alone. Cells get lost, damaged or worn out all the time. So you also **replace** millions of cells. You probably make about 200 000 000 000 (200 billion) red blood cells <u>every day</u> plus billions of other cells.

2 Copy and complete the sentence.

You make new cells for _____ and to _____ lost cells.

3 Write down <u>two</u> reasons why you have to replace cells.

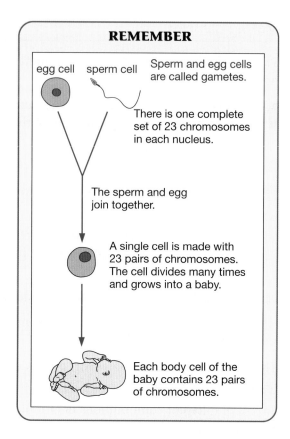

REMEMBER

egg cell   sperm cell

Sperm and egg cells are called gametes.

There is one complete set of 23 chromosomes in each nucleus.

The sperm and egg join together.

A single cell is made with 23 pairs of chromosomes. The cell divides many times and grows into a baby.

Each body cell of the baby contains 23 pairs of chromosomes.

How you keep the chromosome number the same

The kind of division that produces new body cells is different from the kind that makes gametes.

Look at the diagram.

4 Copy and complete the sentences.

Before a body cell divides, each chromosome makes a _____ of itself. So, the nucleus of each new cell has the same _____ of chromosomes as the original cell. It also contains exactly the same _____ information. We call this type of division _____.

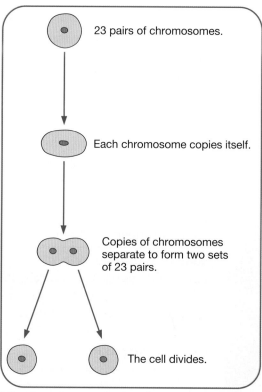

23 pairs of chromosomes.

Each chromosome copies itself.

Copies of chromosomes separate to form two sets of 23 pairs.

The cell divides.

Mitosis makes new body cells. Nuclei also divide by mitosis during asexual reproduction.

Mitosis in animal cells

Look at the pictures of a dividing cell with two pairs of chromosomes.

5 Write down the captions of the pictures, in the order that shows what happens in mitosis.

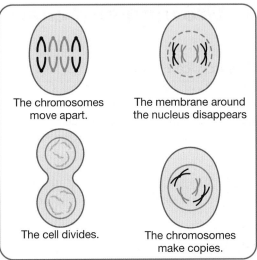

The chromosomes move apart.

The membrane around the nucleus disappears

The cell divides.

The chromosomes make copies.

Mitosis results in cells with the same number of chromosomes as the original cell.

Mitosis for asexual reproduction

Some plants and animals reproduce without making sex cells. Single-celled organisms may just divide into two.

Larger organisms sometimes grow parts that separate from the **parent** and live independently. The parent and offspring are genetically identical. We call them a clone.

6 Are cells of clones produced by meiosis or mitosis? Explain your answer.

This tiny Hydra will soon be ready to separate from its parent.

What you need to remember *Copy and complete using the* **key words**

Making new body cells

Gametes join at _____ to form a single cell. Its nucleus contains new pairs of _____. It divides by _____ over and over again to produce the new individual.

Your body has to make new cells to _____ lost and worn out cells as well as for _____. In body cells, the chromosomes are in _____.

Some living things produce offspring by asexual reproduction. Their cells are made by mitosis from the _____ cells. So they are genetically the same as their parent.

4 Growing and changing

One new cell

Animals and plants that reproduce by sexual reproduction start life as just one cell. This cell divides and grows over and over again. At first the cells of the embryo are identical and can develop into any kind of cell.

1 Suggest why each cell in an eight-cell stage embryo could develop into a complete embryo.

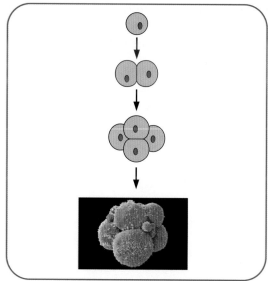

Each of these cells <u>could</u> grow into a complete embryo. The genes are the same in all these cells and they are all able to work.

To lots of different cells

Soon, different genes start to work in different cells. Cells become specialised. We say that they **differentiate**. Large animals such as humans make about 200 different kinds of cells. Some cells remain unspecialised. They are the embryonic **stem cells**.

2 Copy and complete the sentences.

The cells in an _____ grow and divide over and over again. Some cells continue to grow and _____. Others specialise. We say that they _____.

3 Look at the photograph.
Name <u>three</u> kinds of specialised cells in mice.

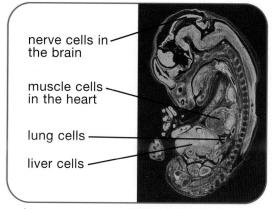

In this mouse embryo, different genes are working in these different specialised cells. Some genes are no longer working.

Specialised cells in humans and other animals can't develop into other kinds of cells. But tissues do contain cells that can grow and **divide**. For example, your skin produces millions of cells each day to **repair** damage and to replace the cells that get rubbed off.

4 Write down <u>two</u> reasons why an adult has to make new cells.

Most plant cells are different. They don't lose the ability to differentiate. That's why roots can grow on a stem cutting.

5 What must the root cells on a stem cutting have developed from?

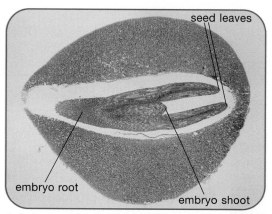

Cells in an embryo plant do specialise. But they can develop into other kinds of cells.

Cells in adult humans that can differentiate

There are some unspecialised cells in adults that can differentiate too. They are also stem cells. Some of them can develop into only a few different kinds of cells. Others can develop into many kinds.

6 Write down <u>three</u> parts of an adult human that contain stem cells.

Blood from the umbilical cord of newborn babies contains stem cells that can develop into different kinds of blood cells.

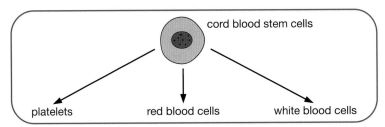

Some doctors think that we should collect and store a baby's cord blood. In future years, they might be able to use the stem cells to help that person. For example, some people need bone marrow transplants to treat conditions such as leukaemia. Often, there isn't a suitable donor. A person's own cord blood stem cells could be used instead.

7 In future, cord blood may be stored. Explain why.

8 Suggest some problems of setting up stores of cord blood.

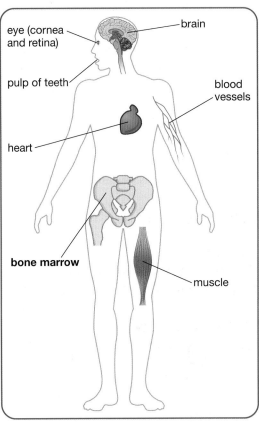

Scientists are developing ways of cloning and using stem cells from these parts of adults.

What you need to remember *Copy and complete using the **key words***

Growing and changing

Many plant cells keep the ability to _____. Most animal cells don't. In mature animals, cells _____ mainly to provide new cells for _____ and replacement. However, special cells called _____ _____ can differentiate into many different types of cells. Embryos and adult _____ _____ are sources of stem cells.

5 Why are stem cells useful?

When a stem cell divides, each cell can either remain a stem cell or develop into a specialised cell such as a brain cell. Scientists hope to be able to use stem cells to repair damaged parts. Imagine being able to grow replacement

- heart muscle destroyed by a heart attack
- brain tissue damaged by a stroke
- nerve tissue to repair a paralysed patient's damaged spinal cord.

Some experimental treatments have worked.
However, there are a lot of problems to overcome.
Scientists warn that solving them will take many years.

1 Read the magazine article. Why did the doctors use the patient's own stem cells?

2 Why did the doctors need to compare the two sets of patients?

3 Suggest why doctors and scientists

    a don't offer this treatment to everyone with heart damage

    b are trying to find new sources of adult stem cells.

Some problems with the science

Scientists have done a lot of experiments using embryonic stem cells. Unfortunately, stem cells sometimes grow into tumours or into the wrong kind of cells. Bone cells are not much use in a heart.

4 Why do many scientists expect stem cells from embryos to be more useful than adult stem cells?

5 Copy and complete the sentence.

Scientists have to overcome the problems of

- _____ by a person's immune system of stem cells that are not their own
- making only the _____ kinds of specialised _____
- stopping growth before _____ develop.

REMEMBER

Stem cells are unspecialised.

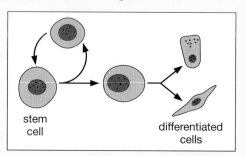

stem cell   differentiated cells

Stem cells from embryos can grow into more specialised types of cells than adult stem cells.

Adult stem cells repair hearts

Doctors have used injections of stem cells to repair failing hearts. Ten patients with heart failure volunteered for this revolutionary treatment.

Doctors carried it out during open-heart surgery. They took marrow from the patients' hip-bones and injected it into damaged parts of their heart muscle.

One in 10 000 cells in bone marrow is a stem cell. Because they used the patient's own stem cells, there was no problem of rejection. Rejection is what happens when the immune system destroys cells that are not the same as a patient's own cells.

For the next 6 months, doctors compared the patients with others who'd had the same operations but no stem cells. Only the stem cell patients had developed new heart muscle and stronger hearts.

Embryonic stem cells

Scientists are trying to make use of two ideas to produce embryonic stem cells to match the patient that needs them.

- The first idea is that you can transplant an adult cell nucleus into an egg cell and make it develop into an embryo. This is the same idea that produced Dolly the sheep.
- The second is that embryonic stem cells can grow into any kind of cell.

Look at the diagram.

6 Copy and complete the sentences.

We can fuse an empty _____ cell and an adult cell _____ to produce an embryo. The _____ then contains _____ cells that are a match for the adult. They will not be rejected when doctors use them to _____ that adult.

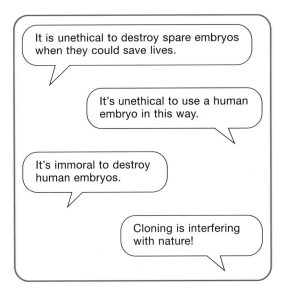

patient

transplant into patient

remove a cell

human egg cell

stimulate the cells to grow into a particular cell type

remove the nucleus

fuse the adult cell and the 'empty' egg cell

remove stem cells

stimulate it to grow and divide

embryonic stem cells

embryo

Some social and ethical issues

In the UK, cloning to produce new adults is not allowed. But scientists can clone embryos up to 14 days old to produce stem cells for research and for treatment of serious disorders.

Often, IVF treatment produces more embryos than are needed. These embryos are usually destroyed.
With permission, scientists can use them. Although this is legal, not everyone agrees with it.

7 Write a short letter to a newspaper giving arguments for <u>or</u> against cloning embryos to produce stem cells.

It is unethical to destroy spare embryos when they could save lives.

It's unethical to use a human embryo in this way.

It's immoral to destroy human embryos.

Cloning is interfering with nature!

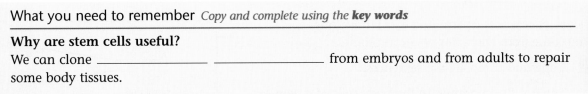

What you need to remember *Copy and complete using the* **key words**

Why are stem cells useful?
We can clone _____ _____ from embryos and from adults to repair some body tissues.

You need to be able to consider social and ethical issues surrounding the use of embryonic stem cells in medical research and treatments.

6 What makes you male or female?

Human body cells contain 23 pairs of chromosomes.
They are in the nucleus of each cell.

Your 23 pairs of chromosomes look like this: or like this:

> **1** Describe one difference between the two sets of chromosomes.

The last two chromosomes in each set carry the genes that make you male or female. We call them sex chromosomes.
There are two different kinds of sex chromosome.
They are called X and Y chromosomes.

> **2** Look at the photograph. What difference can you see between an X and a Y chromosome?

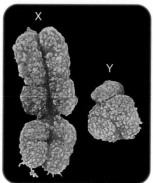

Sex chromosomes.

Each person has either one **X** and one **Y** or two **X** chromosomes.

> **3** Look at the pictures. What do you notice about the sex chromosomes of all the females?

> **4** What can you say about the sex chromosomes of all the males?

> **5** Look back at the two sets of chromosomes at the top of the page.
> Which set belongs to a female and which belongs to a male?

Chromosomes in sperm and eggs

Gametes, or sex cells (sperm and eggs), have one chromosome from each pair of chromosomes.

> **6** Copy and complete the sentences.
>
> The sex chromosomes in the body cells of a woman are both _____. So all her egg cells have one _____ sex chromosome.
> In men, body cells have one _____ and one _____ sex chromosome. So half of a man's sperm contain an _____ and the other half a _____ sex chromosome.

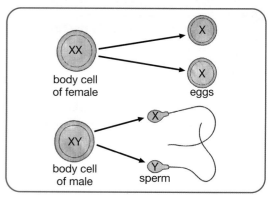

A boy or a girl?

Whether a baby is a **girl** or a **boy** depends on which **sperm** fertilises an **egg**.

7 Copy and complete the table.
Use the diagrams to help you.

Egg cell	Sperm	Fertilised egg cell	Sex of the child
X	X		
X	Y		

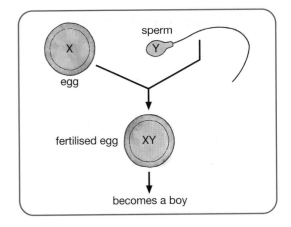

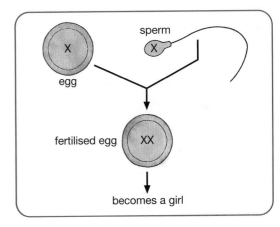

During the first few weeks inside the womb, boys and girls are exactly the same. Then part of the Y chromosome starts working in a boy. It makes the growing sex organs develop into testes instead of ovaries.

How many girls, how many boys?

8 We would expect equal numbers of baby girls and baby boys to be born.
Explain why.

9 In fact, 105 boys are born for every 100 girls.
Suggest some possible reasons.

What you need to remember *Copy and complete using the key words*

What makes you male or female?

One of your 23 pairs of chromosomes carries the genes that determine sex.
In females, both sex chromosomes are the same; they are both _____.
In males, one sex chromosome is an _____ and the other a _____.
All the _____ cells of a woman contain an X chromosome.
_____ cells contain an X or a Y chromosome.

X egg cell + Y sperm cell ⟶ a baby _____
X egg cell + X sperm cell ⟶ a baby _____

7 Some human genes

Genes control many of your characteristics

Each of your 23 pairs of chromosomes is made up of lots of genes. Genes control your **characteristics**.
Sometimes only one pair of genes controls a characteristic.
Most characteristics are controlled by more than one gene.
The environment also has an effect.

Chromosomes are made of long molecules of a substance called DNA. So each gene is a section of a DNA molecule.

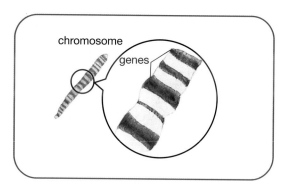

> **1** Some people compare the genes on a chromosome to beads on a necklace.
> Explain why.

Chromosomes come in pairs, so genes are also in pairs.
The two members of a pair of genes can have different forms. They are called **alleles**. A baby may get different alleles from each parent.

The DNA in each form is slightly different, so each produces a different effect.

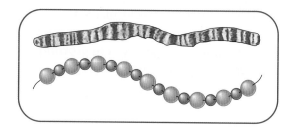

> **2** What do we call different forms of a gene?

When sex cells join

When two sex cells or **gametes** join, we call the process fertilisation. The new cell gets half of its chromosomes from each **parent**.

> **3** **a** Copy and complete the diagram.
> **b** Explain why the new cell divides by mitosis.

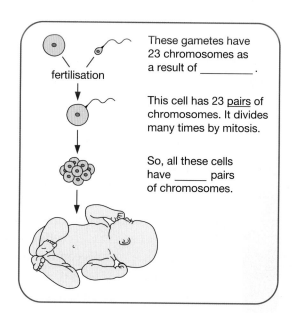

These gametes have 23 chromosomes as a result of _____ .

This cell has 23 <u>pairs</u> of chromosomes. It divides many times by mitosis.

So, all these cells have _____ pairs of chromosomes.

REMEMBER

A cell with only two pairs of chromosomes ...   ... can make these different sex cells.

Genes separate into sex cells in the same way.
So we can draw diagrams like the one above for genes.

Passing on blood group genes

Humans have several blood group systems.
One of them has three different alleles. We call them A, B and O. Another blood group system is the rhesus system (D). There are several other blood group systems in addition to these, too.

Look at the diagrams.

> **4** Why does a person have only two of the alleles A, B and O?

> **5** Draw the missing gamete.

You have about 20 000 to 25 000 different genes. So it's hard to imagine the number of different gametes that you can make.

Also, gametes fuse at random. So sexual reproduction leads to lots of **variation** between the offspring.

The next pages take these ideas further.

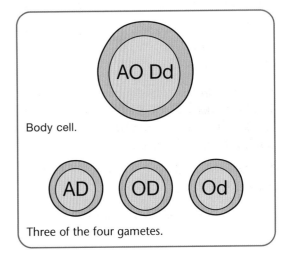

Body cell.

Three of the four gametes.

What you need to remember *Copy and complete using the **key words***

Some human genes
Just one gene controls some _____. A gene may have different forms called

_____.

When _____ or sex cells fuse, one of each pair of alleles comes from each

_____. So sexual reproduction leads to _____.

8 Why are some alleles hidden?

Why are blood groups important?

If you lose a lot of blood, you may need to be given blood from a donor. We call this a blood transfusion. It has to be the right blood group. When doctors first tried transfusing blood, many people died. Doctors didn't know that the donor's and recipient's blood needed to match.

If blood groups don't match, the red blood cells clump together. The clumps block blood vessels and the person dies. An Austrian called Karl Landsteiner discovered this in 1901.

> **1** Why is the blood group on the donor card?

You inherit your blood group

One **gene** on chromosome 1 controls the rhesus blood group. It has two different forms or **alleles**. They are rhesus positive (D) and rhesus negative (d). Either one of these can be present on each of a person's two copies of **chromosome** 1.

> **2** One set of alleles on the chromosome pair could be Dd.
> Write down the other <u>two</u> possible sets.

We call an allele that can hide the effect of another allele, the **dominant** allele. We say that the 'hidden' allele is **recessive**.

> **3** For the rhesus blood group, which allele is dominant?
> Explain your answer.

The recessive allele controls the development of a **characteristic** <u>only</u> when the dominant allele isn't present.

> **4** Someone with blood group alleles AO is group A.
>
> **a** Which allele, A or O, is dominant?
> **b** Which alleles does a person with blood group O have?

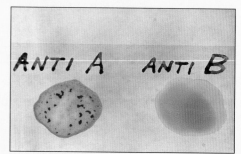

REMEMBER

One blood group system is ABO. Another is the rhesus system.

Group B blood has antibodies against group A (anti-A). So group B blood clumps the red cells in a person with group A blood. Anti-B antibodies wouldn't affect the red cells of someone with group A blood.

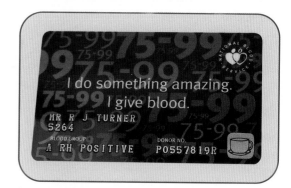

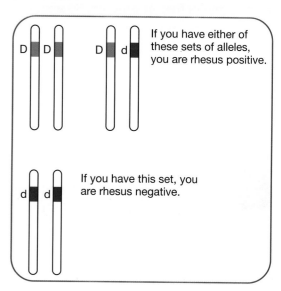

If you have either of these sets of alleles, you are rhesus positive.

If you have this set, you are rhesus negative.

The inheritance pattern

Look at the diagram.
Each sex cell has only one rhesus allele. Sex cells fuse at random.

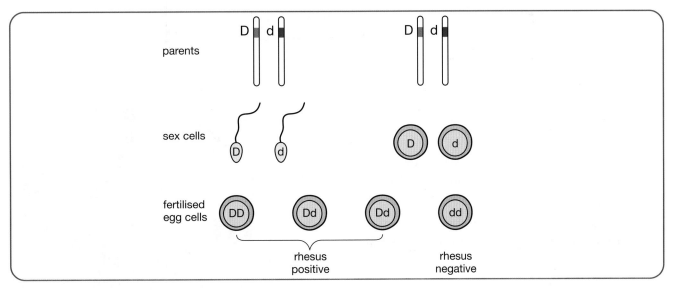

5   What are the chances of these two rhesus positive parents having a rhesus negative child?

6   The diagram on the right is one of the ways we usually draw an inheritance pattern.
Draw a similar diagram for parents who are Dd and dd.

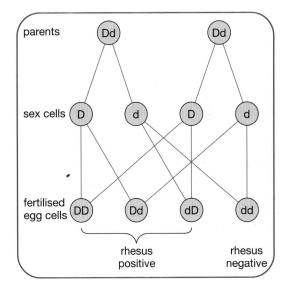

What you need to remember *Copy and complete using the **key words***

Why are some alleles hidden?

Some characteristics are controlled by one _____. This gene may have different forms called _____. If an allele controls the development of a _____ when it is on one _____ only, we call it a _____ allele. An allele that doesn't show up if the dominant allele is present is called a _____ allele.

You need to be able to construct genetic diagrams like you did in question 6.

9 DNA and the genetic code

How does inheritance work?

In 1859 a scientist called Friedrich Miescher separated some large **molecules** from cell nuclei. He called this nuclein.

Then, in 1944, other scientists showed that his nuclein is our genetic material and that it controls what we are like.

We call it **DNA** or deoxyribonucleic acid. It is the chemical that our chromosomes are made from. Each **gene** is a section of DNA.

In 1953, Francis Crick and James Watson worked out the chemical structure and built a model of DNA.

> **1** Look at the Box.
> Write down <u>two</u> patterns observed by other scientists that helped Crick and Watson to work out the structure of DNA.

Finding the structure of DNA

Erwin Chargaff found a pattern in the amounts of the four bases in DNA.

amount of base A = amount of base T

amount of base C = amount of base G

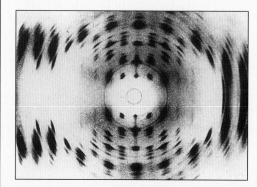

Rosalind Franklin and Maurice Wilkins took this X-ray picture that showed a repeating pattern in the structure of DNA.

A model of DNA

> **2** DNA is made of two strands linked together.
>
> **a** What is the shape of the molecule?
> **b** What links the two strands together?

There was still the problem of how DNA did its job.
No one knew how DNA coded for the genetic information.

Think of a DNA molecule as a bit like a ladder. The base pairs that link the two strands are like the rungs of the ladder. They are either A–T or C–G.

The shape of the DNA molecule turned out to be a double helix. So think of a ladder twisted into a spiral.

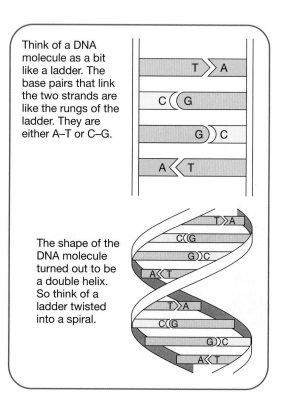

Cracking the genetic code

There are over 20 different **amino** acids. Cells combine them in different numbers and different orders to make different proteins. So we can make lots of different proteins.

> **3** It is possible to make hundreds of different proteins from just 20 amino acids.
> Explain why.

Our cells make proteins in tiny structures in the cytoplasm called ribosomes. They get their instructions in code from the DNA in the nucleus. Scientists knew that one gene codes for one **protein**. What they needed to find out was the codes for the amino acids which make up proteins.

In 1961, Crick worked out the code.

> **4** Look at the diagrams.
> There are 20 naturally occurring amino acids.
> Explain why the code must have more than two of the bases A, T, G and C.

If one base codes for one amino acid, four bases can only code for four amino acids.

If two bases code for each amino acid, 16 different amino acid codes are possible.

	A	T	G	C
A	AA	AT	AG	AC
T	TA	TT	TG	TC
G	GA	GT	GG	GC
C	CA	CT	CG	CC

If three bases code for each amino acid, there are more possible codes than there are amino acids.

GCA	GCG	GTA	CAT	ATA
AAT	TAG	TTT	CAA	AAG
...	...	...	...	...

How does the code work?

The code has to have three bases to produce all the different amino acids. Each group of three bases is the code for one amino acid.

> **5** The diagram above shows only ten three-base codes.
> Work out at least another <u>ten</u> of the 64 possible codes for yourself.

The order of the bases on the DNA molecule controls the order of the amino acids in a protein.

> **6** This is the code for a small part of a protein molecule.
>
> GTT ATG TGG TTT GTT
>
> Write down the sequence of amino acids that this codes for.

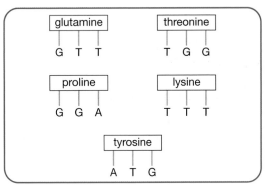

These are the codes for five amino acids. You do not need to remember them. You do need to remember that three bases code for one amino acid.

What you need to remember *Copy and complete using the **key words***

DNA and the genetic code

Chromosomes are made up of large _____ of deoxyribonucleic acid.
We usually call it _____. A _____ is a small section of DNA.
Each gene codes for a particular combination of _____ acids that makes a particular _____.

10 DNA fingerprinting

Just like your fingerprints, your DNA is **unique** to you. Only **identical** twins have identical DNA. So we can use some of the patterns of bases to identify an individual.

1 Suggest why identifying someone from a DNA sample is called DNA or genetic fingerprinting.

In 1984, Alec Jeffreys was investigating DNA in connection with inherited disorders in families. He wanted to identify genes that caused these disorders.

He noticed that there were bits of DNA with repeating patterns that seemed to be unique to an individual.

He checked this idea using DNA from people in his research assistant's family. He found matches and realised that he should be able to use the patterns to **identify** individuals. It took him about 3 months to get the process working properly.

How to take a DNA fingerprint

Look at the diagram.

2 What must samples for DNA fingerprinting contain?

3 What do scientists use to cut up the DNA?

4 What does a gene probe do?

5 Suggest why the DNA strand has to be single or open for the gene probe to join with it.

At first, the markers were radioactive and detected using X-ray film. Newer methods use fluorescent or coloured markers.

By making lots of copies of DNA, scientists can now test much smaller samples.

6 How can scientists now do a DNA fingerprint from the few cells at the base of two or three hairs?

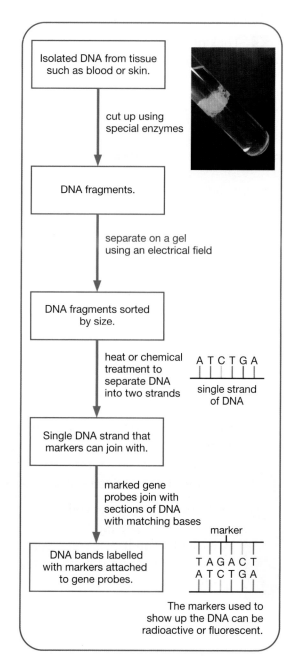

Isolated DNA from tissue such as blood or skin.

cut up using special enzymes

DNA fragments.

separate on a gel using an electrical field

DNA fragments sorted by size.

heat or chemical treatment to separate DNA into two strands

A T C T G A
single strand of DNA

Single DNA strand that markers can join with.

marked gene probes join with sections of DNA with matching bases

marker

DNA bands labelled with markers attached to gene probes.

T A G A C T
A T C T G A

The markers used to show up the DNA can be radioactive or fluorescent.

What is a DNA fingerprint like?

The original DNA fingerprints looked a bit like bar codes. Now the data is often computerised.

Look at the picture.

The top two charts show the genetic fingerprints of a mother, child and one possible father. The one on the right shows the bars that match the mother's DNA. The bars in the child's DNA fingerprint must be in either the mother's or the father's DNA.

> **7** Which of the two possible fathers, the one on the bottom left or the one on the bottom right, is the real father? Explain your answer.

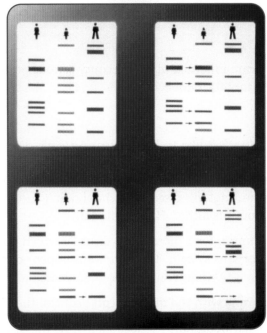

DNA fingerprinting to find out who was the father of a child.

Uses of DNA fingerprinting

The first use of DNA fingerprinting was in an immigration case.

A Ghanaian boy tried to join his mother in the UK. She couldn't prove that he was her son. Her solicitor asked Jeffreys to help. He was able to prove that the boy was her son and brother to her other children.

> **8** What might Jeffreys' evidence have looked like? Explain in words or use a drawing.

Another early use was in a murder case called the Pitchfork murders. Blood tests indicated that the same man carried out two murders. DNA tests showed that the suspect wasn't the murderer. Police then asked Jeffreys to test the DNA of all the men with the same blood group in three nearby villages. The actual murderer got a friend to take his test for him so he wasn't found out at first. But Pitchfork, the murderer, boasted about it and was arrested. His DNA was a match.

> **9** Some people want the DNA fingerprint of everyone in the UK to be stored on a database. Suggest <u>one</u> reason for and <u>one</u> against this.

DID YOU KNOW?

We now use DNA **fingerprinting** to solve crimes, to identify bodies, and to identify relationships in plants and animals as well as humans. There is a national database of 2.5 million DNA fingerprints in the UK.

What you need to remember *Copy and complete using the key words*

DNA fingerprinting

Apart from _____ twins, each person has _____ DNA. Scientists can use this to _____ individuals in a process called DNA _____.

11 Huntington's disease

Some inherited disorders cause serious problems or disability. Others don't.

What's it like to have Huntington's disease?

Michael and his father both have a disorder called Huntington's disease. Michael didn't catch the disorder from his father. He inherited it.

Huntington's disease is a disorder which damages your **nervous** system. The symptoms appear as you get older, usually when you are about 35 years old.

People with the disorder can't control their muscles.

Their bodies may jerk suddenly. As the disorder gets worse they can't think clearly. There is no cure, and people die from it in middle age.

1 Michael feels healthy now.
How will the disorder affect him as he gets older?

How do people get Huntington's disease?

A faulty allele causes Huntington's disease. The allele is **dominant**. So just one faulty allele, from **one** of your parents, is enough to give you this disorder. Everyone who has this allele develops the disorder.

Because symptoms don't show until a person is 30–40 years old, a person may have passed on the allele to children before he or she knows that they have it.

2 Which parent passed on the faulty allele to Michael?

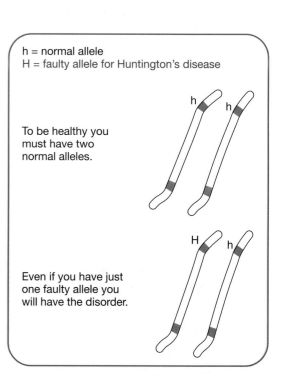

h = normal allele
H = faulty allele for Huntington's disease

To be healthy you must have two normal alleles.

Even if you have just one faulty allele you will have the disorder.

Michael's family tree

Look at the family tree. Michael has the disorder.
His brother Wayne has had a test. He has only normal
alleles. Paul, aged 21, can't decide whether to have the test
or not.

3 Why does everyone with the Huntington's disease
allele always develop symptoms?

4 Draw a diagram to show what Paul's alleles would
be like if he had Huntington's disease.

5 For Paul, write down some advantages and
disadvantages of having a test.

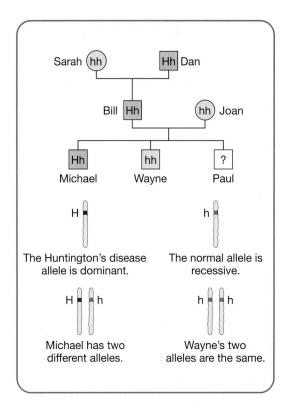

The Huntington's disease allele is dominant.

The normal allele is recessive.

Michael has two different alleles.

Wayne's two alleles are the same.

6 The diagram shows the allele combinations possible
in Bill and Joan's children.
What is the probability that Paul has only normal
alleles?

7 Copy and complete the sentences.

Chromosomes and genes are in _____.
Sometimes the two _____ in a pair of
genes are different. We call the one that shows up,
the _____ allele. When only one parent
has a dominant allele, there is a 50:50
_____ of passing it to a child.

8 **a** Draw diagrams like the ones for Bill and Joan
to show the children that Michael could have
with a woman who also had the alleles Hh.
b What are the chances of Michael and a woman
who also had the alleles Hh having a child with
Huntington's disease?

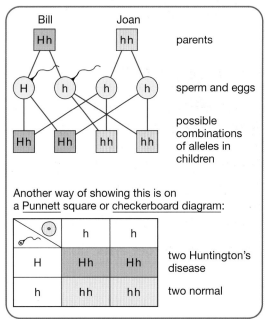

parents

sperm and eggs

possible combinations of alleles in children

Another way of showing this is on
a Punnett square or checkerboard diagram:

two Huntington's disease

two normal

What you need to remember *Copy and complete using the* **key words**

Huntington's disease
This is a disorder of the _____ system. The allele that causes it is
_____ so it takes only _____ parent with the disorder to pass it on.

You need to be able to draw and interpret genetic diagrams just like you did in question 8.

12 Cystic fibrosis

You can catch a cold or measles. Microorganisms cause these diseases. You can't catch cystic fibrosis. It is an **inherited** disorder.

> **1** Imagine you have cystic fibrosis. You are in hospital for a check-up. A friend is worried about coming to see you.
> Write her a note explaining why she cannot catch the disorder from you.

What is it like to have cystic fibrosis?

Laura has cystic fibrosis. It's a disorder of **cell** membranes, so it affects Laura in many ways.

She has to have physiotherapy every day to help her get rid of the very thick and sticky mucus that blocks the tubes to her lungs.

This mucus affects her breathing. Also, her lungs are easily infected because microorganisms are trapped in this mucus.

Another problem is that Laura's digestive glands, such as her pancreas, don't work properly. She has to take enzymes every time she has a meal. If she forgets to take them, she can't digest her food properly.

> **2** Laura soon gets breathless when she plays sports. Why is this?

> **3** Laura is smaller than most other girls of her age. Write down <u>one</u> possible reason for this.

How do people get cystic fibrosis?

The allele for cystic fibrosis is **recessive**. So you get cystic fibrosis only if you inherit it from **both** parents.

> **4** Explain why you need a faulty allele from both parents to get cystic fibrosis.

People who have one faulty allele but don't have the disorder are called **carriers**.

> **5** A person with two healthy parents could still get cystic fibrosis.
> Explain how.

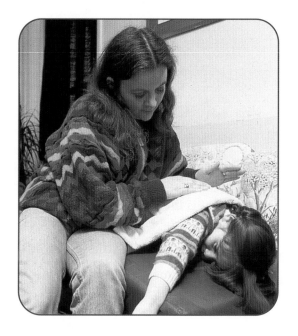

C = normal allele
c = faulty allele for cystic fibrosis

If you have two normal alleles you are healthy.

If you have one normal allele and one faulty allele you are healthy.

If you have two faulty alleles you have the disorder.

How do you know if you are a carrier?

One in 20 people carries the cystic fibrosis allele.

Until Laura was born, her parents had no idea that they were carriers of cystic fibrosis. After Laura was born, they were worried about the risk of having another child with the disorder.

Their doctor sent them to a genetic counsellor.

6 Look at the diagrams the counsellor used.

    a Write down the alleles of Laura and her parents.
    b Why do we call her parents carriers?

7 Complete the sentence to explain what the counsellor said to Laura's parents.

    If both parents are _____ of cystic fibrosis, there is a one in _____ chance of a child having the disorder.

There is a test to find out whether or not you are a carrier of the cystic fibrosis **allele**. Some people think that anyone wanting to start a family should have the test. It's not very expensive. Caring for a cystic fibrosis child is costly in time and money, and it is stressful to watch a loved one suffer.

8 Suggest <u>one</u> argument for and <u>one</u> against testing everyone for cystic fibrosis before they start a family.

9 There is a clue in this family tree that a recessive allele causes the characteristic shown in green. What is the clue?

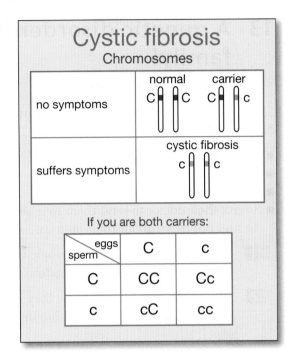

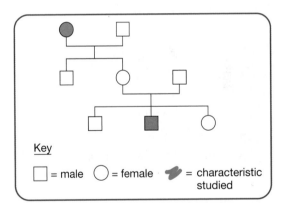

Key

☐ = male   ◯ = female   ⬗ = characteristic studied

What you need to remember *Copy and complete using the **key words***

Cystic fibrosis
Some disorders are passed on by genes. We say they are _____.
Cystic fibrosis is a disorder of _____ membranes. The cause is a _____ allele.
So to get cystic fibrosis you must inherit a faulty allele from _____ of your parents.
People who have one copy of the allele are called _____. They don't have the disorder but they can pass on the faulty _____.

You need to be able to construct genetic diagrams and to predict and explain the results of crosses just like you have done on these pages.

13 A genetic disorder in the family!

Sometimes people know that they carry **alleles** for disorders. They may decide

- not to have children
- to adopt a child
- to let nature take its course
- to ask their doctor to send them to a genetic counsellor to find out more about their options.

1 Write down <u>two</u> ways that people find out whether or not they have alleles for serious genetic disorders.

2 Where can people who know they have a genetic disorder go for advice about having a baby?

Counselling for Laura's parents

Laura's parents want to have another child. The genetic counsellor told them that their chances of having another affected child were one in four.

They know that they haven't the time and energy to look after two children with cystic fibrosis. They dread the day when Laura can't fight off an infection, or when she needs a heart–lung transplant and can't get one. Transplants can save the lives of people with cystic fibrosis.

3 Laura's parents love her.
Suggest why having another child with cystic fibrosis would be a problem for

    a Laura
    b her parents
    c the new baby.

4 Suggest why Laura's heart could be given to someone else if Laura had a heart–lung transplant.

I couldnt bear to watch another child suffer – or cope with the work.

It's hard for a second child with this disorder to watch an older child suffer and know this will happen to them.

I'm worried about her future. We'll be lucky if she lives until she is 30.

It's a struggle for all of us coping with physiotherapy, illness and all these pills.

Problems when there is cystic fibrosis in the family.

Testing a fetus

One option that the counsellor discusses with Laura's parents is testing cells from a fetus for the cystic fibrosis alleles. We call it pre-natal diagnosis.

Look at the diagram.

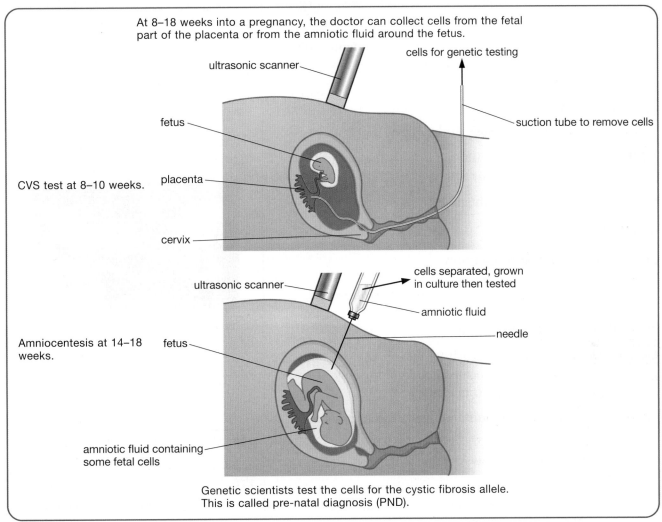

At 8–18 weeks into a pregnancy, the doctor can collect cells from the fetal part of the placenta or from the amniotic fluid around the fetus.

cells for genetic testing

ultrasonic scanner

suction tube to remove cells

fetus

CVS test at 8–10 weeks.

placenta

cervix

ultrasonic scanner

cells separated, grown in culture then tested

amniotic fluid

needle

Amniocentesis at 14–18 weeks.

fetus

amniotic fluid containing some fetal cells

Genetic scientists test the cells for the cystic fibrosis allele. This is called pre-natal diagnosis (PND).

Sampling like this involves a small risk of losing the baby.
The test is not 100% accurate.

If the fetus has two copies of the cystic fibrosis allele, they would offer a termination. Another word for a termination is an abortion.

5 Why would they only terminate a fetus with two copies of the allele?

6 Laura's parents decide against embryo testing. Suggest two reasons why many people turn down this option.

Views on abortion

- Some people think that abortion is morally wrong in all circumstances.
- Some think that it's wrong to allow the birth of a very sick child.
- Others think that it's always the mother's right to decide whether or not to continue a pregnancy.

Continued on next page

13 A genetic disorder in the family! continued

Another option

An option that avoids possible termination of a pregnancy is to use in vitro fertilisation or IVF.

IVF is a standard fertility treatment for a woman who can't become pregnant. Often, women whose egg tubes are blocked have this treatment.

Look at the flow chart.

7 In IVF treatment, where does fertilisation happen?

8 IVF doesn't always result in a baby being born. Suggest <u>two</u> reasons for this.

Doctors can combine <u>IVF</u> with <u>embryo screening</u>.

Embryo screening and selection

Several embryos are usually produced in IVF treatment. When the embryos are at the eight-cell stage, scientists can screen them for cystic fibrosis alleles.

Doctors remove one cell from each for testing and the embryos continue to grow. Doctors then implant only embryos without cystic fibrosis alleles.

We call this process pre-implantation genetic diagnosis or PGD.

9 Put the sentences below into the correct order to describe PGD. The first one is correct.

- The woman takes fertility drugs to make eggs mature in her ovaries.

- The doctor implants one or two healthy embryos in her womb.

- The eggs are fertilised in a dish.

- The embryos are screened for the cystic fibrosis allele.

- The embryos grow to the eight-cell stage.

- The doctor collects mature eggs from her ovaries.

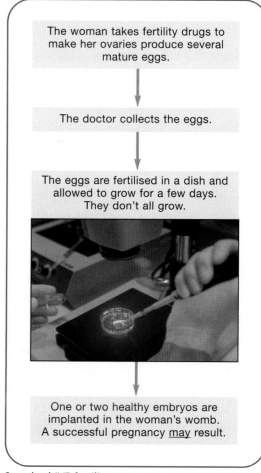

The woman takes fertility drugs to make her ovaries produce several mature eggs.

↓

The doctor collects the eggs.

↓

The eggs are fertilised in a dish and allowed to grow for a few days. They don't all grow.

↓

One or two healthy embryos are implanted in the woman's womb. A successful pregnancy <u>may</u> result.

Standard IVF fertility treatment.

Pre-implantation genetic diagnosis

- <u>Pre-implantation</u> means before implantation.

- <u>Genetic diagnosis</u> means finding out whether the embryo has an allele for a genetic disorder.

A brother for Laura

Laura's parents decided that they would like to try to have a baby by embryo screening and selection. They felt uncomfortable about terminating a pregnancy, but not about destroying balls of cells before implantation.

The doctor implanted two embryos and one, now called Jamie, survived.

10 Suggest why some people object to selecting some embryos and destroying others.

11 Doctors can only do what the law allows. Name the organisation that decides what is lawful in embryo selection.

12 For the three examples shown on the right, suggest why the HFEA made each decision.

Designer babies

Some people argue against the use of embryo screening. They say that it is a step on the road to producing 'designer babies'.

Laura's brother is a 'selected baby', not a 'designer baby'. To produce a baby with the characteristics you wanted, scientists would have to add or remove genes from a fertilised egg cell. This is genetic modification. The law doesn't allow this on human embryos.

13 Suppose in the future, designing babies were possible and lawful. Suggest some problems that this could cause.

Normally, sex selection is not allowed.

Doctors can select female embryos in cases where it is only the male embryo that is at risk of a genetic disorder such as haemophilia.

Embryo selection to provide matching cord blood for a dying family member has been allowed after appeal. It is not allowed if a baby is wanted <u>only</u> to save another child.

Some uses of embryo screening.
The Human Fertilisation and Embryology Authority (HFEA) decides which uses of embryo screening are within the law.

What you need to remember *Copy and complete using the **key words***

A genetic disorder in the family!
Embryos can be screened for the _____ that cause genetic disorders such as Huntington's disease and _____ _____.

You need to be able to make informed judgements based on economic, social and ethical issues concerning embryo screening.

H

14 More genetic crosses

> **REMEMBER**
>
> You have already looked at inheritance patterns of some genes. You can use what you have learnt because other genes, such as sickle cell disorder, have the same patterns.

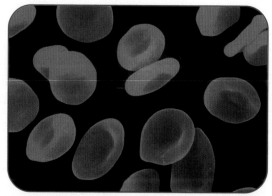

Normal red blood cells.

The inheritance pattern for sickle cell disorder

People with this disorder have abnormal haemoglobin in their red blood cells. Sometimes they feel well. At other times, they are tired and catch infections easily. Their red blood cells can go out of shape and block capillaries, causing painful swellings. They spend a lot of time in hospital.

1 Describe <u>two</u> differences between the red blood cells of people with sickle cell and normal alleles.

Sickle cells don't carry oxygen as well as normal red blood cells.

How is sickle cell disorder inherited?

The normal haemoglobin allele is <u>dominant</u>, so one recessive sickle cell allele produces no symptoms. A person with one sickle cell allele is called a carrier. When both parents are carriers, there is a one in four chance of a child having the disorder.

2 The diagram below shows the inheritance pattern for cystic fibrosis.
Compare it to the pattern for sickle cell disorder.

	eggs C	c
sperm		
C	CC normal	Cc carrier
c	cC carrier	cc cystic fibrosis

Cystic fibrosis.

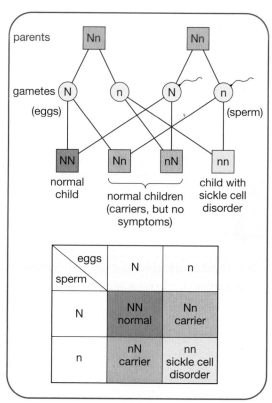

Sickle cell disorder.

More patterns

You can predict the outcome of crosses because of the way alleles are inherited. The patterns apply to any of the genes that you've studied.

Look at the chart on the right.

3 In rows 1, 3 and 6 in the chart, there is only one possible outcome.
Explain why.

4 Complete this diagram to show that the prediction in row 2 of the chart is correct.

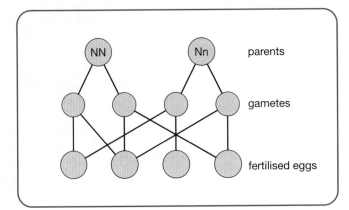

5 What are the characteristics of children with

a NN alleles?
b Nn alleles?

6 a Draw a genetic diagram for the cross in row 4.
b What characteristics do these children have?

Read the information in the Box.

7 a Two parents with polydactyly produce a child with the normal number of fingers and toes. What are the alleles of the parents?
b Draw a genetic diagram to show how they can produce a child with the normal number of fingers and toes.
c What are their chances of producing a child with a normal number of fingers and toes?

	Cross (alleles of parents)	Predicted outcome (possible children)
1	NN × NN	NN only
2	NN × Nn	NN or Nn (all normal)
3	NN × nn	Nn only
4	Nn × nn	Nn or nn (1 normal to 1 sickle)
5	Nn × Nn	NN, nN, Nn or nn (3 normal to 1 sickle)
6	nn × nn	nn only

In this example, N is normal (dominant) and n is sickle cell haemoglobin. But the pattern is the same for other genes with a dominant and a recessive allele.

Polydactyly

There is a dominant allele that causes the growth of extra fingers or toes. This allele is called polydactyly.

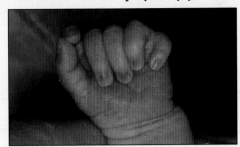

People with two recessive alleles have the normal number of fingers and toes.

What you need to remember

More genetic crosses
There is nothing new for you to <u>remember</u> in this section.

You need to be able to predict and explain the results of crosses for all the possible combinations of dominant and recessive alleles of the same gene.

1 What are atoms made of?

The diagram shows what is inside a helium atom.
In the centre of the atom is the **nucleus**.

> **1** **a** What two sorts of particles do you find in the
> nucleus of an atom?
> **b** What is the same about these two particles?
> **c** What is different?

> **2** Copy and complete the table.

Name of particle	Mass	Electrical charge
proton	1	+1
neutron		
electron		

> **3** The complete helium atom has no electrical charge
> overall. Why is this?

The number of protons is always **equal** to the number of
electrons in an atom. This means that the positive and the
negative charges balance in an atom.

> **4** Explain why atoms have no overall electrical charge.

The symbols that tell us what atoms contain

This diagram tells you everything you need to know about
a helium atom.

> **5** Copy and complete the following sentences.
>
> The helium atom has _____ protons.
> So it must also have _____ electrons.
> The helium atom has a mass number of
>
> _____ .
>
> So it must contain two _____ in its
> nucleus.

The atomic number of an atom tells us which element the
atom is. So an atom with two protons must be a helium
atom.

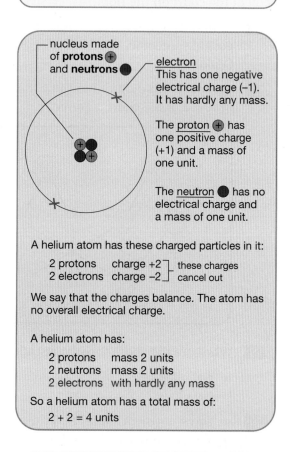

REMEMBER

In the centre of an atom there is the nucleus.
Around the nucleus there are particles called **electrons**.

nucleus made of **protons** ⊕ and **neutrons** ●

electron
This has one negative electrical charge (–1). It has hardly any mass.

The proton ⊕ has one positive charge (+1) and a mass of one unit.

The neutron ● has no electrical charge and a mass of one unit.

A helium atom has these charged particles in it:

2 protons   charge +2 ⎤ these charges
2 electrons   charge –2 ⎦ cancel out

We say that the charges balance. The atom has no overall electrical charge.

A helium atom has:

2 protons   mass 2 units
2 neutrons   mass 2 units
2 electrons   with hardly any mass

So a helium atom has a total mass of:
2 + 2 = 4 units

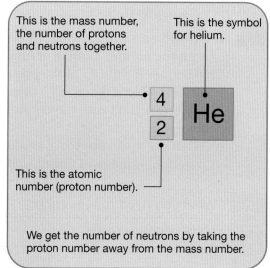

This is the mass number, the number of protons and neutrons together.

This is the symbol for helium.

4
2
He

This is the atomic number (proton number).

We get the number of neutrons by taking the proton number away from the mass number.

All of the atoms of an element have the **same** number of protons.

Atoms of different elements have **different** numbers of protons.

The diagrams show a hydrogen atom and a lithium atom.

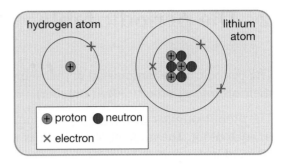

6 Write down the following symbols. Add the mass number and the atomic number for each one.

   a H
   b Li

7 Copy and complete the sentence.

   A sodium atom has _____ protons, _____ electrons and _____ neutrons.

$$^{23}_{11}Na \qquad \text{a sodium atom}$$

8 Why can we also call the atomic number the proton number?

What you need to remember *Copy and complete using the* **key words**

What are atoms made of?
The centre of an atom is called the _____.
The nucleus can contain two kinds of particle:

■ particles with no charge called _____
■ particles with a positive charge called _____.

Every element has its own special _____ _____ (proton number) which is equal to the number of protons.
Atoms of the same element always have the _____ number of protons.
Atoms of different elements have _____ numbers of protons.
Around the nucleus there are particles with a negative charge called _____.
In an atom the number of electrons is _____ to the number of protons.
This means that atoms have no overall electrical charge.

2 The periodic table

The periodic table contains all of the elements in order of their **atomic number** (proton number).

The atomic number also tells you the number of **electrons** in each atom. The number of electrons is what gives an element its properties.

Looking for patterns in a list of elements

The diagram below shows the first 20 elements in the order of their proton numbers.

$_1$H $_2$He $_3$Li $_4$Be $_5$B $_6$C $_7$N $_8$O $_9$F $_{10}$Ne $_{11}$Na $_{12}$Mg $_{13}$Al $_{14}$Si $_{15}$P $_{16}$S $_{17}$Cl $_{18}$Ar $_{19}$K $_{20}$Ca

○ alkali metal   ○ halogen   ○ noble gas

1 Look carefully at the list of elements.

   a What kind of element comes straight after each noble gas?

   b What kind of element usually comes just before each noble gas?

Making the list of elements into a periodic table

To make the list of elements into the periodic table:

- we place hydrogen and helium as shown opposite
- we start a new row of the table every time we reach an element that is an alkali metal.

2 Copy and complete the table.

Group	What we call the elements in the group
1	
	halogens
0	

hydrogen doesn't belong to any group

Group							0
1	2	3	4	5	6	7	
				$_1$H hydrogen			$_2$He helium
$_3$Li lithium	$_4$Be beryllium	$_5$B boron	$_6$C carbon	$_7$N nitrogen	$_8$O oxygen	$_9$F fluorine	$_{10}$Ne neon
$_{11}$Na sodium	$_{12}$Mg magnesium	$_{13}$Al aluminium	$_{14}$Si silicon	$_{15}$P phosphorus	$_{16}$S sulfur	$_{17}$Cl chlorine	$_{18}$Ar argon
$_{19}$K potassium	$_{20}$Ca calcium						

The first 20 elements in the modern periodic table.

Completing the periodic table

The full periodic table shows all the elements that we know about. This makes it look more complicated.

3 There are lots of elements that are not placed in Groups 0 to 7. What do we call these elements?

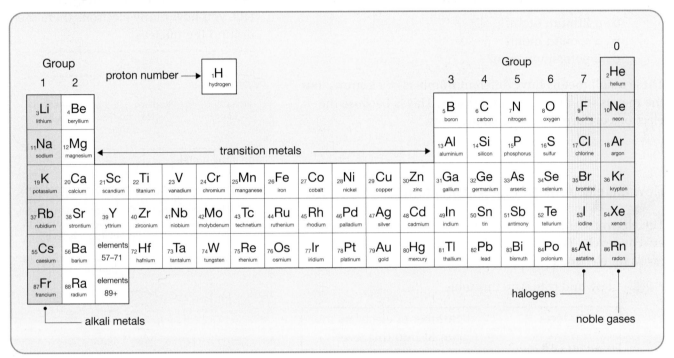

4 Which elements in the periodic table have these atomic numbers?

   a 6

   b 20

   c 12

5 How many electrons do the following elements have?

   a sodium

   b neon

   c oxygen

> **REMEMBER**
>
> The number of protons in an atom is equal to the number of electrons.

What you need to remember *Copy and complete using the key words*

The periodic table

In the modern periodic table, elements are arranged in order of their _____ _____ (proton number).

This tells us the number of protons and also the number of _____ in an atom.

3 Families of elements

What elements are like and the way they react depends on the electrons in their atoms.

1 How many electrons are there in

    a a lithium atom?

    b a sodium atom?

    c a potassium atom?

These alkali metals have different numbers of electrons, but the metals still react in a similar way. This is because the electrons are arranged in a similar way.

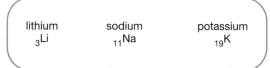

Some alkali metals.

How are electrons arranged in an atom?

The electrons around the nucleus of an atom are in certain **energy levels**. The diagram shows the first three energy levels for electrons.

2 Copy and complete this table.

Energy level	Number of electrons that can fit into this level
first (lowest energy)	
second	
third	

How electrons fill up the energy levels

The first energy level is the **lowest**. The electrons start to fill up this level first. When the first energy level is full, electrons start to fill up the second level.

The diagrams show where the electrons are in the first three elements.

3 Draw the same kind of diagram for

    a a carbon atom, $_6$C

    b an oxygen atom, $_8$O.

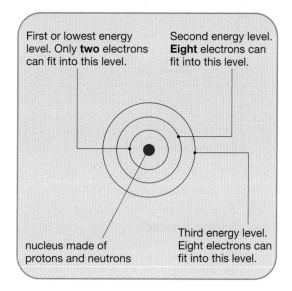

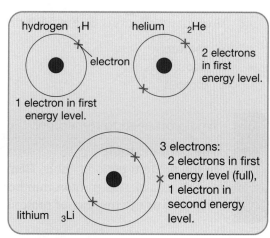

Why alkali metals are in the same family

Lithium, sodium and potassium are very similar elements. We call them alkali metals and put them in Group 1 of the periodic table.

The diagrams show why these elements are similar. The **top** energy level is the one on the outside of the atom.

4 Copy and complete the following sentences.

The elements in Group 1 are similar to each other. This is because they all have just _____ electron in their top energy level.

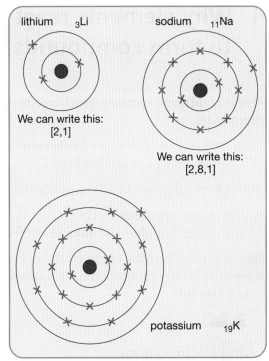

lithium $_3$Li   sodium $_{11}$Na

We can write this:
[2,1]

We can write this:
[2,8,1]

potassium $_{19}$K

These show the arrangement of electrons in the alkali metals of Group 1.

A simple way to show electrons

Drawing electron diagrams takes time. Here is a quicker way to show how electrons are arranged in atoms.

5 Write down the electron arrangement for potassium.

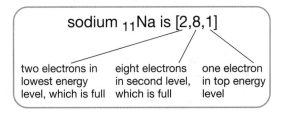

sodium $_{11}$Na is [2,8,1]

two electrons in lowest energy level, which is full

eight electrons in second level, which is full

one electron in top energy level

What you need to remember *Copy and complete using the **key words***

Families of elements
In atoms, the electrons are arranged in certain _____ _____.
The first level has the _____ energy. It can take up to _____ electrons.
The second and third energy levels can each take up to _____ electrons.
Elements in the same group have the same number of electrons in their _____ energy level.

You need to be able to show how the electrons are arranged in the first 20 elements of the periodic table.

4 Why elements react to form compounds

Atoms of different elements react together to form compounds.

1 What joins the atoms of elements together when they make a compound?

Atoms form chemical bonds in one of the following ways.

- The atoms can **share** electrons.
- The atoms can **give and take** electrons.

Elements react because of the electrons in their atoms. Atoms are more stable when their **highest energy level** is completely full.

Giving electrons away

Sodium reacts with other elements by losing an electron. When an atom loses an electron, it forms an **ion**.

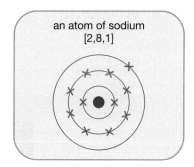

an atom of sodium
[2,8,1]

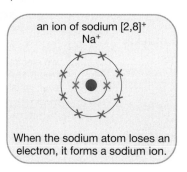

an ion of sodium [2,8]⁺
Na⁺

When the sodium atom loses an electron, it forms a sodium ion.

2 How many electrons are there in the highest energy level of the sodium atom?

When it gives the electron away, the next lowest energy level becomes the highest one. It is completely full.

3 How many electrons are there in the highest energy level of the sodium ion?

> **REMEMBER**
>
> A **compound** is a substance in which two or more elements are not just mixed together. They are joined with chemical bonds.

> **REMEMBER**
>
> - Atoms have electrons in different energy levels around the nucleus.
> - The highest energy level is the level on the outside of an atom.
> - There is room for:
>
>   2 electrons in the first energy level
>   8 electrons in the second energy level
>   8 electrons in the third energy level.
>
> - The number of electrons in an atom is the same as the number of protons.
> - The proton number tells us how many protons are in the nucleus.
> - Electrons have a charge of –1. Protons have a charge of +1.
> - Atoms have no charge overall because there are equal numbers of protons and electrons in each atom.

Taking electrons

An atom can also become an ion by gaining electrons. The highest energy levels of some elements are nearly full. A chlorine atom has seven electrons in its highest energy level.

4 Copy and complete the sentences.

The easiest way for chlorine to fill its highest energy level is to _____ one electron.
This makes the atom more _____.

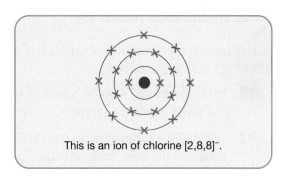

The chlorine atom [2,8,7] needs to gain an electron to make it more stable.

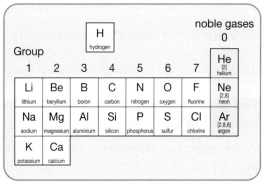

This is an ion of chlorine [2,8,8]⁻.

Like noble gases

The **noble gases** are very unreactive elements. This is because their highest energy levels are already full.

5 Which group do the noble gases belong to?

6 Draw the arrangement of electrons in an atom of

   a neon
   b argon.

Look at the way the electrons are arranged in an atom of neon. It is the same as the electron arrangement in a sodium ion.

An atom is most stable when its highest energy level is full, like the atoms of the noble gases.

7 Which noble gas has the same arrangement of electrons as an ion of chlorine?

8 How is an atom of this noble gas different from an ion of chlorine?

Group							noble gases 0
			H hydrogen				He [2] helium
1	2	3	4	5	6	7	
Li lithium	Be beryllium	B boron	C carbon	N nitrogen	O oxygen	F fluorine	Ne [2,8] neon
Na sodium	Mg magnesium	Al aluminium	Si silicon	P phosphorus	S sulfur	Cl chlorine	Ar [2,8,8] argon
K potassium	Ca calcium						

Group 0 elements are also called the noble gases.

What you need to remember *Copy and complete using the **key words***

Why elements react to form compounds

When two or more elements are joined together with a chemical bond, they form a _____.

Atoms form chemical bonds when they _____ electrons or _____ _____ _____ electrons.

For an atom to be stable, its _____ _____ _____ must be full.

When an atom gives or takes electrons, it forms an _____.

Ions have electron arrangements like those in the _____ _____.

111

5 Group 1 elements

The metals lithium, sodium and potassium are all very similar.
They belong to Group 1 of the periodic table and are also known as the **alkali metals**.

> **REMEMBER**
> A vertical column in the periodic table is called a group.

What are the alkali metals like?

Alkali metals are similar to other metals in some ways. There are also some differences.

1   Write down <u>two</u> ways in which the alkali metals are the same as other metals.

2   Write down <u>three</u> ways in which the alkali metals are different from other metals.

Most metals are hard, but your teacher can cut alkali metals with a knife as easily as cutting cheese.

Why are they called the alkali metals?

Alkali metals have similar **chemical properties**. They are all very reactive and react very fast with cold water.
This means that we have to store them under oil away from the air and water.

When they react with water, they fizz and move around on the surface. They produce the gas called hydrogen.
They also turn the water into a solution that is alkaline.
That is why we call the metals the alkali metals.

3   Why do we store the alkali metals under oil?

4   Copy and complete the sentences.

   When the alkali metals react with water, they produce _____ gas. They also turn the water into an _____ solution.

5   Why are the Group 1 elements called the alkali metals?

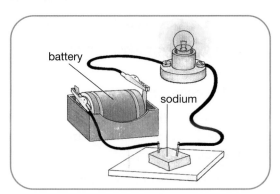

Like other metals, alkali metals conduct electricity and heat, but they melt more easily than most other metals.

Potassium, like lithium and sodium, is lighter (less dense) than other metals. It is so light that it floats on water. The potassium darts about as it reacts with the water, making it fizz.

Looking at the atoms of Group 1 elements

All of the Group 1 elements, like sodium, have just **one** electron in their highest energy level.

> **6** Which is the easiest way for a sodium atom to fill its highest energy level?

When atoms give electrons away, they become **positively charged**. We call an atom which has lost or gained electrons an ion.

> **7** What is the charge on the sodium ion?

We can show the electron arrangement in an atom or ion without drawing all of the energy levels. For example, the electron arrangement in a lithium atom is [2,1].

> **8** Write down the electron arrangement in a sodium ion.

All the same

The other alkali metals like potassium and lithium all form ions with a single positive charge.

> **9** Lithium has three electrons.
> Draw a diagram to show the electron arrangement in
>
> **a** an atom of lithium
>
> **b** an ion of lithium.

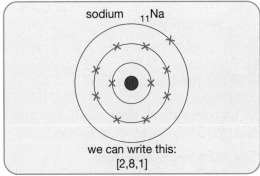

sodium ₁₁Na

we can write this:
[2,8,1]

The easiest way for a sodium atom to become stable is for it to lose an electron.

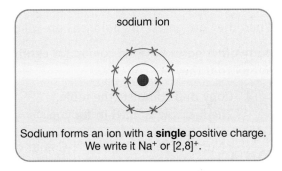

sodium ion

Sodium forms an ion with a **single** positive charge.
We write it Na⁺ or [2,8]⁺.

What you need to remember *Copy and complete using the **key words***

Group 1 elements
Another name for the Group 1 elements is the _____ _____.
All of the elements in this family have similar _____ _____.
Group 1 elements all have _____ electron in their highest energy level.
When they react, they give away this electron.
Atoms which lose electrons become _____ _____ ions.
Group 1 elements form ions with a _____ positive charge.

6 Group 7 elements

We have just learnt about the family of elements called the alkali metals. They are in Group 1 of the periodic table.

In Group 7, there is another family of elements.
We call them the **halogens**.

1 Write down the names of <u>four</u> elements in the halogen family.

Group	1	2	3	4	5	6	7	0
	Li						F	
	Na						Cl	
	K				halogens		Br	
							I	

F is fluorine
Cl is chlorine
Br is bromine
I is iodine

What are the halogens like?

The halogens are all non-metals. The photos show you what they look like at room temperature.

2 At room temperature

   a which halogen is a solid?
   b which two halogens are gases?
   c which halogen is a liquid that gives off a gas?

When they are gases, the halogens are all coloured.

Many other gases have no colour, for example oxygen. We say that they are colourless.

3 Copy and complete the table.
The first row is filled in for you.

Name of the halogen	Colour of the gas
fluorine	pale yellow

Fluorine and chlorine.

Liquid bromine

Iodine crystals

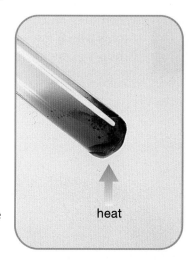

Iodine crystals produce iodine gas when you heat them.

heat

The halogens can react with metals

Although they look different, the halogens have similar **chemical properties**.

They all react with the alkali metals. The alkali metal sodium reacts with chlorine to produce sodium chloride. This is ordinary salt.

> **4** What are the <u>two</u> elements in ordinary salt?

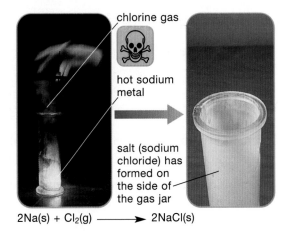

chlorine gas

hot sodium metal

salt (sodium chloride) has formed on the side of the gas jar

$2Na(s) + Cl_2(g) \longrightarrow 2NaCl(s)$

Looking at the atoms of Group 7 elements

All of the Group 7 elements have **seven** electrons in their top energy level.

> **5** Which is the easiest way for a chlorine atom to get a full top energy level?

When atoms gain electrons, they become **negatively charged** ions.

> **6** Copy and complete the sentences.
>
> The chloride ion (Cl^-) has a _____
> negative charge.
> We can show the arrangement of electrons in the ion if we write _____.

> **7** Fluorine has nine electrons.
> Draw a diagram to show the electron arrangement in
>
> **a** an atom of fluorine
> **b** a fluoride ion.

> **REMEMBER**
>
> We call an atom which has lost or gained electrons an ion.

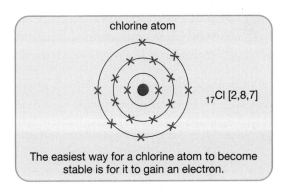

chlorine atom

$_{17}Cl$ [2,8,7]

The easiest way for a chlorine atom to become stable is for it to gain an electron.

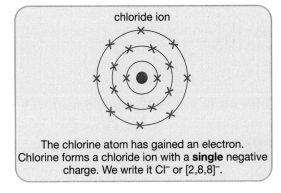

chloride ion

The chlorine atom has gained an electron. Chlorine forms a chloride ion with a **single** negative charge. We write it Cl^- or $[2,8,8]^-$.

What you need to remember *Copy and complete using the* **key words**

Group 7 elements
Another name for the Group 7 elements is the _____.
All of the elements in this family have similar _____ _____.
Group 7 elements all have _____ electrons in their top energy level. When they react, they gain one electron.
Atoms which gain electrons become _____ _____ ions.
Group 7 elements form ions with a _____ negative charge.

7 Metals reacting with non-metals

What happens when sodium reacts with chlorine?

The metal sodium reacts with the non-metal chlorine to produce a compound. We call it sodium chloride.

The diagram shows what happens when sodium reacts with chlorine.

1 Copy and complete the sentences.

The sodium atom gives the _____ in its highest energy level to the _____ atom. This makes both atoms more _____. Both atoms now have an electrical

_____.

We call Na^+ a sodium _____.
We call Cl^- a _____ ion.

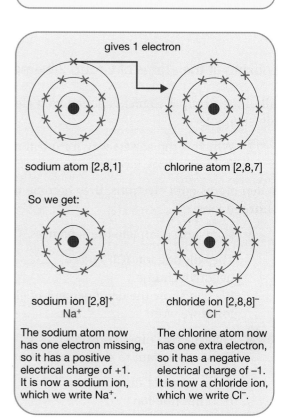

gives 1 electron

sodium atom [2,8,1]   chlorine atom [2,8,7]

So we get:

sodium ion [2,8]⁺
Na^+

chloride ion [2,8,8]⁻
Cl^-

The sodium atom now has one electron missing, so it has a positive electrical charge of +1. It is now a sodium ion, which we write Na^+.

The chlorine atom now has one extra electron, so it has a negative electrical charge of −1. It is now a chloride ion, which we write Cl^-.

Other alkali metals like lithium react with halogens in the same way.

2 Copy the diagram of a lithium atom and a fluorine atom. Then add an arrow to show how the electron moves when they react together.

3 Which atom becomes

a the positively charged ion?
b the negatively charged ion?

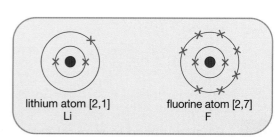

lithium atom [2,1]
Li

fluorine atom [2,7]
F

Ionic substances

Compounds made from ions are called **ionic compounds**. Ionic compounds form when metals react with non-metals.

The diagrams show two examples.

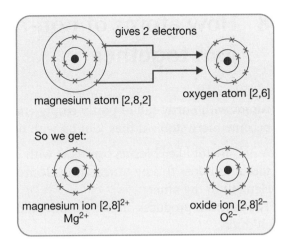

4 Copy the table. Complete it for all of the ions shown in the diagrams. The first one is done for you.

Name of ion	Symbol for the ion
magnesium	Mg^{2+}

5 Now draw a diagram to show how sodium oxide is formed.

The formula of an ionic substance

Sodium chloride has <u>one</u> chloride ion for each sodium ion. We write its formula as NaCl.

In calcium chloride there are <u>two</u> chloride ions for each calcium ion. We write its formula as $CaCl_2$.

6 Write down the formula for magnesium oxide.

7 Sodium oxide has two Na^+ ions for every one O^{2-} ion. Write down the formula for sodium oxide.

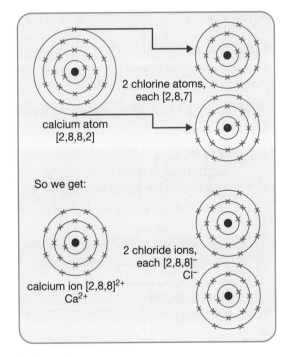

You need to be able to show how the electrons are arranged in the ions for sodium chloride, magnesium oxide and calcium chloride. You can do this in the following forms:

 and [2,8]$^+$ for the sodium ion.

8 How atoms of non-metals can join together

Atoms with partly full or partly empty energy levels can become more stable if they join up with other atoms.

A non-metal like chlorine can react with a metal like sodium. It does this by transferring electrons from one element to the other.
The reaction produces an ionic compound called sodium chloride.

Atoms of non-metals can also join together. For example chlorine can react with the non-metal hydrogen.

What happens when chlorine and hydrogen react?

When two non-metals such as chlorine and hydrogen react, they do it by **sharing** electrons. The diagram shows what happens to the shared electrons.

1   Copy and complete the sentences.

A hydrogen atom and a chlorine atom share one pair of _____.
Each atom is then more stable.
The hydrogen atom has a total of _____ electrons in its first energy level. This level is now _____.

The chlorine atom has a total of _____. electrons in its third energy level. This level is also _____.

This makes a _____ of hydrogen chloride.

2   Write down the formula of hydrogen chloride.

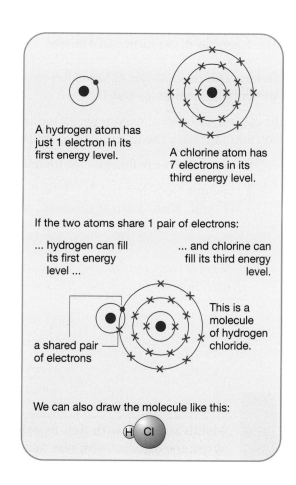

A hydrogen atom has just 1 electron in its first energy level.

A chlorine atom has 7 electrons in its third energy level.

If the two atoms share 1 pair of electrons:

... hydrogen can fill its first energy level ...

... and chlorine can fill its third energy level.

a shared pair of electrons

This is a molecule of hydrogen chloride.

We can also draw the molecule like this:

H Cl

Other covalently bonded molecules

When atoms share electrons we say they form **covalent** bonds.

Covalent bonds are very **strong**.

3 Write down the names of <u>four</u> molecules made from atoms of

    a two different non-metals

    b the same non-metal element.

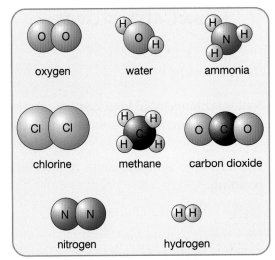

These simple molecules are all made from elements joined with covalent bonds.

Other ways to show covalent bonds

An ammonia molecule (NH_3) is formed when a nitrogen atom shares electrons with three hydrogen atoms. We can show the bonding in three different ways.

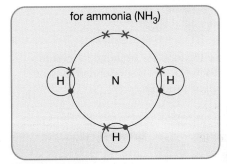

This shows how the electrons are shared in the top energy levels.

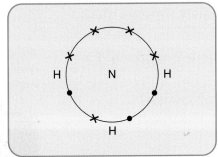

The dots are electrons from the hydrogen atoms. The crosses are electrons from the nitrogen atoms.

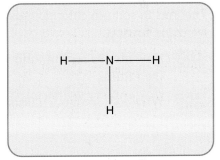

This simply shows that three hydrogen atoms are bonded to one nitrogen atom.

4 Show the covalent bonds in a hydrogen chloride molecule in each of these ways.

What you need to remember *Copy and complete using the **key words***

How atoms of non-metals can join together
Atoms can join together by _____ electrons. The bonds that they form are called _____ bonds and are very _____.

You need to be able to show the covalent bonds in molecules like water, ammonia, hydrogen, hydrogen chloride, methane and oxygen in the following forms:

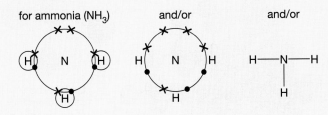

9 Giant structures

Ionic structures

Sodium chloride is an ionic compound. There are strong **forces of attraction** between Na^+ and Cl^- ions. This is because the sodium and chloride ions have **opposite** charges.

The forces act in all directions and we call this **ionic bonding**.

1 What is the charge on

    a a sodium ion?

    b a chloride ion?

2 Why are there strong forces of attraction between the sodium and chloride ions?

The ions in sodium chloride make a giant structure which we call a **lattice**.

3 How are the sodium and chloride ions arranged in the lattice?

4 Why does sodium chloride form crystals?

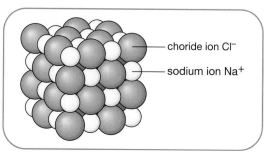

choride ion Cl^-

sodium ion Na^+

This is how the ions are arranged in sodium chloride. Each Na^+ ion is surrounded by six Cl^- ions in a giant structure.

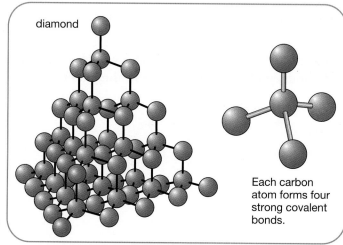

Sodium chloride makes crystals with a regular shape. This is because the ions are arranged in a pattern.

Covalent structures

Many substances with covalent bonds have simple molecules, for example water and oxygen. However, some substances like **silicon dioxide** have giant covalent structures.

5 Copy and complete the sentences.

Two substances which have giant covalent structures are _____ and

_____ _____.

Another name for these structures is

_____.

Many covalently bonded substances are simple molecules, e.g. _____ and _____.

Diamond is a form of carbon. The carbon atoms form a giant covalent structure. We call structures like these **macromolecules**.

diamond

Each carbon atom forms four strong covalent bonds.

Giant structures of metals

Metals allow electric currents and heat (thermal energy) to pass through them easily. We say that they are good conductors of heat and electricity. The diagrams help to explain why metals have these properties.

The electrons in the metals that are free to move

- can carry electric current through the metal
- can carry heat (thermal energy) through the metal.

6 Copy and complete the sentences.

Electrons can move through the structure of metals. They hold the _____ together in a regular pattern.
The free electrons allow metals to be good conductors of _____ and

_____.

7 Which electrons are free to move in the metal?

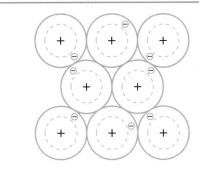

In a piece of metal, the electrons from the highest energy level are **free** to move anywhere in the metal. The electrons hold all of the atoms together in a single giant structure.

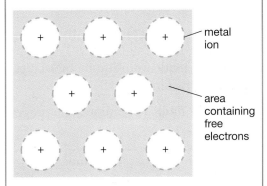

The metal atoms become ions with a positive charge. Because the electrons are free, we can show them as a grey area where we are likely to find them.

Opposites attract

Because the metal atoms lose electrons, they become ions. These **positively** charged ions are held together by the sea of **negatively** charged electrons.
We call these strong **electrostatic** attractions.

8 Explain why the metal atoms form ions with a positive charge.

What you need to remember *Copy and complete using the key words*

Giant structures
Many substances form giant structures.
Ionic compounds form giant structures of ions. We call these a _____. The ions have _____ charges and there are strong _____ _____

_____ between them. The forces act in all directions and this is called

_____ _____.

Some substances with covalent bonds form giant structures, for example _____ and _____ _____. We call these giant structures _____.
Metals also form giant structures. Electrons from the top energy level of the atoms are

_____ to move. The metal atoms form _____ charged ions. The free electrons are _____ charged. The metal ions and free electrons are held together by strong _____ attractions.

121

1 Simple molecules

Many substances are made from simple molecules, for example water and oxygen.

1 What is the formula for

    a water?
    b oxygen?
    c methane?

2 What type of bonds hold the atoms together in simple molecules like these?

> **REMEMBER**
>
> Atoms of non-metals can join together by sharing electrons. The bonds that they form are called covalent bonds and are very strong.
>
> There are covalent bonds in these simple molecules:
>
> | | |
> |---|---|
> | water | H_2O |
> | ammonia | NH_3 |
> | hydrogen | H_2 |
> | hydrogen chloride | HCl |
> | methane | CH_4 |
> | oxygen | O_2 |

Properties of substances with simple molecules

Substances made from simple molecules have several properties in common.

Look at the table. It compares the properties of different chemicals.

Substance	Is it made from simple molecules with covalent bonds?	Melting point (°C)	Boiling point (°C)	Solid, liquid or gas at room temperature?
water	yes	0	100	liquid
methane	yes	−182	−161	gas
sodium chloride	no	801	1413	solid
ammonia	yes	−77	−34	gas
calcium chloride	no	782	1600	solid
magnesium oxide	no	2852	3600	solid
iodine	yes	114	184	solid

3 Copy and complete the sentences.

Substances made from simple molecules have low _____ _____ and low _____ _____.

These substances can be _____, _____ or _____ at room temperature. Solids made from simple molecules have very low melting and _____ _____.

4 Write down what happens if we try to pass electricity through substances with simple molecules.

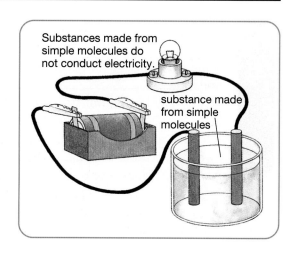

Substances made from simple molecules do not conduct electricity.

substance made from simple molecules

Explaining the properties of simple molecules

The covalent bonds which hold the atoms together in simple molecules are very strong.

There are also forces **between** the simple molecules which are quite **weak**.

5 What name do we give to the weak forces between molecules?

When a substance melts or boils, it uses enough energy for the molecules to overcome the forces holding them together.

If the forces between its molecules are weak, only a small amount of energy is needed to overcome these forces.

That is why substances with simple molecules have low melting points and boiling points.

6 Copy and complete the sentences.

A solid uses _____ when it melts to allow the _____ to slide over each other.
A liquid uses _____ to boil to allow the _____ to escape from the surface of the liquid.
Substances made from simple molecules have weak _____ forces. This means that their melting and boiling points are _____.

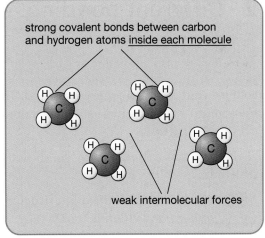

strong covalent bonds between carbon and hydrogen atoms <u>inside each molecule</u>

weak intermolecular forces

There are only weak forces <u>between</u> these molecules. We call these **intermolecular** forces.

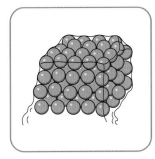

This substance is melting. Its simple molecules do not need much energy to slide over each other.

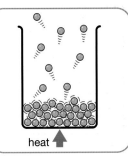

This substance is boiling. Its simple molecules do not need much energy to escape from the surface of the liquid.

heat

Simple molecules like those in methane don't have an overall **electrical charge**. This is why they don't **conduct electricity**.

7 Explain why substances made from simple molecules do not conduct electricity.

What you need to remember *Copy and complete using the **key words***

Simple molecules
Substances that consist of simple molecules can be a _____, a _____ or a _____ at room temperature. They all have a low _____ _____ and _____ _____.
This is because there are only _____ forces _____ the molecules.
We say there are weak _____ forces. When the substance melts or boils, these forces are overcome but the covalent bonds are not affected.
Substances that consist of simple molecules do not _____ _____ because the molecules do not have an overall _____ _____.

2 Different bonding – different properties

Sodium chloride is an ionic compound. The forces between the sodium Na$^+$ and chloride Cl$^-$ ions are very strong and act in all **directions**.

Each Na$^+$ ion is surrounded by six Cl$^-$ ions in a giant structure.

> **1** What do we call the giant structure formed by sodium and chloride ions?

The ions in sodium chloride have opposite charges and are held together by **electrostatic** forces.
These are strong forces and give it a very high melting point (801 °C) and boiling point (141°C).

All ionic compounds have very high **melting points** and **boiling points**.

> **2** What type of force holds the ions together in sodium chloride?

> **3** Look at the table.
> Write down the letters of
>
> **a** a substance which could be sodium chloride
> **b** two other substances which could be ionic compounds.

Substance	Melting point (°C)	Boiling point (°C)
A	0	100
B	−165	−142
C	3078	4300
D	−94	−22
E	654	1987
F	801	1413

Ionic compounds and electricity

Ionic compounds will **conduct electricity** if we dissolve them in water or heat them until they melt.

> **4** If we want to make sodium chloride conduct electricity, what temperature must we heat it to?

> **5** What else can we do to sodium chloride to make it conduct electricity?

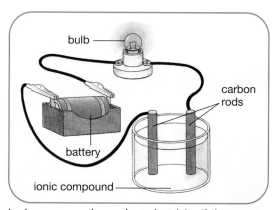

Ionic compounds conduct electricity if they are melted or dissolved in water.

Setting the ions free

The ions in a sodium chloride lattice are particles with an electrical charge. An ionic compound like this can only conduct electricity if its charged particles can move about.

When we melt an ionic compound or dissolve it in water, the ions are free to **move**.

6   Copy and complete the sentences.

The ions in the sodium chloride lattice have _____ charges. This means that the ions _____ each other.

7   Why can electricity flow in an ionic compound once the ions are free to move?

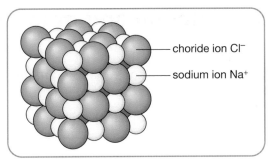

In ionic compounds, each ion is surrounded by, and strongly attracted to, oppositely charged ions.

Chlorine from salt

Passing electricity through a solution of sodium chloride in water is a very important chemical process.

One of the substances we produce in this way is chlorine gas. We can use chlorine to make bleach and a plastic called PVC.

8   Write down the two things we must do to solid sodium chloride in order to produce chlorine gas.

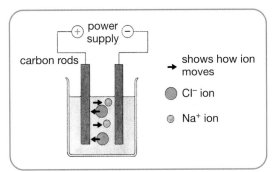

These ions are free to move. They can carry the **current**.

What you need to remember   *Copy and complete using the key words*

Different bonding – different properties

The ions in compounds like sodium chloride are arranged in a giant _____.

There are strong _____ forces between the oppositely charged ions. These act in all _____.

Ionic compounds like sodium chloride have very high _____ _____ and _____ _____.

When they are dissolved in water or melted, they can _____ _____.

This is because their ions are free to _____ about and carry the _____.

3 Diamond and graphite

The element carbon can exist as **diamond** and **graphite**. These two substances are very different.

1 Copy and complete the table.

Substance	Diamond	Graphite
Element it is made from		
Is it hard or soft?		
What we use it for		

Diamond is a form of the element carbon.
It's the hardest material on Earth.
We can use it for drilling and cutting tools.

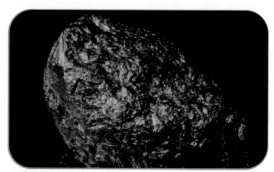

Graphite is also a form of the element carbon.
It's a very soft substance.
We use it for the 'lead' in pencils and for lubricating the moving parts of machines.

We can explain the differences in these two substances if we look at their structures. Both diamond and graphite form giant covalent structures.

The atoms in both carbon and graphite are linked to other atoms by **strong** covalent bonds. This gives them very high **melting points**.

2 What is another name for a giant covalent structure?

3 Copy and complete the sentences.

Diamond and graphite both melt at high _____.

This is because their carbon atoms form strong _____ bonds.

REMEMBER

Some substances with covalent bonds form giant structures, for example diamond and silicon dioxide. We call these giant structures **macromolecules**.

Diamond – four strong covalent bonds

In diamond, each carbon atom forms **four** covalent bonds with other carbon atoms.

The carbon atoms form a **rigid**, giant covalent structure.

4 Copy and complete the sentences.

A diamond is made from a giant structure of _____ atoms. Another name for this giant structure is a _____.
Each carbon atom is joined to _____ other carbon atoms.
This is why diamond is so _____.

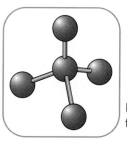

Each carbon atom forms four strong covalent bonds.

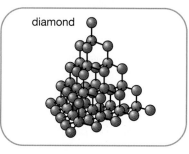

diamond

Carbon atoms in a diamond make a strong, rigid three-dimensional structure or **lattice**. This is why diamonds are so **hard**.

Graphite – another giant structure

In graphite, each carbon atom bonds to **three** others.
This forms **layers** which are free to slide over each other.
This is why graphite is **soft** and slippery.

5 Copy and complete the sentences.

In graphite, the bonds between the carbon atoms in the layers are _____. But the bonds between the layers are _____.

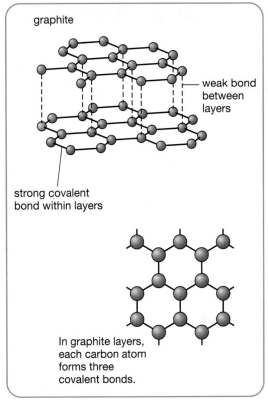

graphite

— weak bond between layers

strong covalent bond within layers

In graphite layers, each carbon atom forms three covalent bonds.

In graphite, bonds between carbon atoms in the layers are strong covalent bonds. But the bonds between layers of carbon atoms are weak, so the layers slide over each other. This makes the surface flaky and soft. Graphite has a high melting point.

What you need to remember *Copy and complete using the key words*

Diamond and graphite
The atoms of some substances can share electrons to form giant structures. We call these
_____.

Two examples of this are the two forms of carbon, _____ and _____.
Both of these substances have high _____ _____ because the
covalent bonds between their atoms are very _____.
The table shows how the properties of diamond and graphite are linked to their structure.

Substance	Hard or soft?	How many covalent bonds each carbon atom makes	Type of structure
diamond	_____	_____	_____ structure called a _____
graphite	_____	_____	forms _____ which can slip over each other

You need to be able to relate the properties of substances like diamond and graphite to their uses.

4 More giant structures – metals

We can explain the properties of metals if we look at the way in which their atoms are arranged.

1 Write down <u>two</u> properties of metals.

Metals conduct heat and electricity because there are electrons in them that are free to move. We say these electrons are **delocalised**. The delocalised electrons carry electric current. They also allow a metal to conduct heat.

2 Where do the delocalised electrons in a metal come from?

3 Copy and complete the sentences.

The delocalised electrons can carry electric
_____. This allows metals to conduct
_____.

It also allows metals to conduct _____.

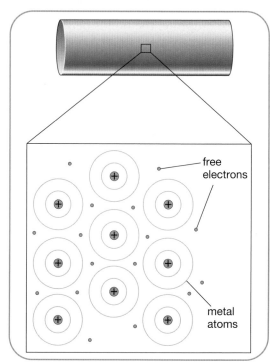

Electrons from the top energy level of metal atoms are free to move. The positively charged ions are held together in a regular pattern by a 'sea' of negatively charged electrons.

More metal properties

Metals are also useful to us because we can **bend** and **shape** them.

4 Write down the name of <u>one</u> metal we can form into different shapes.

5 Write down a word to describe this property of metals.

We can bend metals and make them into different shapes. We say they are malleable. Aluminium is so malleable that we can make it into shapes like this drinks can.

Layers of atoms

Metals are built up from **layers** of atoms. When we bend metals, the layers **slide** over each other.

> **6** Copy and complete the sentences.
>
> The atoms in metals are arranged in _____. These can _____ over each other. This is why we can _____ and _____ metals.
> The atoms are still held in a regular pattern by the delocalised (free) _____.

A non-metal that can conduct electricity

Although graphite is a non-metal, it is also a good conductor of **electricity** and **heat**. This makes it useful for making electrodes and parts of electric motors.

The reason graphite conducts electricity and heat is because it has free electrons in its structure.
Each carbon atom has <u>four</u> outer shell electrons but, in graphite, only three electrons are used for bonding with other carbon atoms. So the other electron is **delocalised** (free to move).

The delocalised electrons in the graphite structure can carry an electric current.

> **7** Why can graphite conduct electricity?
>
> **8** How is this property of graphite useful to us?
>
> **9** Explain why graphite has free (delocalised) electrons.

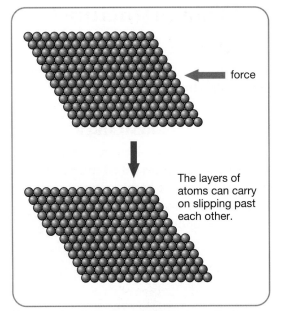

If we apply a force to a metal like iron, the layers slide over each other. The metal atoms can slide over each other but are still held together by the free electrons.

The layers of atoms can carry on slipping past each other.

force

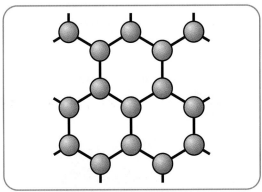

In graphite layers, each carbon atom forms three covalent bonds.

What you need to remember *Copy and complete using the **key words***

More giant structures – metals
The _____ of atoms in metals are able to _____ over each other.
This is why we can _____ and _____ metals.
Metals conduct heat and electricity because their structures contain _____ electrons.
The non-metal graphite can also conduct _____ and _____. This is because one electron from each carbon atom is _____.

You need to be able to relate the properties of substances to their uses.

5 Which structure?

The properties of a substance can help us to suggest the type of structure it has.

REMEMBER

Atoms that share electrons can form giant covalent structures called macromolecules. These have very <u>high melting points</u> because their atoms are linked together with strong covalent bonds.

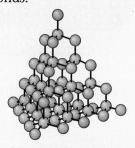

REMEMBER

Substances that consist of simple molecules have relatively <u>low melting points</u> and boiling points.
This is because there are only weak forces between the molecules. They don't <u>conduct electricity</u>.

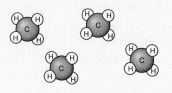

REMEMBER

Metals <u>conduct heat and electricity</u> because their structures contain delocalised (free) electrons. The layers of atoms in metals are able to slide over each other. This is why <u>we can bend and shape metals</u>.

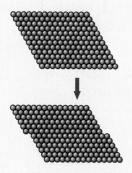

REMEMBER

Compounds made from ions are called ionic compounds. The ions are arranged in a giant lattice. Ionic compounds have very <u>high melting points and boiling points</u>.
When they are dissolved in water or melted, they can <u>conduct electricity</u>. This is because their ions are free to move about and carry the current.

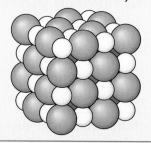

Silicon dioxide is the hard compound on the surface of sandpaper. We all know it as sand.

1. Which property of silicon dioxide suggests that it has a giant covalent structure?

2. Explain why silicon dioxide has these properties.

3. Give an example of another substance which has these properties.

The silicon dioxide on sandpaper is very hard. It melts at 1610 °C.

We use liquid nitrogen to freeze foods very quickly without damaging them.

4 What properties of nitrogen suggest that it is made from simple molecules?

5 Explain why liquid nitrogen has these properties.

6 Give an example of another substance which has these properties.

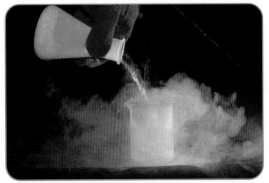

Liquid nitrogen has a boiling point of −196 °C. It does not conduct electricity.

Aluminium has many uses. We can shape it and draw it out into wires.

7 What properties of aluminium suggest that it is made from a regular metallic structure?

8 Explain why aluminium has these properties.

9 Give an example of another substance which has these properties.

These electric cables are made from aluminium, which is a good conductor of electricity.

The properties of the compound calcium chloride tell us what type of structure it has.

10 What properties of calcium chloride suggest that it is made from an ionic lattice?

11 Explain why calcium chloride has these properties.

12 Give an example of another substance which has these properties.

Calcium chloride has a melting point of 782 °C. It will conduct electricity when we dissolve it in water or melt it.

What you need to remember *Copy and complete using the* **key words**

Which structure?
Another example of a compound with a giant covalent structure is

_____ _____ .

You need to be able to use information about the properties of a substance to suggest the type of structure it has.

6 What is nanoscience?

Can you imagine an MP3 player the size of an earring? Or a nanobot (tiny robot) that could enter your bloodstream and attack cancer cells?

Both of these things may be possible in the future owing to an exciting new area of science called **nanoscience**.

Nanoscience is the study of materials on a very, very small scale. It's about things which are between 1 and 100 nanometres in length.

To help us to understand the scale of nanoscience we need to compare the **nanometre** (nm) to the size of things we know.

> **1** What is the width of a human hair in nanometres?
>
> **2** How many nanometres are there in a millimetre?
>
> **3** About how many atoms of a solid material would fit into a nanometre?

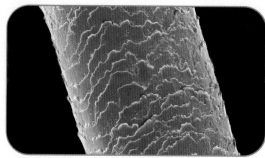

A human hair is around 80 000 nanometres wide.

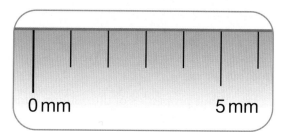

0 mm   5 mm

A nanometre is a millionth of a millimetre!

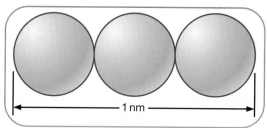

1 nm

You could fit about three atoms of a solid material into a nanometre.

Nanoparticles

Nanoparticles are particles of less than 100 nm in diameter. If we compare them with larger particles of the same material we find that they have very different **properties**.

> **4** Copy and complete the sentences.
>
> Nanoparticles of zinc oxide are used in
> _____ because they absorb and reflect
> _____ _____.
>
> Nanoparticles often have different
> _____ from larger particles of the same
> _____.

This sunscreen contains nanoparticles of zinc oxide. The nanoparticles absorb and reflect ultra-violet radiation. They also make the sunscreen smooth and transparent, not sticky and white.

Why do nanoparticles have different properties?

A large particle has many atoms inside the particle and only a few on its surface.
Nanoparticles are so small that more of their atoms are actually on the surface of the particle.

Look at the diagrams of the particles.

5 Copy and complete the sentences.

There are _____ atoms on the surface of the large particle and _____ atoms inside. This means that for every atom inside the particle we find _____ on the surface.

6 Look at the small particles.
What is the <u>total</u> number of atoms

a on their surface?

b on the inside?

7 How many atoms do we find on the surface of the small particles for every atom that is inside?

Of course particles actually exist in three dimensions, and so the differences between the numbers of atoms on the surface are even greater than we can show here.

We say that nanoparticles have a high **surface area to volume ratio**.

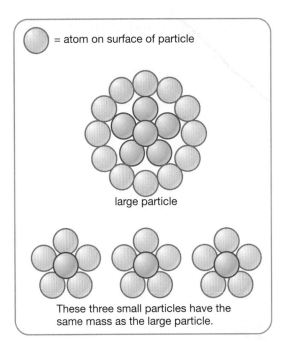

= atom on surface of particle

large particle

These three small particles have the same mass as the large particle.

Coatings

Because nanoparticles are so small, they can form thin layers on surfaces. We can use them to produce new **coatings**. Titanium dioxide nanoparticles are also used to coat glass.

8 What is the advantage of windows coated with a thin layer of titanium dioxide?

Visitors to the Dragon's Lair at London Zoo can have a clear view of the Komodo dragon. The glass used has a self-cleaning coating made from a layer of titanium dioxide nanoparticles.

What you need to remember *Copy and complete using the key words*

What is nanoscience?
_____ is the study of materials on a very small scale.
A _____ is a millionth of a millimetre.
_____ are particles which are smaller than 100 nm. They have different _____ from bigger particles of the same substance.
Because nanoparticles are so small, they have a high _____ _____
_____ _____ _____.
We can use them to make new _____, for example for glass.

7 More new materials

Nanoparticles may have many important uses in the future. For example, they could provide us with new and improved **catalysts**.

We use catalysts to speed up chemical reactions and they work better if they have a large surface area.

1. Which property of nanoparticles makes them good for making new catalysts?

2. Write down <u>two</u> ways in which nanoprocessors may improve the computers of the future.

We already use **sensors** to measure things. For example, temperature sensors help us to control the heat in buildings. But we don't have sensors to measure everything. Nanoscience could help us to produce sensors that are more <u>selective</u>.

It would be very useful to have sensors that could continuously check the quality of our drinking water or the air.

3. Copy and complete the sentences.

   Nanoscience may lead to the development of

   - new sensors that are more _____ than the ones we already use
   - lighter and stronger _____ materials.

4. Write down <u>two</u> advantages that carbon nanotubes have over steel.

Soon the microprocessors we use in our **computers** will reach their limits. New nanoprocessors could be much faster, and of course much smaller!

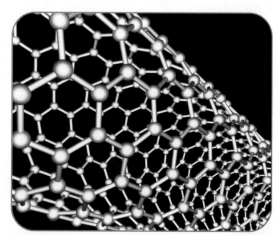

These carbon nanotubes are many times stronger than steel. Nanoscience may help us to develop new **construction materials**.

Worries about new materials

Nanoscience is a new area of science. So it is important to consider how safe it is. Many people were worried by a book written about how nanoscience could develop in the future.

> **5** Copy and complete the sentences.
>
> The book suggested that tiny _____
> could make _____ of themselves.
> They would get so out of _____ that
> they would cover the Earth.

Nobody takes this threat seriously these days, but it is still important to consider the safety of nanoscience.

Certain nanoparticles could cause us health problems. For example, researchers have already found that molecules known as buckyballs can harm human cells.

> **6** Why did scientists test buckyball molecules?

> **7** What did they find out?

The properties of nanoparticles are very different from those of bigger particles of the same substance. So it's important to test nanoparticles to find out how safe they are.

> **8** Why must scientists test nanoparticles for safety even if they know that bigger particles of the substance are not harmful?

In 1986, Eric Drexler (an American nanoscientist) wrote a book called <u>Engines of Creation</u> in which he warned that tiny robots that were designed to build objects from scratch, atom by atom, could eventually build copies of themselves. This could get out of control, with the robots using natural materials as building blocks.

'In less than a day, they would weigh a tonne, in less than two days, they would outweigh the Earth,' he wrote. He called the scenario 'grey goo' because it predicts that the whole surface of the Earth would become just a pile of goo. Most scientists, including Drexler himself, now think that this is highly unlikely.

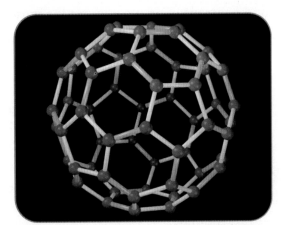

Buckyballs may some day be used in industry, so scientists carried out experiments to see if they are harmful to living things.

What you need to remember *Copy and complete using the **key words***

More new materials
The properties of nanoparticles may lead to the development of new _____, improved _____, selective _____ and
_____ _____ which are stronger and lighter.

You need to be able to use information like this to weigh up the advantages and disadvantages of using new materials like nanomaterials and smart materials.

1 Masses of atoms

Inside an atom like sodium there are three types of particles – protons, neutrons and electrons.

1. Which particle has a very small mass?

2. Copy and complete the sentences.

   Protons and neutrons are the particles in the _____ of an atom.
   One proton has a mass of _____ mass unit.
   One neutron also has a mass of _____ mass unit.

Mass number

Most of the mass of an atom comes from the protons and the neutrons. If we add together the number of **protons** and **neutrons** in an atom we get the **mass number**.

3. How do we work out the mass number of an atom?

4. If an atom has 5 protons and 6 neutrons, what is its mass number?

We can work out the number of neutrons an atom contains if we know its mass number and the atomic number.
We simply take the atomic number away from the mass number.

5. Write down <u>two</u> things we need to know about an atom to work out the number of neutrons an atom contains.

6. Explain how the symbol $^{23}_{11}$Na tells us that sodium has 12 neutrons in its nucleus.

The diagram shows a hydrogen atom and a lithium atom.

7. Write down the following symbols. Add the mass number and the atomic number for each one.

   a H
   b Li

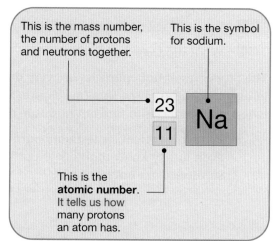

This is the mass number, the number of protons and neutrons together.

This is the symbol for sodium.

23
11
Na

This is the **atomic number**. It tells us how many protons an atom has.

An atom of sodium has 23 – 11 = 12 neutrons in its nucleus.

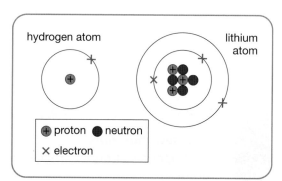

hydrogen atom   lithium atom

⊕ proton ● neutron
✕ electron

Hydrogen atom and lithium atom.

Three kinds of carbon

All carbon atoms contain 6 protons, so they have an atomic number of 6.

Carbon atoms can have different numbers of **neutrons**. This gives the atoms different masses. Atoms of the same element that have different masses are called **isotopes**.

8 | Copy and complete the table. The first row has been filled in for you.

Mass number of carbon isotope	Number of protons	Number of neutrons
12	6	6

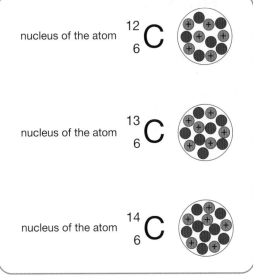

Three isotopes of the element carbon.

Carbon 14 – a useful isotope

The isotope of carbon with a mass number of 14 is also known as carbon 14.

9 | Write down <u>one</u> use of the isotope carbon 14.

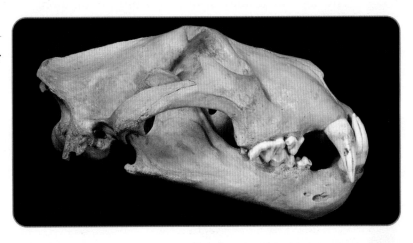

Carbon 14 was used to date this lion skull, found in the grounds of the Tower of London. It lived when King John reigned in England (around AD 1200).

What you need to remember *Copy and complete using the key words*

Masses of atoms

The symbol $^{23}_{11}$Na tells us that sodium has a _____ _____ of 23 and an _____ _____ of 11.

The mass number tells us the total number of _____ and _____ in an atom.

We can show the relative masses of protons, neutrons and electrons in the following way.

Name of particle	Mass
_____	very small
proton	_____
neutron	_____

Atoms of the same element can have different numbers of _____. These atoms are called _____ of that element.

2 How heavy are atoms?

Can we weigh atoms?

Atoms are the very small particles that make up all of the elements. Atoms of different elements have different masses.

Atoms are so small that you can't weigh them, even with the best scientific balance.

   1   Copy and complete the sentences.

       The element made with the heaviest atoms is called

       _____ .

       One atom of this element has a mass of

       _____ grams.

Numbers as small as these aren't easy to write down or use in calculations.

   2   Why don't we usually measure the mass of an atom in grams?

How many atoms?

Atoms of uranium are the heaviest atoms that we find in nature. Even so, there is a huge number of atoms in just 1 gram of uranium.

There are lots of dots in this box.

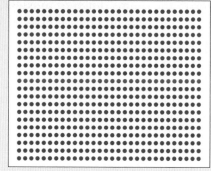

But in 1 gram of uranium, there are over 4 million million million times more atoms than dots in the box.

This means that one uranium atom has a mass of 0.000 000 000 000 000 000 000 4 g.

H ## Comparing the masses of atoms

Chemists can't weigh separate atoms. But they can compare how heavy different atoms are. They compare the mass of an atom to the mass of a carbon atom.

Carbon exists as different isotopes so they compare masses of atoms to the ^{12}C **isotope**.

   3   What is an isotope?

   4   Copy and complete the sentence.

       Scientists compare the mass of atoms of an element with the _____ isotope.

REMEMBER

- Isotopes are atoms of the same element with different numbers of neutrons.
- The isotopes of an element, e.g. carbon, have different mass numbers.

Inventing a scale of mass for weighing atoms

The lightest atom is hydrogen. Twelve hydrogen atoms have the same mass as one atom of the ^{12}C isotope.

If we say that one atom of the ^{12}C isotope has a mass of 12 units then an atom of hydrogen has a mass of 1 unit.

We call the mass of an atom in these units its **relative atomic mass**. We use the symbol A_r for short.

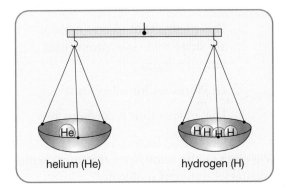

1 carbon atom
mass 12 units
$A_r = 12$

12 hydrogen atoms
mass 1 unit each
$A_r = 1$

5 Copy and complete the sentence.

A_r is a quick way of writing _____

_____ _____ .

6 Copy and complete the table.

Atom	A_r
hydrogen	
	12
helium	

helium (He)

hydrogen (H)

Which isotope?

Carbon isn't the only atom which exists as different isotopes. 75% of the atoms of chlorine have a mass number of 35, whereas 25% have a mass number of 37.

REMEMBER

The mass number is the total number of protons and neutrons in an atom.

7 What is the mass number of

a the heavier isotope of chlorine?
b the lighter isotope of chlorine?

To work out the relative atomic mass of chlorine, scientists take an **average** value of the isotopes. This gives chlorine an A_r of 35.5.

What you need to remember *Copy and complete using the key words*

How heavy are atoms?
We compare the masses of atoms with the mass of the _____ _____ .
We call this the _____ atomic mass, or _____ for short.
Many atoms exist as different isotopes so the A_r is an _____ value.

3 Using relative atomic mass

In molecules, atoms are joined together. Substances are called compounds if their molecules are made from atoms of different elements.

> **1** Copy the picture of the two molecules. For each molecule, write down whether it is an element or a compound.

> **2** Copy and complete the sentences.
>
> The formula for ammonia is _____.
>
> This means that in one molecule of ammonia there are three hydrogen atoms and _____ nitrogen atom.
>
> The formula for nitrogen is _____.
>
> This means that it contains two _____ of nitrogen.

We can use the relative atomic mass scale to compare the masses of different molecules.

The mass of a molecule is called its relative formula mass. We call this M_r for short.

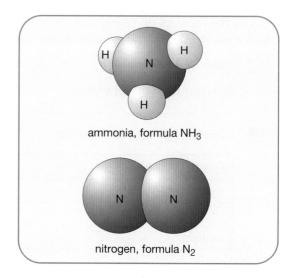

ammonia, formula NH_3

nitrogen, formula N_2

Calculating the mass of molecules

If we know the formula of a molecule then it is easy to work out the relative formula mass.

We look up the relative **atomic** masses of the elements. Then we **add** the masses of all the atoms in the formula.

i The formula for carbon dioxide is CO_2.
It contains one carbon atom and two oxygen atoms.
Adding the relative atomic masses together, we get:

$$\begin{array}{ccccc} & C & O & O & CO_2 \\ \text{relative formula mass} = & 12 + & 16 + & 16 = & 44 \end{array}$$

ii A molecule of oxygen, formula O_2, has got two oxygen atoms in the molecule.
Each oxygen atom has a mass of 16.
Therefore the two oxygen atoms have a total mass of 32.

$$\begin{array}{cccc} & O & O & O_2 \\ \text{relative formula mass} = & 16 + & 16 = & 32 \end{array}$$

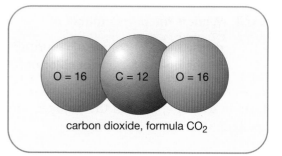

carbon dioxide, formula CO_2

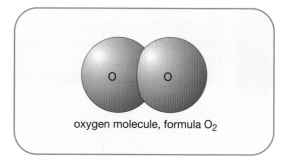

oxygen molecule, formula O_2

3 a Draw a molecule of ammonia.
   b Write the relative atomic mass of each atom on your diagram.
   c Now work out the relative formula mass, M_r, for ammonia.

4 Calculate the relative formula mass, M_r, for nitrogen in the same way.

Calculating more relative formula masses

Here are some rules for reading a chemical formula.

- Each element has a chemical symbol (e.g. H = hydrogen, O = oxygen).
- A chemical symbol without a number stands for one atom of that element. So, in H_2O (water) there is one atom of oxygen.
- The little number to the right of a symbol tells you how many atoms there are of that element only. So, in H_2O there are two hydrogen atoms.

5 The formula for copper sulfate is $CuSO_4$.

   a How many atoms of copper does it have?
   b How many atoms of sulfur does it have?
   c How many atoms of oxygen does it have?

- The number to the right of a bracket gives us the number of atoms of every element inside the bracket. So, in $Ca(OH)_2$ there are two atoms of oxygen and two atoms of hydrogen.

6 Now calculate the relative formula mass for each compound shown in the diagram.

The relative atomic masses of some elements.

Element	Symbol	A_r
aluminium	Al	27
bromine	Br	80
calcium	Ca	40
carbon	C	12
chlorine	Cl	35.5
copper	Cu	63.5
helium	He	4
hydrogen	H	1
iron	Fe	56
magnesium	Mg	24
nitrogen	N	14
oxygen	O	16
sulfur	S	32

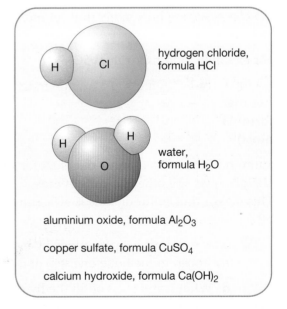

hydrogen chloride, formula HCl

water, formula H_2O

aluminium oxide, formula Al_2O_3

copper sulfate, formula $CuSO_4$

calcium hydroxide, formula $Ca(OH)_2$

What you need to remember *Copy and complete using the **key words***

Using relative atomic mass
To work out a relative formula mass (_____ for short)

- look up the relative _____ masses of the elements
- then _____ together the masses of all the atoms in the formula.

4 Elementary pie

Think about an apple pie you buy from the supermarket.
There is usually a table of information on the packet.
This tells us how much carbohydrate, fat and protein there
are in each 100 g of the pie.

1 Write down how much of each type of food
substance there is in 100 g of the pie. Write the list
in order, starting with what there is most of.

Telling you how much of everything there is in each 100 g
makes it easy to compare different foods.

2 How do the amounts of protein and fat in the apple
pie compare with the amounts in the bread?

Another way of saying 8 g out of 100 g is to say
8 per cent (%). Per cent means 'out of one hundred'.
We call this a **percentage**.

How much of an element is in a compound?

We can easily see how many units of mass of **elements** are
in a compound.

For example, sulfur dioxide is SO_2.

M_r		= mass of S atom + mass of 2 O atoms		
(relative	=	32	+	2 × 16
formula	=	32	+	32
mass)	=		64	

Sulfur gives 32 units of **mass** out of 64 for sulfur dioxide.
Oxygen gives the other 32 units of mass.
This means that sulfur dioxide is 50% sulfur and
50% oxygen by mass.

3 Now work out the percentage by mass of carbon and
hydrogen in methane one step at a time, like this.

a What is the mass of all the hydrogen atoms?
b What is the mass of the carbon atom?
c What is the relative formula mass of methane?
d What is the percentage by mass of hydrogen in
methane?
e What is the percentage by mass of carbon in
methane?

Apple pie Nutritional information Average values per 100 g	
protein	3 g
carbohydrate	54 g
fat	11 g

Bread Nutritional information Average values per 100 g	
protein	8 g
carbohydrate	31 g
fat	2 g

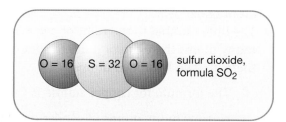

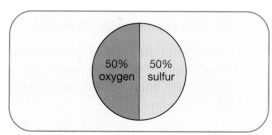

Half is the same as 50%.

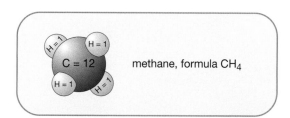

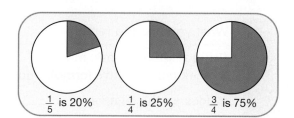

$\frac{1}{5}$ is 20% $\frac{1}{4}$ is 25% $\frac{3}{4}$ is 75%

How to calculate percentages

Percentages don't usually work out as easily as they do for sulfur dioxide and methane.

In water, for example, 2 parts out of 18 are hydrogen. To calculate this as a percentage on your calculator.

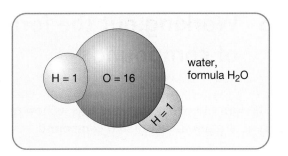

water, formula H_2O

press the number 2
then press ÷
then press the numbers 1, then 8 (18)
then press ×
then press the numbers 1, then 0, then 0 (100)
then press =

4 What is 2 parts out of 18 as a percentage?

You can work out other tricky percentages in a similar way.

The percentages by mass of the elements in ammonia

The diagram shows an ammonia molecule.

5 Work out

    a the total mass of hydrogen atoms in the molecule
    b the relative formula mass, M_r, for the molecule
    c the percentage by mass of hydrogen in the molecule.

6 Work out the percentage by mass of nitrogen in ammonia. (Hint: what percentage isn't hydrogen?)

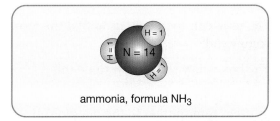

ammonia, formula NH_3

General percentage rule

The percentage by mass of an element in a compound is given by

$$\frac{\text{total mass of the element}}{\text{relative formula mass of the compound}} \times 100\%$$

What you need to remember *Copy and complete using the **key words***

Elementary pie
Chemical compounds are made of _____ (just as an apple pie is made of ingredients).
We can work out the _____ of an element in a compound using the relative _____ of the element in the formula and the _____ _____ _____ of the compound.

You need to be able to work out the percentage by mass of each element in a compound, just like you have on these pages.

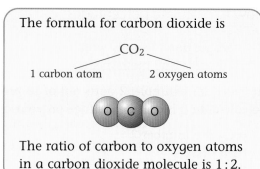

The formula for carbon dioxide is

$$CO_2$$

1 carbon atom   2 oxygen atoms

The ratio of carbon to oxygen atoms in a carbon dioxide molecule is $1:2$.

H 5 Working out the formulae of compounds

The formula of a compound tells us how many of each kind of atom there are in a compound.

To work out the formula of the compound we have to know the ratio of the atoms it contains.

1 What is the ratio of the atoms (or ions) in

   a an ammonia molecule, formula NH_3?
   b a methane molecule, formula CH_4?
   c the compound magnesium oxide, formula MgO?
   d the compound aluminium oxide, formula Al_2O_3?

We can find the masses of the elements that combine by careful weighing in experiments. Using this information, we can find the ratio of atoms in a compound.

The ratio can then help us to find the formula of the compound.

The box below shows how to do this.

> Step 1. Write down the ratio of the masses combining (from information in the question).
>
> Step 2. Write down A_r for each element.
>
> Step 3. Divide each mass by A_r to get the ratio of the atoms of each element.
>
> Step 4. Work out the simplest whole-number ratio (in this case divide the larger number by the smaller).

2 1.28 grams of an oxide of sulfur contain 0.64 g of sulfur and 0.64 g of oxygen. Find the ratio of sulfur to oxygen atoms and work out the empirical formula for this compound.
(Set out your answer as in the example.
A_r sulfur = 32; A_r oxygen = 16.)

The formula for sodium chloride is

$$NaCl$$

1 sodium atom   1 chlorine atom

Sodium chloride is an ionic compound.

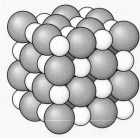

The ratio of sodium atoms (ions) to chlorine atoms (ions) is $1:1$

Example

A chemist found that 0.12 g of magnesium combined with 0.8 g of bromine.
What is the ratio of magnesium to bromine atoms in the compound magnesium bromide?

magnesium	:	bromine
0.12 g	:	0.8 g
$A_r = 24$	:	$A_r = 80$
$0.12 \div 24 = 0.005$	:	$0.8 \div 80 = 0.01$
1	:	2

The ratio of magnesium to bromine atoms is $1:2$.
The ratio Mg : Br is $1:2$.
The simplest formula for the compound is $MgBr_2$.
This is called the **empirical formula**.

Finding a formula by experiment

The diagram shows an experiment to find the empirical formula of copper oxide. The results (weighings) taken are shown in the table.

3 **a** Copy the table of results and then complete it.
   b Use the results to work out the empirical formula for copper oxide.
   (Set out your answer as in the example on page 144. A_r copper = 63.5.)

You do not usually get exact whole-number ratios from the results of an experiment. So if, for example, you get a ratio of 2.1 : 1, you would assume that the correct answer is 2 : 1.

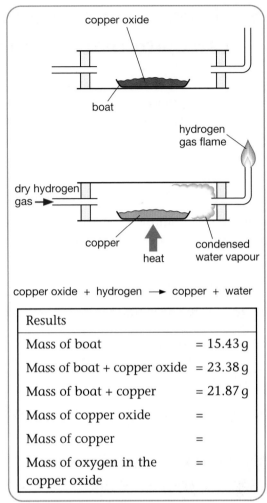

copper oxide + hydrogen ⟶ copper + water

Results	
Mass of boat	= 15.43 g
Mass of boat + copper oxide	= 23.38 g
Mass of boat + copper	= 21.87 g
Mass of copper oxide	=
Mass of copper	=
Mass of oxygen in the copper oxide	=

Finding the formula of copper oxide.

What you need to remember *Copy and complete using the* **key words**

Working out the formulae of compounds
The simplest formula of a compound is called its _____ _____.

You need to be able to calculate chemical quantities using empirical formulae.

H 6 Using chemical equations to calculate reacting masses

> You will find it helpful to look at page 310 about balancing equations before you cover this section.

A balanced symbol equation is a useful shorthand way of describing what happens in a chemical reaction.

1 What does this equation tell you?

$$CH_4 + 2O_2 \rightarrow 2H_2O + CO_2$$

(CH_4 is the formula for methane.)

We can use a **balanced symbol** equation to work out the masses of substances which react together and the masses of the products.

These are the steps to follow.

Step 1. Write down the balanced symbol equation.

Step 2. Decide what each formula tells you about the numbers of each kind of atom. (You may find it helpful to write this down.)

Step 3. Find out the relative atomic masses of each of the elements in the equation.

Step 4. Write in the relative atomic masses.

Step 5. Work out the mass of each reactant used and of each product that is made. The mass of reactant(s) equals the mass of product(s). This is because all the same atoms are still there.

Step 6. Write in words what this means. (You can use any units. Normally, you should use the units given in the question.)

2 Follow steps 1–6 to work out the masses of reactants and products in these two chemical reactions.

a $C + O_2 \rightarrow CO_2$

b $CH_4 + 2O_2 \rightarrow 2H_2O + CO_2$

Set out your answers as in the example.

Element	Symbol	A_r
aluminium	Al	27
carbon	C	12
copper	Cu	63.5
iron	Fe	56
magnesium	Mg	24
oxygen	O	16

Relative atomic masses A_r of some atoms.

Example 1

Magnesium reacts with oxygen to form magnesium oxide. Work out the reacting masses and the product mass.

$$2Mg + O_2 \rightarrow 2MgO$$

2 magnesium atoms		2 magnesium atoms
+	$\rightarrow$	+
2 oxygen atoms		2 oxygen atoms

Mg = 24   O = 16

$(2 \times 24) + (2 \times 16) = [(2 \times 24) + (2 \times 16)]$

48 + 32 = [48 + 32]

48 + 32 = 80

For the product, work out the inner brackets first.

48 + 32 → 80

48 grams of magnesium react with 32 grams of oxygen to form 80 grams of magnesium oxide.

You may be asked to calculate the mass of a product from a given mass of reactant in a chemical reaction.

Use only the quantities of the substances about which you are asked.

Example 1 shows how you should set out your answer so that what you are doing is clear.

3 Calculate the mass of calcium oxide (CaO) that is produced from heating 10 g of limestone ($CaCO_3$).

$$CaCO_3 \rightarrow CaO + CO_2$$

Set out your answer as in Example 2.

Sometimes you will be asked to calculate the mass of one of the reactants.
Again, use only the quantities about which you are asked.
Example 3 shows how you should set out your answer so that what you are doing is clear.

4 $CuO + H_2 \rightarrow Cu + H_2O$

How much copper oxide (CuO) is needed to produce 16 kg of copper in this reaction?

Set out your answer in a similar way to Example 3. But, this time, the calculation isn't exactly the same.

Example 2

$$2Al + Fe_2O_3 \rightarrow Al_2O_3 + 2Fe$$

In this reaction, what mass of iron is produced from 8 grams of iron oxide (Fe_2O_3)?

$$Fe_2O_3 \rightarrow 2Fe$$

2 iron atoms + 3 oxygen atoms → 2 iron atoms

$$[(2 \times 56) + (3 \times 16)] \rightarrow (2 \times 56)$$
$$[112 + 48] \rightarrow 112$$
$$160 \rightarrow 112$$

So 160 g of iron oxide produces 112 g of iron.
So 1 g of iron oxide produces $\frac{112}{160}$ g of iron.
So 8 g of iron oxide produces
$\frac{112}{160} \times 8$ g = 5.6 g of iron

Example 3

$$2Al + Fe_2O_3 \rightarrow Al_2O_3 + 2Fe$$

How much aluminium is needed to react completely with 8 kg of iron oxide in this reaction?

$$2Al + Fe_2O_3$$

2 aluminium atoms   2 iron atoms + 3 oxygen atoms

$$(2 \times 27) \qquad [(2 \times 56) + (3 \times 16)]$$
$$54 \qquad\qquad [112 + 48]$$
$$54 \qquad\qquad 160$$

So 160 kg of iron oxide reacts with 54 kg of aluminium.

So 1 kg of iron oxide reacts with $\frac{54}{160}$ kg of aluminium.

So 8 kg of iron oxide reacts with $\frac{54}{160} \times 8$ kg = 2.7 kg of aluminium.

What you need to remember *Copy and complete using the* **key words**

Using chemical equations to calculate reacting masses
We can work out the masses of reactants and products from _____
_____ equations.

You need to be able to work out masses of products and reactants just like you have on these pages.

7 Reactions that go forwards and backwards

In <u>most</u> chemical reactions:

substances at the   →   new substances at
start of the reaction   the end of the reaction

reactants   →   products

In <u>some</u> reactions, the products can change back into the original reactants.

A + B   ⇌   C + D

reactants ⇌ products

> This sign means that the reaction can go both ways. It is reversible.

This kind of reaction can go in both directions.
So we call it a **reversible reaction**.

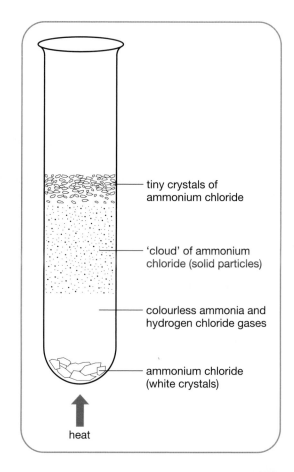

tiny crystals of ammonium chloride

'cloud' of ammonium chloride (solid particles)

colourless ammonia and hydrogen chloride gases

ammonium chloride (white crystals)

heat

What happens when we heat ammonium chloride?

1. Look at the diagram. When we heat ammonium chloride, it decomposes to form two colourless gases. What are they?

2. Copy and complete the equation.

   ammonium _____ ⇌ **ammonia** + **hydrogen chloride**

   (_____ solid)   (_____ gases)

3. What does the symbol ⇌ in the equation tell you?

What you need to remember *Copy and complete using the **key words***

Reactions that go forwards and backwards
In some chemical reactions, the products of the reaction can react to produce the original reactants.
A + B ⇌ C + D
We call this kind of reaction a _____ _____.

ammonium chloride ⇌ _____ + _____ _____
  (white solid)   (colourless gases)

8 How much do we really make?

In a chemical reaction, atoms are never lost or gained. But often when we carry out a reaction we don't make the **mass** of a product that we calculated we should.

There are several reasons for this.

- Some of the product may **escape** into the air.

- If we have to separate the product from a mixture, some of it may get **left behind**.

- Sometimes reactants react in a **different** way from the way we expect them to. They make a different product from the one we were measuring.

- **Reversible** reactions can give us less product than we expected. Some of the product may turn back into reactants.

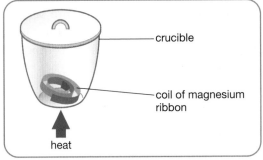

When we heat magnesium in air we have to lift the lid to allow oxygen in. Some of the magnesium oxide produced can escape into the air.

1. Write down the word equation for magnesium reacting with oxygen.

2. Explain why we may get less magnesium oxide than we expect to produce.

3. Write down the mass of carbon dioxide we expect to make when we burn 12 g of carbon.

4. Explain why the mass we get may be less than this.

5. Copy and complete the sentences.

   Often, reversible reactions do not go to

   _____.

   This means that not all of the reactants turn into

   _____.

Burning 12 g of carbon in oxygen should give us 44 g of carbon dioxide but we may get less than this. Some of the carbon may react with oxygen to make carbon monoxide instead of carbon dioxide.

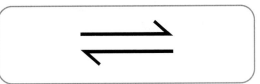

In reversible reactions, the reactants may not all turn into products. We say that the reaction may not go to **completion**.

What you need to remember *Copy and complete using the **key words***

How much do we really make?
Atoms are not gained or lost in a chemical reaction. But when we carry out a chemical reaction we don't always obtain the _____ of a product we expect.
This could be because

- some of the product may _____ or get _____ _____ in a mixture
- the reaction may be _____ from the one we expected
- the reaction is _____ and may not go to _____.

9 Catching nitrogen to feed plants – the Haber process

> **REMEMBER**
>
> A chemical reaction
>
> $$A + B \rightleftharpoons C + D$$
>
> is a reversible reaction.

Plants need nitrogen to grow well, but growing crops in the same fields year after year uses up the nitrogen in the soil.

Plants can't use nitrogen from the air so farmers have to use a nitrogen fertiliser to feed them.

Chemists make nitrogen fertiliser in several stages. The first stage involves 'catching' the nitrogen from the air. They use the nitrogen to make a compound called ammonia.

This process is used all over the world and is called the Haber process.

> **1** Why is the process chemists use to make ammonia called the Haber process?

This is Fritz Haber. He developed the process for making ammonia from nitrogen and hydrogen. Thanks to him, we make over 60 million kilograms of fertiliser containing nitrogen each day.

Making ammonia by the Haber process

The Haber process involves this reaction

nitrogen + hydrogen $\rightleftharpoons$ ammonia

> **2** What does the symbol $\rightleftharpoons$ in the equation tell you about the reaction?

Because the reaction is **reversible**, not all the nitrogen and hydrogen change into ammonia. Chemists and chemical engineers had to work out the way to get the best **yield** of ammonia. The yield is the amount of a **product** that we make in a reaction.

> **3** Write down the names of the <u>two</u> raw materials which react to produce ammonia.

H

> **4** Write down the conditions that help to give us the best yield of ammonia.

> **5** What do we use to speed up the reaction between the nitrogen and hydrogen?

> ## Making ammonia
>
> The best conditions for producing ammonia are
>
> - a **high temperature** (about **450 °C**)
> - a **high pressure** (about **200** times the pressure of the atmosphere).
>
> The reaction between the nitrogen and hydrogen is speeded up using a hot **iron** catalyst.

Nitrogen and hydrogen

Nitrogen and hydrogen gases are passed into the reaction vessel to react.

6 Copy and complete the sentences.

Nitrogen gas we need for the Haber process is obtained from the _____.
We get the hydrogen we need from
_____ _____, which is methane.
The ammonia we make is cooled and turns into a _____.

We remove the liquid ammonia.

In the reaction vessel, not all of the nitrogen and hydrogen react.

7 How do we separate the ammonia from the unreacted nitrogen and hydrogen?

8 What then happens to any unreacted nitrogen and hydrogen?

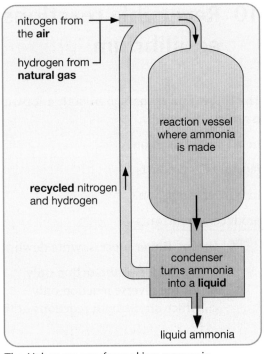

The Haber process for making ammonia.

We can't put ammonia on the soil

Ammonia is a corrosive chemical and not suitable to put straight onto the soil. It has to go through two more stages to become a fertiliser which farmers can use.

9 What is the name of a common fertiliser that farmers use?

Ammonium nitrate fertiliser.

What you need to remember *Copy and complete using the **key words***

Catching nitrogen to feed plants – the Haber process
The raw materials for the Haber process are _____ (from the _____)
and _____ (from _____ _____).
We pass the gases over a catalyst of _____ at a _____
_____ (about _____) and a _____ _____
(_____ atmospheres).
These conditions give us the best _____ of ammonia. The yield is the amount of
_____ we obtain in a reaction.
This equation shows us that the reaction is _____:
nitrogen + hydrogen ⇌ ammonia
When the ammonia is cooled it turns into a _____. The remaining hydrogen
and nitrogen is _____.

10 Reversible reactions and equilibrium

The Haber process can go in both a forwards direction and a reverse direction.

In a forward reaction,

reactants → products

In a reverse reaction,

products → reactants

1 For the Haber process, write down the equation

   a for the forward reaction only
   b for the reverse reaction only
   c which shows both reactions at the same time.

> **REMEMBER**
>
> The Haber process is a reversible reaction. It can go both ways.
> We can show it like this:
> nitrogen + hydrogen ⇌ ammonia

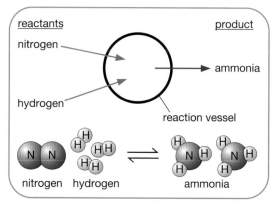

The Haber process.

H Equilibrium

When the Haber process reaction begins, there will be many reacting molecules of nitrogen and hydrogen but few ammonia molecules. This means that the forward reaction will be fast, but the reverse reaction will be slow.

We say that the rate, or speed, of the forward reaction is greater than that of the reverse reaction.

As the reaction continues, the numbers of nitrogen and hydrogen molecules will decrease and the number of ammonia molecules will increase. So the **rate** of the forward reaction will decrease and the rate of the reverse reaction will increase.

Eventually a point is reached where the rate of the forward reaction and the rate of the reverse reaction are equal. This point is called **equilibrium**.

2 Copy and complete the sentences.

At equilibrium, the _____ of the forward and reverse reactions are equal.
At equilibrium, in the Haber process reaction vessel there will be <u>three</u> substances: _____
_____ and _____.

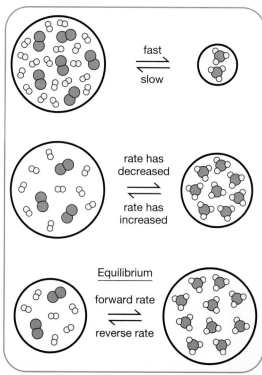

At equilibrium, the rates of the forward and reverse reactions are the <u>same</u>.

We can only reach equilibrium if we prevent the products and the reactants from leaving the reaction vessel. We call this a **closed system**.

3   Copy and complete the sentences.

For the reactants and products to reach equilibrium, they must be in a _____ system. This means that they must not _____ the reaction vessel.

How much?

The amount of product in the mixture at equilibrium depends on the particular reaction and on the reaction **conditions** (that is, the temperature and pressure).

4   How much ammonia is there in the equilibrium mixture at normal temperature and pressure?

5   How can we increase this percentage?

The graph shows the percentage of nitrogen and hydrogen which is converted to ammonia at different temperatures and pressures.

6   a From the graph, what happens to the yield of ammonia as we increase the pressure?
    b What happens to the yield of ammonia as we increase the temperature?
    c Under what conditions of temperature and pressure is the yield of ammonia greatest?

7   Suggest a combination of temperature and pressure that would give an even higher yield.

Yield of ammonia
In the Haber process, under normal temperature and pressure (25 °C and 1 atmosphere), the amount of ammonia at equilibrium is only about 1%. We can increase this by changing the reaction conditions.

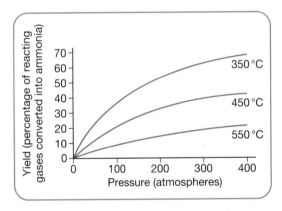

What you need to remember *Copy and complete using the key words*

Reversible reactions and equilibrium
In a reversible reaction, when the forward reaction occurs at the same _____ as the reverse reaction we say it has reached _____. We can only reach equilibrium in a _____ _____, when products and reactants can't leave the reaction vessel.
How much of each reacting substance there is at equilibrium depends on the reaction _____.

11 As much as possible!

All manufacturers try to make their products as economically as possible.

Ammonia is usually manufactured at a temperature of about 450 °C and a pressure of about 200 atmospheres. The reasons for using these conditions are that they give a reasonable **yield** of ammonia and that they produce the ammonia **quickly**.

1   **a** How do these conditions compare with those for the highest yield shown on the graph?
    b Estimate the yield under these conditions.

A lower temperature would give a greater yield of ammonia but the reaction would take place very slowly. This would increase the cost of manufacture.

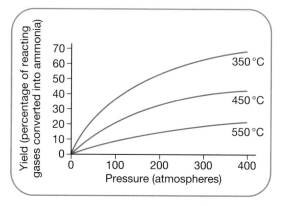

A higher pressure would also increase the yield of ammonia but the vessel would have to be much thicker and stronger. It would cost much more to build and the process would have more safety risks.

2   Write down <u>two</u> reasons why we don't use a lower temperature of 350 °C for producing ammonia.

3   Write down <u>two</u> reasons why we don't use a higher pressure for producing ammonia.

Although reversible reactions like the Haber process may not go to completion (the reactants may not all turn into products) they can still be **efficient**.

Reactants are put in and products are removed continuously over a long period of time. So we call this a **continuous** process.

4   Copy and complete the sentences.

Unreacted _____ and _____ are recycled back into the reaction vessel.
_____ is constantly being removed from the reaction mixture.
We say the Haber process is a _____ process.

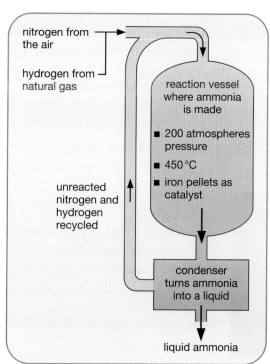

Working out the yield

The yield is the amount of a product we obtain.

To work out the **percentage yield** we divide the yield by the amount that would have been obtained if all of the reactant had been converted to product (the maximum possible amount).

We do the following calculation.

$$\text{Percentage yield} = \frac{\text{amount of product obtained}}{\text{maximum possible amount}} \times 100\%$$

Matt calculated that he would make 4.0 g of magnesium oxide, but he only actually made 2.1 g. He worked out the percentage yield like this:
percentage yield = $\frac{2.1}{4.0} \times 100\% = 52.5\%$

5   Look at the experiment.

   a What mass of copper oxide did Sam predict that she would produce?

   b What mass of copper oxide did Sam actually produce?

   c What was the percentage yield in her experiment?

6   Write down <u>one</u> possible reason why Sam did not obtain as much copper oxide as she predicted she would.

What you need to remember *Copy and complete using the **key words***

As much as possible!
The Haber process for producing ammonia is a _____ process. This type of process makes reversible reactions more _____.
The reaction conditions used in the Haber process are chosen because they produce a reasonable _____ of ammonia _____.
The _____ _____ is the amount of product we make when compared with the amount we should make. We can work it out if we do the following calculation:

$$\text{percentage yield} = \frac{\text{amount of product obtained}}{\text{maximum possible amount}} \times 100\%$$

12 Atom economy

Chemical manufacturers take raw materials and make them into a product that is more useful and worth more. They can then sell the product for a profit (to make money).

To make the most profit, the manufacturers need to make as much product as possible from their starting materials.

H

1 What do we call the amount of product that we make in a chemical reaction?

Although it's important to make as much product as possible, we must also consider the amount of **starting materials** we are using. Sometimes a lot of the atoms in the starting material are wasted because they don't go into the final product.

> **REMEMBER**
>
> The yield is the amount of product we obtain in a chemical reaction.

Less wasted materials

Ibuprofen is a widely used painkiller. About 3000 tonnes of it are sold every year in the UK alone.

2 What is ibuprofen?

3 Who first developed ibuprofen?

In the mid-1980s, other companies were allowed to produce ibuprofen. The process that Boots had been using was quite wasteful because many of the atoms used to make the drug did not go into the final product.

Boots developed the process to make ibuprofen. Until the mid-1980s, only Boots had the right to make and sell the drug.

A company called BHC developed a method of producing ibuprofen which was much less wasteful.

4 Copy and complete the sentences.

The BHC method for producing ibuprofen uses less _____ _____ than the _____ method. It _____ fewer atoms.

Method of producing ibuprofen	Mass of ibuprofen (g)	Mass of starting materials (reactants) used to make ibuprofen (g)
Boots	206	514.5
BHC	206	266

We can work out the amount of starting materials that end up as useful products.
We call this the **atom economy** (atom utilisation).

Calculating atom economy

We calculate atom economy using the following equation.

$$\% \text{ atom economy} = \frac{\text{mass of useful products}}{\text{mass of reactants}} \times 100\%$$

So, for the Boots process of making ibuprofen:

mass of useful product = 206 g

mass of reactants = 514.5 g

$\% \text{ atom economy} = \frac{206\,g}{514.5\,g} \times 100\% = 40\%$

5 Now use the figures on page 156 to calculate the atom economy for the BHC method of producing ibuprofen.

Sustainable development

Improving the atom economy of a process helps us to meet the aims of **sustainable development**.

It helps to conserve raw materials. It also reduces the waste that we make.

6 Write down the aims of sustainable development.

7 How does the BHC method of making ibuprofen contribute to sustainable development?

8 Explain how reducing the amount of waste in a process can increase the profit a company makes.

Aims of sustainable development

In meeting our needs today, it's important that we don't

- damage the environment
- use up resources which will be needed by future generations.

Method of ibuprofen production	Waste produced (tonnes per year)
Boots	1800
BHC	690

Conserving raw materials and reducing waste can also help manufacturers to make new chemicals more **cheaply**.

What you need to remember *Copy and complete using the **key words***

Atom economy
We can measure the amount of _____ _____ that end up as useful products. This is the _____ _____.
Using reactions with a high atom economy is important for
_____ _____. It can also help manufacturers make chemicals more
_____.

You need to be able to calculate the atom economy for industrial processes.

You need to be able to say whether they meet the aims of sustainable development.

1 Using heat to speed things up

Some chemical reactions are very fast. Others are slow.
The reactions go at different speeds or **rates**.

The explosion takes a fraction of a
second.

The tablet reacts with water in about
a minute.

The nail takes a few hours to start
rusting. It takes many months to rust
completely.

> **1** Describe <u>one</u> example each of a chemical reaction
> that is
>
> **a** very slow, taking hours or days
> **b** very fast, taking seconds or less
> **c** medium speed, taking one minute or so.

Speeding up reactions in the kitchen

When we cook food, there are chemical reactions going on.
How fast the food cooks depends on how hot we make it.

> **2** Look at the pictures.
>
> **a** Which is faster, cooking in boiling water or in
> cooking oil?
> **b** Why do you think this is?

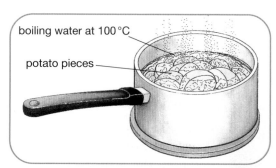

boiling water at 100 °C

potato pieces

The pieces of potato take about 20 minutes to cook.

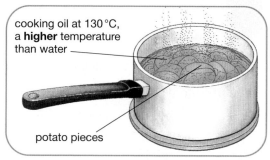

cooking oil at 130 °C,
a **higher** temperature
than water

potato pieces

The potatoes take less than 10 minutes to cook.

How much difference does temperature make?

Look at the colour change reaction. The table shows how long it takes for the mixture to change colour.

3 Copy and complete the sentences.

The higher the temperature, the _____ the time the reaction takes.
This means that the rate of reaction is

_____ .

4 How long do you think the reaction will take at temperatures of

a 60°C?
b 10°C?

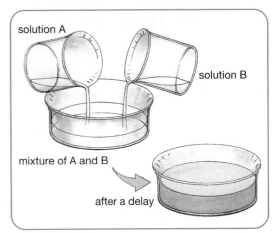

A colour change reaction.

Temperature (°C)	20	30	40	50
Time taken to go blue (seconds)	400	200	100	50

Using temperatures to control reactions

If you increase the temperature by 10°C, chemical reactions go about twice as fast. To **slow down** a chemical reaction you must reduce the temperature.

5 Where can you put milk to slow down the chemical reactions that make it go bad?

6 About how long will it take the milk to go sour in the fridge?

7 **a** How many times faster do the potatoes cook in the pressure cooker?
   b What does this tell you about the temperature of the water inside the pressure cooker?

Chemical reactions make food go bad.

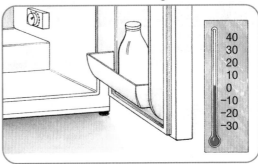

Inside a fridge, the milk takes many days to go sour.

water boiling at 100 °C

pressure cooker

The potatoes take about 24 minutes to cook.

The potatoes take about 6 minutes to cook.

Outside, the milk goes sour in 2 days.

What you need to remember *Copy and complete using the **key words***

Using heat to speed things up
Chemical reactions go at different speeds or _____ .
Chemical reactions go faster at _____ temperatures.
At low temperatures, chemical reactions _____ _____ .

2 Making solutions react faster

Some substances will dissolve in water to make a **solution**.
We can use solutions for many chemical reactions.
The speed of these chemical reactions depends on how
strong the solutions are.

1 What is the chemical solution in a car battery?

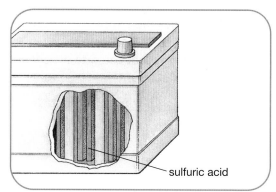

The chemical reactions in a car battery need
sulfuric acid of just the right strength.

'Strong' and 'weak' solutions

Your friend likes her tea to taste sweet, but not too sweet.

one spoonful — sugar
not sweet enough
sugar solution is too weak

two spoonfuls
just right

three spoonfuls
too sweet
sugar solution is too strong

2 Look at the diagrams. Copy and complete the table.

Spoonfuls of sugar	What the tea tasted like	Strength of solution
1		
2		perfect
3		

3 A mug of tea is 1.5 times bigger than one of the
cups shown above.
How many spoonfuls of sugar should your friend put
into a mug of tea? Give a reason for your answer.

We call a 'strong' solution a **concentrated** solution.
To make a solution 'weaker', we **dilute** it with water.

4 Look at the diagrams. Copy and complete the
sentences.

The orange drink in the bottle is _____.
To make it good to drink we need to
_____ it.

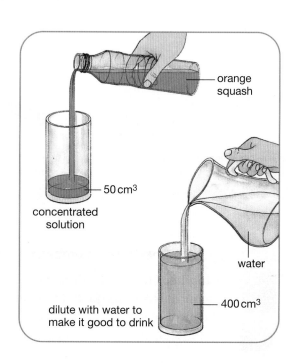

orange squash

50 cm³
concentrated solution

water

dilute with water to make it good to drink
400 cm³

How does concentration affect the speed of a chemical reaction?

Look at the pictures of the reaction between a chemical we call thio and an acid.

5 Copy and complete the sentences.

The most concentrated solution contains _____ spatulas of thio crystals.
The reaction with the most concentrated thio solution takes the _____ time.
This means that this reaction has the _____ rate.

Making gases react faster

Some gases will react together to make new substances. For example, we can make ammonia gas by reacting together a mixture of nitrogen and hydrogen gases.

We can squeeze gases into a smaller space. This is like making a more concentrated solution. The gases will then react together faster. A **high** pressure gas is like a very concentrated solution.

6 A chemical factory makes ammonia gas. They already make the hydrogen and nitrogen as hot as they can. What else should they do to make the reaction go faster?

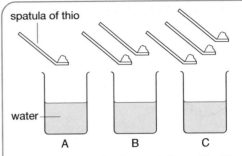

spatula of thio

water

A   B   C

Some students make three solutions with different strengths of sodium thiosulfate ('thio' for short).

dilute acid

They add 5 cm³ of acid to each solution.

black cross marked on paper

The solution gradually goes cloudy.

Eventually you can't see the cross when looking down through the solution.

Results.

Solution	Time for cross to disappear
A	8 minutes
B	4 minutes
C	2.5 minutes

What you need to remember *Copy and complete using the **key words***

Making solutions react faster
When we dissolve a substance in water we make a _____.
A solution that contains a lot of dissolved substance is a _____ solution.
To make a concentrated solution react more slowly, we can _____ it.
To make gases react faster, we need a _____ pressure.

3 Making solids react faster

The pictures show a chemical reaction between a solid and a solution.

1 Write down

    a the name of the solid in the reaction
    b the name of the solution used
    c the name of the gas produced.

2 Copy and complete the word equation for this reaction.

$$\underline{\hspace{3cm}} + \underline{\hspace{2cm}} \text{acid} \rightarrow \underline{\hspace{2cm}} \text{dioxide} + \underline{\hspace{2cm}}$$

bubbles of carbon dioxide gas

dilute hydrochloric acid

limestone pieces

During the reaction.

solution of calcium chloride

limestone pieces (now smaller)

When all the acid has been used up, the reaction stops.

Making the reaction faster

One way to make the reaction faster is by using more concentrated acid. But how fast the limestone reacts also depends on how big the pieces of limestone are.

3 Look at the pictures.
Copy and complete the table.

Size of solid pieces	Time taken to react	Speed of reaction
one large piece		
several small pieces		
lots of very small pieces		

4 Copy and complete the sentence.

The smaller the bits of limestone, the
_____ they react with the acid.

With one large piece of limestone, the gas bubbles continue for 10 minutes.

50 cm³ acid

50 cm³ acid

With smaller pieces, the gas bubbles continue for 1 minute. The bubbling is faster.

50 cm³ acid

With very small pieces, the gas bubbles continue for a few seconds. The bubbling is very fast.

Do you suck or crush sweets?

Think about eating a hard sweet. If you suck the sweet in one piece it lasts quite a long time. If you crush the sweet into little pieces it doesn't last so long.

5 Why does the crushed sweet dissolve faster? Explain your answer as fully as you can.

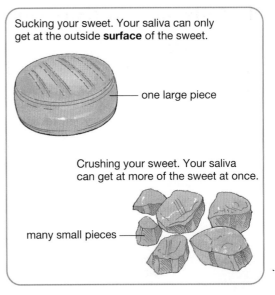

Sucking your sweet. Your saliva can only get at the outside **surface** of the sweet.

one large piece

Crushing your sweet. Your saliva can get at more of the sweet at once.

many small pieces

Why small bits react faster

The same amount of limestone in smaller bits reacts **faster**. The acid can get at smaller bits better. This is because they have more **surface area**.

6 Look at the large cube of limestone in the diagram.

   a How many little squares are there on one face of the large cube?

   b How many faces are there on the cube?

   c What is the total number of small squares on the surface of the cube? This is the surface area of the cube.

7 Now look at the large cube broken up into smaller cubes.

   a What is the surface area of each small cube?

   b What is the total surface area of all the small cubes added together?

   c How many times more surface area do the small cubes have than the large cube?

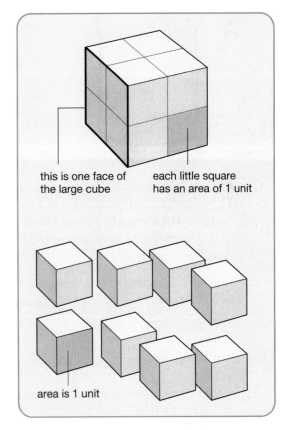

this is one face of the large cube

each little square has an area of 1 unit

area is 1 unit

What you need to remember *Copy and complete using the **key words***

Making solids react faster

A solid can react with a liquid only where they touch. The reaction is on the _____ of the solid.

If we break up the solid, we increase the total _____ _____.

This means that smaller pieces react _____.

4 Substances that speed up reactions

People use hydrogen peroxide to bleach their hair. It works by releasing oxygen. The oxygen turns the hair a very pale blonde colour.

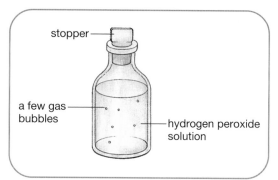

1 Copy and complete the word equation for this reaction.

hydrogen peroxide → _____ + _____

In the bottle, the hydrogen peroxide very slowly splits up into oxygen gas and water.

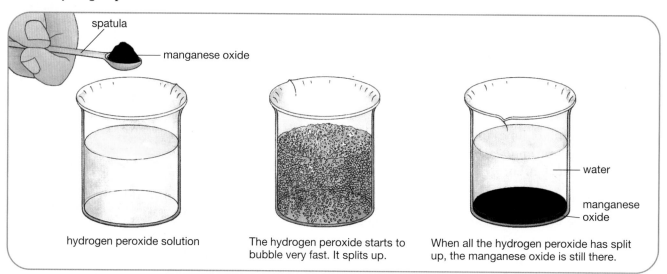

hydrogen peroxide solution

The hydrogen peroxide starts to bubble very fast. It splits up.

When all the hydrogen peroxide has split up, the manganese oxide is still there.

2 Look at the diagram above. What happens if we put a tiny amount of manganese oxide into some hydrogen peroxide?

A substance which speeds up a chemical reaction in this way has a special name. We call it a **catalyst**.

Why don't you need much of the catalyst?

3 Copy and complete the sentences, using the diagram to help you.

The _____ _____ is not used up in the chemical reaction. It is still there at the end. We can use it over and over again to split up more _____ _____.

4 How could we collect the catalyst so that we could use it again?

5 How does this experiment show that a catalyst is not used up in the reaction?

A catalyst does not get **used up** in a reaction. We can use the same manganese oxide **over** and **over** again. First filter the water and manganese oxide.

Put the manganese oxide into some fresh hydrogen peroxide.

It starts to bubble quickly.

We can show that the catalyst is not one of the ordinary chemicals that react, by writing the equation like this.

hydrogen peroxide $\xrightarrow{\text{manganese oxide}}$ oxygen + water

We write the name of the catalyst above the arrow.

What can we make using catalysts?

We can make lots of useful substances using catalysts. These substances **cost** less to make when you use one. Usually each chemical reaction needs its own **special** catalyst.

Sunflower oil is a vegetable oil. This oil can be reacted with hydrogen to make margarine, using nickel as a catalyst.

> 6   What is the catalyst we use to make margarine?

Why do cars have catalytic converters?

Look at the diagrams.

The catalytic converter changes harmful gases into safer gases.
The catalyst is not used up in the reactions.

> 7   Why do we fit cars with catalytic converters?

> 8   We often have to fill up a car with fuel.
> We don't have to add more catalyst to the converter.
> Why is this?

What you need to remember *Copy and complete using the **key words***

Substances that speed up reactions
A substance that speeds up a chemical reaction is called a _____.
The catalyst increases the rate of reaction but is not _____ _____.
We can use catalysts _____ and _____ again.
Each chemical reaction needs its own _____ catalyst.
Useful materials like margarine _____ less to make when we use a catalyst.

5 More about catalysts

Catalysts are very important to the chemical industry. This is because 80% of industrial processes use catalysts. We use about half the elements in the periodic table to speed up reactions in some way.

> **REMEMBER**
>
> A catalyst increases the rate of reaction but is not used up.
> We can use it over and over again.

1 What does a catalyst do?

2 Why do we need so many different kinds of catalyst?

Advantages of using catalysts

If we use a catalyst, the reaction can take place quickly at a lower temperature. This saves energy.

3 Copy and complete the sentence.

Catalysts can speed up reactions without the need to use so much _____.

In a reaction mixture, sometimes the reactants can react in more than one way. This can give us products we don't actually want.

We can use a catalyst to increase the rate of the reaction that we <u>do</u> want. The catalyst helps to reduce the amount of waste in the chemical reaction.

4 Copy and complete the sentences.

Sometimes in a chemical reaction, the reactants make substances that we don't _____, as well as those we do.

The correct catalyst can speed up the reaction that makes the _____ we need.

5 Which type of chemical reaction does a zeolite catalyst speed up?

This zeolite catalyst helps to split up (crack) long hydrocarbon molecules into smaller, more useful molecules.

Disadvantages of some catalysts

Although catalysts aren't used up in reactions it can be difficult to re-use them.

 6 Write down the name of the catalyst that Boots used to make the drug ibuprofen.

 7 Why couldn't this catalyst be re-used?

 8 Write down the names of <u>two</u> substances which are now used as catalysts for making ibuprofen.

 9 Write down <u>one</u> advantage of using these substances as catalysts.

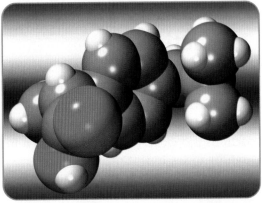

This is a molecule of the painkiller ibuprofen. Boots first made ibuprofen using a catalyst of aluminium chloride. The catalyst couldn't be separated out after the reaction so it had to be thrown away.
A new method for making ibuprofen uses two catalysts – hydrogen fluoride and an alloy of nickel and aluminium. The manufacturers can separate these out and reuse them lots of times.

Enzymes

Enzymes are sometimes called biocatalysts.

They control the reactions in living things and are very useful to the food and drug industries.

In industry many processes need high temperatures or pressures. This means that they use expensive equipment and large amounts of energy.

Using enzymes to carry out chemical reactions is much cheaper. This is because enzymes work at normal temperatures and pressures.

 10 Copy and complete the sentences.

The catalysts in living things are called

_____ .

It is cheaper to use enzymes to carry out some chemical reactions because they do not need high

_____ or high _____ to work.

What you need to remember

More about catalysts
There is nothing new for you to <u>remember</u> in this section.

You need to be able to

■ weigh up the advantages and disadvantages of using catalysts in industry
■ explain why the development of catalysts is important.

6 Investigating rates of reaction

Looking and timing

All we need to measure the speed of many chemical reactions is a clock. We can then watch the reaction carefully to see how it changes.

We need to look out for different things in different reactions.

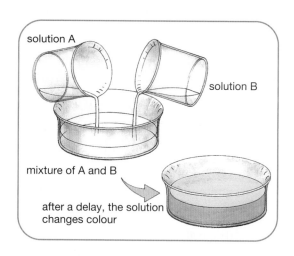

solution A

solution B

mixture of A and B

after a delay, the solution changes colour

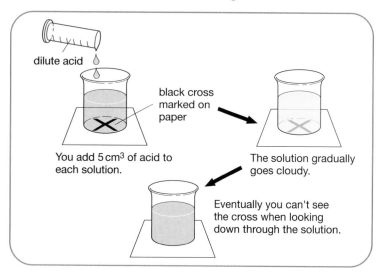

dilute acid

black cross marked on paper

You add 5 cm³ of acid to each solution.

The solution gradually goes cloudy.

Eventually you can't see the cross when looking down through the solution.

> **1** Write down **three** different things you might look for when you are timing a chemical reaction.

How much gas is produced?

Some chemical reactions produce a gas.

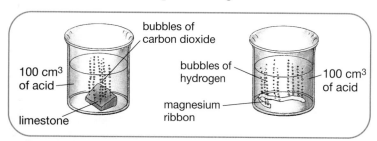

bubbles of carbon dioxide

100 cm³ of acid

limestone

bubbles of hydrogen

magnesium ribbon

100 cm³ of acid

> **2** Write down the name of the gas produced when
>
> **a** limestone reacts with acid
> **b** magnesium reacts with acid.

We can collect the gas and measure how much there is. Then we can use the results to draw a graph.

> **3** How can we collect and measure a gas produced during a reaction?

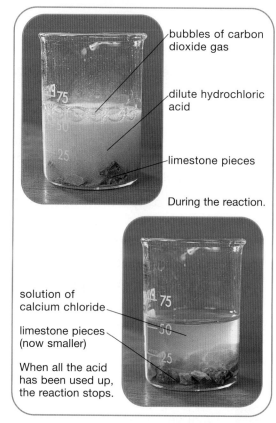

bubbles of carbon dioxide gas

dilute hydrochloric acid

limestone pieces

During the reaction.

solution of calcium chloride

limestone pieces (now smaller)

When all the acid has been used up, the reaction stops.

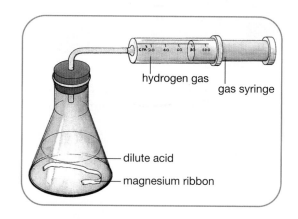

hydrogen gas

gas syringe

dilute acid

magnesium ribbon

Look at the graph. It shows the results of the experiment of magnesium reacting with acid.

A gas syringe was used to collect the gas.

4 Copy and complete the sentences.

During the first 2 minutes, the reaction is _____.

Then for the next 2 minutes, the reaction is _____ _____.

After 4 minutes, the reaction is _____ and no more _____ is produced.

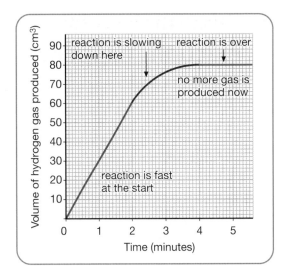

How does the mass change?

We can also measure the rate of reaction by weighing. If a gas escapes into the air during a reaction, the mass of what is left goes down.

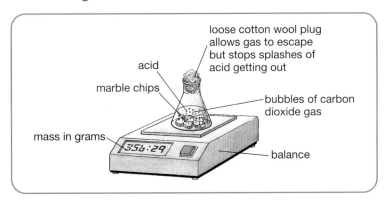

The graph shows some students' results for this experiment.

5 Look at the graphs.

  a Which reaction takes longer to finish?
  b Which reaction has the faster rate?
  c How much carbon dioxide gas is produced in each reaction?

6 Why is there a cotton wool plug in the neck of the flask?

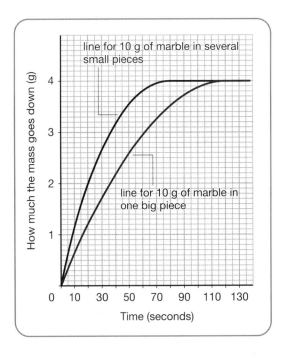

What you need to remember

Investigating rates of reaction
There is nothing new for you to <u>remember</u> in this section.

You need to be able to understand what graphs like the ones on this page are telling you about rates of reactions.
The graphs show how much of a product is formed (or how much of a reactant has been used up) over time.

7 What makes chemical reactions happen?

Chemical reactions can only happen when the particles of different substances **collide** with each other.

The diagram shows what happens when carbon burns in oxygen.

1   Copy and complete the sentences.

A molecule of oxygen contains ———————— oxygen atoms.

When the molecule collides with some hot carbon, the oxygen atoms join with a ———————— atom to make a molecule of ———————— ————————.

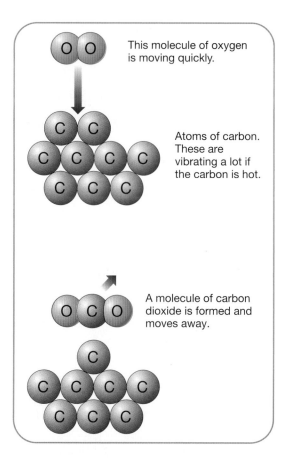

This molecule of oxygen is moving quickly.

Atoms of carbon. These are vibrating a lot if the carbon is hot.

A molecule of carbon dioxide is formed and moves away.

Why do reactions speed up when you increase the temperature?

The higher the temperature, the **faster** the oxygen molecules move.

2   Write down <u>two</u> reasons why faster-moving oxygen molecules react more easily with carbon.

The smallest amount of energy that particles must have for a reaction to occur is called the **activation** energy.

We say that increasing the temperature increases the rate of reaction.

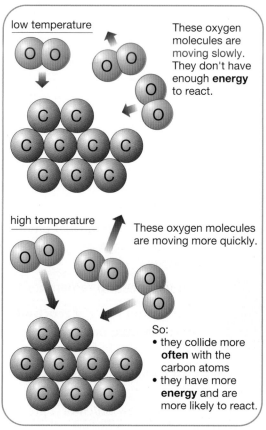

low temperature

These oxygen molecules are moving slowly. They don't have enough **energy** to react.

high temperature

These oxygen molecules are moving more quickly.

So:
• they collide more **often** with the carbon atoms
• they have more **energy** and are more likely to react.

Why does breaking up a solid make it react faster?

A lump of iron doesn't react very quickly with oxygen, even if it is very hot. But the tiny specks of iron in a sparkler burn quite easily.

3   Why do tiny specks of iron react more easily than a big lump of iron?

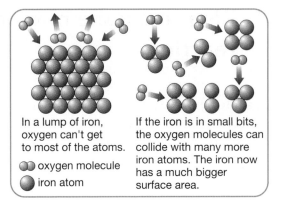

In a lump of iron, oxygen can't get to most of the atoms.

⬤⬤ oxygen molecule

⬤ iron atom

If the iron is in small bits, the oxygen molecules can collide with many more iron atoms. The iron now has a much bigger surface area.

Why do strong solutions react faster?

Magnesium metal reacts with acid.

The reaction is faster if the acid is made more concentrated.

4   Explain why the reaction is faster in more concentrated acid.

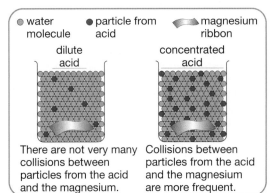

⬤ water molecule   ⬤ particle from acid   magnesium ribbon

dilute acid   concentrated acid

There are not very many collisions between particles from the acid and the magnesium.

Collisions between particles from the acid and the magnesium are more frequent.

Another way to make gases react faster

Gases react faster if they are hot. The diagrams show another way to make gases react faster.

5   Explain why increasing the pressure increases the rate of reaction of gases.

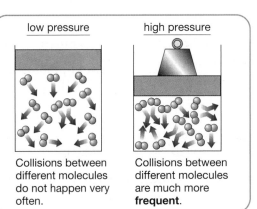

low pressure   high pressure

Collisions between different molecules do not happen very often.

Collisions between different molecules are much more **frequent**.

What you need to remember *Copy and complete using the **key words***

What makes chemical reactions happen?
For substances to react:

■ their particles must _____

■ the particles must have enough _____ when they do this.

The smallest amount of energy they need to react is called the _____ energy.

If you increase the temperature, reactions happen faster. This is because the particles collide more _____ and with more _____.

Breaking solids into smaller pieces, making solutions more concentrated and increasing the pressure of gases all make reactions _____.

All these things make the collisions between particles more _____.

8 Measuring the rate of reaction

The rate of a reaction is the speed of the reaction. It doesn't tell us 'how much' of a product we make, but instead 'how quickly' a reaction happens.

When zinc reacts with hydrochloric acid, there are two ways we can measure the rate of reaction.

zinc + hydrochloric acid → zinc chloride + hydrogen

$Zn(s) + 2HCl(aq) → ZnCl_2(aq) + H_2(g)$

We could

■ measure how quickly a **product** is made
■ measure how quickly a **reactant** (e.g. the zinc) seems to disappear.

1 Which product could we measure as it is produced?

2 Which reactant could we measure as it disappears?

We work out the rate of a chemical reaction in the following way:

$$\text{rate of reaction} = \frac{\text{amount of reactant used}}{\text{time}}$$

or

$$\text{rate of reaction} = \frac{\text{amount of product formed}}{\text{time}}$$

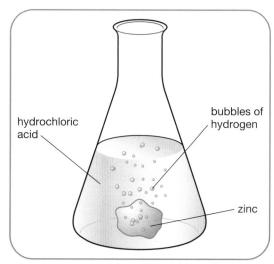

When zinc reacts with hydrochloric acid it makes a gas which we can collect. The zinc and acid are used up in the reaction.

How quickly a product is made

In this experiment we measure the volume of hydrogen (in cm^3) made every 30 seconds.

We can work out the rate of the reaction for the first 30 seconds:

$$\text{rate of reaction} = \frac{\text{volume of hydrogen}}{\text{time}}$$

$$= \frac{6}{30} = 0.2 cm^3 \text{ per second}$$

3 Now work out the rate of reaction between 60 and 90 seconds.

4 What do you notice about the rate of reaction compared with the rate in the first 30 seconds?

Time (seconds)	Total volume of gas produced (cm^3)
0	0
30	6
60	10
90	13
120	15
150	17
180	19
210	20
240	20
270	20
300	20
330	20
360	20

How quickly we lose mass

When the zinc reacts with the hydrochloric acid, hydrogen escapes and there is a loss of mass.

We can also measure the rate of reaction by working out the loss in mass (of the zinc and hydrochloric acid) every 30 seconds.

Look at the graph for the reaction.

We can work out the rate of reaction for the first 30 seconds.

$$\text{rate of reaction} = \frac{\text{loss in mass}}{\text{time}}$$

$$= \frac{0.45}{30}$$

$$= 0.015 \, \text{g/s}$$

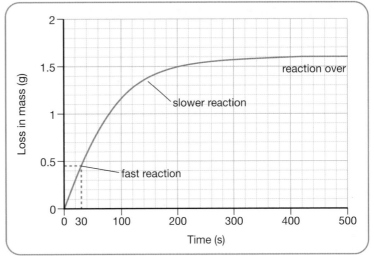

A graph can give us information about the rate of a reaction between zinc and hydrochloric acid.

The slope of the graph also gives us information about the rate of the reaction.

5 What do the following slopes tell us about the rate of reaction?

a a steep slope
b a shallower slope
c a flat (horizontal) slope.

What you need to remember *Copy and complete using the key words*

Measuring the rate of reaction
We can find the rate of a chemical reaction if we measure

■ the amount of _____ used over time or
■ the amount of _____ formed over time.

$$\text{rate of reaction} = \frac{\text{amount of reactant used}}{\text{time}} \quad \text{or} \quad \frac{\text{amount of product formed}}{\text{time}}$$

9 Particles, solutions and gases

When we compare rates of reaction, we need to know what concentration of a solution we are using.

Two solutions with the same concentration must have the same <u>number of particles</u> of the dissolved substance (solute) in the same volume of solution.

But dissolving the same <u>mass</u> of different solutes in the same amount of solution would not be fair.

Mohan weighed out 40 g of sodium hydroxide and dissolved it in 1 dm^3 of water. He wanted to make a solution of potassium hydroxide with the same concentration. In other words, he wanted to make a solution with the same number of particles in it.

> **1** The formula of potassium hydroxide is KOH. What is its relative formula mass? Show how you worked it out.

For solutions of two compounds to have the same concentration, they must have the same number of formula masses in the same volume of solution.

> **2** Copy and complete the sentence.
>
> Mohan made the solution the same concentration by adding ＿＿＿＿ g of potassium hydroxide to ＿＿＿＿ dm^3 of water.

> **3** Why would dissolving the same masses of sodium hydroxide and potassium hydroxide not give us solutions with the same concentration?

> **4** Suppose you dissolve 20 g of sodium hydroxide in water to make 500 cm^3 of sodium hydroxide solution. How many grams of potassium hydroxide would you need to make 500 cm^3 of potassium hydroxide solution with the same concentration?

Introducing the mole

So, to make solutions of the same concentration, we need to use the relative formula mass of the solute in grams. We call this a mole.

> **5** How many particles are there in 1 mole of
>
> **a** sodium hydroxide? **b** potassium hydroxide?

> **6** What is the mass of 1 mole of
>
> **a** sodium hydroxide? **b** potassium hydroxide?

REMEMBER

The atoms of different elements have different masses. These are compared on a scale that is called relative atomic mass.

Element	Relative atomic mass
hydrogen (H)	1
oxygen (O)	16
sodium (Na)	23
potassium (K)	39

Sodium hydroxide has the formula NaOH.
So the relative formula mass of sodium hydroxide is:
Na   O   H
23 + 16 + 1 = 40

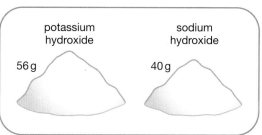

Dissolving these masses of chemical compounds in equal volumes of water produces solutions with the same concentration.

The mole

A mole of any substance contains the same number of **particles**.
This number is
602 000 000 000 000 000 000 000!
We can write this as 6.02 × 10^{23} for short.

Comparing concentrations

We can write the concentration of a solution in **moles per cubic decimetre**. We write this **mol/dm³** for short.

If we dissolve 1 mole of potassium hydroxide in $1\,dm^3$ of water, the solution has the same **molar concentration** as 1 mole of sodium hydroxide in $1\,dm^3$ of water.

7 Calcium chloride has a relative formula mass of 111. What is the mass of 1 mole of calcium chloride?

8 How would you make a solution of calcium chloride

  a with a concentration of $1\,mol/dm^3$?
  b with a concentration of $0.5\,mol/dm^3$?

Particles in a gas

It's hard to measure the mass of a gas formed in a chemical reaction and much easier to measure its volume. The volume of a gas can tell us about the number of **particles** it contains.

9 Copy and complete the sentences.

The balloons contain the same _____ of the gases helium and oxygen. Each balloon also contains the same number of _____ of gas. We can only compare volumes of gases if they are at the same _____ and _____.

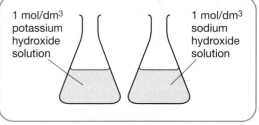

1 mol/dm³ potassium hydroxide solution   1 mol/dm³ sodium hydroxide solution

These two flasks each contain solutions with the same molar concentration. They each contain the same number of particles.

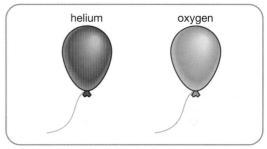

helium   oxygen

These two balloons have the same volume of gas inside. They also contain the same number of particles.

I'm sure this balloon was bigger in the shop.

If we want to compare volumes of gases we must do it at the same **temperature** and **pressure**.

What you need to remember *Copy and complete using the key words*

Particles, solutions and gases
We can measure the concentration of a solution in _____ _____
_____ _____ or _____.
Equal volumes of solutions with the same _____ _____ contain the same number of _____.
Equal volumes of gases at the same _____ and _____ contain the same number of _____.

You can learn more about the mole on page 312.

1 Getting energy out of chemicals

We can buy meals and drinks in packaging which will heat them up. We say that they are self-heating.
A chemical reaction inside the packaging produces the heat.

1 Which <u>two</u> chemicals react to produce heat in a self-heating coffee can?

Many other chemical reactions can transfer **energy** to the surroundings. This energy is often in the form of **heat**.

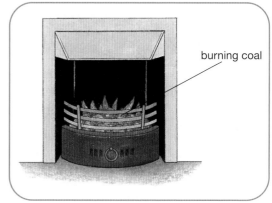

We can heat up the coffee in these cans to 60 °C by pushing a button on the base. This starts a chemical reaction between quicklime and water which gives out heat.

Heat from burning

Burning substances also produces energy in the form of heat. Another word for burning is **combustion**.

2 What form of energy do we want when we burn fuels like coal?

3 What is another word that means burning?

burning coal

We burn substances like coal because they produce heat. We call them fuels.

Naming reactions

Chemical reactions which release energy are called **exothermic** reactions.

4 Copy and complete the sentences.

'Ex' means _____.
'Therm' means something to do with

_____.

So 'exothermic' means _____ going

_____.

An <u>exit</u> sign is where you go <u>out</u>.

A <u>thermo</u>meter tells you how <u>hot</u> something is. A <u>Thermo</u>s™ flask keeps the <u>heat</u> in.

Other exothermic reactions

Chemical reactions which happen in solutions can also be exothermic. As the reaction happens the solution gets warmer.

5 What happens to the temperature of the acid when we add alkali to it?

6 What do we call this type of exothermic reaction?

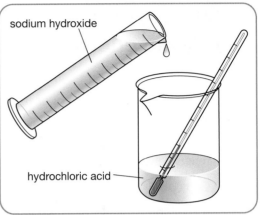

sodium hydroxide

hydrochloric acid

Adding the right amount of alkali to an acid can make it turn neutral. The reading on the thermometer increases during the reaction. **Neutralisation** is an exothermic reaction.

There are many other chemical reactions which are exothermic, for example the reaction between magnesium and oxygen.

Magnesium powder is one of the chemicals we find in fireworks. When it reacts with oxygen from the air, it forms magnesium oxide.

magnesium + oxygen → magnesium oxide

We call this an **oxidation** reaction. Many oxidation reactions are exothermic.

7 Copy and complete the sentences.

When magnesium combines with oxygen we call it an _____ reaction. When fireworks explode, many _____ reactions take place.

8 When fireworks explode they give out heat energy. Write down <u>two</u> other forms of energy which are released when the chemicals in fireworks react.

The silver colour we see when fireworks explode is from the oxidation of magnesium. The fast reactions in fireworks are exothermic.

What you need to remember *Copy and complete using the key words*

Getting energy out of chemicals
Some chemical reactions release (transfer) _____ into their surroundings.
The energy they release is often _____ energy. We say that these reactions are
_____ .

Some examples of exothermic reactions are _____ , _____ and
_____ .

2 Do chemical reactions always release energy?

Many chemical reactions release, or transfer, energy **to** their surroundings.

> **1** Write down <u>two</u> examples of chemical reactions that release energy.

> **2** Copy and complete the sentence.
>
> A reaction that releases heat energy is called an _____ reaction.

Other reactions will happen only if **energy** is taken in **from** the surroundings. We call these **endothermic** reactions.

You have to supply energy to cook the egg.

> **3** Write down <u>one</u> everyday example of an endothermic reaction.

Taking in energy from the surroundings

Endothermic reactions often take in heat energy.

Many of the cool packs athletes use to relieve pain and inflammation are just a mixture of ammonium nitrate and water.

> **4** What must the athlete do to make the cold pack work?

> **5** Where does this endothermic process take its heat from?

> **6** Why do we call this an endothermic process rather than an endothermic reaction?

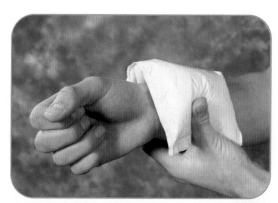

There is a water bag inside this cool pack. When you break it, the ammonium nitrate dissolves in the water. This uses heat from the surroundings – your body.
Although dissolving isn't a chemical reaction, this is still an example of an endothermic process.

Using heat to split up compounds

We can make some chemical reactions happen by supplying energy in the form of heat. This is why a Bunsen burner is so useful; it supplies heat energy.

7　Look at the diagrams.

Copy and complete the word equations for the endothermic reactions.

copper _____ + ⟨energy⟩ → copper _____ + _____

calcium carbonate + ⟨energy⟩ → _____ + _____

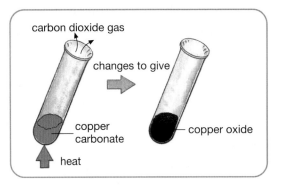

carbon dioxide gas

changes to give

copper carbonate

copper oxide

heat

Both of these reactions use **heat** to split up the metal carbonates.

8　What do we call the type of reaction which splits up a compound using heat?

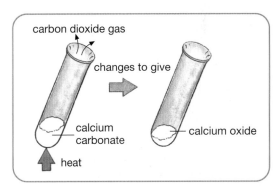

carbon dioxide gas

changes to give

calcium carbonate

calcium oxide

heat

What you need to remember *Copy and complete using the **key words***

Do chemical reactions always release energy?

When chemical reactions occur, energy is transferred _____ or _____ the surroundings. When a reaction takes in energy from the surroundings we call it an _____ reaction. Often the _____ it takes in is heat energy.

Examples of endothermic reactions include _____ _____ reactions.

In these reactions, _____ is taken in to split up a compound.

3 Backwards and forwards

What happens when we heat copper sulfate?

Look at the photos of the two forms of copper sulfate.
It is easy to change one into the other. The reaction can go
both ways. We say this change is reversible.

1 What is a reversible reaction?

2 Copy the equation for the reaction.
   The spaces are there for you to write in the colours.

hydrated copper sulfate + energy ⇌ anhydrous copper sulfate + water
(_____)   (_____)

3 Is making anhydrous copper sulfate this way an
   exothermic or an endothermic reaction? Explain
   your answer.

These crystals of copper sulfate have water
molecules in them as well as copper sulfate.
We say that they are **hydrated**.

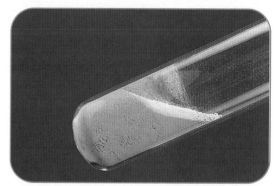

This powder is **anhydrous** copper sulfate.
It has no water in it.

The diagram shows what happens when we add water to
anhydrous copper sulfate.

4 Describe the energy transfer when we add water to
   anhydrous copper sulfate.

So when we add water to anhydrous copper sulfate, energy
is transferred to the surroundings.

Exactly the **same** amount of energy from the surroundings
is needed to drive water out of the hydrated crystals.

Testing for water

Sometimes in a chemical reaction, we make a substance
which looks like water. We can use anhydrous copper
sulfate to **test** if this liquid contains **water**.

5 Describe the colour change you would see if you
   added a liquid containing water to anhydrous
   copper sulfate.

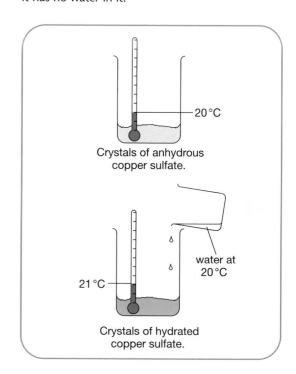

20 °C

Crystals of anhydrous
copper sulfate.

water at
20 °C

21 °C

Crystals of hydrated
copper sulfate.

Energy transfers in the Haber process

The Haber process is another example of a reversible reaction.

6 Write down the word equation for the reversible reaction we call the Haber process.

Just like the reaction with copper sulfate, this reaction is **exothermic** in one direction and **endothermic** in the opposite direction. Again, the same amount of energy is transferred in both the forward and reverse reactions.

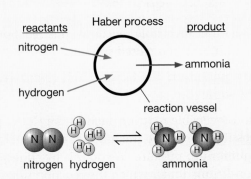
Equilibrium and the closed system

7 What do we call it if the rate of the forward reaction is the same as the rate of the reverse reaction?

The Haber process can only reach equilibrium if the reactants and products cannot leave the reaction vessel. We call this a **closed system**.

8 Write down the names of the three substances there are in the reaction vessel for the Haber process at equilibrium.

9 Explain what we mean by a closed system.

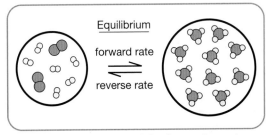

At equilibrium, the **rate** of the forward reaction and the rate of the reverse reaction are the same.

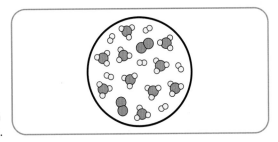

These are the three substances in the reaction vessel at equilibrium.

What you need to remember *Copy and complete using the **key words***

Backwards and forwards

If a reversible reaction is _____ in one direction it is _____ in the opposite direction. The amount of energy that is transferred is the _____.
When we heat _____ copper sulfate it produces _____ copper sulfate. We can use the reverse reaction as a _____ for _____.
We reach equilibrium in a _____ _____ when the forward and reverse reactions occur at exactly the same _____.

H 4 Equilibrium and temperature

The reaction used in the Haber process is reversible:

$$N_2 + 3H_2 \rightleftharpoons 2NH_3$$

Like other reversible reactions, this reaction reaches equilibrium in a closed system.

At equilibrium, the forward and reverse reactions occur at the same rate.

In a reversible reaction such as the Haber process, it is possible to change the amount of product in the equilibrium mixture. We do this by changing the **conditions** under which the reaction takes place.

We need to know which conditions will give us the best yield of ammonia.

> **1** What is the yield of a chemical reaction?

> **2** Write down <u>two</u> conditions we can change inside the reaction vessel used in the Haber process.

In the Haber process, we produce ammonia in the forward reaction:

$$N_2 + 3H_2 \rightarrow 2NH_3$$

> **3** Copy and complete the sentence.
>
> To produce more ammonia, we need to choose conditions that will favour the _____ reaction.

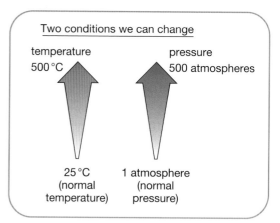

Two conditions we can change

temperature 500 °C

pressure 500 atmospheres

25 °C (normal temperature)

1 atmosphere (normal pressure)

Changing the temperature

The energy changes in a reversible reaction are also reversible.

> **4** In the Haber process which reaction, forward or reverse, is
>
> **a** exothermic?
> **b** endothermic?

$$N_2 + 3H_2 \underset{\text{endothermic}}{\overset{\text{exothermic}}{\rightleftharpoons}} 2NH_3$$

The forward reaction in the Haber process is exothermic. The reverse reaction is endothermic.

By changing the temperature of an equilibrium mixture of nitrogen, hydrogen and ammonia, we can change the amount of product in the equilibrium mixture.

5. What happens to the yield of the endothermic reaction if we raise the temperature of the equilibrium mixture?

6. Do we produce more or less ammonia in the equilibrium mixture if we raise the temperature?

7. What happens to the yield of the exothermic reaction if we decrease the temperature of the equilibrium mixture?

8. Do we produce more or less ammonia in the equilibrium mixture if we decrease the temperature?

The temperature that manufacturers actually use for making ammonia is 450 °C. Although a lower temperature gives a better yield of ammonia, the rate of reaction is very slow.

9. Copy and complete the sentence.

Ammonia is usually manufactured at a temperature of _____.

10. Explain why manufacturers choose a high temperature to make ammonia even though the yield is not very high.

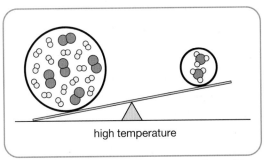

high temperature

Increasing the temperature **increases** the yield from the endothermic reaction. It **decreases** the yield from the exothermic reaction.

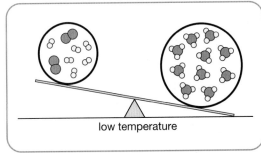

low temperature

Decreasing the temperature **decreases** the yield from the endothermic reaction. It **increases** the yield from the exothermic reaction.

What you need to remember *Copy and complete using the* **key words**

Equilibrium and temperature
At equilibrium, the relative amounts of the substances in the equilibrium mixture depend on the _____ of the reaction.
If we raise the temperature, the yield from the endothermic reaction _____ and the yield from the exothermic reaction _____.
If we lower the temperature, the yield from the endothermic reaction _____ and the yield from the exothermic reaction _____.

You need to be able to describe the effects of changing the temperature on a reaction like the Haber process.

H 5 Equilibrium and pressure

What causes pressure in gases?

In a gas like nitrogen, the molecules move around quickly, colliding with each other and with the walls of the container. This is what gives a gas its pressure.

1 Copy and complete the sentences.

If we increase number of gas molecules in a container then we _____ the pressure. The higher the number of particles, the _____ the pressure.

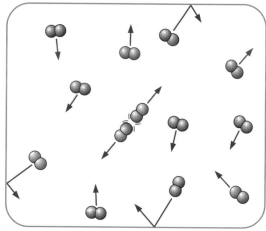

This gas is at a low pressure.

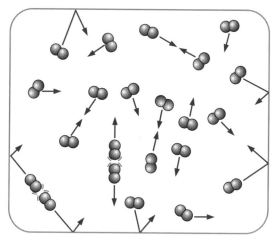

This gas in this container is at a higher pressure than the gas above because it contains more molecule in the same space.

Making ammonia and pressure

We make ammonia gas when two other gases, nitrogen and hydrogen, react together.

2 Look at the equation for this reaction.

   a How many reactant molecules are there?
   b How many molecules of ammonia are produced from the reactant molecules?

So if we produce more ammonia, we reduce the total number of molecules in the reaction vessel. This reduces the pressure in the vessel.

3 What effect does reducing the number of molecules have on the pressure in the reaction vessel?

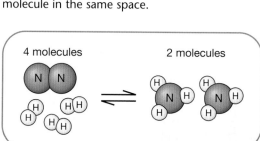

The **equation** shows us that the forward reaction forms <u>two</u> ammonia molecules for every <u>four</u> reactant molecules.

More pressure

We can change the equilibrium in the reaction mixture if we increase the pressure.

If we increase the pressure on an equilibrium mixture of nitrogen, hydrogen and ammonia, the rate of the forward reaction increases more than the rate of the reverse reaction.

We say that increasing the pressure **favours** the forward reaction. This is because the forward reaction **reduces** the number of molecules.

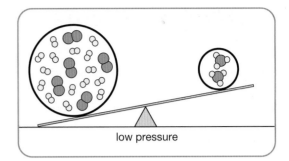

low pressure

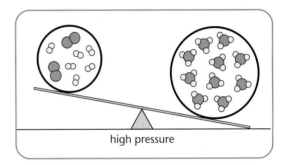

high pressure

4   Copy and complete the sentences.

If we increase the pressure this favours the

_____ reaction.

This is because it produces _____ molecules in the mixture.

5   Explain why increasing the pressure doesn't affect the reaction shown by the equation below.

$$CO + H_2O \rightleftharpoons CO_2 + H_2$$

Too much pressure

The graph shows what happens to the yield of ammonia as we increase the pressure at 450°C.

6   Write down the yield of ammonia we obtain when the pressure is 400 atmospheres.

7   Write down <u>one</u> reason why manufacturers do not use this pressure to make ammonia.

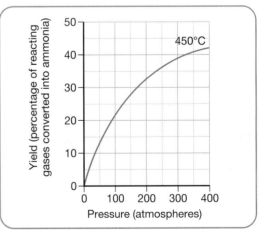

Increasing the pressure increases the yield of ammonia. However, if we increase the pressure in the reaction vessel, we also increase the safety risks.

What you need to remember *Copy and complete using the key words*

Equilibrium and pressure
In reactions with gases, if we increase the pressure, the equilibrium _____ the reaction which _____ the number of molecules.
We can see the number of molecules in the products and the reactants if we look at the
_____ .

You need to be able to describe the effects of changing the pressure on a reaction like the Haber process.

6 Using less energy

H

Chemical manufacturers need to find the best conditions for making their products.
They need to consider the effects of **temperature** and **pressure**. They also need to consider the **rate** of the reaction.

The best conditions for a manufacturer to use are known as the **optimum conditions**.

1 Copy and complete the sentences.

A manufacturer needs to consider the best

_____, _____ and rate of

_____ for a process.

We call these the _____ conditions.

2 Look at the table.
Which conditions give the highest yield of ammonia?

3 Explain why, in the Haber process, ammonia is manufactured at

a a higher temperature than the optimum

b a lower pressure than the optimum.

> **REMEMBER**
>
> ■ In the Haber process, ammonia is usually manufactured at a temperature of about 450 °C and a pressure of about 200 atmospheres.
> ■ A lower temperature gives a greater yield of ammonia but the reaction only takes place very slowly.
> ■ A higher pressure also increases the yield of ammonia but the vessel has to be much thicker and stronger. It costs much more to build and the process has more safety risks.

Pressure (atmospheres)	Yield at		
	100 °C	300 °C	500 °C
25	91.7%	27.4%	2.9%
100	96.7%	52.5%	10.6%
400	99.4%	79.7%	31.9%

This table shows the yield of ammonia as a percentage at different temperatures and pressures in the Haber process.

Less energy

Manufacturers have to pay for the **energy** they use. Using large amounts of energy can make the product expensive to make. We say there are **economic** reasons for using as little energy as possible.

Using large amounts of energy also has an effect on the **environment**.

4 Write down <u>two</u> ways energy use may affect the environment.

This power station uses natural gas to provide heat energy. Natural gas is non-renewable and cannot be replaced. Burning it also releases carbon dioxide into the air. Many scientists believe that increasing carbon dioxide levels are causing the temperature of the Earth to rise.

Chemical manufacturers can reduce the amount of energy they use in several ways.

They can prevent energy from being **wasted** by using insulation and checking that their equipment is working properly.

Another way to **use** less energy is to choose a reaction that works at lower temperatures and pressures. We call these **non-vigorous** conditions. These conditions also **release** less wasted energy into the environment.

5 Copy and complete the sentences.

Reactions which take place under non-vigorous conditions use and release less _____.
This is because they take place at lower
_____ and _____.

In the Haber process, thermal energy is released during the reaction. This is then used to make steam to drive turbines. Some factories use the heat to provide heating and hot water on the site.

Many chemical reactions are exothermic and give out large amounts of heat.

6 Write down <u>two</u> ways in which waste thermal energy can be used for another process.

Sustainability

We now use much less energy in chemical production than we did in the past. This is important for **sustainable development**.

7 Explain how using less energy is important for sustainable development.

> **REMEMBER**
>
> In meeting our needs today, it's important that we don't
>
> ■ damage the environment
> ■ use up resources which will be needed by future generations.

What you need to remember *Copy and complete using the **key words***

Using less energy
Manufacturers have to find the best _____, _____ and
_____ of reaction for producing chemicals. We call these the _____
_____.

It is important for industries to use as little _____ as possible and to reduce the
amount that is _____.
This is because using energy

■ is expensive (for _____ reasons)
■ can affect the _____.

Using _____ conditions for chemical reactions helps to _____ less
energy and to _____ less energy into the environment. This is important for
_____ _____.

You need to be able to weigh up the conditions that industrial processes use in terms of the energy they require.

7 Saving steam!

Many chemical manufacturers have made reductions in their energy consumption over recent years.

One chemical company near Bradford, UK, has dramatically reduced the amount of energy it uses, its carbon dioxide emissions and its costs.

> **1** Write down <u>two</u> products which are made using chemicals from the site near Bradford.

This site produces many different types of chemicals.

Its products include chemicals for use in cosmetics, agriculture and cleaning products.

The company wanted to reduce the amount of energy it was using. The manufacturers knew they were losing heat energy from pipes carrying steam so they carried out a survey. Using an infra-red camera they found out exactly where they were losing the energy from.

> **2** What did the manufacturers use to detect the energy which they were losing?

> **3** What did they do to prevent further energy loss?

Other energy savings

There were other ways in which the site was wasting energy too.

They installed computers to check how electricity is used and to prevent any waste. They also used thermostats and timers to control temperatures and save energy.

The company decided to generate its own electricity on the site. This wastes less energy than taking it from the National Grid.

> **4** Write down <u>three</u> things the company now does which reduce the amount of energy used.

These images are of steam pipes. The bright spots in the lower photo show where thermal energy was being lost. The company provided better insulation at these places. They spent £11 000 on surveying and repairing the pipes. This reduced costs by £23 500 per year in saved heat!

Evidence for energy savings

We can show the reduction in energy use at the site on a graph.

5 Copy and complete the sentences.

In 1992 the amount of energy used per tonne of product was _____ GJ.

This reduced to _____ GJ by 1997.

6 Approximately what fraction of the energy used in 1992 was used in 2001?

7 There was a slight increase in energy consumption between 1997 and 1999. Write down a possible reason for this.

By 2001 the site also produced much less carbon dioxide than it did in 1992. We say there is a correlation between the amount of energy used and the amount of carbon dioxide produced at the site.

8 Explain how the decrease in energy used at the site may have caused the reduction in the amount of carbon dioxide produced.

9 Can you suggest any factors which might have caused less carbon dioxide to be produced at the site?

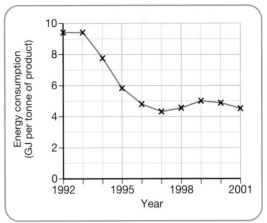

This graph shows us the amount of energy used at the site per tonne of product. A gigajoule (GJ) is a unit of energy (1 GJ = 1 billion joules).

REMEMBER

We burn fuels to give us energy. Most of the fuels we burn produce carbon dioxide gas.

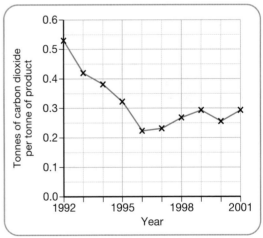

This graph shows the amount of carbon dioxide produced at the site per tonne of product.

What you need to remember

Saving steam!

There is nothing new for you to <u>remember</u> in this section.

You need to be able to weigh up the conditions that industrial processes use in terms of how much energy they use.

1 Using electricity to split up compounds

Some compounds contain **elements** which are very useful to us. If a compound contains **ionic** bonds we can split it up using electricity.

Solid ionic substances, like sodium chloride, will not let electricity pass through them. We must first **dissolve** the compound in water or **melt** it.

1 Why can't we split up a solid ionic substance using electricity?

2 Write down the <u>two</u> ways we can make electricity pass through an ionic compound.

Splitting up copper chloride

Copper chloride is another ionic substance. The diagram shows what happens when an electric current passes through copper chloride solution. The electricity splits it up.

3 Copy and complete the sentences.

A coating of copper forms at the _____ electrode.
Bubbles of chlorine gas are released at the _____ electrode.

In the copper chloride solution

■ the copper ions have a positive charge
■ the chloride ions have a negative charge.

When we dissolve solid copper chloride in water, the ions are free to **move** about.

4 Copy and complete the sentences.

The copper ions have a _____ charge.
They move to the _____ electrode.
The chloride ions have a _____ charge.
They move to the _____ electrode.

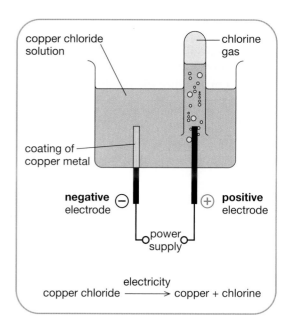

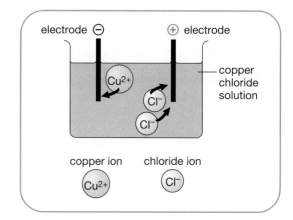

Splitting up lead bromide

When we split up a compound using electricity we call it **electrolysis**.

Like copper chloride, lead bromide is an ionic substance. But lead bromide doesn't dissolve in water.
To make electricity pass through lead bromide we must first melt it.

The diagram shows what happens if we melt lead bromide and then pass an electric current through it.

5 What is electrolysis?

6 Write down the names of the <u>two</u> substances we make when we split up lead bromide using electricity.

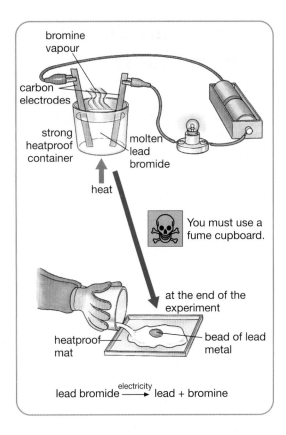

bromine vapour

carbon electrodes

strong heatproof container

molten lead bromide

heat

You must use a fume cupboard.

at the end of the experiment

heatproof mat

bead of lead metal

lead bromide $\xrightarrow{\text{electricity}}$ lead + bromine

Opposites attract

Like copper chloride, lead bromide is made from ions. When we melt solid lead bromide, the ions are free to move about.

7 Copy the diagram showing the ions in lead bromide. Mark on the diagram the way that the ions move during electrolysis.

8 Why do ions move towards the electrode with the opposite charge?

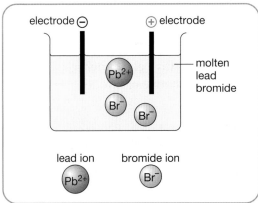

electrode ⊖   ⊕ electrode

Pb²⁺

Br⁻   Br⁻

molten lead bromide

lead ion   bromide ion

Pb²⁺   Br⁻

The ions move to the electrode with the opposite charge. Opposite charges attract.

What you need to remember *Copy and complete using the key words*

Using electricity to split up compounds

We can use electricity to split up _____ compounds into _____.
We call this _____.
First we must _____ the compound or _____ it in water.
When we do this the ions are free to _____ about in the liquid or solution.
When we pass electricity through an ionic substance

■ the positive ions move to the _____ electrode
■ the negative ions move to the _____ electrode.

2 What happens at the electrodes?

If we dissolve or melt ionic substances, they will conduct electricity. When we pass electricity through the liquid or solution, the substance splits up.

1 What do we call it when we split up a compound using electricity?

2 Copy and complete the table.

Charge on ion	Which electrode does it move towards?
positive	
negative	

When we dissolve copper chloride in water the ions are free to move about.

■ Copper ions have a positive charge. We can show them as Cu^{2+}.

■ Chloride ions have a negative charge. We can show them as Cl^-.

3 Which ions, copper or chloride, will move towards the

a positive electrode?
b negative electrode?

Losing and gaining electrons

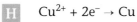

At the negative electrode, the copper ions gain electrons. They form copper atoms.

H $Cu^{2+} + 2e^- \rightarrow Cu$

($2e^-$ represents two electrons)

At the positive electrode, chloride ions lose electrons to form chlorine molecules.

H $2Cl^- \rightarrow Cl_2 + 2e^-$

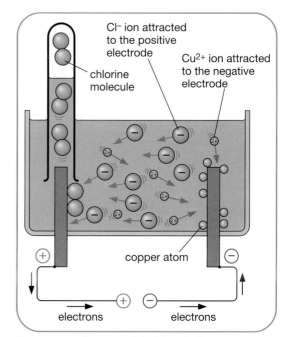

Electrolysis of copper chloride solution.

Oxidation without oxygen?

Oxidation and reduction are not just about the addition or removal of oxygen. They also involve atoms gaining and losing electrons.

So we can use the terms **oxidation** and **reduction** for other reactions, even if oxygen doesn't take part.

- When atoms of an element are oxidised, they **lose** electrons.
- When atoms of an element are reduced, they **gain** electrons.

4 Copy and complete the sentence.

During electrolysis

- at the negative electrode, positively charged ions _____ electrons
- at the positive electrode, negatively charged ions _____ electrons.

5 At which electrode are ions

a oxidised?
b reduced?

REMEMBER

When we combine a substance with oxygen, we call it oxidation.
When we remove oxygen from a substance, we call it reduction.

In this equation
copper oxide + zinc → copper + zinc oxide

- the zinc has been oxidised (gained oxygen)
- the copper oxide has been reduced (lost oxygen).

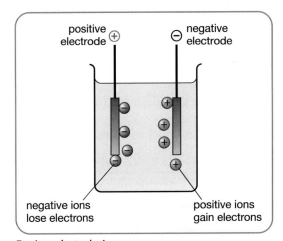

positive electrode ⊕   negative electrode ⊖

negative ions lose electrons

positive ions gain electrons

During electrolysis
- electrons flow into the positive electrode
- electrons flow out of the negative electrode.

What you need to remember *Copy and complete using the **key words***

What happens at the electrodes?
At the negative electrode, positively charged ions _____ electrons. We call this _____.

At the positive electrode, negatively charged ions _____ electrons. We call this _____.

3 Which ion?

When we pass electricity through a solution of an ionic compound, the elements in the compound are often produced at the electrodes.

1   Write down the <u>two</u> substances we produce if we split up a solution of copper chloride.

However, sometimes the **water** in the solution can become involved in the electrolysis. The electricity splits up the water and hydrogen is produced at the negative electrode.

2   What is produced at the negative electrode when we pass electricity through a solution of sodium chloride?

3   Where has this element come from?

Substance we are splitting up	What is produced at the negative electrode?
sodium chloride solution	hydrogen
potassium bromide solution	hydrogen
copper chloride solution	copper

What do we produce at the negative electrode?

There are rules which help us to predict the products of electrolysis.

At the negative electrode

During electrolysis, we always produce a <u>metal</u> or <u>hydrogen</u> at the negative electrode.

■ If the metal in the compound is low in the reactivity series, for example lead or copper, the <u>metal</u> is produced.

■ If the metal in the compound is high in the reactivity series, for example sodium or potassium, <u>hydrogen</u> is produced.

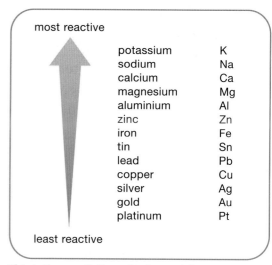

This is the reactivity series for metals. It tells us how **reactive** a metal is.

4   Copy and complete the sentences.

When we pass electricity through a solution of potassium bromide, we produce _____ at the negative electrode. We don't produce the metal _____ because it is too

_____ .

5   Predict what would be produced at the negative electrode if we passed electricity through the following solutions:

a   lead nitrate

b   silver chloride

c   potassium sulfate.

What do we produce at the positive electrode?

In a solution of an ionic substance, negative ions move towards the positive electrode. There is another rule which helps us to predict what is produced.

6   a What is produced at the positive electrode when we pass electricity through lead nitrate solution?
     b Where does this element come from?

7   Copy and complete the sentences.

If we pass electricity through a solution of potassium bromide, we produce _____ at the positive electrode.
Splitting up a solution of lead iodide produces _____ at the positive electrode.

Putting it all together

We can use the two rules together to predict the products formed when we pass electricity through a solution.

8   Copy and complete the diagrams.
     Use the rules to predict what is formed at the positive and negative electrodes.

Substance we are splitting up	What is produced at the positive electrode?
sodium chloride solution	chlorine
potassium bromide solution	bromine
lead nitrate solution	oxygen

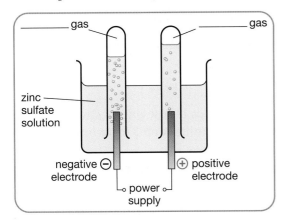

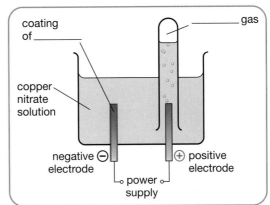

What you need to remember *Copy and complete using the key words*

Which ion?
When we pass electricity through a dissolved substance, the _____ in the solution can split up too. The products formed at the electrodes depend on how _____ the elements are.

You need to be able to predict the products of passing electricity through a solution.

H

4 Half equations

Chemical changes occur during the electrolysis of ionic substances.

At the negative electrode, positively charged ions gain electrons from the electrode. They produce atoms or molecules which have no charge.

At the positive electrode, negatively charged ions lose electrons to produce atoms or molecules with no charge.

The diagram in the Box shows the electrolysis of molten lead bromide. The information below the diagram shows how we can show the change at each electrode using **half equations**. It also shows you how to **balance** the half equations.

1. For the electrolysis of lead bromide, copy the <u>balanced</u> half equations to show what happens to the ions at

    a   the positive electrode
    b   the negative electrode.

2. Copy and then balance these half equations for the electrolysis of molten sodium chloride.

    a Cl^- → Cl_2 + e^-
                (chlorine molecule)
    b Na^+ +   →   Na
                (sodium atom)

3. Complete and balance these half equations for extracting aluminium from aluminium oxide.

    a O^{2-} → O_2 + e^-
    b Al^{3+} + e^- → Al

Electrolysis of lead bromide

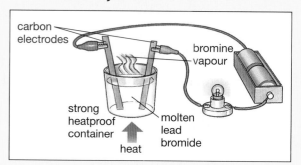

In the electrolysis of molten lead bromide

■ lead atoms are released at the negative electrode
■ bromine molecules are released at the positive electrode.

At the negative electrode, lead ions gain electrons (e^-) to become lead atoms.

$$Pb^{2+} + e^- \rightarrow Pb$$

But an ion with a charge of 2+ needs to gain two electrons to become an atom.
We have to balance the half equation like this.

$$Pb^{2+} + 2e^- \rightarrow Pb$$

lead ion   two electrons   lead atom
                from the electrode   (no charge)

At the positive electrode, bromide ions lose electrons to form bromine molecules.

$$Br^- \rightarrow Br_2 + e^-$$

Each bromide ion needs to lose one electron to become an atom. Bromine atoms form molecules containing two atoms.
We have to balance the half equation like this

$$2Br^- \rightarrow Br_2 + 2e^-$$

two bromide   one bromine   two electrons
ions   molecule   to the electrode
                 (no charge)

What you need to remember *Copy and complete using the **key words***

Half equations

We can show the reactions that take place during electrolysis using _____
_____, for example
$2Cl^- \rightarrow Cl_2 + 2e^-$
It is important to _____ these.

You need to be able to complete and balance half equations like the ones on this page.

5 Useful substances from salt

Ordinary salt, or sodium chloride, is a very important substance. We can use it to make other chemicals if we dissolve it in water and split up the solution by electrolysis.

We can use salt to make substances like bleach, margarine, plastics and soap.

1 Write down the names of <u>three</u> materials we can make using chemicals from salt.

2 Copy and complete the sentences.

Passing electricity through brine produces the gases _____ and _____.
It also produces a solution of _____ _____.

These three chemicals are very important to the _____ _____.

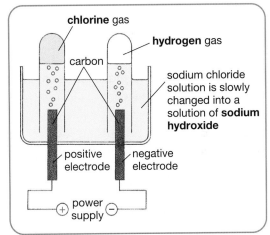

The electrolysis of sodium chloride solution (brine) produces useful raw materials for the **chemical industry**.

The chemicals we make during the electrolysis of sodium chloride are very corrosive. So manufacturers use specially designed cells. There are three different kinds of cell. Look at the table below.

3 Write down the names of the <u>three</u> types of cell that are used for the electrolysis of sodium chloride.

4 The mercury cell is the oldest type of cell. It is still used widely. Write down <u>two</u> reasons why it is now being phased out.

5 If you were a manufacturer, which type of cell would you replace your mercury cells with? Explain your answer.

Type of cell used for the electrolysis of sodium chloride	Power used (kilowatt hours) to make 1 tonne of chlorine	Quality of sodium hydroxide produced by the cell	Environmental issues
mercury cell	3440	very good	minor traces of poisonous mercury in products
diaphragm cell	2900	poor	uses asbestos (harmful and difficult to dispose of safely)
membrane cell	2700	quite good	no known problems

What you need to remember *Copy and complete using the key words*

Useful substances from salt
The electrolysis of sodium chloride solution produces _____, _____ and _____ _____ solution. These are important reagents for the _____ _____.

You need to be able to weigh up the good and bad points of chemical processes, just like you did for the electrolysis of sodium chloride.

6 Purifying copper

Why we need pure copper

We all use many different electrical appliances such as computers, DVD players, mobile phones, TVs and electric kettles.

We need copper to make these appliances. We also need copper to be able to use them.

1 Write down <u>two</u> reasons why a mains TV set depends on copper.

The copper we need to make cables or electrical circuits must be very pure indeed.

Copper is used inside the cables that carry electricity to electrical appliances.

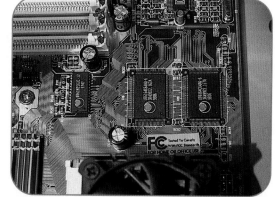

Copper is used to make the printed circuits inside TVs, MP3 players and computers.

How to make copper very pure

We make copper pure by **electrolysis**. The diagrams show how we do this.

2 Copy and complete the sentences.

At the positive electrode, copper _____ become copper _____.

At the negative electrode, copper _____ become copper _____.

3 a What happens, over a period of two weeks, to all of the copper from the positive electrode?
b What happens to the impurities?

In this electrolysis reaction the copper sulfate is not decomposed (broken down). It remains unchanged. Copper ions enter the solution at the positive electrode and leave the solution at the negative electrode.

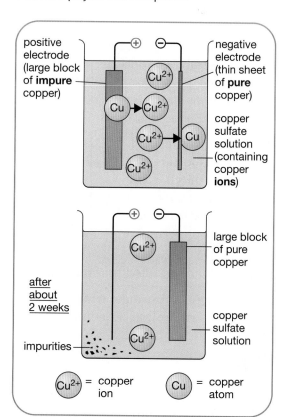

Losing and gaining electrons

We can explain what is happening when we purify copper if we look at the transfer of electrons.

At the positive electrode:

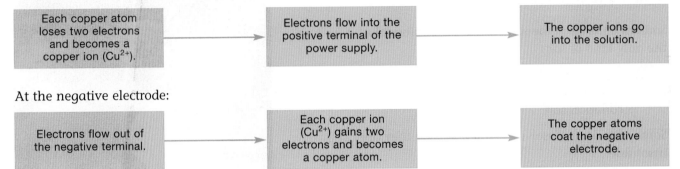

Each copper atom loses two electrons and becomes a copper ion (Cu^{2+}).	→ Electrons flow into the positive terminal of the power supply.	→ The copper ions go into the solution.

At the negative electrode:

Electrons flow out of the negative terminal.	→ Each copper ion (Cu^{2+}) gains two electrons and becomes a copper atom.	→ The copper atoms coat the negative electrode.

4 Complete and balance these half equations for purifying copper.

a At the positive electrode

$$Cu \rightarrow Cu^{2+} + \quad e^-$$

b At the negative electrode

$$+ \quad e^- \rightarrow Cu$$

5 Copy and complete the sentences.

When we purify copper, copper _____ lose electrons at the positive electrode.
We call this _____.
At the negative electrode copper _____ gain electrons.
We call this _____.

> **REMEMBER**
>
> **O**xidation **I**s **L**oss of electrons.
> **R**eduction **I**s **G**ain of electrons.

What you need to remember *Copy and complete using the **key words***

Purifying copper
We purify copper by a process called _____. We use a positive electrode made from the _____ copper and a negative electrode made from _____ copper.
The solution we use for the process contains copper _____.

You need to be able to explain processes using the terms oxidation and reduction, just like you did here for the purification of copper.

7 Making salts that won't dissolve

Different kinds of salt

Sodium chloride is the salt we put on our food. But it isn't the only kind of salt.

1 Look at the photograph.
Write down the names of <u>two</u> different salts besides common salt.

Some salts don't dissolve in water. We say they are **insoluble**.

When we mix certain salt solutions together they form a new salt which does not dissolve. This is how we make insoluble salts.

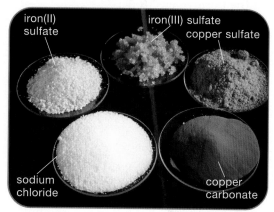

Some salts.

Making a salt from two other salts

Sodium chloride and silver nitrate are both salts that will dissolve in water. Diagrams A and B show what happens if we mix together solutions of these two salts.

2 **a** What happens when we mix together solutions of sodium chloride and sodium nitrate?
b Why does this happen?
c What do we call a solid substance that forms when two solutions mix?

We say that the silver chloride has been produced by a **precipitation** reaction.

Diagrams C and D show what you can then do to get pure silver chloride from the solution.

3 Put these instructions in the correct order to show how you would produce some pure silver chloride.

■ Use a filter to separate out the precipitate of silver chloride.
■ Mix the two solutions together to form a precipitate.
■ Add silver nitrate solution to a solution of sodium chloride.
■ Wash the precipitate with distilled water and leave it to dry.

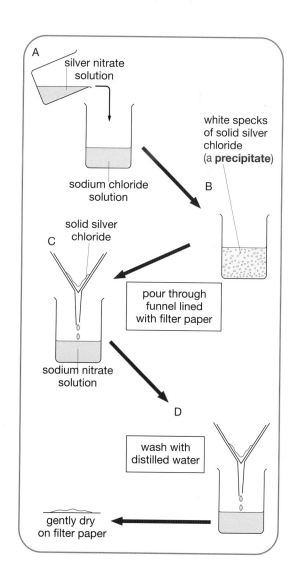

How does precipitation work?

Salts are ionic compounds. When a soluble salt dissolves in water the ions separate from each other and spread out amongst the water molecules.

The diagram shows what happens when the ions in sodium chloride are mixed with the ions in silver nitrate solution.

> **4** Copy and complete the sentences.
>
> The silver ions from the _____
> _____ solution join up with the
> _____ ions from the sodium chloride
> solution to form specks of solid
> _____ _____.
>
> The _____ ions and the
> _____ ions stay in the solution.
> We say they are _____ ions.

The equation for this precipitation reaction is

silver nitrate	+	sodium chloride	→	silver chloride	+	sodium nitrate
$AgNO_3$	+	$NaCl$	→	$AgCl$	+	$NaNO_3$

> **5** Add state symbols to the formula equation to show what happens in the reaction.

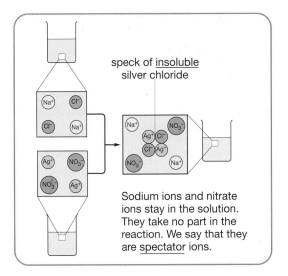

speck of insoluble silver chloride

Sodium ions and nitrate ions stay in the solution. They take no part in the reaction. We say that they are spectator ions.

REMEMBER

We can show the states of a substance in an equation using state symbols.
(s) means solid
(aq) means dissolved in water
(l) means a liquid
(g) means a gas.

Cleaning things up

Precipitation reactions can be very useful. Water companies add aluminium salts to our **drinking water** before it reaches our homes. This removes any **unwanted** ions from the water.

> **6** Write down <u>two</u> other ways in which we can use precipitation reactions.

We use precipitation reactions

■ to clean up swimming pool water
■ to treat our **effluent** (waste water).

What you need to remember *Copy and complete using the key words*

Making salts that won't dissolve

If a salt won't dissolve we say it is _____.
We can make insoluble salts by mixing certain solutions which form a _____.
Reactions like this are called _____ reactions. We can use them to remove
_____ ions from solutions, e.g. for treating _____
_____ and _____.

You need to be able to suggest the ways you could make a named salt. You will learn more of these on pages 202–206.

8 Making salts using acids and alkalis

Many salts will dissolve in water. We say that they are **soluble** in water.

We can use acids to produce soluble salts. One way to do this is to react the acid with an alkali.

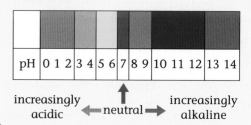
The diagram shows what happens as we add acid to an alkali. We can use an **indicator** to tell us about the reaction.

  1 What colour is the indicator in diagram B?

  2 Is the solution in the flask in diagram B acidic, alkaline or neutral?

The indicator tells us when the acid and alkali have completely **reacted**. If we add just the right amount of acid to an alkali we produce a solution that is neutral (not an acid or an alkali). We say that the acid and alkali have neutralised each other.

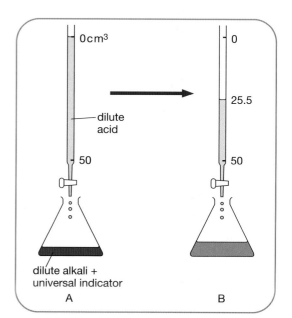

dilute acid

dilute alkali + universal indicator

A   B

What's in the neutral solution?

The neutral solution still contains all of the particles from the acid and the alkali. They have reacted to form a new substance called a salt, as well as some water.

If we want to obtain the **solid** salt we have to evaporate the water from the solution. This leaves crystals of the salt behind.

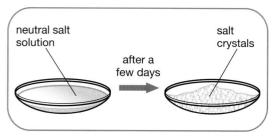

neutral salt solution   after a few days   salt crystals

Producing a solid salt.

We say the solution has **crystallised**.

  3 Complete the sentences.

    The neutral solution contains a _____ .
    We evaporate the _____ out of the
    solution to give us the _____ salt.
    We say that we have _____ the
    solution.

How do we know which salt we have made?

The salt that we make depends on:

- the acid
- the metal in the alkali that we use.

When we neutralise hydrochloric acid, the salt we make is a **chloride**.
Any salt of nitric acid is a **nitrate**.
Any salt of sulfuric acid is a **sulfate**.

The salt takes the first part of its name from the **metal** in the alkali that we use. So if we neutralise sodium hydroxide with hydrochloric acid we make the salt called sodium chloride.

4 Copy and complete the word equation.

sodium hydroxide + hydrochloric acid → _____ + _____

5 Which salt do we make if we neutralise potassium hydroxide with hydrochloric acid?

6 Copy and complete the word equations.

a potassium hydroxide + sulfuric acid → _____ + water

b _____ hydroxide + _____ acid → sodium nitrate + water

7 The diagrams show how to make potassium chloride.

a Why do we add litmus to the acid?
b Why do we boil the neutral solution with charcoal and then filter it?

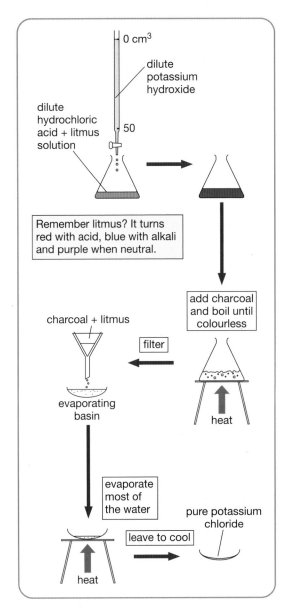

0 cm³

dilute potassium hydroxide

dilute hydrochloric acid + litmus solution

50

Remember litmus? It turns red with acid, blue with alkali and purple when neutral.

add charcoal and boil until colourless

charcoal + litmus

filter

evaporating basin

heat

evaporate most of the water

leave to cool

pure potassium chloride

heat

What you need to remember *Copy and complete using the **key words***

Making salts using acids and alkalis

We can make a _____ salt by reacting an acid with an alkali. We use an _____ to tell us when the acid and alkali have completely _____.
The _____ salt can be _____ from the salt solution we make.
The type of salt we make depends on the acid we use.

- To make a _____, we use hydrochloric acid
- To make a _____, we use sulfuric acid
- To make a _____, we use nitric acid.

The salt we make also depends on the _____ in the alkali.

9 Other ways to make soluble salts

We can't use acid + alkali reactions to make all the salts we need. We make some salts by reacting an acid with

- a **metal** or
- an insoluble base.

Making salts using acid + metal

When a metal reacts with an acid it produces the salt of that metal and bubbles of hydrogen gas.

1 Which salt do we make if we react magnesium with hydrochloric acid?

2 Write a word equation for the reaction.

3 How do we know when the reaction is complete?

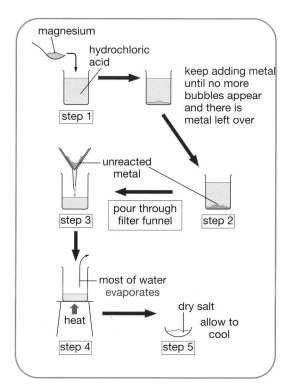

This method of making a salt will only work for metals which are quite reactive. It is not safe to use if a metal is too **reactive**.

4 Write down the name(s) of

  a <u>three</u> metals whose salts are safe to make by this method

  b <u>one</u> metal which is not reactive enough for this method to be used

  c <u>two</u> metals which are too reactive for this method to be safe.

5 a Write down a set of instructions for making some pure zinc sulfate crystals. Use short numbered sentences.

  b Write a word equation for the reaction.

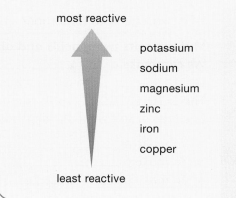

Salts from insoluble bases

A base is a metal **oxide** or **hydroxide**. Bases react with an acid to produce a salt and water.

acid + base → salt + water

Some bases dissolve in water and some don't.

An **alkali** is a base which dissolves in water. We have already seen how to make salts using acids and alkalis.

There are also many **insoluble bases** (bases which don't dissolve in water). We can still use them to neutralise acids and make salts.

6 Copy and complete the sentences.

We can't use copper oxide to make an alkaline solution because it is _____ in water. We can tell that the copper oxide reacts with the acid because the acid turns into a solution which is

_____.

In the reaction between copper oxide and hydrochloric acid we produce _____ _____ and _____.

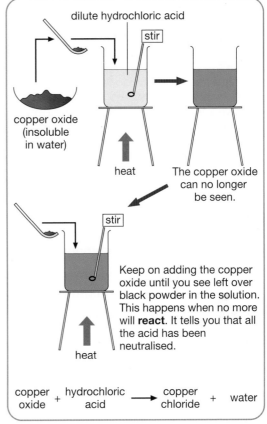

copper oxide (insoluble in water)

dilute hydrochloric acid

stir

heat

The copper oxide can no longer be seen.

stir

Keep on adding the copper oxide until you see left over black powder in the solution. This happens when no more will **react**. It tells you that all the acid has been neutralised.

heat

copper oxide + hydrochloric acid ⟶ copper chloride + water

We can remove any unreacted base by passing the mixture through a **filter**.

How can we tell when all of the acid has been neutralised?

When we neutralise an acid with an insoluble base like copper oxide, we don't need an indicator.

7 **a** What do we see left in the solution when all of the acid has been neutralised?

b Why do we see this?

c How do we separate the salt solution from any insoluble base that is left over?

What you need to remember *Copy and complete using the* **key words**

Other ways to make soluble salts

We can make a salt from an acid if we react it with a _____. Not all metals are suitable because some are too _____ while other metals are not reactive enough.

We can also use _____ _____ to produce salts. A base is a metal _____ or _____. A base which will dissolve is called an _____.

To make a salt from an insoluble base we add it to the acid until no more will _____. Then we _____ off the solid that is left over.

10 Making salts that don't contain metals

Some of the salts that are most important to us don't contain metals at all. They are the ammonium salts that we use as **fertilisers**.

We make ammonium salts from the compound ammonia.

> **1** Why are ammonium salts so important?

> **2** Which elements is ammonia made from?

When ammonia gas dissolves in water it produces an **alkaline** solution called ammonium hydroxide.

We can use ammonium hydroxide to neutralise an acid. The salt that we make is an **ammonium** salt.

> **3** Copy and complete the sentences.
>
> We make ammonium hydroxide by dissolving _____ gas in water. It is able to neutralise an acid because it is an
>
> _____ .

> **4** This equation shows how we can make ammonium chloride.
>
> ammonium + hydrochloric → ammonium + water
> hydroxide   acid   chloride
>
> Write down a word equation to show how we can make ammonium nitrate.

Every year in the UK over 1 million tonnes of ammonia are made into ammonium salts. We use these as fertilisers.

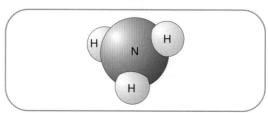

A molecule of ammonia, formula NH_3.

> **REMEMBER**
>
> The type of salt we make depends on the acid we use. To make
>
> ▪ a chloride we use hydrochloric acid
> ▪ a sulfate we use sulfuric acid
> ▪ a nitrate we use nitric acid.

What you need to remember *Copy and complete using the **key words***

Making salts that don't contain metals
When we dissolve ammonia in water it produces an _____ solution. We use this to produce _____ salts.
Farmers use large amounts of ammonium salts as _____ .

11 What happens during neutralisation?

Acidic solutions are acidic because they contain **hydrogen ions**. These have a positive charge.

The symbol for a hydrogen ion is H^+.

Alkaline solutions are alkaline because they contain **hydroxide ions**. These have a negative charge. The symbol for a hydroxide ion is OH^-.

> **1** Copy and complete the sentences.
>
> Hydrogen _____, H^+, make solutions
>
> _____.
>
> _____ ions, OH^-, make solutions
>
> _____.

Some solutions are more strongly acidic (or alkaline) than others. We can compare the strengths of different acids and alkalis using the **pH scale**.

> **2** In the diagram, what is the pH of
>
> **a** the acidic solution?
> **b** the alkaline solution?

Acidic and alkaline solutions will react together to produce neutral solutions. We call this **neutralisation**.
Each hydrogen ion in the acid joins up with a hydroxide ion to form a molecule of **water**.

> **3** What is the pH of the neutral solution?
>
> **4** Copy and complete the sentence.
>
> In all acid + alkali neutralisation reactions,
>
> _____ ions react with
>
> _____ ions to produce water.

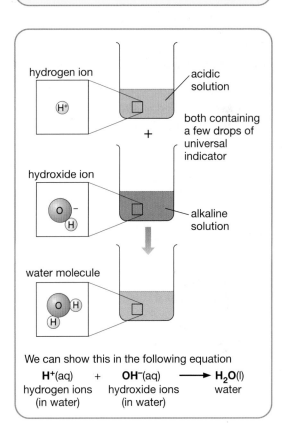

hydrogen ion — acidic solution

H^+

both containing a few drops of universal indicator

hydroxide ion — alkaline solution

O^- H

water molecule

O H H

We can show this in the following equation

$$H^+(aq) + OH^-(aq) \longrightarrow H_2O(l)$$
hydrogen ions (in water)   hydroxide ions (in water)   water

What you need to remember *Copy and complete using the **key words***

What happens during neutralisation?

_____ _____ (H^+) make solutions acidic.

_____ _____ (OH^-) make solutions alkaline.

The _____ _____ measures how acidic or alkaline a solution is.

When hydroxide ions react with hydrogen ions to produce _____ we call it

_____.

We can show this by the equation

_____(aq) + _____(aq) → _____(l)

1 Travelling at speed

Ideas you need from KS3

Calculating speed

A sprinter runs 10 metres in 1 second. His speed is 10 metres per second (m/s). Speed in metres per second tells you how many metres you travel in 1 second.

You can work out speed like this:

$$\text{speed (metres per second)} = \frac{\text{distance travelled (metres)}}{\text{time taken (seconds)}}$$

Example: on a motorway, a car travels 300 metres in 10 seconds.

distance travelled = 300 metres (m)
time taken = 10 seconds (s)
speed = ?

so speed $= \dfrac{300\,\text{m}}{10\,\text{s}} = 30$ metres per second (m/s)

On your calculator: 300 ÷ 10 = 30

1 Look at the examples in the picture and work out the missing item for each one.

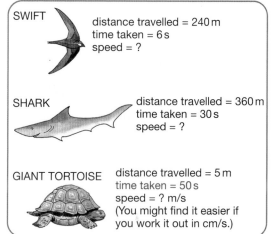

SWIFT
distance travelled = 240 m
time taken = 6 s
speed = ?

SHARK
distance travelled = 360 m
time taken = 30 s
speed = ?

GIANT TORTOISE
distance travelled = 5 m
time taken = 50 s
speed = ? m/s
(You might find it easier if you work it out in cm/s.)

A distance–time graph

A man is running at a steady speed in a straight line. This graph shows the distance he travels against time taken, so it is called a distance–time graph.

You can read from the graph the distance he travels in a period of time. For example, it takes him 4 seconds to run 20 metres.

2 What speed is this?

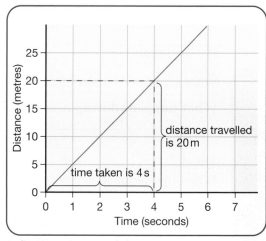

A distance–time graph.

Jane's journey

This example shows how we can describe a journey on a distance–time graph. Look at it carefully and use it to answer the questions.

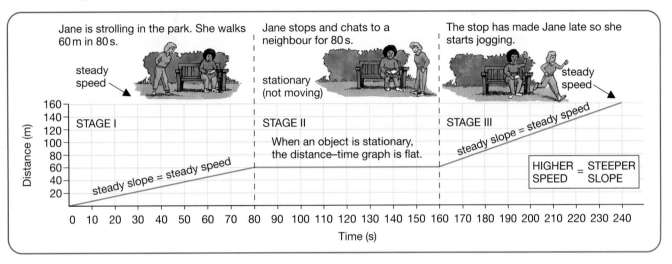

3 Look at stage I of the journey, when Jane is walking.

   a How many metres does Jane walk?
   b How long does it take Jane to walk this distance?
   c What is her speed for this part of her journey?

4 Look at stage II of the journey.

   a What is Jane's speed while she chats?
   b Describe the shape of the graph for this stage.
   c Write down a rule for telling when something is stationary on a distance–time graph.

5 **a** Which part of the graph is steeper, I or III?
   b Which stage of the journey is faster, I or III?
   c What is the connection between speed and slope on a distance–time graph?

The **slope** of a distance–time graph tells you about the **speed**.

If the object is **stationary**, the graph is a horizontal line.

If an object has a higher speed, the graph has a steeper slope.

What you need to remember *Copy and complete using the **key words***

Travelling at speed
The _____ of a distance–time graph represents _____.
A horizontal line on a distance–time graph shows that the object is _____.

You need to recall and be able to use the formula

$$\text{speed (metres per second)} = \frac{\text{distance travelled (metres)}}{\text{time taken (seconds)}}$$

2 Velocity and acceleration

Same speed but different velocity

The diagram shows three aircraft taking part in a display.

1 What is the same about the motion of the planes?

2 What is different?

All three aircraft have the same speed, but they are moving in different <u>directions</u>. We say that they have different velocities. **Velocity** is speed in a given direction.

Look at the aircraft flying in a circle.

3 Is its speed constant?

4 Is its velocity constant?

Give a reason for your answers.

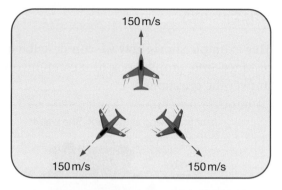

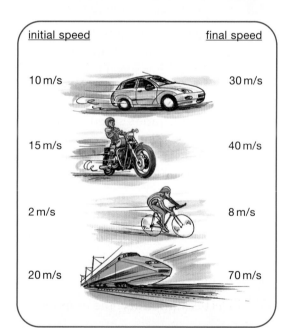

Changing velocity

The drawing shows a car travelling on a straight road. The car speeds up from 10 m/s to 30 m/s. Its velocity changes by 20 m/s because

30 m/s – 10 m/s = 20 m/s

5 Calculate the change of velocity for each of the other examples in the diagram.

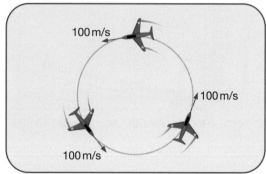

initial speed	final speed
10 m/s	30 m/s
15 m/s	40 m/s
2 m/s	8 m/s
20 m/s	70 m/s

Acceleration

When your velocity changes, we say that you accelerate. Racing drivers want a very large **acceleration**. This means they want to go from a low speed to a high speed in a very short **time**.

6 Copy and complete the sentence.

A big _____ means you reach the top speed in a short _____.

A note about speed and velocity

Velocity is speed in a given direction. When an object only moves in one direction along a straight line you can talk about its speed or velocity as the same thing, but if the direction changes you must use <u>velocity</u> to calculate acceleration.

At the start of a race, this car can accelerate up to 50 m/s in just 5 s. (50 m/s is more than 100 mph.)

How to calculate acceleration

The racing car in the photo on p.210 takes 5 seconds to reach a velocity of 50 metres per second. So, every second, its velocity increases by 10 metres per second. This is its acceleration. You can work out acceleration like this:

$$\text{acceleration} = \frac{\text{change in velocity}}{\text{time taken}}$$

So for the racing car,

$$\text{acceleration} = \frac{50 \, \text{m/s}}{5 \, \text{s}} = 10 \, \text{m/s}^2$$ (On your calculator: $50 \div 5 = 10$)

The **change** in velocity is measured in metres per second (m/s). The time taken is measured in seconds (s). So the units of acceleration are metres per second, per second. We call these **metres per second squared** (m/s^2).

> **7** Look at the examples in the picture and work out the missing items in each one.

Why we use velocity to calculate acceleration

The diagram shows a ball being thrown into the air.
When the ball comes back down it is moving at the same speed as you threw it up. But it is moving in the opposite direction. Its velocity has changed.

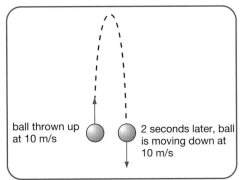
ball thrown up at 10 m/s — 2 seconds later, ball is moving down at 10 m/s

The speed of the ball has not changed. The velocity of the ball has changed by 20 m/s.

> **8** a How much has the velocity of the ball changed?
> b What was the time taken for this change?
> c What is the ball's acceleration?

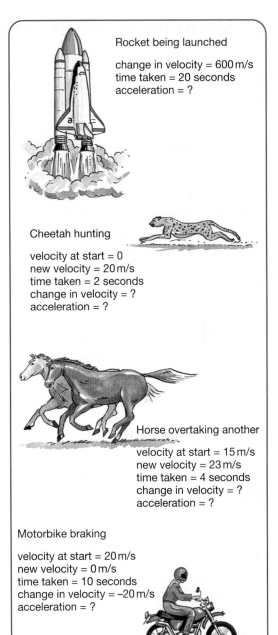

Rocket being launched
change in velocity = 600 m/s
time taken = 20 seconds
acceleration = ?

Cheetah hunting
velocity at start = 0
new velocity = 20 m/s
time taken = 2 seconds
change in velocity = ?
acceleration = ?

Horse overtaking another
velocity at start = 15 m/s
new velocity = 23 m/s
time taken = 4 seconds
change in velocity = ?
acceleration = ?

Motorbike braking
velocity at start = 20 m/s
new velocity = 0 m/s
time taken = 10 seconds
change in velocity = –20 m/s
acceleration = ?

What you need to remember *Copy and complete using the **key words***

Velocity and acceleration
The speed of an object in a particular direction is called its _____.
The rate at which the velocity of an object changes is called its _____.
The units of acceleration are _____ _____ _____
_____ (m/s^2).

Acceleration can be calculated like this: acceleration = $\dfrac{\text{_____ in velocity}}{\text{_____ taken}}$

3 Velocity–time graphs

The diagram shows three cars moving in different ways. The velocity–time graph for each car is shown as well.

1 What does a horizontal line on a velocity–time graph tell you about the velocity?

2 What feature of a velocity–time graph tells you that the object is accelerating?

3 The velocity–time graph for an object is a horizontal line through the origin. What can you say about the object's motion?

Velocity–time graphs look very similar to distance–time graphs but beware, they are quite different. Do not confuse the two.

4 Copy the velocity–time graphs for the three cars. Sketch distance–time graphs underneath with the same time axes.

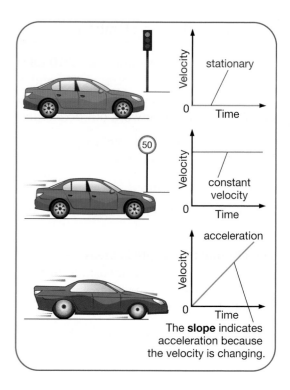

The **slope** indicates acceleration because the velocity is changing.

A cyclist's journey

A cyclist is riding along a straight road. Look at the velocity–time graph for the cyclist. The slope of the velocity–time graph tells you how the velocity is changing.

5 In which parts of the journey is the velocity steady?

6 What is the cyclist's velocity
  a in section A?
  b in section C?

7 How does the graph show an acceleration?

8 How does the graph show that the cyclist slows down quicker than she speeds up?

A **steeper** slope on a velocity–time graph means a bigger acceleration (or deceleration).

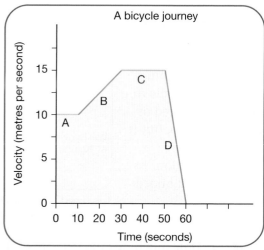

First the cyclist is moving at a steady speed (A) then she slowly accelerates to a higher speed (B). She travels at this higher speed for a while (C) then she quickly slows down (decelerates) and stops (D).

Deceleration

When something speeds up it accelerates. When it slows down we say that it <u>decelerates</u>. We sometimes describe deceleration as <u>negative acceleration</u>.

Rocket launch

The data in the table are for a rocket launch.

9 Plot a velocity–time graph for the rocket as it lifts off.

10 How does the velocity–time graph show the rocket is accelerating as it leaves the launch pad?

11 Draw a line of best fit through the points. Measure the gradient of this line to find the rocket's acceleration.

Time (s)	Velocity (m/s)
0.0	0.0
1.0	2.9
2.0	6.1
3.0	9.0
4.0	11.9
5.0	15.2
6.0	17.9
7.0	21.2

Performance figures

Two sports cars are tested against each other from a standing start.

Look at their velocity–time graphs.

12 Which car accelerates more quickly to 60 mph?

13 Which car has the greater top speed?

14 Which car decelerates faster when it brakes?

Give reasons for your answers.

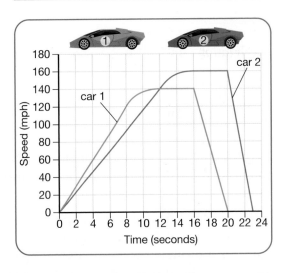

What you need to remember *Copy and complete using the **key words***

Velocity–time graphs

The _____ of a velocity–time graph represents acceleration.

The _____ the slope the higher the acceleration.

You need to be able to construct velocity–time graphs for a body moving with a constant velocity or a constant acceleration.

H 4 More about motion graphs

Calculating speed from a distance–time graph

$$\text{Speed} = \frac{\text{distance}}{\text{time}}$$

So, for part A of the graph on the right,

$$\text{speed} = \frac{20\,\text{m}}{5\,\text{s}} = 4\,\text{m/s}$$

To calculate the speed for other parts of the graph, you need to use the slope or gradient of the graph. Example 1 shows you how to do this for part B of the graph.

1 **a** Make a copy of the graph but mark the changes for part C instead of part B.
 b Calculate the speed for part C of the graph. Show your working.

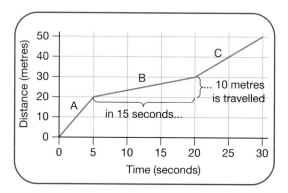

Example 1

In part B of the graph

$$\text{speed} = \frac{\text{distance}}{\text{time}} = \frac{10\,\text{m}}{15\,\text{s}} = 0.67\,\text{m/s}$$

Calculating acceleration from a velocity–time graph

$$\text{Acceleration} = \frac{\text{change in velocity}}{\text{time taken}}$$

So for part P of the graph on the right

$$\text{acceleration} = \frac{2\,\text{m/s}}{2\,\text{s}} = 1\,\text{m/s}^2$$

To calculate the acceleration for other parts of the graph, you need to use the slope or gradient of the graph. Example 2 shows you how to do this for part Q of the graph.

2 **a** Make a copy of the graph but mark the changes for part R instead of part Q.
 b Calculate the acceleration for part R of the graph. (Show your working.)

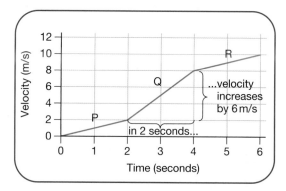

Example 2

$$\text{acceleration} = \frac{\text{change in velocity}}{\text{time}}$$

$$= \frac{6\,\text{m/s}}{2\,\text{s}} = 3\,\text{m/s}^2$$

Calculating distance travelled from a velocity–time graph

The **area** beneath a velocity–time graph tells you the
distance that an object has travelled.
The diagrams explain why.

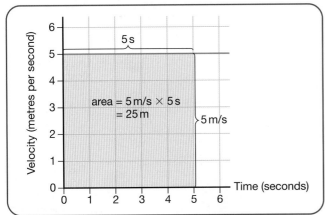

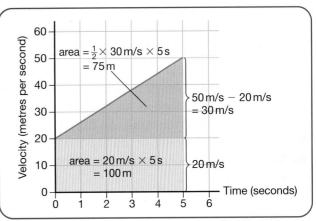

The speed of this object is constant and equal to 5 m/s.
Distance travelled in 5 s = speed × time
                           =   5 m/s × 5 s = 25 m
This is equal to the area shown under the velocity–time
graph when you work it out using the units given on the
axes of the graph.

The speed of this object is increasing steadily.
You can find the area under the graph by dividing it into a
rectangle and a triangle as shown.
Distance travelled   =   100 m + 75 m   =   175 m

Example 3 shows how you can work out from the
graph on the right the distance travelled in the first
5 seconds.

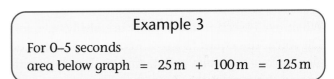

Example 3

For 0–5 seconds
area below graph = 25 m + 100 m = 125 m

3 Make a copy of the graph. Mark the area
under the graph for between 5 and 10 seconds.
Then calculate the distance travelled during
this period.
(Show your working.)

4 Find the total distance travelled by the object
between 0 and 15 seconds.

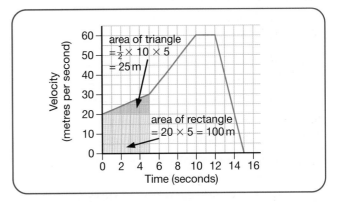

What you need to remember *Copy and complete using the **key words***

More about motion graphs
The _____ under a velocity–time graph represents the _____ travelled.

You need to be able to:

- calculate the speed of a body from the slope of a distance–time graph
- calculate the acceleration of a body from the slope of a velocity–time graph
- calculate the distance travelled by a body from a velocity–time graph.

1 Applying forces

Interactions

When you clap your hands, they apply forces to each other. Your right hand applies a force to your left and your left hand applies an equal and opposite force to your right.

When two objects apply forces to each other, we say that they **interact**. Some objects interact when they touch, your hands for example. Magnets and electrical charges interact at a distance without touching. All things interact at a distance through the force of gravity, but the force is very small unless one of the objects is very big, like the Earth or the Moon.

1 Name <u>two</u> ways in which electrical charges can interact.

2 How do the Earth and the Moon interact?

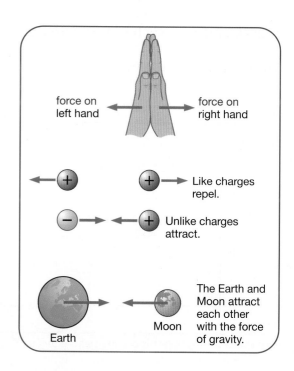

Equal and opposite

When two objects interact, there are always two forces. The forces are **equal** in size and **opposite** in direction. One force acts on one object. An equal and opposite force acts on the second object.

3 Look at the weight on the spring.
Then copy and complete the sentences.

The weight pulls _____ on the spring.
The spring pulls _____ on the weight.
The forces are _____ and

_____.

4 Copy the diagrams of the other three pairs of interacting objects. In each case, the arrow shows the force on one of the objects. The label describes the force. Add an arrow to show the force on the second object. Label the arrow.

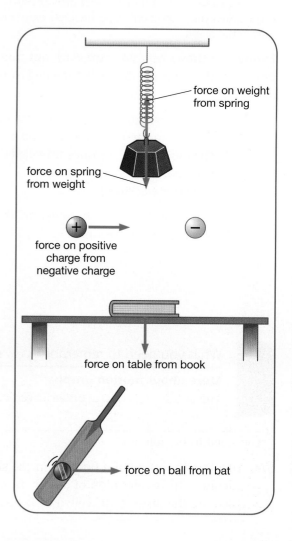

More than one force

The horse in the first diagram is pulling the tree trunk with a 1000 N force.

In the second diagram, two horses are pulling. Their forces are in the same direction so they add together. They have the **same effect** as if a **single force** equal to both the forces added together was acting.

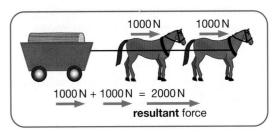

5 Copy and complete the sentence.

The single force that has the same effect as two or more forces acting on a body is called the _____ force.

Forces that balance

In this diagram, the horses pull with forces that are equal in size but in opposite directions.
The forces cancel each other out.

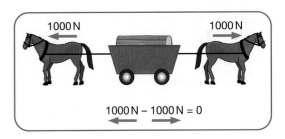

6 What is the resultant force when two equal but opposite forces act on a single object?

Finding the resultant

The first two examples here show how to find the resultant of two or more forces that are not equal. The forces all act along the same line.

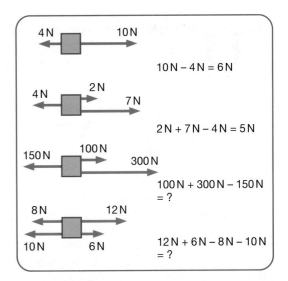

$10 N - 4 N = 6 N$

$2 N + 7 N - 4 N = 5 N$

$100 N + 300 N - 150 N = ?$

$12 N + 6 N - 8 N - 10 N = ?$

7 Find the resultant force for the other two examples. Draw a diagram for each to show its size and direction.

What you need to remember *Copy and complete using the **key words***

Applying forces
When two bodies _____, the forces they exert on each other are _____ and _____.
A number of forces acting on a body may be replaced by a _____ _____ which has the _____ _____ on the body as the original forces all acting together. The force is called the _____ force.

2 Staying still

Tug of war

You might think that things stay still only when <u>no</u> forces act on them. A tug of war shows that this isn't so. The rope is stationary. When both teams pull with equal forces in opposite directions, the forces balance each other. The **resultant** force on the rope is **zero** and so it remains **stationary**.

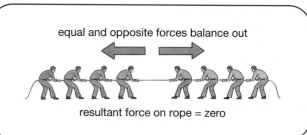
equal and opposite forces balance out

resultant force on rope = zero

1 Copy and complete the sentence.

If something remains stationary, the resultant force on it must be _____.

2 Look at the picture of a dumb-bell being held still.

    a What force is acting downwards on the dumb-bell?
    b What force is acting upwards on the dumb-bell?
    c Copy and complete the sentence.

    The dumb-bell stays still because the resultant of the force acting upwards and the force acting downwards is _____.

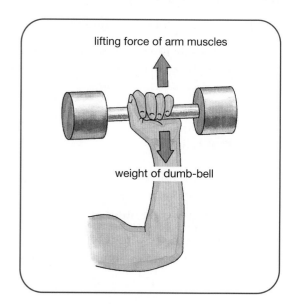
lifting force of arm muscles

weight of dumb-bell

Why you don't fall through the floor

Your weight pulls you down. The floor holds you up, so it must be pushing upwards on you.

When you stand still, the two forces on your body are equal in size but act in opposite directions.

So the forces balance and you stay where you are.

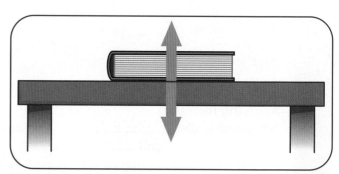
weight of person pulls him down

equal and opposite forces balance out

floor pushes up on person

People don't fall through floors.

3 Look at the picture of a book on a table. Explain, as fully as you can, why the book doesn't fall through the table.

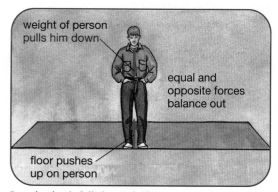
Books don't fall through tables.

How can a helicopter hover?

When people are lifted from a boat, the helicopter has to keep very still. This is difficult because the weight of the helicopter is always pulling it downwards.

4 **a** What force is acting upwards on the helicopter?
   b Explain how the helicopter can keep still.

5 What would happen to the helicopter if

   a the uplift was greater than the weight?
   b the weight was greater than the uplift?

   Give reasons for your answers.

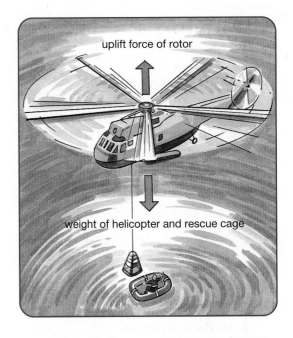

uplift force of rotor

weight of helicopter and rescue cage

Using forces to keep still

6 Look at the pictures of stationary objects.
   For each one

   a copy the picture
   b mark on the <u>two</u> forces that are acting on the underlined object
   c label the forces that you have marked on the picture
   d explain why the object keeps still.

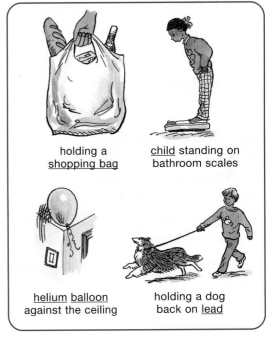

holding a <u>shopping bag</u>

<u>child</u> standing on bathroom scales

helium <u>balloon</u> against the ceiling

holding a dog back on <u>lead</u>

What you need to remember *Copy and complete using the **key words***

Staying still
If the _____ force acting on a stationary body is _____, the body will remain _____ .

3 Moving at constant speed

Why do things slow down?

If you stop pedalling your bicycle, air resistance and other **friction** forces slow you down. Friction forces always act in the **opposite** direction to movement. A similar thing happens if you stop paddling a canoe – the main friction force on a canoe is water resistance.

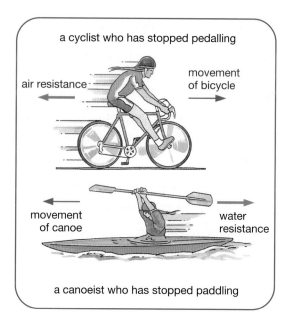

a cyclist who has stopped pedalling

air resistance

movement of bicycle

movement of canoe

water resistance

a canoeist who has stopped paddling

1 Copy and complete the sentences.

When a bicycle moves through the _____, a force of friction acts in the opposite _____.
This force _____ the bicycle down.
When a canoe moves through the water, a force of friction acts in the _____ direction.
This _____ the canoe down.

Keeping going

When there is friction, you need another force to keep going at constant speed.

When a sailboard is moving, water resistance acts against it. To move at a steady speed, the force of the wind on the sail must balance the friction force.

2 What is the resultant force on the sailboard when it is travelling at constant speed?

Look at the passenger jet flying at constant speed through the air.

3 What force balances the air resistance on the moving jet?

4 What is the resultant force on the jet?

These examples show that if the **resultant force** acting on a moving body is **zero**, the body continues to move at the **same speed** and in the **same direction**.

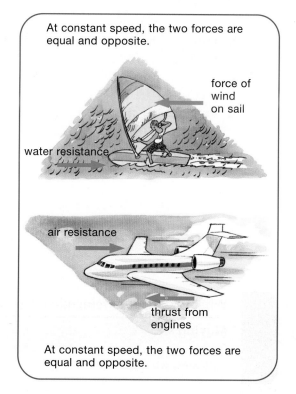

At constant speed, the two forces are equal and opposite.

force of wind on sail

water resistance

air resistance

thrust from engines

At constant speed, the two forces are equal and opposite.

Life without friction

Without friction, a cyclist could freewheel forever in a straight line. She would not need to pedal to keep going at a constant speed.

You can get some idea of what life would be like without friction at an ice rink.

5 Copy and complete the sentences.

An ice rink is almost _____ free. If there was no friction at all, a curling stone would carry on moving at _____ speed in a _____ line. It would _____ stop.

Motion in space

Space is an almost perfect vacuum. There is no air to cause friction. In deep space, where the gravity of stars and planets is negligible, a spacecraft will travel in a straight line at constant speed.

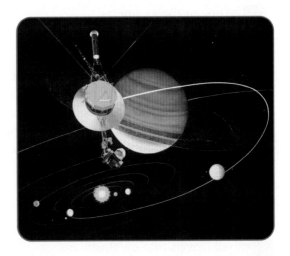

In the sport of curling, competitors slide granite stones along the ice. The friction force is very small. The curling stone travels in a straight line at almost constant speed.

6 When was the space probe Voyager 1 launched?

7 How fast is Voyager travelling away from the Sun?

8 Voyager has no engine, so why does it keep moving?

9 Explain why Voyager is now moving in an almost straight line.

The Voyager 1 space probe was launched by a rocket in 1977 to fly past Jupiter and Saturn. It passed by Saturn in 1980.
There is no friction in space to slow Voyager down, so it will keep moving forever without an engine. In 2005, Voyager left the solar system. It was 14.2 billion kilometres from the Sun (more than twice as far as Pluto) and travelling at 61 500 kilometres per hour.

What you need to remember *Copy and complete using the key words*

Moving at constant speed
Air resistance and water resistance are _____ forces. They always act in the _____ direction to movement.
If the _____ _____ acting on a moving body is _____, the body will continue to move at the _____ _____ and in the _____ _____.

4 Accelerating

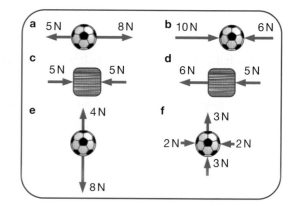

Accelerating from rest

You need a **force** to **speed up** a bobsleigh. The bigger the force, the faster the bobsleigh speeds up. A bigger force makes the bobsleigh **accelerate** faster.

Look at the picture of the bobsleigh.

The bobsleigh starts from rest.

1 How does the team apply a force to the sleigh to make it accelerate?

2 In which direction does the team push?

3 In which direction does the sleigh accelerate?

In which direction is the acceleration?

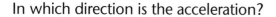

If the **resultant** force on a stationary object is not zero, the object will accelerate in the same direction as the resultant force.

4 Look at the examples.
In each case

- draw the body
- find the resultant force and mark its size and direction with an arrow on your drawing
- decide whether the body will remain stationary or accelerate (start to move and speed up)
- draw and label an arrow to show the direction of any acceleration.

Slowing down

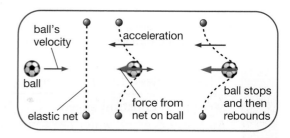

A football travels into an elastic net.
As the net stretches, the ball will **slow down**, stop, and then speed up in the opposite direction to which it started.

5 In which direction does the force from the net act on the ball?

6 In which direction does the ball accelerate?

Deceleration

When something slows down, we say that it decelerates. We can think of deceleration as acceleration in the opposite direction to the movement. If this acceleration continues, the object will come to rest, and then reverse its direction of motion.

Changing direction

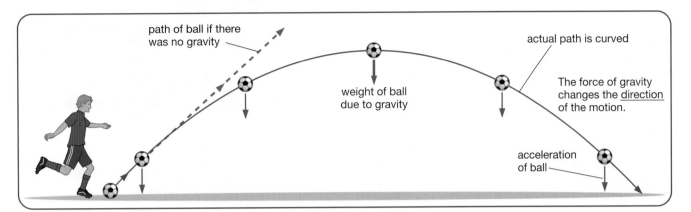

path of ball if there was no gravity

actual path is curved

weight of ball due to gravity

The force of gravity changes the <u>direction</u> of the motion.

acceleration of ball

A force can make a **moving** body **change direction**.
A ball follows a curved path through the air.

7 What force pulls the ball towards the ground?

8 In which direction does this force make the ball accelerate?

9 Describe <u>one</u> way in which the acceleration affects the ball's movement.

> **REMEMBER**
>
> Velocity involves speed <u>and</u> direction. Acceleration is the change in velocity in a given time – so an acceleration can be a speed change, a direction change or both.

Force and acceleration are in the same direction

A family is playing blow football. They blow through straws to move the ball. The ball accelerates in the **direction** of the force.

10 Explain how the movement of the ball changes in each situation shown. Will the ball speed up, slow down or change direction?

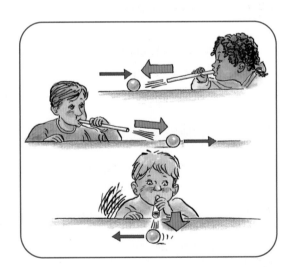

What you need to remember *Copy and complete using the **key words***

Accelerating

If the _____ force acting on a stationary body is not zero, the body will _____ in the direction of the resultant force.

If the resultant _____ acting on a _____ body is not zero, the body will accelerate in the _____ of the resultant force. This may cause the body to

_____ _____, _____ _____ or

_____ _____.

5 Force, mass and acceleration

Applying a force

Students investigate the relationship between force, mass and acceleration in the laboratory.

1 How do the students apply a constant force to accelerate the trucks?

2 When they apply the same force to different masses, which accelerates faster – the larger mass or the smaller mass?

3 If they keep the mass constant but increase the force, how does the acceleration change?

4 Give <u>one</u> reason why it's difficult to do the experiment accurately.

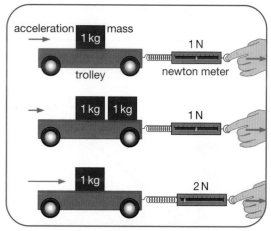

The students <u>compare</u> how fast the trucks accelerate. Accurate <u>measurements</u> are difficult with the trucks because of friction.

Experiments in space

A spaceship is a better place to measure the accelerations produced by different forces.

5 Why is a spaceship a good place to do experiments on force and acceleration?

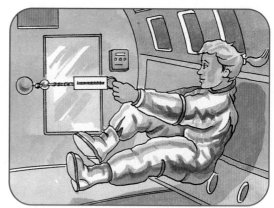

In space, friction and gravity don't mess up our experiments with forces.

How force affects acceleration

The diagrams show some experiments in a spaceship. The same 1 kg mass is accelerated using different forces.

6 a How much acceleration does a 1 N force give to the 1 kg mass?
   b How much acceleration does a 2 N force give?

7 Copy and complete the sentence.

When the force on an object is doubled, its acceleration is _____ .

Changing the force

speed increases by 1 m/s every second
acceleration is 1 m/s^2 (metre per second squared)

1 N force

speed increases by 2 m/s every second
acceleration is 2 m/s^2

2 N force

speed increases by 3 m/s every second
acceleration is 3 m/s^2

3 N force

How mass affects acceleration

A 1 N force is then used to accelerate different masses.

8 **a** How much acceleration do you get when the mass is twice as big?

b How much acceleration do you get when the mass is three times as big?

c Copy and complete the sentence.

If the force stays the same, an object with twice as much mass is given half as much

_____ .

A **force** of 1 N acting on a **mass** of 1 kg produces an **acceleration** of 1 m/s^2.

9 **a** Copy and complete the table using the results of all <u>six</u> experiments shown in the diagrams.

Force (N)	Mass (kg)	Acceleration (m/s^2)	Mass × acceleration
1	1	1	1

b What do you notice about the first and last columns in the table?

The force is always the same as the mass times the acceleration.

  force   =   mass   ×   acceleration
(**newtons**, N)   (kilograms, kg)   (**metres/second**^{2}, m/s^2)

10 Look at the examples in the picture.
Use the formula to work out the missing items.
The first one is done for you.

Changing the mass

speed increases by 1 m/s every second
acceleration is 1 m/s^2

speed increases by $\frac{1}{2}$ m/s every second
acceleration is $\frac{1}{2}$ m/s^2

speed increases by $\frac{1}{3}$ m/s every second
acceleration is $\frac{1}{3}$ m/s^2

Force (F)   = Mass (m) × Acceleration (a)
Acceleration = Force ÷ Mass
Mass   = Force ÷ Acceleration

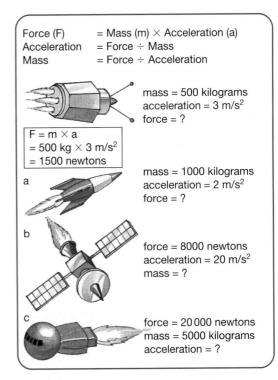

mass = 500 kilograms
acceleration = 3 m/s^2
force = ?

F = m × a
= 500 kg × 3 m/s^2
= 1500 newtons

a

mass = 1000 kilograms
acceleration = 2 m/s^2
force = ?

b

force = 8000 newtons
acceleration = 20 m/s^2
mass = ?

c

force = 20 000 newtons
mass = 5000 kilograms
acceleration = ?

What you need to remember *Copy and complete using the **key words***

Force, mass and acceleration
Force, mass and acceleration are related by the formula

_____ = _____ × _____

(_____, N)   (kilograms, kg)   (_____/_____, m/s^2)

6 Stop that car!

Braking force

When a car driver brakes, the braking **force** between the brakes and the wheels slows the wheels down.

> **1** Explain why you must brake harder to stop in the same distance when you are travelling at higher **speed**.

Tyres must grip

Friction between the tyres and the road makes the tyres grip the road. When you brake, the wheels slow down. The friction with the road must then increase to slow the whole car. The friction force depends on the tyre design and the road surface.

> **2** Why does the car skid if you brake too hard?
>
> **3** Why must the driver brake carefully when the road is wet?
>
> **4** Why must the driver brake very carefully when there is ice on the roads?
>
> **5** Why is it safer to have a rough road surface before a pedestrian crossing?

Why do tyres have tread?

You need good tyres to stop quickly. Tyres can grip the road only if they are touching it. They lose their grip when the road is wet. The tread on a tyre is designed to push away the water. In dry conditions, the tread doesn't help. In dry weather, racing cars use tyres with no tread.

> **6** Why do racing drivers stop to change their tyres when it starts raining?
>
> **7** Why do **worn** tyres increase the chance of a skid?

REMEMBER

Force = mass × acceleration.
You need a bigger force to produce a bigger acceleration or deceleration.

The faster car must decelerate more quickly to stop in the same **distance**. This needs a larger braking force.

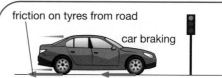

friction on tyres from road

car braking

Friction slows the whole car as the wheels slow.

skid

If you brake too hard, the wheels lock (stop turning) and the car skids. The friction from the road cannot slow the car as fast as the brakes slow the wheels.

There is less friction on a **wet**, oily or **icy** road, so a skid is more likely when you brake or try to turn.

You can't stop instantly

If someone steps out in front of a car, it takes time for the driver to react. This is called the reaction time. The distance the car travels during the reaction time is called the **thinking** distance.

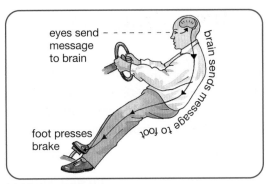

eyes send message to brain

brain sends message to foot

foot presses brake

Making a quick stop.

8 Look at the diagram. Why does it take time to react?

9 Look at the table.

  a What is the thinking distance when travelling at 30 miles per hour?

  b What happens to the thinking distance if the speed is doubled?

When the driver presses the brake pedal, it takes time for the brakes to slow the car down. During this time, the car travels a distance called the **braking** distance.

10 Look at the table.

  a What is the braking distance for a speed of 30 miles per hour?

  b What happens to the braking distance if the speed is increased?

  c Copy and complete the formula.

$$\frac{\text{stopping}}{\text{distance}} = \frac{\text{thinking}}{\text{distance}} + \frac{\underline{\quad\quad}}{\text{distance}}$$

Speed in miles per hour	Thinking distance in metres	Braking distance in metres	Stopping distance in metres
20	6	6	12
30	9	14	23
40	12	24	36
50	15	38	53
60	18	55	73
70	21	75	96

Stopping distances on dry roads.

After drinking **alcohol**, people may feel perfectly normal but their reactions are actually much slower.

11 Why is it a bad idea for people to drive after drinking alcohol?

12 What other factors could affect the reaction time?

Tiredness can kill
Take a break

DRUG DRIVING.
NOT A SAFE TRIP.

What you need to remember *Copy and complete using the **key words***

Stop that car!
The higher your _____, the greater the braking _____ needed to stop in a given _____.
Stopping distance = _____ distance + _____ distance
A driver's reaction time can be affected by tiredness, drugs and _____.
A skid is more likely when the roads are _____ or _____, or the tyres are _____.

7 It's a drag!

When an object moves through a **fluid** such as air or water, there is a force of friction acting on it in the opposite direction. Air resistance and water resistance oppose motion. They are **drag** forces.

1 Copy and complete the sentence.

To keep a car moving at a constant velocity, the driving force from the engine must exactly _____ the frictional forces.

2 You need a bigger driving force to keep a car going at 70 miles per hour than at 50 miles per hour. Explain why.

3 How does a car's shape affect the drag force?

4 The table below gives the fuel consumption for a car at different speeds. Explain why the car travels fewer miles per gallon at higher speeds.

Speed (mph)	Fuel consumption (miles per gallon)
30	56
50	54
70	47
90	35

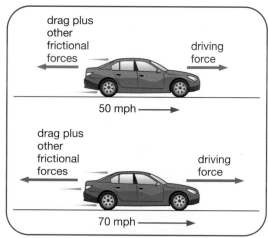

At constant velocity, the frictional forces (including the drag) **balance** the **driving force**. Air resistance (drag) increases with speed, so a bigger driving force is needed at a higher speed.

Car designers try to produce streamlined shapes that make the air flow smoothly around the car. This reduces the drag force.

Making the most of air resistance

Drag can be very useful if you actually want to slow down. The space shuttles use this idea. As the shuttle lands, a parachute opens to help the braking. The parachute provides a bigger surface to increase the air resistance.

5 Why do you think the shuttle needs a large parachute?

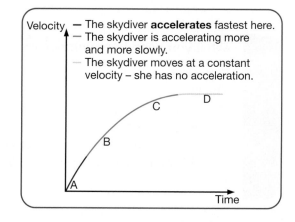

movement of shuttle

air resistance slows shuttle down

Terminal velocity

A skydiver jumps out of an aeroplane.
The graph shows what happens to her velocity as she falls.

Copy and complete the sentences.

As the skydiver falls, she _____.
This happens quickly at first and then more and more _____.
Eventually she stops accelerating and falls at a _____ velocity.

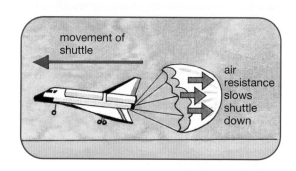

Velocity
— The skydiver **accelerates** fastest here.
— The skydiver is accelerating more and more slowly.
— The skydiver moves at a constant velocity – she has no acceleration.

Time

Why does the skydiver stop accelerating?

The skydiver accelerates when there is an unbalanced force acting on her.

The diagram shows the forces acting on the skydiver at points A, B, C and D on the graph.

7 Which force causes the skydiver to accelerate?

8 What happens to the air resistance as she speeds up?

9 What is the **resultant** force at terminal velocity (D)?

Making a safe landing

Well before she reaches the ground, the skydiver opens her parachute.

10 Explain why opening her parachute gives her a much smaller terminal velocity.

Large area gives more air resistance. This balances gravity at a much lower speed.

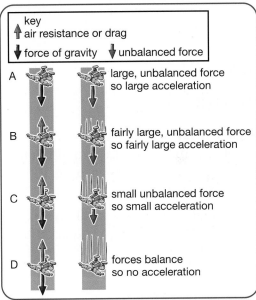

key
↑ air resistance or drag
↓ force of gravity ↓ unbalanced force

A large, unbalanced force so large acceleration

B fairly large, unbalanced force so fairly large acceleration

C small unbalanced force so small acceleration

D forces balance so no acceleration

When the skydiver stops accelerating, we say that she has reached her **terminal velocity**.

What you need to remember *Copy and complete using the **key words***

It's a drag!
When a car travels at a steady speed, the frictional forces _____ the

_____ _____ .

The faster a body moves through a _____ , the greater the _____

force which acts on it.

A body falling through a fluid initially _____ owing to the force of gravity.

Eventually the _____ force on the body will be zero and it will fall at its

_____ _____ .

You need to be able to draw and interpret velocity–time graphs for bodies that reach terminal velocity, including a consideration of the forces acting on the body.

8 Mass and weight

Now that Malcolm is older and less active, he has started to put on weight. Malcolm wants to lose weight. He would weigh less on Mars, but his body would still be exactly the same. There is just as much of him. He still has exactly the same mass.

ON EARTH
bathroom scales
read 90

ON MARS
bathroom scales
read 36

What is mass?

Mass tells you how much there is of something. A 10 kg bag of potatoes contains twice as much potato as a 5 kg bag, so it has twice the mass. We measure the mass of things in **kilograms** (kg).

> **1** Malcolm says his weight is 90 kg. This is wrong. Which of Malcolm's characteristics really measures 90 kg?

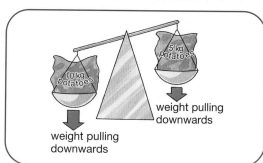

More mass means more weight.

What is weight?

When you drop something, gravity makes it fall. We call the force of gravity on the object its weight. Objects with more mass have more weight. That is because there is more mass for gravity to act on. We measure forces in **newtons**.

> **2** **a** What causes an object to have weight?
> **b** In which direction does weight act?

> **3** Copy and complete the sentence.
>
> Weight is a _____ so we should measure it in _____ .

What's the difference?

Mass and weight are different. You have the same mass wherever you are because you have the same amount of body. But your weight depends on the strength of gravity where you are.

> **4** Look at the picture of the astronaut.
> Why do astronauts weigh less on the Moon?
> Explain your answer.

An astronaut who weighs 900 N on Earth weighs only about 150 N on the Moon. This is because the Moon's gravity is about one-sixth the strength of Earth's gravity.

Working out weight

Weight depends on how much mass an object has.
It also depends on the strength of gravity.
The diagrams show the weights of two objects on Earth.

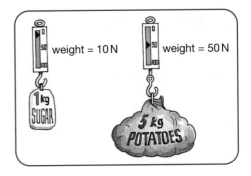

5 Copy and complete the sentence.

On Earth, each 1 kilogram of mass has a weight of
about _____ newtons.

We say that the strength of the Earth's gravity is
10 newtons per kilogram (10 N/kg). We call this the Earth's
gravitational field strength. We can work out the weight
of an object as follows:

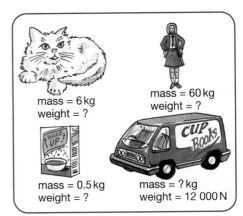

weight	=	mass	×	gravitational field strength
(newtons, N)		(kilograms, kg)		(newtons/kilogram, N/kg)

6 Look at the examples in the pictures and work out
the missing numbers.

Malcolm goes planet hopping

Malcolm has a mass of 90 kg. On Earth, the gravitational
field strength is 10 N/kg. Therefore, his weight is
90 × 10 = 900 N.

7 Copy and complete the table to show
how Malcolm's weight would change
in different parts of the solar system.

	Malcolm's mass (kg)	Gravitational field strength (N/kg)	Malcolm's weight (N)
Earth	90	10	900
Moon	90	1.6	
Mars		4	
Jupiter		23	

What you need to remember *Copy and complete using the **key words***

Mass and weight
An object always has the same mass. We measure this in _____.
The weight of an object is the force of gravity that acts on it. We measure this in

_____.

On Earth, the force of gravity is about _____ N/kg. We call this the Earth's

_____ _____ _____.

You need to be able to calculate the weight of a body using the formula

weight	=	mass	×	gravitational field strength
(newtons, N)		(kilograms, kg)		(newtons/kilogram, N/kg)

1 Doing work

Trolleys won't push themselves

You move a shopping trolley by applying a force to it.
When you push the trolley, you transfer **energy** to it.
We say that you are doing **work**. Work, like energy, is
measured in joules.

1 Copy and complete the sentences.

To make an object move, you must transfer
_____ to it. You can do this by moving
the object with a _____. The energy you
transfer like this is called _____ .

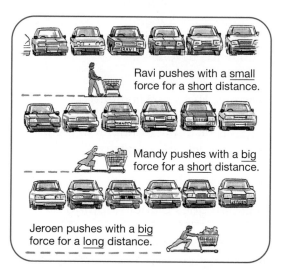

Ravi pushes with a <u>small</u>
force for a <u>short</u> distance.

Mandy pushes with a <u>big</u>
force for a <u>short</u> distance.

Jeroen pushes with a <u>big</u>
force for a <u>long</u> distance.

Who does the most work?

The diagram shows three shoppers pushing trolleys to their
cars.

2 **a** Who does more work, Ravi or Mandy?
Explain why.
b Who does more work, Mandy or Jeroen?
Explain why.

The amount of work done depends on how much force is
used and what distance is moved. In fact, we can calculate
it like this:

work done = **force** × distance moved
(joules, J) (newtons, N) **(metres, m)**

3 Look at the pictures and work out the missing
numbers. The first one is done for you.

Work done = force × distance
Distance = work done ÷ force
Force = work done ÷ distance

model train

force = 5 N
distance moved = 3 m
work done = force × distance
= 5 × 3
= 15 J

crane

force = 7000 N
distance moved = 6 m
work done = ?

barrow

force = 300 N
distance moved = ?
work done = 12 000 J

weight-lifter

force = ?
distance moved = 2 m
work done = 1400 J

Friction is a waste of work

When you first push a shopping trolley, it starts to move. But you then have to keep on pushing to keep it moving at the same speed. You are then doing work against the force of friction. All the work you do ends up as heat (thermal energy).

4 Copy and complete the sentences.

When you start a trolley moving, work done is transferred as _____ energy.
When you keep a trolley moving, work done is transferred as _____ energy.

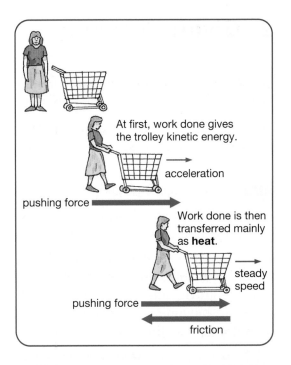

At first, work done gives the trolley kinetic energy.

acceleration

pushing force

Work done is then transferred mainly as **heat**.

steady speed

pushing force

friction

Working your way up the stairs

When you walk up stairs, you are doing work. You are lifting your own weight so you are working against gravity. The distance you move your weight is the height of the stairs.

6 How much work must the person in the diagram do against gravity to climb the stairs?

7 To what form of energy is this work transferred?

3 m

8 m

To climb the stairs, the girl must lift a force of 600 N up a distance of 3 m.

She must do work to increase her gravitational potential energy.

weight = 600 N

Climbing stairs.

What you need to remember *Copy and complete using the* **key words**

Doing work
When a force moves an object, _____ is transferred and _____ is done.
You can calculate the amount of work done like this:

work done   =   _____   ×   distance moved
(_____, __)   (newtons, N)   (_____, __)

Work done against friction is mainly transferred as _____.

233

2 Giving it energy

The athletes shown are doing work to make things move. The work they do transfers energy, but in different ways.

The bodybuilder is stretching springs. The work he does transfers energy to the springs. The energy is stored as **elastic** potential energy.

> **1** Copy and complete the sentence.
>
> Elastic potential energy is energy stored in an object when work is done to change its _____.

The work done to change the **shape** of a spring is stored as elastic potential energy.

The weight-lifter applies a force to lift the weight against gravity, so he is doing work. The energy he transfers is stored as gravitational potential energy. A weight lifted above the ground has more gravitational potential energy than a weight on the ground.

> **2** **a** How much work does the weight-lifter do?
> **b** How much potential energy does the lifted weight gain?

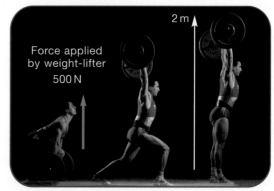

Force applied by weight-lifter 500 N

2 m

The work done to lift a weight increases its gravitational potential energy.

The shot-putter pushes the shot to make its speed as high as possible. By doing work, she transfers energy to the shot. The moving shot has kinetic energy (movement energy). Objects with a lot of **kinetic energy** are more difficult to stop.

> **3** Which shot would be more difficult to stop if you tried to catch it:
>
> **a** A or B?
> **b** C or D?

The shot-putter straightens her arm to put the shot. The work done increases the shot's kinetic energy. If the push is upwards, the shot also gains gravitational potential energy.

> **4** Copy and complete the sentences.
>
> An object has more kinetic energy when it has _____ **mass**.
> An object has more kinetic energy when it has _____ **speed**.
>
> **5** What other form of energy does the shot-putter give the shot?

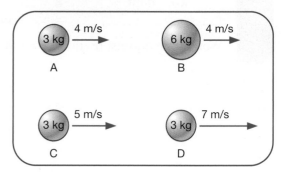

A: 3 kg, 4 m/s
B: 6 kg, 4 m/s
C: 3 kg, 5 m/s
D: 3 kg, 7 m/s

A closer look at kinetic energy

You can work out the kinetic energy of a moving object using this formula:

kinetic energy = $\frac{1}{2}$ × mass × speed^2
(joules, J)   (kilograms, kg)   (m/s)^2

The figure shows how to work out the kinetic energy of a ball that is thrown up into the air.

> **6** A car of mass 750 kg is moving at a speed of 20 metres per second. Calculate its kinetic energy. (Start by writing out the formula. Show your working.)

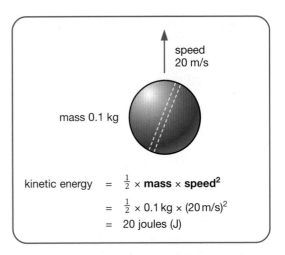

speed 20 m/s

mass 0.1 kg

kinetic energy $\quad = \frac{1}{2}$ × **mass** × **speed**^{2}

$\qquad\qquad\qquad = \frac{1}{2}$ × 0.1 kg × (20 m/s)^2

$\qquad\qquad\qquad =$ 20 joules (J)

Why fast-moving things can do a lot of damage

In most collisions, the kinetic energy of the objects that collide is transferred to the materials from which they are made. This can bend or break the objects. It also usually makes them warmer.

The more kinetic energy a moving object has, the more damage it can do in a collision. It can do this damage to itself, to whatever it collides with or to both. The diagram explains an important consequence of the higher energy of a car with more speed.

> **7** How many more times kinetic energy does a car travelling at 40 mph have than a car travelling at 20 mph?
>
> **8** Suggest why most pedestrians hit by a car travelling at 20 mph survive, but 9 out of 10 hit at 40 mph are killed.
>
> **9** Road safety campaigners want the speed limit in residential areas reduced to 20 mph. Why?

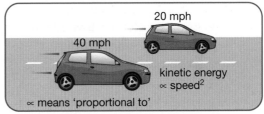

20 mph

40 mph

kinetic energy ∝ speed^2

∝ means 'proportional to'

The overtaking car has twice the speed. So it has 2^2 times = 4 times as much kinetic energy (for the same mass).

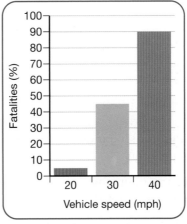

Fatalities (%) — Vehicle speed (mph)

The chance of being killed when hit by a motor vehicle.

What you need to remember *Copy and complete using the **key words***

Giving it energy

_____ potential energy is the energy stored in an object when work is done on the object to change its _____.

The _____ _____ of a body depends on its _____ and its _____.

You can calculate the kinetic energy of a body with the formula

kinetic energy = $\frac{1}{2}$ × _____ × _____
(joules, J)   (kilograms, kg)   (m/s)^2

3 Energy thrills

Springboard dive

Brian is a diver. He stands on a springboard, then bounces to start his dive.

1 Copy and complete the sentences.

When the springboard is bent, it has

_____ _____ energy.

As the board straightens, it transfers its energy to Brian, pushing him into the air. At the highest point of his dive, Brian has maximum _____

_____ energy.

As Brian accelerates towards the water, his gravitational energy transforms to

_____ energy.

His kinetic energy is a _____ just before he enters the water.

Water resistance slows Brian down. Brian's kinetic energy is transferred to the water, stirring it up, making it splash and creating waves. In the end, all the energy is transformed to _____

_____ .

Brian uses energy from his muscles to begin the dive.

The bent springboard has elastic potential energy.

At the highest point of the dive, Brian has maximum gravitational potential energy.

As he enters the water, Brian has maximum kinetic energy. This energy is transferred to the water, ending up as thermal energy.

Bungee jump

Andy runs a bungee jump from a river bridge in New Zealand. The bridge is 43 metres above the water. He explains that making a good jump is all about understanding energy.

2 What form of energy does the bungee jumper have just before jumping?

3 To what form is this energy transformed as the jumper falls?

4 Describe the energy transformation that takes place as the bungee rope stretches.

5 Why must the bungee length be adjusted for every jumper?

'Gravitational potential energy and kinetic energy depend on mass. The more mass you have, the further the bungee will stretch, so we need to get the rope length right for each jumper. If we have done the calculation correctly, you will stop just above the water surface!'

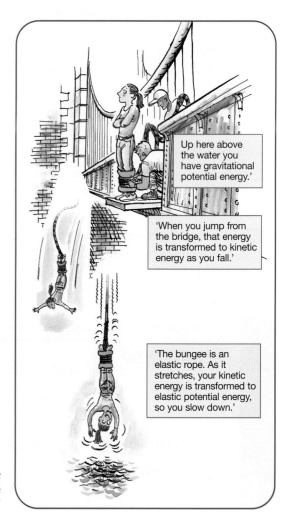

'Up here above the water you have gravitational potential energy.'

'When you jump from the bridge, that energy is transformed to kinetic energy as you fall.'

'The bungee is an elastic rope. As it stretches, your kinetic energy is transformed to elastic potential energy, so you slow down.'

Pole vault

Irena is a pole-vaulter. She is attempting a new world record of 5 metres – as high as a house! To vault this high she must also be a world-class sprinter. The illustration explains why.

The pole straightens, lifting Irena over the bar. The pole's elastic potential energy is transformed to gravitational potential energy.

As Irena falls, her gravitational energy is transformed to kinetic energy.

As she reaches the jump, she places her pole. Her speed makes it bend. Her kinetic energy is transformed to elastic potential energy.

Irena increases her kinetic energy by sprinting as fast as she can. She needs to sprint at 10 m/s to have enough energy to clear a record height.

Irena comes to rest when she lands on soft air-filled cushions. All her kinetic energy finally ends up as thermal energy (heat).

6   Why must Irena be able to sprint at 10 m/s?

7   To what form of energy is her kinetic energy transformed as she bends the pole?

8   What form of energy does Irena have as she clears the bar?

9   What energy transformation takes place as she falls back towards the ground?

10 What finally happens to this energy after she lands on the cushions?

What you need to remember

Energy thrills
There is nothing new for you to <u>remember</u> in this section.

You need to be able to discuss the transformation of kinetic energy to other forms of energy in particular situations.

1 Momentum

How hard it is to stop a moving object depends on the mass of the object and on how fast it is moving.

1 Look at the diagrams. Which is it harder to stop:

a a 30 tonne lorry or a 1 tonne car that are moving at the same speed?

b a car that is moving at 10 metres per second or the same car when it is moving at 20 metres per second?

Give reasons for your answers.

The greater the mass of an object, and the faster it is moving, the harder it is to stop the object.

We say that the object has more momentum.

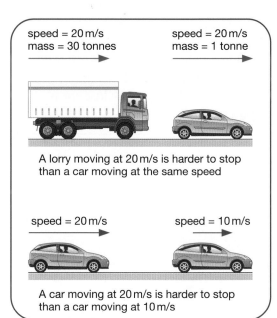

speed = 20 m/s
mass = 30 tonnes

speed = 20 m/s
mass = 1 tonne

A lorry moving at 20 m/s is harder to stop than a car moving at the same speed

speed = 20 m/s

speed = 10 m/s

A car moving at 20 m/s is harder to stop than a car moving at 10 m/s

Calculating momentum

You can calculate the momentum of a moving object like this:

momentum	=	mass	×	velocity
(kilogram metre / second, kg m/s)		(kilogram, kg)		(metre / second, m/s)

Example

A 25 kg supermarket trolley is moving at 2 m/s. Calculate its momentum.

momentum = mass × velocity
= 25 kg × 2 m/s
= 50 kg m/s

Momentum has magnitude and direction

The velocity of an object is its speed in a particular direction.

momentum = **mass** × **velocity**

This means that momentum not only has a size, or **magnitude**, but it also has a **direction**.

2 What is meant by the velocity of an object?

3 What is the formula for calculating momentum?

4 How much momentum does this car have?

5 How many times more momentum has a 30 tonne lorry than a 1 tonne car travelling at the same speed?

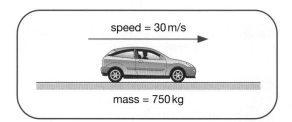

speed = 30 m/s

mass = 750 kg

Changing momentum

You can change the **momentum** of a moving object.
The diagram shows how you can do this.

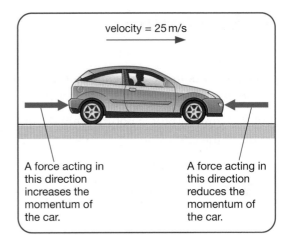

velocity = 25 m/s

A force acting in this direction increases the momentum of the car.

A force acting in this direction reduces the momentum of the car.

6 Copy and complete the sentences.

To change the momentum of a moving object, you must exert a _____ on it. To increase the momentum of the moving object, the force must act in the same _____ as the object is moving.
To reduce the momentum of an object moving in a particular direction, you must exert a force on the object in the _____ direction.

You can also give a stationary object some momentum by exerting a force on it that makes it move.

Calculating changes in momentum

To produce a bigger change in momentum, you can

■ use a bigger **force**
■ apply the force for a longer **time**.

You can calculate the change in momentum produced by applying a force, like this:

change in momentum = force × time
(kilogram metre / second,   (newton, N)   (second, s)
    kg m/s)

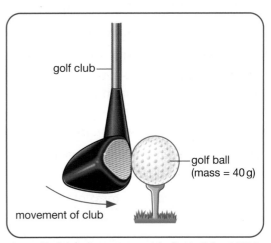

golf club

golf ball (mass = 40 g)

movement of club

The golf club is in contact with the ball for 1/100 of a second. During this time, it exerts an average force of 200 N.

7 a Calculate the momentum given to the golf ball shown in the diagram.
(Begin by stating the above formula.)
b Use your answer to **a** to calculate the speed of the ball just after it has been hit.

What you need to remember *Copy and complete using the **key words***

Momentum
You can calculate the momentum of an object with the formula:

momentum = _____ × _____
(kilogram metre / second, kg m/s)   (kilograms, kg)   (metres/second, m/s)

Momentum has both _____ and _____.
A force acting on a body that is moving, or able to move, changes its _____.
You can calculate the change of momentum with the formula

change in momentum = _____ × _____
(kilogram metre / second, kg m/s)   (newton, N)   (second, s)

2 Explosions

When a cannon fires, an explosion sends a cannon ball flying very quickly out of the barrel.

But the cannon ball is not the only thing that moves as a result of the explosion.

Look at the diagram

1 Describe the <u>two</u> movements that occur when a cannon is fired.

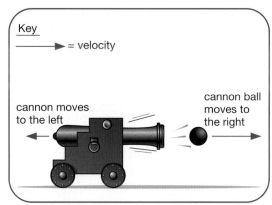

When the cannon is fired, the cannon ball moves in one direction and the cannon moves in the opposite direction. We say that the cannon <u>recoils</u>.

Momentum in explosions

When the cannon fires, no **external** (outside) forces act on the cannon and the cannon ball. This means that their total momentum does not change.

We say that momentum is **conserved**.

Before the explosion, the cannon and ball are stationary, so the total momentum is zero. After the explosion, the momentum of the cannon ball moving to the right is balanced by the momentum of the cannon moving in the opposite direction. The total momentum is still zero.

The total momentum can be zero after the explosion because momentum has <u>direction</u> as well as size (magnitude).

2 Look at the diagrams of the cannon before and after it is fired.

   a What is the total momentum of the cannon and the cannon ball inside it before firing?

   b What is the total momentum of the cannon and the cannon ball after firing?

   c What happens to the total momentum of the object(s) involved during any explosion?

   d How does the <u>magnitude</u> of the cannon's momentum compare with that of the cannon ball after firing?

   e How does the <u>direction</u> of the cannon's momentum compare with that of the cannon ball after firing?

> ### REMEMBER
> - To change the momentum of an object, you must exert a <u>force</u> on it.
> - Momentum has <u>magnitude</u> (size) and direction.

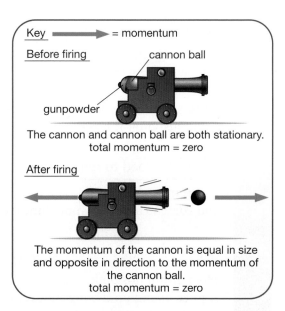

Key ——▶ = momentum

Before firing   cannon ball

gunpowder

The cannon and cannon ball are both stationary.
total momentum = zero

After firing

The momentum of the cannon is equal in size and opposite in direction to the momentum of the cannon ball.
total momentum = zero

> In any explosion, total momentum is conserved provided no external forces act on the exploding object(s).

Calculating what happens in an explosion

The first part of the diagram shows

- the mass of a cannon
- the mass of a cannon ball
- the velocity of the cannon ball after firing.

You can use this information to calculate the velocity of recoil of the cannon.

Before firing, the total momentum of the cannon and the cannon ball is zero. So the total momentum after firing is also zero.

So

momentum of cannon = momentum of cannon ball

$$\begin{array}{c}\text{mass of}\\\text{cannon}\end{array} \times \begin{array}{c}\text{velocity of}\\\text{cannon}\end{array} = \begin{array}{c}\text{mass}\\\text{of ball}\end{array} \times \begin{array}{c}\text{velocity}\\\text{of ball}\end{array}$$

$$\text{velocity of cannon} = \frac{\text{mass of ball} \times \text{velocity of ball}}{\text{mass of cannon}}$$

$$= \frac{5\,\text{kg} \times 150\,\text{m/s}}{500\,\text{kg}}$$

$$= 1.5\,\text{m/s}$$

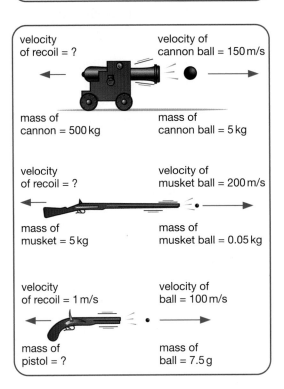

3 Use the information on the diagrams to calculate

  a the velocity of recoil of the musket
  b the mass of the pistol.

What you need to remember *Copy and complete using the* **key words**

Explosions
Momentum is _____ in any explosion provided no _____ forces act on the exploding bodies.

You need to be able to use the conservation of momentum to calculate the mass, velocity or momentum of a body involved in an explosion.

3 Collisions

When two objects collide, each exerts a force on the other.

1 Copy and complete the sentences.

When two objects collide, the forces they exert on each other are _____ in size and _____ in direction.
These forces change the _____ of the two objects by equal but _____ amounts.
This means that the overall change in momentum for the collision is _____.
So in any collision, total momentum is _____ provided no _____ forces act on the colliding objects.

Collision calculations

The figure shows a collision between two balls. We can use momentum to calculate the velocity of the second ball after the collision.

Initial momentum (kg m/s)

ball 1 →	ball 2 ←	total →
2 kg × 5 m/s = 10 kg m/s	2 kg × 2 m/s = 4 kg m/s	10 kg m/s – 4 kg m/s = 6 kg m/s

Final momentum:

ball 1 ←	ball 2 →	total →
2 kg × 2 m/s = 4 kg m/s	2 kg × velocity	2 kg × velocity – 4 kg m/s

Momentum is conserved so:
final momentum = initial momentum
$2\,kg \times velocity - 4\,kg\,m/s = 6\,kg\,m/s$
$2\,kg \times velocity = 6\,kg\,m/s + 4\,kg\,m/s = 10\,kg\,m/s$
$velocity = 10\,kg\,m/s \div 2\,kg = 5\,m/s$

2 Use momentum conservation to calculate

a the velocity of the railway trucks after they latch together

b the mass of the car.

Before collision

During collision

The objects apply equal but opposite forces to each other. These forces change their momentum by equal but opposite amounts, so the total change in momentum is zero.

After collision

Momentum is **conserved** (provided no **external** forces act). The final momentum is equal to the initial momentum.

	5 m/s	2 m/s
before collision	2 kg	2 kg

	2 m/s	velocity = ?
after collision	2 kg	2 kg

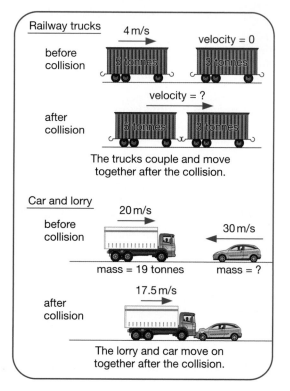

Railway trucks
4 m/s
velocity = 0
before collision 5 tonnes 3 tonnes
velocity = ?
after collision 5 tonnes 3 tonnes

The trucks couple and move together after the collision.

Car and lorry
20 m/s
before collision
30 m/s
mass = 19 tonnes   mass = ?

17.5 m/s
after collision

The lorry and car move on together after the collision.

Surviving collisions

When a car crashes, it stops suddenly. A force has to act on the passenger to change their momentum from the value when they are moving to zero. The force is usually provided by a seatbelt or an airbag. You can calculate this force from the formula

$$\text{force} = \frac{\text{change in momentum}}{\text{time}}$$

This equation tells us that the shorter the time for the momentum change, the bigger the force.

3 Look at the pictures.
Then copy and complete the sentences.

The momentum change for the person not wearing a seatbelt happens when he hits the windscreen. This takes place in a very _____ time so the force is very _____.
A large force applied to the head is usually fatal.

The momentum change for someone wearing a seatbelt takes a _____ time as the seatbelt brings him to rest.
This means that the force is _____. An airbag prevents the driver making a sudden impact with the _____ _____.

A sudden impact changes the passenger's momentum in a very short time, so the force is very large.

Seatbelts and airbags change the passenger's momentum more gradually. The time is longer so the force is smaller. This prevents the driver being injured by the steering wheel.

4 Modern cars are designed to crumple in a collision. Use momentum change to explain why a car that crumples gradually is safer than a car that is rigid and comes to rest in a very short time.

A modern car crumples in a collision. This means the momentum takes longer to change, so the forces are smaller.

What you need to remember *Copy and complete using the **key words***

Collisions
Momentum is _____ in any collision provided no _____ forces act on the colliding bodies.

You need to be able to use the conservation of momentum to calculate the mass, velocity or momentum of a body involved in a collision.
You need to be able to use the ideas of momentum to explain safety features.

1 Electricity that can make your hair stand on end

Electricity doesn't always flow through circuits.
Electricity can also stay just where it is.
This is called **static** electricity.

You can produce static electricity by rubbing together two **different** materials. We say that we have **charged** the materials with electricity.

> **1** Combing your hair can produce static electricity.
>
> **a** Why does this happen?
> **b** Write down <u>two</u> ways in which you can tell when it happens.

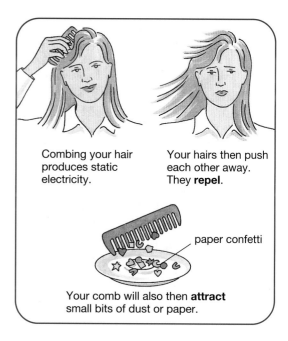

Combing your hair produces static electricity.

Your hairs then push each other away. They **repel**.

paper confetti

Your comb will also then **attract** small bits of dust or paper.

Is all static electricity the same?

You can rub two strips of plastic with a cloth.
This charges them with static electricity. The diagrams show what the charged strips of plastic will then do.

> **2** Copy the sentences. Then use the words <u>attract</u> and <u>repel</u> to complete them.
>
> Two charged strips made from the same plastic _____ each other.
>
> A charged polythene strip and a charged acetate strip _____ each other.
>
> Both charged strips will also _____ light objects that do not have a charge.

Charged objects sometimes attract and sometimes repel.

This means that there must be <u>different types</u> of electrical charge.

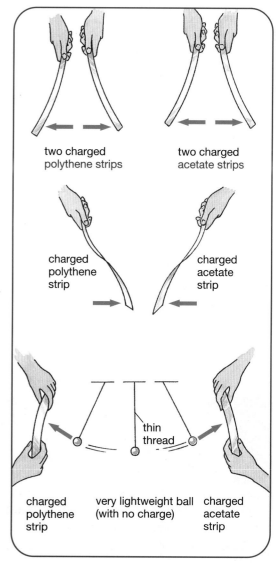

two charged polythene strips

two charged acetate strips

charged polythene strip

charged acetate strip

charged polythene strip

very lightweight ball (with no charge)

thin thread

charged acetate strip

Two types of charge

Two polythene strips that are rubbed with the same cloth must have the same kind of charge. These charges repel. Two acetate strips rubbed with the same cloth must have the same kind of charge. These charges also repel.

3 Copy and complete the sentences.

Objects that have the _____ type of electrical charge repel each other. So if two charged objects attract each other they must have _____ electrical charges.

Here is a simple way to remember what happens:

■ **like** charges repel, **unlike** charges attract.

The charge you get on a polythene strip when you rub it is called **negative** (–).

The charge you get on an acetate strip when you rub it is called **positive** (+).

4 Copy and complete the table.

Charge		Do the strips attract or repel?
First strip	Second strip	
+	+	
+	–	
–	–	

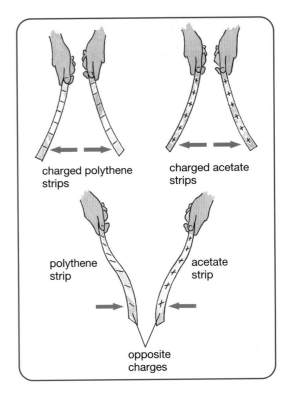

charged polythene strips

charged acetate strips

polythene strip

acetate strip

opposite charges

Really making hair stand on end

You can use an electrostatic machine to make hair really stand on end.

5 Explain how this happens, as fully as you can.

large charge on metal dome

drive pulley

Electrostatic generator. The belt becomes charged as it rubs against the drive pulley. The charge on the belt transfers to the dome.

What you need to remember *Copy and complete using the **key words***

Electricity that can make your hair stand on end

When you rub two _____ materials together, they become _____ with electricity. This is called _____ electricity.
There are two types of charge, called _____ (+) and _____ (–).
Charges of the same type _____ each other.
Charges of different types _____ each other.
We say that _____ charges repel and _____ charges attract.

2 Why rubbing things together produces electricity

It's all down to electrons

When you rub two different materials together, **electrons** are rubbed off one material and onto the other. These electrons are very tiny. Each electron carries a small electrical charge.

If you rub two pieces of the same material together, electrons don't move.

1 When you rub two different materials together, they become charged. Why?

2 What type of electrical charge does each electron carry?

The materials that you rub together must not only be different. At least one of them, and usually both of them, must be an electrical **insulator**.

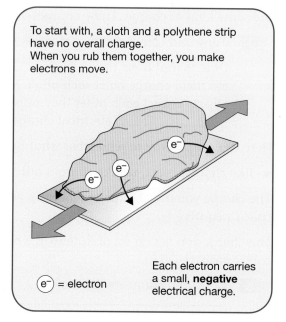

To start with, a cloth and a polythene strip have no overall charge.
When you rub them together, you make electrons move.

(e⁻) = electron

Each electron carries a small, **negative** electrical charge.

Why rubbing polythene gives it a negative charge

The diagrams show what happens when you rub polythene with a cloth.

3 Copy and complete the sentence.

When you rub a piece of polythene with a cloth, you make electrons move from the _____ to the _____.

4 Explain the following, as fully as you can.

a The polythene ends up with a negative charge.

b The cloth ends up with a positive charge.

5 The negative charge on the polythene is exactly **equal** to the positive charge on the cloth. Why is this?

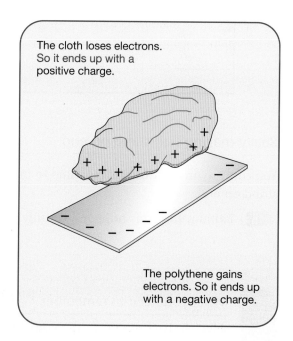

The cloth loses electrons. So it ends up with a positive charge.

The polythene gains electrons. So it ends up with a negative charge.

Why rubbing acetate gives it a positive charge

When you rub a piece of acetate with a cloth, the acetate becomes positively charged.

6   **a** What type of charge do you get on a cloth when you rub a piece of acetate with it?

     b What happens to the electrons as you rub the acetate with a cloth?

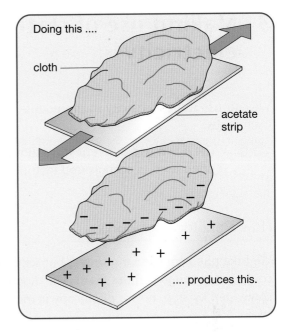

Doing this ....

cloth

acetate strip

.... produces this.

Peeling things apart

Peeling two different materials apart has the same effect as rubbing them together. Electrons are transferred from one material to the other.

7   Copy and complete the sentence.

When you peel different materials apart, one of them becomes _____ charged and the other becomes _____ charged.

8   When you peel some sticky tape from a roll, it often tends to go back on again.
Explain, as fully as you can, why it does this.

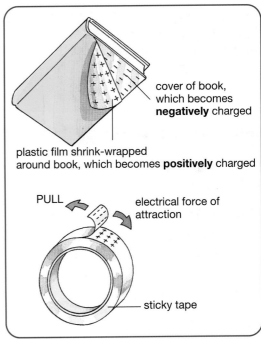

cover of book, which becomes **negatively** charged

plastic film shrink-wrapped around book, which becomes **positively** charged

PULL

electrical force of attraction

sticky tape

What you need to remember *Copy and complete using the **key words***

Why rubbing things together produces electricity
When two different materials are rubbed together, _____ are rubbed off one material and onto the other.
One, or both, of the materials must be an electrical _____ .
Each electron carries a small, _____ electrical charge.
The material that gains electrons becomes _____ charged.
The material that loses electrons becomes _____ charged.
These two charges are exactly _____ in size.

3 Making use of static electricity

We can use static electricity in many different ways to do useful jobs.

1 Write down <u>two</u> different ways that static electricity is often used in schools and factories.

making photocopies

removing dirt from smoke

before   after

spraying car bodies

spraying crops

How a photocopier works

We take photocopiers for granted, but schools and offices could not manage without them. The diagrams below show, step by step, how a photocopy is made.

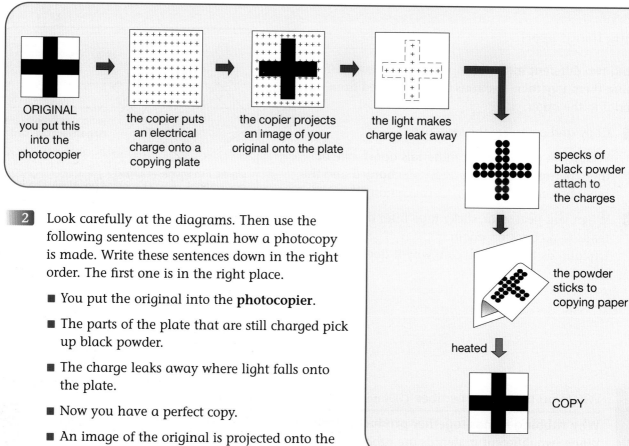

ORIGINAL
you put this into the photocopier

the copier puts an electrical charge onto a copying plate

the copier projects an image of your original onto the plate

the light makes charge leak away

specks of black powder attach to the charges

the powder sticks to copying paper

heated

COPY

2 Look carefully at the diagrams. Then use the following sentences to explain how a photocopy is made. Write these sentences down in the right order. The first one is in the right place.

- You put the original into the **photocopier**.

- The parts of the plate that are still charged pick up black powder.

- The charge leaks away where light falls onto the plate.

- Now you have a perfect copy.

- An image of the original is projected onto the plate.

- The copying plate is charged with electricity.

- The powder is transferred to a piece of paper and heated so that it sticks.

How to remove the dirt from smoke

Smoke contains lots of tiny bits of dirt. This dirt falls on houses and gardens. If people breathe in the dirt, it can damage their lungs.

The diagram shows how the dirt can be removed from factory chimneys using a **smoke precipitator**.

3 Copy and complete the sentences.

A metal grid and antenna are connected to the positive side of a high _____ supply.
The metal chimney is connected to the _____ side of the supply.
Tiny bits of dirt pick up a _____ charge as they pass through the grid. They are then repelled by the antenna and _____ by the chimney.
So the dirt collects (precipitates) on the inside of the _____ and is removed every so often.

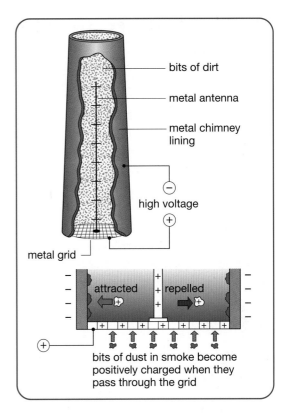

bits of dirt

metal antenna

metal chimney lining

high voltage

metal grid

attracted   repelled

bits of dust in smoke become positively charged when they pass through the grid

How to make a spray hit its target

When a liquid is sprayed out of a nozzle, it becomes electrically charged. Sprays can be made to charge the droplets as much as possible. The diagrams show how this helps the spray to find its target.

4 Explain why a pesticide spray works better if it charges the droplets of pesticide.

5 Car makers want most of the paint from a spray to end up on a car body. What can they do to the car body to make sure this happens?

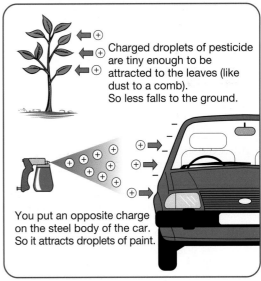

Charged droplets of pesticide are tiny enough to be attracted to the leaves (like dust to a comb). So less falls to the ground.

You put an opposite charge on the steel body of the car. So it attracts droplets of paint.

What you need to remember *Copy and complete using the **key words***

Making use of static electricity
Electrostatic charges can be useful, for example in a _____ and a _____ _____ .

You need to be able to explain how static electricity is used in the operation of devices such as the photocopier and the smoke precipitator.

4 Conductors and insulators

How to test for good conductors

Some materials let electricity pass through them very easily. A material like this is called a good **conductor**. You can find out which materials are good conductors. The diagram shows you how.

> **1** What happens if you test a good conductor?

The table shows the results of some tests.

> **2** Write down the materials that are good conductors.

> **3** If you tested your body in the same way, the lamp would not light. What does this tell you about your body?

How to test for good insulators

You can do the same tests with a sensitive electrical meter instead of a lamp. A good insulator does not let any electricity pass through it, so the meter stays at zero. This table shows the results of some tests.

Material	Meter reading
flexible plastic	zero
body (hands dry)	small
body (hands wet)	larger
hard plastic	zero
rubber	zero

> **4** Which materials are good insulators?

> **5** Is your body a good insulator? Answer as carefully as you can.

What's the difference?

An electric current is a flow of electrical charges. Electrical charges can move easily through **metals** and some other substances. These materials are conductors. Charges cannot move through insulators.

> **6** Copy and complete the sentences.
>
> In a metal wire, an electric current is a flow of
>
> _____.
>
> In a liquid, the current is a flow of _____.

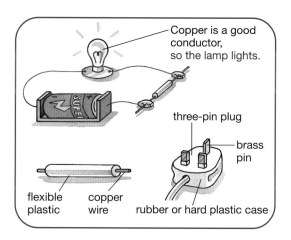

Copper is a good conductor, so the lamp lights.

three-pin plug

brass pin

flexible plastic   copper wire   rubber or hard plastic case

Material	Does lamp light?
flexible plastic	no
copper	yes
hard plastic	no
rubber	no
brass	yes

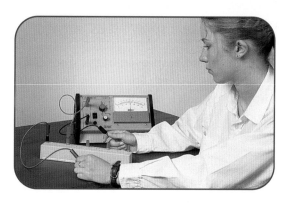

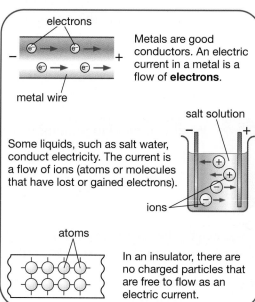

electrons

metal wire

Metals are good conductors. An electric current in a metal is a flow of **electrons**.

salt solution

ions

Some liquids, such as salt water, conduct electricity. The current is a flow of ions (atoms or molecules that have lost or gained electrons).

atoms

In an insulator, there are no charged particles that are free to flow as an electric current.

Feel the current

Look at the two rivers. They are about the same size, but the water is flowing at different rates.

7   In which river is the rate of flow greater?

8   Which river has the bigger current?

Just as we call a flow of water a water current, so we call a flow of electrical charge an electric **current**.

9   Copy and complete the sentence.

The rate of flow of charge through a conductor is the amount of _____ that passes by each _____. This is called the

_____.

Strong current.

Weak current.

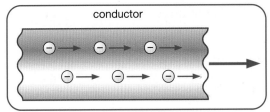

An electric current is the amount of charge that passes by each second.

> ### REMEMBER
>
> You can give some materials an electrical charge by rubbing them together. Electrons are rubbed off one material onto the other. The material that gains electrons becomes negatively charged. The material that loses electrons gains an equal positive charge.

Connecting to earth

When an object has an electrical charge we may wish to **discharge** it – to prevent unwanted sparks or shocks for example. The diagram shows how we can do this. We connect the object to the **earth** with a conductor. The conductor allows electrons to flow through it. This is a current of electricity.

10   Look at the diagrams.
Then copy and complete the sentences.

When a negatively charged, conducting object is earthed, _____ move from the object to earth. When a positively charged object is earthed, electrons move from the _____ to the

_____.

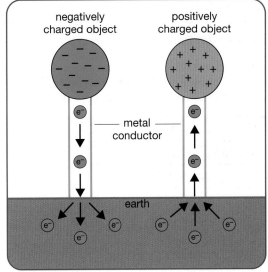

Electrons move until the object is discharged.

What you need to remember *Copy and complete using the **key words***

Conductors and insulators

Electrical charges can move easily through some substances, for example _____.
The rate of flow of electrical charge is called the _____.
We can _____ a charged body by connecting it to _____ with a
_____. _____ then flow through the conductor to the earth.

5 Danger from sparks

H

Making a spark

Look at the diagram. The belt on the electrostatic generator transfers charge to the dome. As the belt turns, the charge on the dome increases.

1 Copy and complete the sentences.

The greater the charge on the dome, the _____ the potential difference between it and _____.
When the potential difference is high enough, a _____ jumps through the air to a nearby _____.

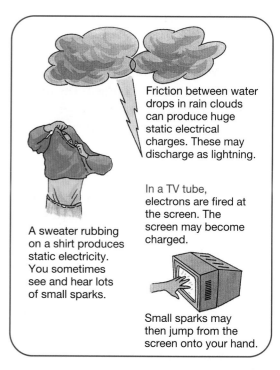

As the charge on the dome gets bigger, the **potential difference** (voltage) between the dome and **earth** increases. Eventually, a **spark** jumps between the dome and the nearby conductor.

Sparks big and small

Static electricity can produce sparks. Often these sparks are very small. But sometimes they are huge.

2 Look at the pictures.
Then copy and complete the table.

	Size of sparks (large or small)	How the static charge is produced
television screen		
lightning		
taking off a sweater		

Friction between water drops in rain clouds can produce huge static electrical charges. These may discharge as lightning.

A sweater rubbing on a shirt produces static electricity. You sometimes see and hear lots of small sparks.

In a TV tube, electrons are fired at the screen. The screen may become charged.

Small sparks may then jump from the screen onto your hand.

Preventing explosions at flour mills

Flour is made by grinding wheat to a very fine powder. The bits of flour make the air very dusty. This mixture of flour and air can be very dangerous. Just a tiny spark can make it explode.

3 Look at the diagrams.
There is a danger of a spark between the pipe and the container. Explain why.

4 How can such a spark be avoided?

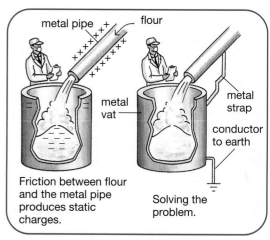

Friction between flour and the metal pipe produces static charges.

Solving the problem.

Fire hazards with petrol tankers

Petrol is very flammable. A tiny spark can cause a serious fire when petrol or petrol vapour is open to the air.

At filling stations, petrol is transferred from tankers to underground tanks. There must be no sparks while this is being done.

5 In what <u>two</u> ways can petrol tankers produce static electricity?

6 Why does static electricity create a hazard when pumping petrol?

7 Write down <u>two</u> things that are done to prevent sparks.

A static charge can build up on a petrol tanker because of the tyres rubbing on the road.

A static charge can also build up as petrol flows through a pipe.

Metal strap. This is connected to the tank before the tank is opened.

from tanker

petrol

underground metal tank connected to earth

Handle chips with care

Technicians who put electronic chips into circuits have special mats on their workbenches. These mats conduct electricity and are connected to earth. The technicians sometimes also wear wrist straps connected to earth.

8 Why are these precautions needed?

9 Explain how these precautions prevent damage to microchips.

The discharge of static electricity through a microchip can damage its microscopic circuits. Earthing the bench and the technician prevents static charge from building up.

What you need to remember *Copy and complete using the **key words***

Danger from sparks

The greater the charge on a body, the greater the _____ _____ between the body and _____.

If the potential difference becomes high enough, a _____ may jump across the gap between the body and any _____ _____ which is brought near it.

You need to be able to explain why static electricity is dangerous in some situations and how precautions can be taken to ensure that the electrostatic charge is discharged safely.

Making a current flow

To make a lamp light up, you must send an electric current through it. You can do this by putting a potential difference across its ends with a battery. Another name for potential difference is voltage.

1. Look at the diagram.
   Then copy and complete the sentences.

   To make the lamp light, you must press the
   _____.

   There is then a _____ across the
   the lamp.
   This makes a _____ flow through the
   lamp.

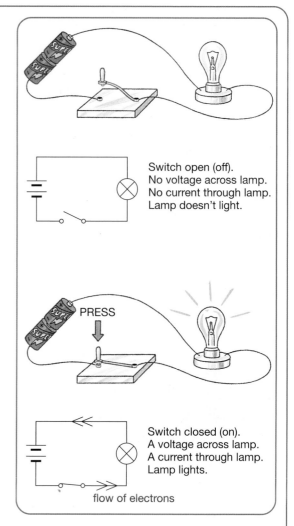

Switch open (off).
No voltage across lamp.
No current through lamp.
Lamp doesn't light.

PRESS

Switch closed (on).
A voltage across lamp.
A current through lamp.
Lamp lights.

flow of electrons

How to measure voltage

You can measure voltage using a voltmeter. To measure the voltage that is pushing a current through a lamp, you connect the voltmeter across the lamp. The diagram shows you how to do this. We say the voltmeter is connected in parallel with the lamp.

Voltage is measured in volts (V for short).

2. What voltage does the battery supply to the lamp?

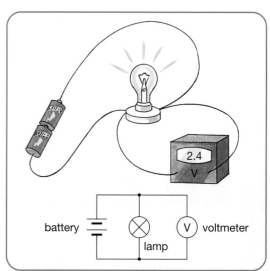

2.4 V

battery   lamp   voltmeter

How to measure current

You can measure an electric current using an ammeter. The diagram shows how you connect an ammeter to measure the current through a lamp.

The current that flows through the lamp must also flow through the ammeter. We say that the ammeter is connected in series with the lamp.

Current is measured in amperes (amps or A for short).

3 What current flows through lamp X

    a when you connect it to just one cell?

    b when you connect it to two cells to get a bigger voltage?

A voltage pushes a current through a lamp.
The lamp resists this current.
We say that it has a resistance.

Comparing resistance

Some lamps resist a current more than others, so they have a bigger resistance.

You need a bigger voltage to push the same current through a bigger resistance.

4 **a** Which has the bigger resistance, lamp X or lamp Y?

    b Give a reason for your answer to **a**.

5 How could you make lamp Y light brightly? Explain your answer as fully as you can.

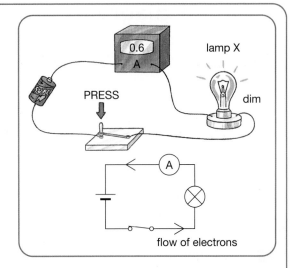

flow of electrons

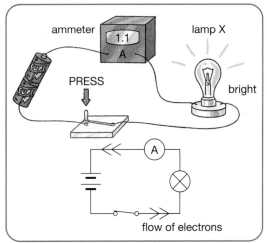

flow of electrons

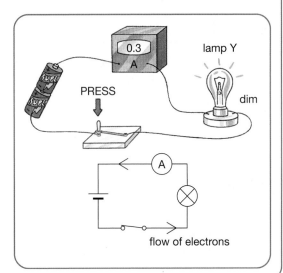

flow of electrons

1 Circuit diagrams

Circuit symbols

You can show an electrical circuit by drawing a picture of what it looks like. But it is a lot easier, and much more convenient, to draw **symbols** for each component in a circuit. You looked at some simple circuits and their diagrams on pages 254 and 255.

For example, instead of drawing a lamp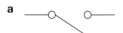

you can draw this symbol —⊗—

> **1** Draw and label the symbols for these components:
>
> **a** cell   **b** thermistor   **c** lamp
> **d** switch (closed)   **e** ammeter   **f** fuse
> **g** variable resistor

> **2** Write down the names of the components shown by these symbols:
>
> **a**    **b** —|⊢--|⊢—
>
> **c** (diode symbol)   **d** (resistor symbol)
>
> **e** —(V)—   **f**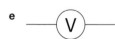

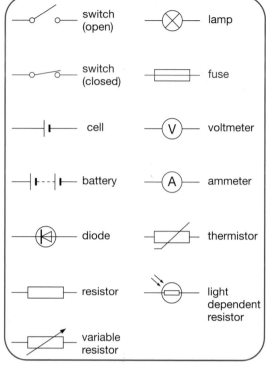

You need to know these symbols for circuit components. You will study the components you have not seen before in the pages that follow.

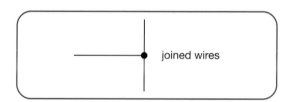

joined wires

Drawing circuit diagrams

On circuit diagrams, you should draw connecting wires as straight lines with right-angled turns. If the wires are joined, you must show this with a dot.

You should be able to draw a circuit diagram from looking at a circuit.

> **3** Draw the circuit diagram for each of these circuits.

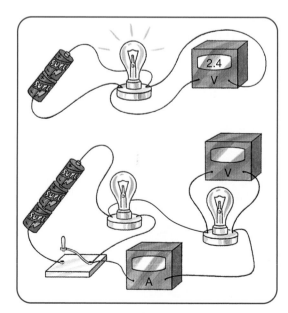

Interpreting circuit diagrams

You should be able to understand, from a circuit diagram, how **components** are connected.

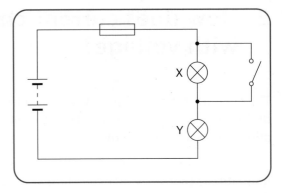

4 Look at the diagram.
Then copy and complete the sentences.

X and Y are both _____.
Making a complete circuit with both X and Y, there is a _____ and a _____.
Connected across the ends of X, there is a
_____ which is _____.

In all of the diagrams

_____→

shows the flow of electrons.

Series and parallel connections

Circuit diagrams A and B show two ways of connecting two lamps to a single cell.

5 Copy and complete the sentences.

When two components are connected in series, the _____ current passes through both components, one after the other.
When two components are connected in _____, the current _____.
Part of the current flows through one component and part flows through the other.

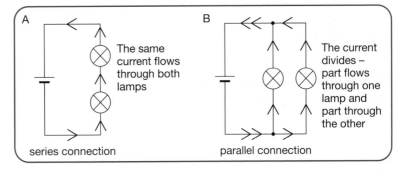

A   The same current flows through both lamps

series connection

B   The current divides – part flows through one lamp and part through the other

parallel connection

Look at circuit diagram C.

6 a Name <u>two</u> components that are connected in parallel with each other.
b Which component is connected in series with the cell and the other components in the circuit?

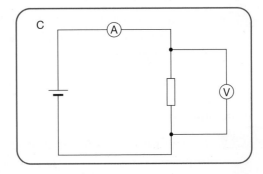

C

What you need to remember *Copy and complete using the **key words***

Circuit diagrams
We use _____ to show _____ in circuit diagrams.

You need to know all the circuit symbols in the table at the top of page 256.
You need to be able to draw and to interpret circuit diagrams like you have on these pages.

2 How does current change with voltage?

The **current** through a lamp depends on the **potential difference** you apply across it. The same is true for any other electrical **component**.

You can use the circuit shown in the diagram to find out how current changes when you change the potential difference.

> 1 Copy and complete the sentences.
>
> Current is measured using an _____.
> This is connected in _____ with the component.
> Potential difference is measured using a
>
> _____.
>
> This is connected in _____ with the component.

Different components give different results. You can show these results on a current–potential-difference graph.

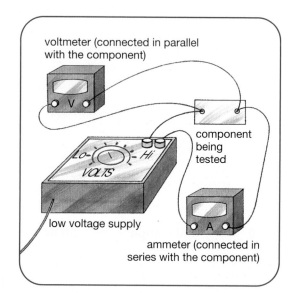

voltmeter (connected in parallel with the component)

component being tested

low voltage supply

ammeter (connected in series with the component)

Current–potential-difference graph for a resistor

The graph shows how the current through a resistor changes when you change the potential difference across it. The graph is like this only if the resistor does not get hot. So you must keep the current through the resistor quite small.

> 2 Describe, as carefully as you can, how the current through the resistor changes as you increase the potential difference.

It sometimes matters which way round you connect a component to the supply. You can check this by connecting it the other way round.

> 3 Look at the second graph. Copy and complete the sentence.
>
> When you connect a resistor the other way round to a supply, the size of the current that flows through it is the _____.

The resistance of the resistor **stays the same** provided its temperature does not change.

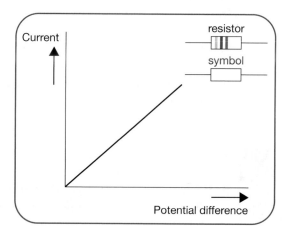

Current

resistor symbol

Potential difference

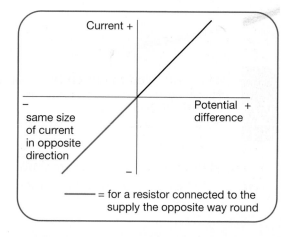

Current +

Potential + difference

same size of current in opposite direction

——— = for a resistor connected to the supply the opposite way round

Current–potential-difference graph for a diode

Some circuits use a component called a diode. The current–potential-difference graph for a diode shows that it behaves differently from a resistor.

4 Does it matter which way round you connect the diode?
Explain your answer as fully as you can.

5 Write down <u>one</u> other difference between a diode and a resistor.

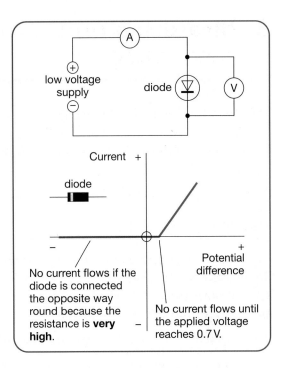

No current flows if the diode is connected the opposite way round because the resistance is **very high**.

No current flows until the applied voltage reaches 0.7 V.

Current–potential-difference graph for a filament lamp

A lamp has a filament that gets very hot. So a lamp may sometimes be called a filament lamp. Look carefully at the current–potential-difference graph for a filament lamp.

6 Does it matter which way round you connect the lamp?
Explain your answer as fully as you can.

7 Copy and complete the sentences.

As the potential difference increases, the current through the filament _____.
But the graph gradually flattens out. This tells you that the _____ is increasing less and less.
This happens because the filament of the lamp becomes very _____, so its resistance increases.

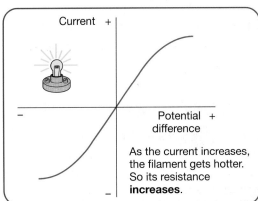

As the current increases, the filament gets hotter. So its resistance **increases**.

What you need to remember *Copy and complete using the **key words***

How does current change with voltage?
A current–_____ _____ graph shows how the _____
through a _____ varies with the potential difference across it.
The current–potential-difference graphs for a resistor, a diode and a filament lamp are as shown:

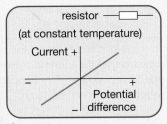

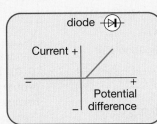

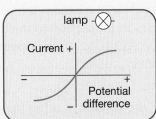

The resistance _____ _____ _____.

Resistance is low in one direction but _____ _____ in the other.

As the filament gets hotter, its resistance _____.

3 Measuring resistance

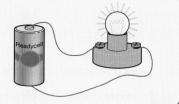

How to measure resistance

We measure **resistance** in units called ohms (symbol, Ω). To measure a resistance you need to know how big a current flows through it when you put a particular **potential difference** (p.d.) across it.

Then you can work out the resistance like this:

$$\frac{\text{resistance}}{\text{(ohms, }\Omega\text{)}} = \frac{\text{potential difference (volts, V)}}{\text{current (amperes, A)}}$$

The example shows how to use this formula.

> **1** The current through a 12 V car headlamp is 3 A. Calculate the resistance of the filament when the lamp is operating.
> (Start by writing down the formula. Show all your working.)

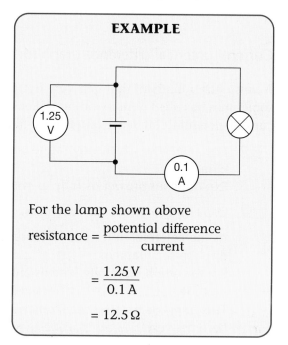

EXAMPLE

For the lamp shown above

$$\text{resistance} = \frac{\text{potential difference}}{\text{current}}$$

$$= \frac{1.25 \text{ V}}{0.1 \text{ A}}$$

$$= 12.5 \, \Omega$$

Calculating resistance from a graph

This graph shows the current through a resistor that stays at a constant temperature.

> **2** **a** Sketch the graph. (You don't need graph paper – it's just the shape you need to get right.)
> **b** Copy and complete the sentences.
>
> For a resistor at constant temperature, the current increases in proportion to the applied _____. This happens because the resistance _____ _____ _____.

> **3** Calculate the resistance using the pairs of values shown by broken lines on the graph.

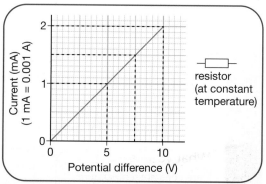

The graph is a straight line through the origin (0, 0). This means that the current is **directly proportional** to the voltage. This happens because the resistance stays the same.

Using resistance to calculate potential difference

We can rearrange the formula

$$\text{resistance (ohms, } \Omega) = \frac{\text{potential difference (volts, V)}}{\text{current (amperes, A)}}$$

to give

$$\begin{array}{ccccc} \text{potential difference} & = & \textbf{current} & \times & \textbf{resistance} \\ \text{(volts, V)} & & \text{(amps, A)} & & \text{(ohms, } \Omega) \end{array}$$

So if you know

- the resistance of a **component** in a circuit, and
- the current flowing through the component,

you can use this version of the formula to calculate the potential difference across the component (see Example).

4   The lamp in the circuit has a resistance of 12 Ω. Calculate the potential difference across the lamp.

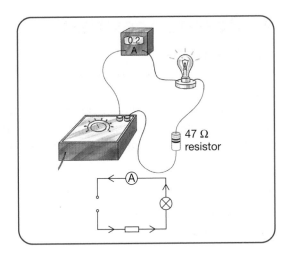

EXAMPLE

In the circuit above, what is the potential difference across the resistor?

potential difference = current × resistance

= 0.2 A × 47 Ω

= 9.4 V

Resistance and current

We can rearrange the formula

$$\begin{array}{ccccc} \text{potential difference} & = & \text{current} & \times & \text{resistance} \\ \text{(volts, V)} & & \text{(amps, A)} & & \text{(ohms, } \Omega) \end{array}$$

to give

$$\text{current (amps, A)} = \frac{\text{potential difference (volts, V)}}{\text{resistance (ohms, } \Omega)}$$

This formula tells us that the current through a component depends on its resistance. If you keep the potential difference the same then making the resistance bigger makes the current **smaller**.

5   Through which resistor in the diagram is the current greater? Explain your answer.

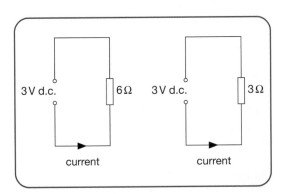

What you need to remember *Copy and complete using the **key words***

Measuring resistance

The current through a resistor (at a constant temperature) is _____ _____ to the _____ _____ across the resistor.

Potential difference, current and resistance are related by the formula

potential difference = _____ × _____

You can find the _____ of a component by measuring the current through and the potential difference across the component.

The current through a _____ depends on its _____. The greater the resistance, the _____ the current for a given _____ _____.

4 Resistances that change

REMEMBER

resistance (ohms, Ω) $=\dfrac{\text{potential difference (volts, V)}}{\text{current (amperes, A)}}$

The resistance of an ordinary resistor stays the same, if its temperature doesn't change. But in a lamp, the temperature of the filament does change, so its resistance changes too.

The resistance of a diode depends on which way the current flows.

Some other electrical components are designed to change their resistance when there are changes in their surroundings.

The resistance of a filament lamp

The graph shows the current through the **filament** of a lamp when different voltages are applied across it.

1 **a** Make a copy of the current–potential-difference graph for the lamp.
   b Underneath your graph, work out the resistance of the filament
      i when the p.d. across it is 0.5 V
      ii when the p.d. across it is 1.0 V.
   c What happens to the resistance of the filament when the p.d. across it increases?
   d Why does this happen?

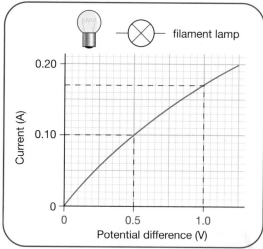

The filament of a lamp becomes hot because it resists the current flowing through it. The graph becomes less and less steep. This means that the current through the filament does not increase as fast as the potential difference across it. This happens because the resistance of the filament **increases** as it gets hotter.

Diodes

Two identical diodes are connected the opposite way around in circuits with lamps.

2 In which circuit does the **diode** have a higher **resistance** – A or B? Explain your answer.

3 Copy and complete the sentences.

The _____ through a diode flows easily in one direction only. The diode has a very high _____ in the reverse direction.

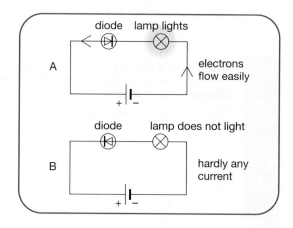

Thermistors

The resistance of a **thermistor** decreases when the **temperature** increases.

4   **a**   Sketch the resistance–temperature graph for the thermistor.

      b   Describe how the resistance of the thermistor changes with temperature.

5   Write down <u>two</u> uses for thermistors.

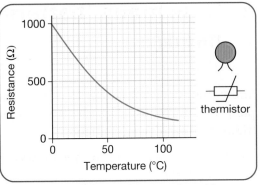

Because their resistance changes a lot with temperature, thermistors are used in electrical thermometers and thermostats.

Light dependent resistors (LDRs)

The resistance of a **light dependent resistor** (LDR) depends on the brightness of the light that falls on it. We call the brightness the **light intensity**.

6   **a**   Sketch the resistance–light-intensity graph for the light dependent resistor (LDR).

      b   Describe how the resistance of the LDR changes with the light intensity.

7   Write down <u>two</u> uses for LDRs.

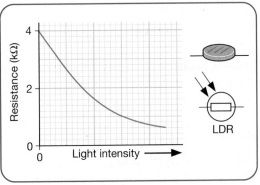

LDRs are used in light meters and in circuits which switch on lights automatically when it gets dark.

What you need to remember *Copy and complete using the* **key words**

Resistances that change

The resistance of a filament lamp _____ as the temperature of the _____ increases.

The current through a _____ flows in one direction only. The diode has a very high _____ in the reverse direction.

The resistance of a _____ _____ _____ (LDR) decreases as _____ _____ increases.

The resistance of a _____ decreases as the _____ increases.

5 How many 'batteries' do I need?

Many things need electricity to work. Some of these things plug in to the mains electricity. The diagram shows some things that work from 'batteries'.

> **1** What is the proper name for what we often call a battery?

> **2** Different things need different numbers of cells to work properly.
> How many cells are needed by each of the things shown in the diagram?

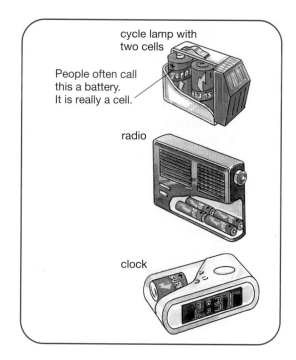

cycle lamp with two cells

People often call this a battery. It is really a cell.

radio

clock

Why does a cycle lamp need two cells?

For a cycle without a dynamo, the cells in a cycle lamp provide the potential difference (voltage) that makes an electric current flow through the lamp. The lamp needs two cells connected **in series** (in line) to provide enough volts to make it light properly.

To make the cycle lamp light normally, you need two cells.

> **3** What potential difference do the two cells on the right provide?

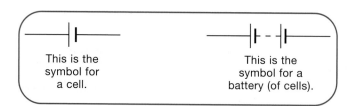

This is the symbol for a cell.

This is the symbol for a battery (of cells).

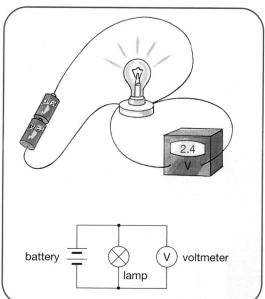

2.4 V

battery   lamp   voltmeter

> **4** The diagram shows two cells connected the opposite way round.
> What potential difference do these two cells give? Give a reason for your answer.

These cells are pushing in opposite directions. Their potential differences cancel out.

What happens if you use the wrong number of cells?

5 Copy the table. Then use the information from the diagrams to complete it.

The diagram for two cells is on page 264.

Number of cells (connected in series)	Total potential difference (voltage) provided
1	
2	
3	

6 What pattern do you see in the voltages when you connect cells together?

7 What voltages do the cycle lamp, radio and clock from question 2 need to work properly?

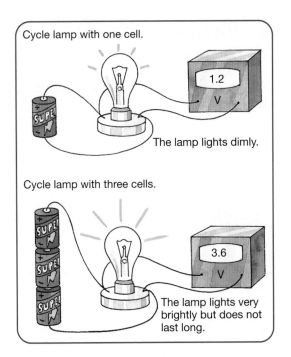

Cycle lamp with one cell.

1.2 V

The lamp lights dimly.

Cycle lamp with three cells.

3.6 V

The lamp lights very brightly but does not last long.

What is a battery?

A **battery** is made up of two or more cells joined together. When you connect cells in series the total potential difference is the **sum** of the potential differences of each **cell**.

8 What voltage does each cell in the car battery provide?

12 volts

one cell

What you need to remember *Copy and complete using the* **key words**

How many 'batteries' do I need?

To get a bigger voltage, you can connect more than one cell _____

_____.

This is called a _____.

The total potential difference is the _____ of the potential difference of each

_____.

6 Parallel circuits

A lamp lights brightly when you connect it as shown in the diagrams below.

> **REMEMBER**
>
> To make a lamp light, you must send a big enough current through it. You can do this by putting a big enough potential difference across the lamp.

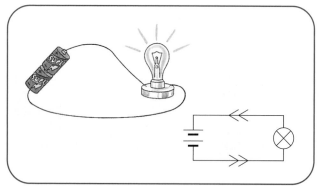

You can connect another lamp to the same battery so that both lamps light brightly.
The diagram on the right shows how you can do this.

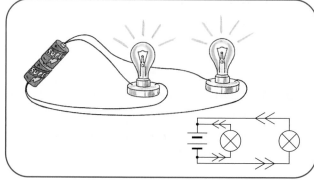

The full potential difference is applied across each lamp. A current flows separately through each lamp. We say the lamps are connected in parallel.

1 Copy and complete the sentence.

The two lamps on the right are connected in

_____.

2 Why do both bulbs light brightly?

3 Suppose one lamp breaks or you take it out. How will this affect the other lamp?

> In all of the diagrams
>
> ————————————>
>
> shows the flow of electrons.

The two lamps in the diagram are connected to the two cells by separate wires. But this isn't the only way to connect things in parallel.

Connecting things in parallel

Connecting wires let electricity flow through them very easily. They have hardly any resistance.

Look at the two circuits. Each lamp is connected directly to both sides of the battery. In each circuit the two lamps are connected in parallel.

4 Copy and complete the sentences.

In these parallel circuits, the current from the battery to both lamps flows through the
_____ wire. Then the current splits and flows through each lamp _____.
Then the current joins back up and flows back to the
_____ through the same wire.

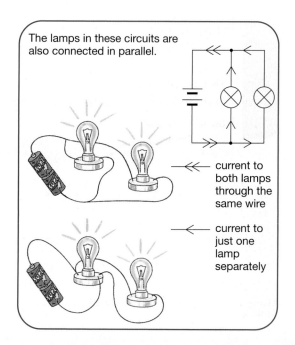

The lamps in these circuits are also connected in parallel.

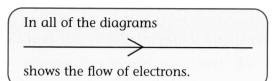

⟵⟵ current to both lamps through the same wire

⟵ current to just one lamp separately

Measuring currents in parallel circuits

When components are connected in parallel, the potential difference across each component is the **same**. So if one component has a smaller resistance, a bigger current will flow through it.

5 Look at the diagram.

    a What is the current through lamp X?
    b What is the current through lamp Y?
    c Which lamp has the bigger resistance?
       Give a reason for your answer.

6 **a** What is the <u>total</u> current supplied by the battery to the two lamps? This is shown by meter A_1.
    b How does this current compare to the separate currents through lamp X and lamp Y?

In a parallel circuit, the **total** current through the whole circuit is the same as the currents through the separate branches added together. It is the **sum** of these **separate** currents.

Safety when connecting things in parallel

When we plug things into the mains supply we are connecting them in parallel. But it isn't safe to take more than 13 A of current from one mains socket. So we need to be very careful about what we plug into it.

7 Copy and complete the table.

Appliances	Total current	Safe to connect current in parallel?
heater + large TV	12 A + 2 A = 14 A	no
lamp + CD player		
small TV + hair dryer		

> **REMEMBER**
>
> To measure the current through a lamp, you must connect an ammeter in series with it.

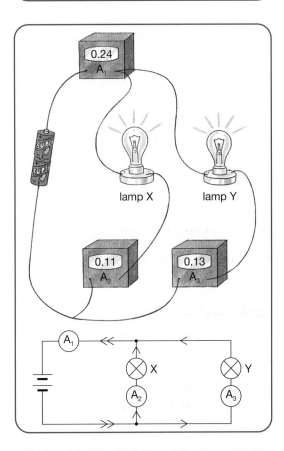

lamp X   lamp Y

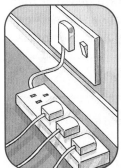

How much current?	
room heater	12 A
hair dryer	3 A
large TV	2 A
small TV	1 A
CD player	1 A
lamp	0.5 A

Parallel connections to the mains.

What you need to remember *Copy and complete using the **key words***

Parallel circuits
For components connected in parallel

- the potential difference across each component is the _____
- the _____ current through the whole circuit is the _____ of the currents through the _____ components.

7 Series circuits

In our homes, lights, power sockets and appliances are usually connected <u>in parallel</u>.

1 Write down <u>two</u> reasons for connecting things to the mains supply in parallel.

In the diagram the switch for each lamp is connected differently. It is connected <u>in series</u> with its lamp.

2 The diagram shows an important component connected in series with <u>all</u> of the lamps and switches in the circuit. What is this component?

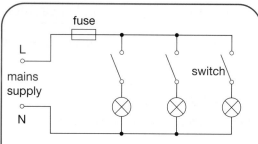

The lights in a house are connected in parallel.

This means that

• they all get the full 230 volts
• they can all be switched on and off separately.

Connecting things in series

The lamp in the first diagram is shining brightly.

The second diagram shows what happens when you connect another lamp in series with it.

3 Copy and complete the sentence.

The current that flows through a series circuit is exactly the _____ in each part of the circuit.

4 **a** What happens to the brightness of the lamps when the second lamp is connected?
   b Explain, as fully as you can, why this happens.

When lamps are connected in series, their total resistance is the same as their separate resistances added together. It is the **sum** of their separate resistances.

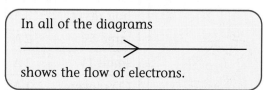

In all of the diagrams

shows the flow of electrons.

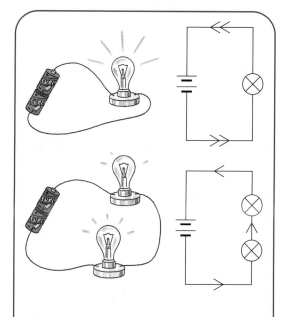

The **same** current flows through one lamp and then through the other. So we say they are connected in series.
The two lamps are dimmer than with one lamp by itself.
So we know that

• the current is smaller
• the resistance of the two lamps is bigger than the resistance of one lamp.

Measuring voltages in a series circuit

The diagram shows the potential differences across the cells and the lamps in a series circuit.

5
  a What is the potential difference across lamp X?
  b What is the potential difference across lamp Y?
  c What is the potential difference across the two cells?
  d How does this potential difference compare with the separate potential differences across the lamps?

In a series circuit, the potential difference of the supply is the same as the potential differences across the separate components added together. Another way of describing this is to say that the **total potential difference** of the supply is **shared** between the components.

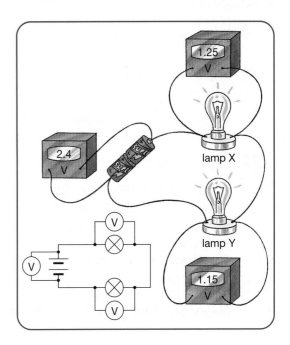

lamp X

lamp Y

Using resistors to control currents

We can put a resistor in series with a component.

This increases the total resistance of the circuit. This means that the current through the component is reduced.
The diagram shows an example.

6   The lamp starts to glow when there is 0.8 V across it. This happens when there is 1.7 V across the variable resistor.
What is the potential difference across the two cells?

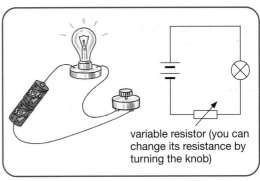

variable resistor (you can change its resistance by turning the knob)

What you need to remember *Copy and complete using the **key words***

Series circuits
For components connected in series

- the total resistance is the _____ of the resistance of each component
- there is the _____ current through each component
- the _____ _____ _____ of the supply is _____ between the components.

8 Using electrical devices

Using a thermistor

A scientist decides to use a thermistor to monitor the temperature in a greenhouse.

> **REMEMBER**
>
> The current through a component depends on its resistance. The greater the resistance, the smaller the current for a given potential difference.

1 What property of the thermistor changes when the temperature changes?

2 When the temperature rises, what happens to

    a the resistance of the thermistor?
    b the current through the thermistor?

3 Copy and complete the sentences.

The scientist connects the thermistor circuit to a data logger and a _____ to monitor the temperature _____.
This means she will not have to be there to take temperature _____, and she will not miss any _____ temperature changes.

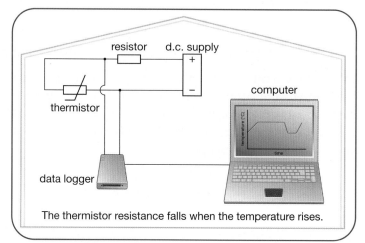

The thermistor resistance falls when the temperature rises.

The computer monitors the temperature continuously, so the scientist doesn't have to be there to take readings. Any sudden temperature changes are recorded.

Calibration

To find the temperature accurately the scientist must measure the resistance of the thermistor at known temperatures. This is called <u>calibration</u>.

Look at the calibration apparatus.

4 What instrument measures the current through the thermistor?

5 What instrument measures the potential difference across the thermistor?

6 How are these instruments connected in the circuit?

7 Write down a formula for calculating the resistance from the voltage and current readings.

8 Use the graph to work out the temperature when the resistance value is 80 Ω.

9 Explain why this thermistor can give more <u>precise</u> temperature readings in the range 20–40 °C than 60–80 °C.

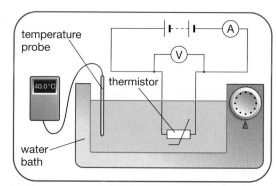

This apparatus is used to calibrate the thermistor. The resistance is measured at different temperatures. The calibration values are stored in the computer so that the temperature can be calculated automatically.

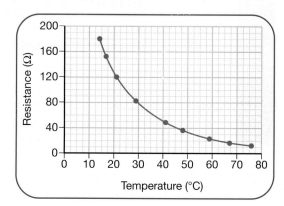

Taking the strain

A strain gauge is an electrical device that can sense how much something is stretched or bent.

10 Why must the gauge be glued firmly to the test object?

11 Why does the resistance of the gauge change when a force is applied to the object?

An engineer attaches a strain gauge to a crane. The gauge will trigger an alarm if the load is too big.

Before the alarm system will work, the engineer must calibrate the gauge. He does this by measuring the gauge resistance when the crane lifts different loads.

12 Draw a circuit that the engineer could use to measure the resistance of the gauge. (Hint: look at the circuit used to calibrate the thermistor on page 270.)

13 The gauge has a voltage of 2 V across it. When the crane is not carrying a load there is a current of 0.05 A through the gauge.
What is the gauge resistance?

14 The crane lifts a load of 2 tonnes. The voltage across the gauge stays the same.
What happens to the current through the gauge?
Explain your answer.

15 The safe working load for the crane is 5 tonnes.
At what resistance value should the engineer set the circuit to trigger the alarm?

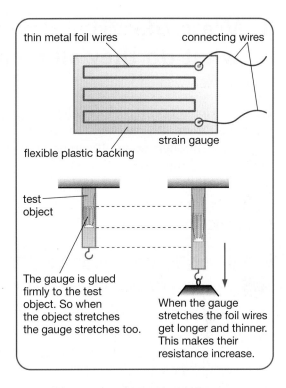

thin metal foil wires

connecting wires

strain gauge

flexible plastic backing

test object

The gauge is glued firmly to the test object. So when the object stretches the gauge stretches too.

When the gauge stretches the foil wires get longer and thinner. This makes their resistance increase.

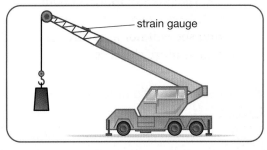

strain gauge

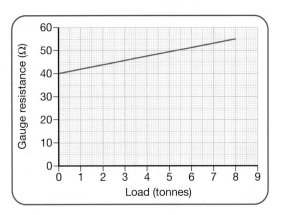

Gauge resistance (Ω) vs Load (tonnes)

What you need to remember

There is nothing new for you to <u>remember</u> in this section.
You have been applying ideas that you have met before.
You may be asked questions like these in tests and examinations.

You need to be able to apply the principles of basic electrical circuits to practical situations.

1 V/a.c./d.c./Hz – what do they all mean?

Electrical appliances have lots of letters and numbers printed on them. It's important for you to know what these letters and numbers mean. If you don't, you could easily damage the appliances or harm yourself.

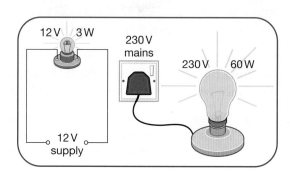

MODEL 8940
SERIAL No. B6KK0297
DIGITAL RADIO RECEIVER
Made in the United Kingdom
220/240V ~ 50/60 Hz

What does the V mean?

Look at the pictures of the lamps. V stands for **volts**.

1 Copy and complete the following sentences.

A 12 V lamp should be used with a _____ supply.

A _____ _____ should be used with a 230-volt supply.

In the UK, the mains supply is about 230 volts.

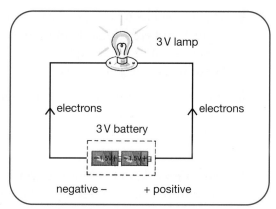

What does d.c. mean?

The diagram shows a battery pushing a current through a circuit.

2 Copy and complete the sentences.

When an electric current flows, _____ are moving around the circuit. They move from the _____ side of the battery, then through the wires and lamp, and then back to the _____ side of the battery.

The electrons always flow in the same **direction**. This is called a **direct** current, or **d.c.** for short.

3 Draw a diagram to show which way the electrons move if the battery is connected the opposite way round.

An electric current is a flow of electrons.

How can you see the direction of a current?

You can use an oscilloscope to draw a graph of the current. The pictures show the current from a battery.

4 Explain how the oscilloscope graph shows the direction in which the electrons flow.

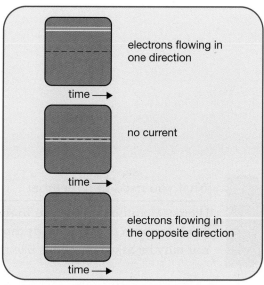

Oscilloscope pictures of a direct current.

What does a.c. mean?

The top circuit diagram shows a lamp connected to a 3 V a.c. supply. The lamp lights up just like it does with a 3 V battery.

The oscilloscope picture shows how the electrons flow around the circuit.

5 Do the electrons always flow in the same direction? Explain your answer.

A current that keeps on **changing** its direction is called an **alternating** current, or **a.c.** for short.

6 How does the oscilloscope picture change when the same lamp is connected to a 6 V a.c. supply?

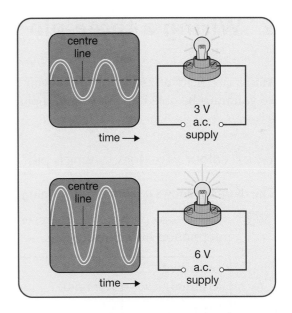

What does Hz mean?

The picture shows the graph of an alternating current. A time scale has been added. The time for the current to change direction then reverse again (1 cycle) is called the <u>period</u>.

7 What is the period of this supply?

8 How many cycles will there be in one whole second?

The number of cycles per second is called the **frequency**. In Europe, mains electricity has a frequency of 50 cycles per second or **50 hertz** (Hz for short).

9 The diagrams show the information on the back of two electrical appliances. Explain, as fully as you can, what this information tells you.

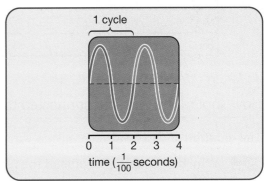

The red line shows one complete cycle of the alternating current.

What you need to remember *Copy and complete using the **key words***

V/a.c./d.c./Hz – what do they all mean?
Cells and batteries supply current which always passes in the same _____.
This is called _____ current (_____).
An _____ current (_____) is one which is constantly
_____ direction. Mains electricity is an a.c. supply.
In the UK it has a _____ of 50 cycles per second
(_____ _____). The UK mains supply is about 230 _____.

You need to be able to interpret oscilloscope pictures for a direct current and an alternating current in the way that you have on these pages.

2 Wiring a three-pin plug

Mains electricity of 230 volts can kill you.
So you must be able recognise when a plug is wired safely.

Which colour wire goes to which pin?

The diagram shows a correctly wired plug.

1 Make a copy of the table. Then complete it using the information from the diagram.

Letter by terminal	Name of terminal	Colour(s) of wires
E		
L		
N		

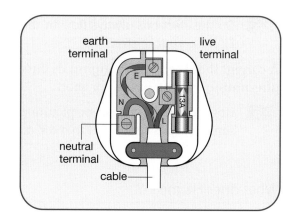

How should the wires be connected to the terminals?

The diagram shows how to connect a wire to its terminal.

2 Why do you remove some of the plastic insulation from a wire before you connect it?

3 Why do you remove only about 5 mm of insulation from each wire?

H Why does a plug have three pins?

The **live** and **neutral** pins of a plug carry the electric current to and from the mains supply. The voltage of the neutral pin is close to **zero**. The voltage of the live pin alternates between **positive** and **negative** compared to the neutral pin to drive the alternating current through the appliance.

The **earth** pin is there for safety. It is very important when using electrical equipment that has a metal case. It can help to stop you getting a shock if something goes wrong. This is explained on page 278.

4 The diagram of the **three-pin** plug shows a cable that has only two wires inside it.
Which terminals are these wires connected to?

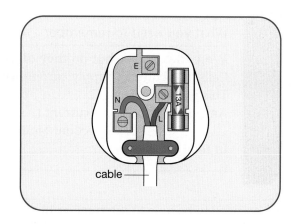

Why is the cable grip important?

The cable connected to a plug often gets pulled. The cable grip means that the whole of the cable takes the strain. Without a cable grip, the copper wires take the strain instead. These are not so strong and can easily break.

5 Copy the table. Then complete it to show what happens if one of the wires inside the plug breaks.

	Brown	Blue	Green and yellow
Will the appliance work?			
Is it safe?			

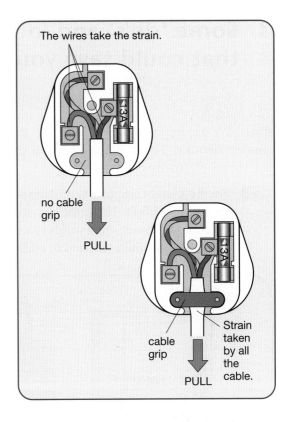

The wires take the strain.

no cable grip

PULL

cable grip

Strain taken by all the cable.

PULL

What's wrong?

The diagrams below show plugs that are unsafe.

6 For each diagram

- explain why the plug is unsafe
- explain what you can do to make it safe.

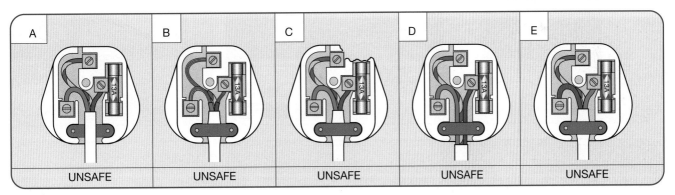

A	B	C	D	E
UNSAFE	UNSAFE	UNSAFE	UNSAFE	UNSAFE

What you need to remember *Copy and complete using the **key words***

Wiring a three-pin plug

Most electrical appliances are connected to the mains using cable and a _____ plug.

The current is supplied through the _____ and _____ pins. The neutral pin is at _____ potential with respect to earth. The live pin alternates between _____ and _____ potential with respect to the neutral pin.

The _____ pin is there for safety.

The colour code for the cable wires is: _____ – live, _____ – neutral, _____ and _____ – earth.

You need to be able to recognise errors in the wiring of a three-pin plug.

3 Some 'do's' and 'don'ts' that could save your life

You must have plugged things into the mains thousands of times. We use mains electricity a lot. So it's very easy to get careless about it. This is dangerous. You can be killed if you use mains electricity carelessly.

> **REMEMBER**
> - The mains supply is 230 volts. This is high enough to give a serious shock, which could be fatal. Higher voltages are even more likely to kill.
> - You will get a worse shock if your skin is wet.

1 An electricity company is making some safety posters for junior schools. The artist has already drawn the posters. She needs some words to finish them off. What words would you add to each of the posters?

NEVER   ALWAYS

PULL

PULL

NEVER

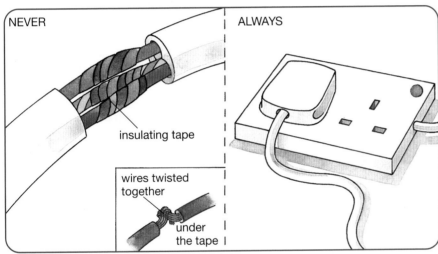

NEVER   ALWAYS

insulating tape

wires twisted together

under the tape

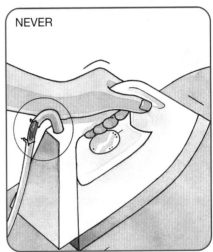

NEVER

2 Think of another thing that it is dangerous to do with mains electricity.
Make a safety poster about it.
Do a drawing, then add the words.

What you need to remember

Some 'do's' and 'don'ts' that could save your life
There is nothing new for you to <u>remember</u> in this section.

You need to be able to spot whenever mains electricity is being used dangerously.
You will find more examples on pages 267 and 275.

4 Why do plugs have fuses?

Why won't a plug work without a fuse?

Electricity won't pass through a plug unless it is fitted with a **fuse**. The diagram shows you why.

1 How does a current get from one end of a fuse to the other?

2 What <u>two</u> parts of a plug does the fuse connect?

3 A plug won't supply a current unless a fuse is fitted. Why not?

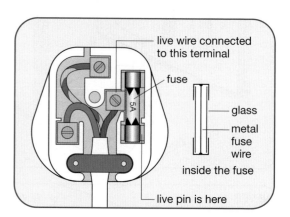

live wire connected to this terminal

fuse

glass

metal fuse wire

inside the fuse

live pin is here

What are fuses for?

Sometimes the current through a circuit becomes too big. The diagrams show why this can be dangerous.

4 Copy and complete the sentences.

If the current flowing through a cable gets too big, the wires get _____. This can make the plastic insulation give off poisonous _____. If the wire gets hot enough, the insulation might burst into _____.

Electrical appliances can also be damaged by a current that is too big. The fuse protects the appliance as well as people.

The fuse makes the circuit safer. The fuse cuts off the current if the current becomes too big.

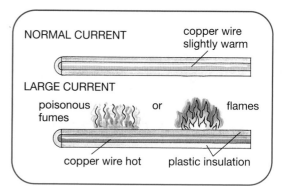

NORMAL CURRENT — copper wire slightly warm

LARGE CURRENT

poisonous fumes — or — flames

copper wire hot — plastic insulation

Making appliances with metal cases safe

If a fault makes the live wire of the mains supply touch the metal case of an appliance, you could get a bad shock.

To make appliances with metal cases safe, we earth them. The diagram shows what then happens if the live wire touches the **earthed** metal case of an **appliance**.

5 Explain, in as much detail as you can, why earthing the metal case of a mains appliance makes it safer.

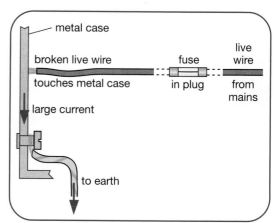

metal case

broken live wire touches metal case

fuse in plug

live wire from mains

large current

to earth

If a broken wire touches an earthed metal case, a large current flows to earth.
This current flows through the fuse.
More thermal energy is transferred by the fuse so it becomes hotter and melts. This disconnects the live wire from the metal case.

How does a fuse do its job?

The diagrams show how a fuse does its job.

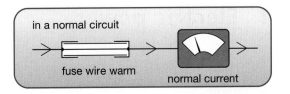

in a normal circuit

fuse wire warm   normal current

6 Copy the table. Then use the information from the diagrams to complete it.

Current to the fuse wire	What happens to the fuse wire
normal	_____ _____
much bigger than normal	_____ _____ and then _____

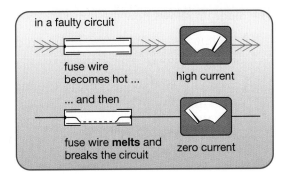

in a faulty circuit

fuse wire becomes hot ...   high current

... and then

fuse wire **melts** and breaks the circuit   zero current

7 Copy and complete the sentences.

If the fuse wire melts, it _____ the circuit.
There is then _____ current.

Circuit breakers

The circuits that carry mains electricity around your home are protected by fuses or circuit breakers in the distribution box. Modern systems always use circuit breakers.

Each **circuit breaker** contains a switch operated by an electromagnet. The switch turns off automatically if the current in the circuit is greater than a safe value. This protects appliances from damage and reduces the risk of fires and shocks.

8 Give <u>two</u> advantages of circuit breakers compared to fuses.

Circuit breakers in a household distribution box.

Plug-in circuit breaker.

> ### Circuit breakers
> The current at which a circuit breaker trips (turns off) can be set more precisely than the current at which a fuse wire melts. When the fault has been identified and repaired, the circuit breaker can be reset rather than replaced.

What you need to remember *Copy and complete using the **key words***

Why do plugs have fuses?
If an electrical fault causes too great a current, the circuit should be switched off by a
_____ or a _____ _____.
When the current exceeds a safe value the fuse _____, breaking the circuit.
Appliances with metal cases are usually _____.
The earth wire and fuse protect the _____ and the user.

1 Electric power

When a lamp lights up, it is transferring energy to its surroundings.

The diagram shows how the lamp is able to do this.

1 What is actually moving round a circuit when a current flows?

2 **a** What happens as an electric current flows through a resistance?

b Where does the energy that is transferred by a lamp filament come from?

The cell is a store of energy.

The lamp filament has a resistance. So when a current is pushed through it gets hot. Energy is transferred to the surroundings as **heat** (thermal energy) and light.

flow of negatively charged electrons

How fast is energy transferred?

The wattage, or **power**, of an electrical appliance tells you how fast it transfers energy. Power is measured in watts (**W**) or in kilowatts (**kW**). 1 kW = 1000 W.

3 How fast does a 100-watt lamp transfer energy?

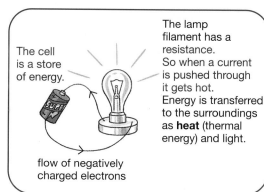

A 60-watt lamp transfers 60 joules of energy per second.

Lift power

The diagram shows two different lifts. Both lifts need the same amount of energy to reach the same height, but the electric motors in the lifts do not supply this energy at the same rate. How fast a motor transfers energy is its power.

4 Which electric motor will have to supply energy faster?

5 Which electric motor will have to be the more powerful?

6 The standard lift has a 5 kW motor. The express lift rises the same height in half the time. How powerful must the electric motor of the express lift be?

The 'standard' lift moves slowly.

The 'express' lift moves faster. It transfers energy more quickly.

How much power?

Power measures the rate (how fast) energy is transferred, so you can work out power like this:

$$\text{power (watts)} = \frac{\text{energy transferred (joules)}}{\text{time taken (seconds)}}$$

So 1 watt is 1 joule of energy transferred every second.

watts (W) = joules per second (J/s)

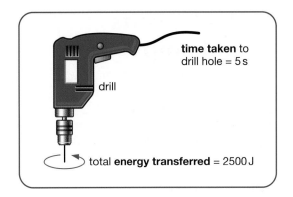

time taken to drill hole = 5 s

drill

total energy transferred = 2500 J

7 Look at the diagram of the drill.
How many joules of electrical energy does the drill transfer each second?

8 What is the drill's power?

How much energy?

You can rearrange the power formula to find out how much energy an electric lamp or kettle uses in a certain time.

Energy transferred = power × time

Look at the diagrams.

9 How much energy has the lamp transferred?

10 How much energy has the kettle transferred?
(Remember that 1 kW = 1000 W.)

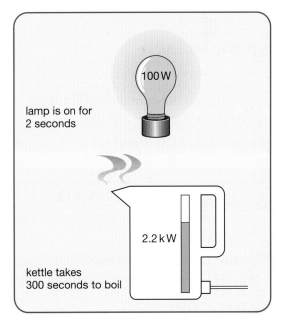

100 W

lamp is on for 2 seconds

2.2 kW

kettle takes 300 seconds to boil

What you need to remember *Copy and complete using the key words*

Electric power
When a current flows through a resistor, electrical energy is transformed into _____ energy.
The rate at which energy is transformed in a device is called the _____.
Power is measured in watts (_____) or in kilowatts (_____).

$$\text{power (watts)} = \frac{\text{_____ _____ (joules)}}{\text{_____ _____ (seconds)}}$$

2 Watts, volts and amps

The voltage of an appliance is the potential difference (p.d.) you should use to make it work. The p.d. makes electrical charge flow through the appliance. The moving charge transfers energy.

1 Copy and complete the sentences.

A _____ voltage supply gives more
_____ to each unit of charge that flows.
If _____ current flows, more energy is
transferred each _____. This means the
_____ is greater.

A power formula

The power of an appliance depends on the potential difference <u>and</u> the current. You can work out the power of an electrical appliance like this:

power = potential difference (p.d.) × **current**
(watts)   (volts)   (amperes)

EXAMPLE

The current through a 230 V fluorescent lamp is 0.1 A. What is the power of the lamp?

power = potential difference (p.d.) × current
(watts)   (volts)   (amps)

power = 230 V × 0.1 A
     = 23 W

2 Look at the diagrams of electrical appliances. Fill in the gaps and work out the missing figures.

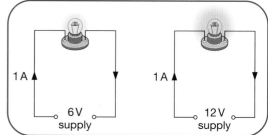

These torch bulbs are designed for different voltages. The current through both bulbs is the same (1 A). But the higher voltage bulb is brighter. A 12 V p.d. gives more energy to the charge that flows than a 6 V p.d. does.

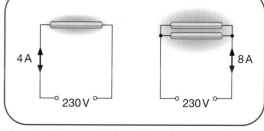

These heaters are designed for the same voltage (23 V). But one heater produces twice the power of the other. More current flows through the more powerful heater, so it transfers more energy each second.

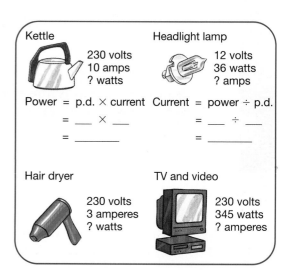

Kettle
230 volts
10 amps
? watts

Headlight lamp
12 volts
36 watts
? amps

Power = p.d. × current   Current = power ÷ p.d.

= ___ × ___   = ___ ÷ ___

= _____   = _____

Hair dryer
230 volts
3 amperes
? watts

TV and video
230 volts
345 watts
? amperes

What size of fuse should I use?

Fuses protect appliances and the people who use them. If the current becomes too high, the fuse wire melts and breaks the circuit (see page 279). The largest current a fuse can carry is called its current rating.

The picture shows the three most common types of fuse in three-pin plugs. These have different current ratings.

> **3** What colour is a 13 A fuse?

> **4** Which type of fuse would you use for the hair dryer in the photo?
> Explain why the two other types of fuse would not be right.

The correct type of fuse will already be fitted in the plug when you buy an appliance. If you need to replace a fuse, you should use one of the same type.

Fuse calculations

If you know the voltage and power of an appliance you can calculate the normal current with the formula

current = power ÷ potential difference (p.d.)
(amps)   (watts)   (volts)

You can use this current value to select the right fuse. You should use the fuse with the <u>lowest</u> current rating that is <u>greater</u> than the normal current.

> **5** Select a fuse for each of the appliances shown below.

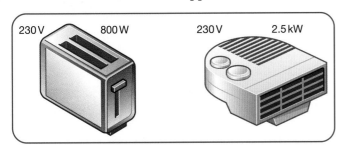

230 V   800 W   230 V   2.5 kW

A 3 A fuse will melt if a current of more than 3 A passes through it.

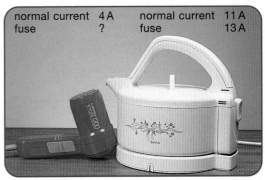

| normal current fuse | 4 A ? | normal current fuse | 11 A 13 A |

The fuse must not melt with the normal current. It must melt if the current is bigger than normal.

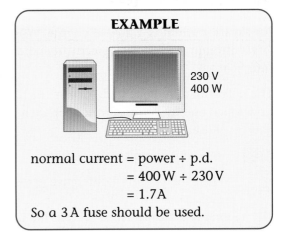

EXAMPLE

230 V
400 W

normal current = power ÷ p.d.
$$= 400\,W \div 230\,V$$
$$= 1.7\,A$$
So a 3 A fuse should be used.

What you need to remember *Copy and complete using the **key words***

Watts, volts and amps
Power, potential difference and current are related by the formula

_____ = _____ _____ (p.d.) × _____
(watts)   (volts)   (amperes)

You need to be able to calculate the current through an appliance from its power and the potential difference of the supply and from this determine the size of fuse needed.

3 Understanding electrical energy

What is a coulomb?

The amount of charge that flows while an electric current is switched on depends on the size of the current and how long it is on. We measure charge in units called coulombs (C, for short).

1 How much charge passes through a wire when

    a a current of <u>one</u> amp flows for <u>one</u> second?
    b a current of <u>two</u> amps flows for <u>two</u> seconds?

You can find the amount of charge with the formula

    charge   =   **current**   ×   **time**
(coulombs, C) (amperes, A) (seconds, s)

2 Work out the charge that flows when a current of 0.8 A is switched on for 60 seconds.

What exactly is a volt?

An electric current is a flow of charge. When the charge flows through a resistance, electrical energy is transformed into heat.

The potential difference (p.d.) across the resistance tells you how much energy is transformed for each coulomb of charge that flows.

3 Copy and complete the sentence.

    When the potential difference across a resistor is

    _____ V, _____ joule of

    energy is transformed to heat for _____
    coulomb of charge that flows.

4 A cell applies a p.d. of 2 V to a lamp. Two coulombs of charge flow through the lamp. How much energy is transformed to heat and light?

You can find the energy transformed with the formula

energy transformed = potential difference × charge
    (joules, J)   (volts, V)   (coulombs, C)

> **REMEMBER**
> ■ Electric current is the rate of flow of electrical charge.
> ■ The size of a current is measured in amps.

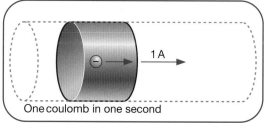

One coulomb in one second

One coulomb is the amount of charge that passes through a wire when a current of one ampere flows for one second.

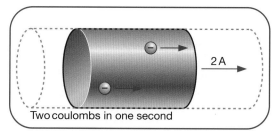

Two coulombs in one second

If the current is two amps then two coulombs of charge pass through the wire each second.

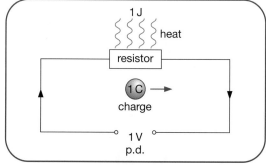

One volt is the potential difference that causes the transfer of one joule of energy for each coulomb of charge that flows.

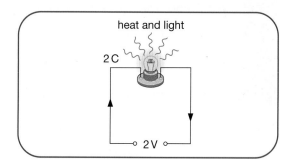

How much energy can a battery supply?

The rechargeable cells in the picture are marked 2000 mA h. This means that, when fully charged, one cell can supply a current of 2000 mA (2 A) for 1 hour. The cell will then be discharged.

REMEMBER

The amount of charge that flows is given by

charge = current × time

The amount of energy transformed when a charge flows is given by

energy transformed = potential difference × charge

1000 mA = 1 A

5 Use the formula
charge = current × time
to work out the amount of charge that one of the cells can make flow.
(Remember 1 hour = 3600 seconds.)

6 The cell voltage is 1.2 V. Use the formula
energy transformed = p.d. × charge
to work out the amount of energy the cell transfers.

7 The 12 V motorcycle battery has a capacity of 10 A h.

a How much charge can the battery make flow?
b How much energy does the battery store when fully charged?

Using your knowledge

8 For each of these calculations, start with the formula you are using. Show all your working.

a Calculate the energy transferred when a potential difference of 12 V is used to make 500 C of charge flow.
b Calculate the potential difference used if the flow of 240 C of charge transfers 9600 J of energy.

9 Use the formulae you have studied on these pages to explain why the power of an electrical appliance (in watts) is given by the formula

power = potential difference (p.d.) × current

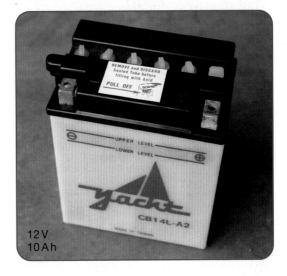

12 V
10 A h

What you need to remember *Copy and complete using the **key words***

Understanding electrical energy
Energy transformed, potential difference and charge are related by the formula
energy transformed = _____ _____ × _____
The amount of electrical charge that flows is related to current and time by the formula
charge = _____ × _____

1 Inside atoms

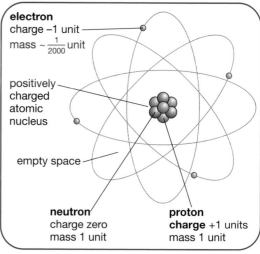

electron
charge −1 unit
mass ~ $\frac{1}{2000}$ unit

positively charged atomic nucleus

empty space

neutron
charge zero
mass 1 unit

proton
charge +1 units
mass 1 unit

The diagram shows one way we picture an atom today.

The numbers of **electrons** and **protons** in an atom are equal. Their charges balance so the atom is electrically neutral.

1 Copy and complete the sentences.

There are three kinds of particle in the atom:
_____, _____ and
_____.
An electron has a _____ charge, a proton has a _____ charge and a neutron has no charge.
The protons and neutrons are in the atomic _____. The nucleus has a _____ charge because of the protons.
The _____ move around the nucleus.
Most of the atom is _____ space.
The whole atom is neutral because it contains _____ numbers of protons and electrons.

2 Copy and complete the table with the masses and charges of the particles that make up atoms.

Particle	Relative mass (mass units)	Relative charge (charge units)
proton	_____	_____
neutron	_____	_____
electron	_____	_____

H An old picture of the atom

The scientist J.J. Thomson discovered the electron in 1897. It was the first particle smaller than a whole atom to be found. Thomson suggested that an atom is like a 'plum pudding'. The negative electrons were like plums or currants inside a soft 'pudding' of positive charge.

3 How did Thomson know that part of the atom must have a positive charge?

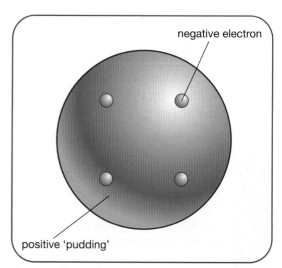

negative electron

positive 'pudding'

Thomson knew that atoms were neutral. His experiments showed that electrons were smaller than whole atoms and had a negative charge – so something else in the atom must be positive.

Rutherford and Marsden's experiment

In 1909, Rutherford, Geiger and Marsden tested Thomson's plum pudding idea. They directed alpha particles from a radioactive source at a very thin sheet of gold.

4 What two observations showed that the plum pudding model was wrong?

The observations led Rutherford to suggest a new model for the atom.

5 Where is the positive charge in Rutherford's atom?

6 Where is most of the mass?

7 Where are the electrons?

The nuclear atom

The diagram shows how Rutherford's nuclear atom was able to explain the experimental observations.

8 Why do most alpha particles pass straight through?

9 What causes some alpha particles to be deflected by large angles?

10 Why do only a few alpha particles bounce back?

> **REMEMBER**
>
> An alpha particle is the nucleus of a helium atom. It contains two protons and two neutrons. Its charge is +2 charge units.

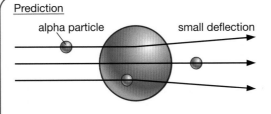

Prediction — alpha particle — small deflection

If the plum pudding model was correct, all the alpha particles should have gone straight, or almost straight, through the soft pudding, like cricket balls through tissue paper.

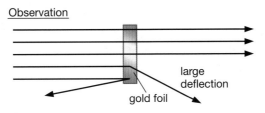

Observation — gold foil — large deflection

But Rutherford and Marsden observed that, although most alpha particles went through, some were deflected by large angles and a few bounced back.

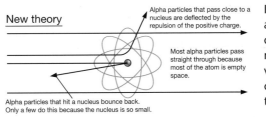

New theory — Alpha particles that pass close to a nucleus are deflected by the repulsion of the positive charge. Most alpha particles pass straight through because most of the atom is empty space. Alpha particles that hit a nucleus bounce back. Only a few do this because the nucleus is so small.

In Rutherford's nuclear atom, all the positive charge and most of the mass is concentrated in a very small nucleus at the centre. The electrons orbit the nucleus.

What you need to remember *Copy and complete using the key words*

Inside atoms

In an atom the number of _____ is equal to the number of _____ in the nucleus. The atom has no net electrical _____.

The relative masses and electrical charges of protons, neutrons and electrons are:

Particle	Relative mass (mass units)	Relative charge (charge units)
_____	1	+1
_____	1	0
_____	1/2000	−1

You need to be able to explain how the Rutherford and Marsden scattering experiment led to the 'plum pudding' model of the atom being replaced by the nuclear model.

2 Can atoms change?

Scientists once thought that atoms were indestructible and could not change. We now know that atoms can change in several ways. To understand how, we must first look at what makes one atom different from another.

Different types of atom

The symbols tell you everything you need to know about a helium atom and a uranium atom.

1   Copy and complete the sentences.

The helium atom has two _____.
So it must have two _____.
The helium atom has a mass number of

_____.

So it must contain two _____ in its nucleus.

All atoms of the same element have the same number of **protons**. Atoms of different **elements** have different proton numbers.

2   What is the proton number of uranium?

3   How many neutrons does the nucleus of this uranium atom contain?

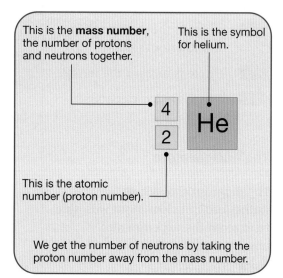

This is the **mass number**, the number of protons and neutrons together.

This is the symbol for helium.

This is the atomic number (proton number).

We get the number of neutrons by taking the proton number away from the mass number.

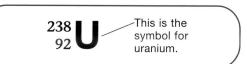

$^{238}_{92}U$ This is the symbol for uranium.

What are isotopes?

All carbon atoms contain 6 protons, so they have a proton number of 6.

Carbon atoms can have different numbers of neutrons. This gives the atoms different masses. Atoms of the same element that have different numbers of neutrons are called **isotopes**.

4   Copy and complete the table. The first row has been filled in for you.

Mass number of carbon isotope	Number of protons	Number of neutrons
12	6	6

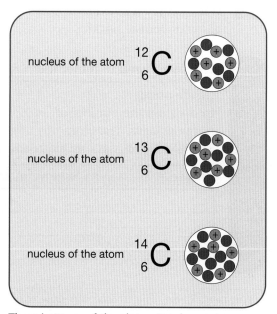

Three isotopes of the element carbon.

How does ionisation change atoms?

Atoms have equal numbers of positive and negative charges. This means that they are neutral. One way atoms can change is by gaining or losing electrons. They then become **ions**.

> **5** A neutral atom gains an extra electron. Is the ion formed positive or negative?

> **6** Explain why an atom that loses an electron becomes a <u>positive</u> ion.

How does radioactive decay change nuclei?

Some atoms have an unstable nucleus. Sooner or later, an unstable nucleus will emit radiation. We say that it <u>decays</u>. If it emits an alpha particle or a beta particle, an atom of a different element is produced.

> **7** In an alpha decay what happens to
>
> **a** the proton number?
> **b** the mass number?

> **8** In a beta decay, what happens to
>
> **a** the proton number?
> **b** the mass number?

> **9** A $^{222}_{86}$Rn nucleus undergoes radioactive decay.
>
> A $^{218}_{84}$Po nucleus is produced. What type of radiation was emitted? Explain your answer.

> **10** The $^{214}_{83}$Bi nucleus emits a beta particle. What is the mass number and the proton number of the element produced? What element is this?
> (Hint: look at question 9.)

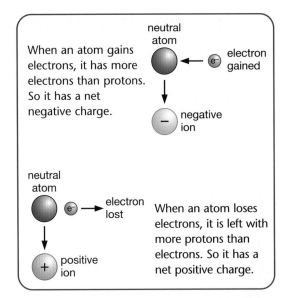

When an atom gains electrons, it has more electrons than protons. So it has a net negative charge.

When an atom loses electrons, it is left with more protons than electrons. So it has a net positive charge.

An alpha particle contains two protons and two neutrons. So when a radioactive nucleus emits an alpha particle its proton number decreases by <u>2</u> and its mass number decreases by <u>4</u>.

A beta particle is an electron emitted from a radioactive nucleus. The beta particle appears when a neutron changes into a proton. So, in a beta decay, the proton number increases by <u>1</u> but the mass number <u>stays the same</u>.

What you need to remember *Copy and complete using the **key words***

Can atoms change?

All atoms of a particular element have the same number of _____.

Atoms of different _____ have different numbers of protons.

Atoms of the same element which have different numbers of neutrons are called

_____.

The total number of protons and neutrons in an atom is called its _____

_____.

Atoms may lose or gain electrons to form charged particles called _____.

You need to know the effects of alpha and beta decay on radioactive nuclei.

3 How much harmful radiation do you get?

X-Rays and the radiation from radioactive substances can definitely cause cancer anywhere in our bodies. So we should avoid these types of radiation if we can.

What amount of radiation is safe?

The amount of radiation your body gets is called your radiation dose. The graph shows how the risk of **cancer** depends on the size of your radiation dose.

1 Copy and complete the sentences.

The bigger the dose of radiation your body gets, the _____ the risk of cancer.

The graph suggests that there is some risk of cancer even with a very _____ radiation dose.

Unfortunately, we're surrounded by harmful radiation. So we can't avoid it all.

Radiation that we can't avoid

We are bombarded with radiation from space, called **cosmic** radiation. There are also **radioactive** substances all around us and even inside the cells our bodies are made from. So our bodies receive radiation all the time, which we call **background** radiation.

2 The boxes on this page and the maps on the next page show the main sources of background radiation.

Copy the table. Then fill in the figures for each source of the background radiation that your body gets.

Source of background radiation	Annual radiation dose (units)
cosmic rays	
buildings	
food and drink	
the ground	
the air	
Total	

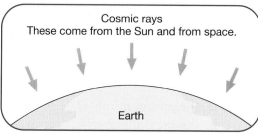

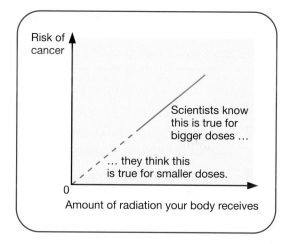

We all get 250 units of cosmic radiation each year. You get one unit more for every 30 m you live above the sea.

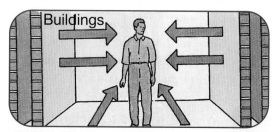

There are radioactive substances in stone, brick and concrete. This gives you about 350 units of radiation a year.

Food and drink

Radioactive substances dissolve. They get in plants, animals that eat the plants and into water. This gives you about 300 units of radiation each year.

Radiation from nuclear power stations

If you live within a mile of a nuclear power station, you should add an extra 5 units a year to your radiation dose.

This is much less than many people think.

Radiation that depends on what you do

The table shows the main sources of any extra radiation which people may receive.

Other sources of radiation	Dose
dental X-ray	20 units each time
chest/leg/arm X-ray	50 units each time
flying	4 units per hour

3   **a** Write down any of these sources that you think have affected you during the past year.

   b Add your radiation dose from these sources to your total from background radiation.

Scientists think that the average annual radiation dose in Britain is reasonably safe.

4   **a** What is the average annual radiation dose in Britain?

   b How does your own annual dose compare with the average?

5   Some people get a bigger radiation dose because of their job.

Write down <u>two</u> jobs that give people a bigger radiation dose.

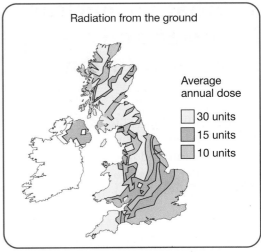

Radiation from the ground

Average annual dose

- 30 units
- 15 units
- 10 units

The soil and rocks beneath your feet contain radioactive substances. How much radiation you get depends on where you live.

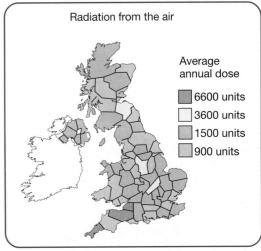

Radiation from the air

Average annual dose

- 6600 units
- 3600 units
- 1500 units
- 900 units

Radioactive radon gas seeps into the air from the ground. The figures in some areas are <u>very</u> high (up to 100 000 units a year).

> The average radiation dose in Britain is about 2500 units each year.

What you need to remember *Copy and complete using the **key words***

How much harmful radiation do you get?

The bigger the dose of radiation you get, the greater the risk of _____.

Our bodies receive radiation all the time from _____ substances in the air, the ground, food, water and building materials.

Our bodies also receive _____ radiation from space.

All this radiation is called _____ radiation.

1 What are nuclear fission and nuclear fusion?

When atomic nuclei change, large amounts of energy may be released. Nuclear **fission** and nuclear **fusion** are two different kinds of nuclear reaction that release **energy**.

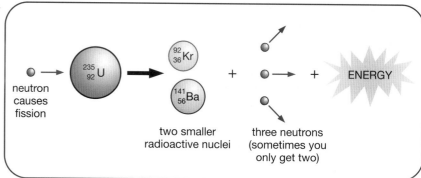

A fission reaction.

Nuclear fission

In nuclear fission, a large atomic nucleus **splits** into **smaller** parts.

1 What particle causes the fission of a $^{235}_{92}$U nucleus?

2 List <u>four</u> different products of the fission reaction.

Chain reaction

The fission of one $^{235}_{92}$U nucleus releases two or three **neutrons**. Each **neutron** may cause another uranium nucleus to split, releasing more neutrons and more energy. The diagram shows how a **chain reaction** may build up if every uranium nucleus releases two neutrons.

3 What is the result of a chain reaction if it is not controlled?

4 Why does dividing the uranium into small pieces prevent an explosion?

In a large sample of $^{235}_{92}$U, the chain reaction can grow so fast that a nuclear explosion happens. The reaction can be controlled by keeping the uranium in small pieces. Neutrons can escape from the surface of the pieces without causing fission. Rods of boron placed between the pieces absorb these neutrons.

Nuclear reactor

In a nuclear reactor, the fuel may be **uranium-235** or **plutonium-239**. The nuclei of these atoms release energy by nuclear fission.

5 How is the nuclear reaction in a reactor controlled?

6 How is the energy released in the reactor used?

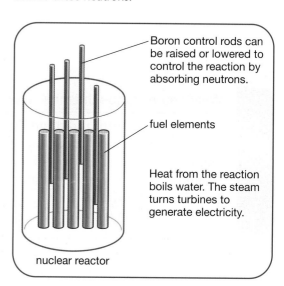

Boron control rods can be raised or lowered to control the reaction by absorbing neutrons.

fuel elements

Heat from the reaction boils water. The steam turns turbines to generate electricity.

nuclear reactor

Nuclear fusion

In nuclear fusion, two small atomic nuclei join together to make a larger one. Energy is released by the reaction.

7 What particles are present in the nucleus of hydrogen-2?

8 List three products of a fusion reaction between two hydrogen-2 nuclei.

Where does the Sun's energy come from?

A series of nuclear fusion reactions that turn hydrogen gas into helium gas makes the **stars** shine. Vast amounts of heat and light are produced.

9 Why don't hydrogen atoms fuse to become helium atoms on Earth?

10 Why won't the Sun keep shining for ever?

11 For how much longer do scientists think the Sun will continue to shine?

Fusion has powered our Sun for about 5 billion years. Its hydrogen fuel will be used up in about another 5 billion years.

A hydrogen-2 nucleus contains one proton and one neutron.
A helium-3 nucleus contains two protons and one neutron.

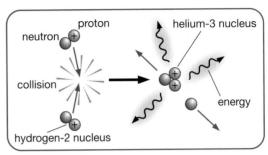

A fusion reaction.

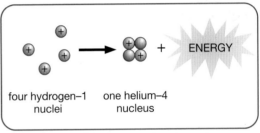

This is the overall fusion reaction that releases energy in a star. The reaction happens in stages. It needs very high temperatures for the reaction to take place.

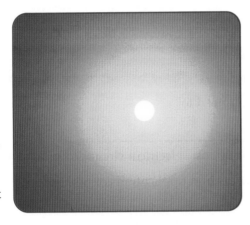

What you need to remember *Copy and complete using the **key words***

What are nuclear fission and nuclear fusion?

Nuclear _____ is the splitting of an atomic nucleus.

Fission may be caused by a _____ entering a nucleus of uranium or plutonium.

The nucleus undergoing fission _____ into two _____ nuclei and

two or three _____, and _____ is released.

The neutrons may go on to start a _____ _____.

_____ and _____ are fuels used in nuclear reactors.

Nuclear _____ is the joining of two atomic nuclei to form a larger one.

Nuclear fusion is the process by which energy is released in _____.

You need to be able to sketch a labelled diagram to illustrate how a chain reaction may occur.

How science works

■ Introduction

Throughout this book, you will have come across examples of how science works.

Scientists

- try to explain the world around us
- gather evidence to try to solve problems
- argue about the reliability and validity of evidence
- make discoveries that lead to technologies that are important for society and for the environment.

You can identify which spreads are concerned with **How science works** by looking at the **What you need to remember** boxes.

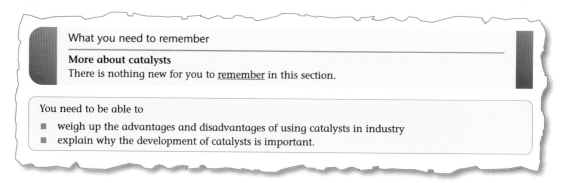

What you need to remember

More about catalysts
There is nothing new for you to <u>remember</u> in this section.

You need to be able to

- weigh up the advantages and disadvantages of using catalysts in industry
- explain why the development of catalysts is important.

Here are some examples of the sorts of issues you need to think about.

- You need to be able to <u>apply</u> the principles of basic electrical circuits to practical situations.

- You need to be able to <u>evaluate</u> developments and applications of new materials, e.g. nanomaterials, smart materials.

- You need to be able to <u>evaluate</u> modern methods of treating diabetes.

- You need to be able to <u>use</u> the idea of momentum to explain safety features.

- You need to be able to <u>explain</u> how the Rutherford and Marsden scattering experiment led to the 'plum pudding' model of the atom being replaced by the nuclear model.

- You need to be able to <u>interpret</u> information about cloning and consider social, economic and ethical issues concerning cloning.

You can learn the skills of dealing with these sorts of issues.

The following pages draw together some of the skills that you will need for your work in class, for tests and examinations and for the centre-assessed unit.

The centre-assessed unit

As part of your normal work in class, you will be asked to

- carry out practical activities on a particular topic
- use the data you collect in a written test taken under examination conditions.

Gathering evidence – observing

Careful observation is a key part of good science. Observing doesn't just mean looking. It can involve all your senses.

You observe similarities and differences when you classify objects, organisms or materials. To do this, you need to be able to recognise which observations are useful for your purpose and which are not. For example, classifying flowers according to the arrangement of petals may be useful. Classifying according to colour isn't.

Observing patterns can lead to investigations. For example, noticing the differences in the rate at which your bread dough rose could lead to a hypothesis or idea that might explain the differences. The next step is to make a testable prediction and to carry out an investigation. The data gathered may or may not support the hypothesis. It may show the need for a new hypothesis.

> Observations of an object, a living thing or something that happens.
>
> ↓
>
> Questions
>
> ↓
>
> Investigations to try to answer these questions, including making
> - further observations
> - measurements
> - experiments.

Designing an investigation

Suppose you were investigating the effect of temperature on the rise of bread dough.

You could do this by making a batch of dough and observing samples kept at different temperatures.

Your investigation must be a <u>fair test</u>. So you need to keep everything but the temperature the same. You need to use

- samples from the same batch of dough
- the same type and size of container
- the same conditions, such as light and humidity.

If your investigation takes the form of a survey, you have to think about a suitable sample size. You may need to consider surveying a group with similar characteristics to make your test fair. You may need a control group. For example, when they trial a new treatment for diabetes, doctors use control groups with similar characteristics who take the 'old treatment'.

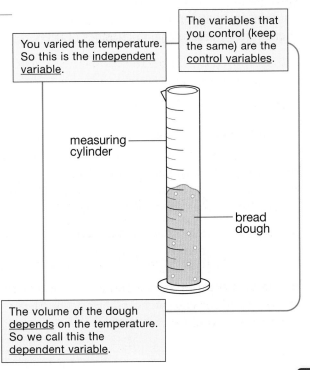

You varied the temperature. So this is the <u>independent variable</u>.

The variables that you control (keep the same) are the <u>control variables</u>.

measuring cylinder

bread dough

The volume of the dough <u>depends</u> on the temperature. So we call this the <u>dependent variable</u>.

■ Gathering evidence – measuring

We use our senses to observe differences between objects and organisms and to observe changes. However, we can support our observations and increase the accuracy of the information we gather by measuring – but only if we measure accurately.

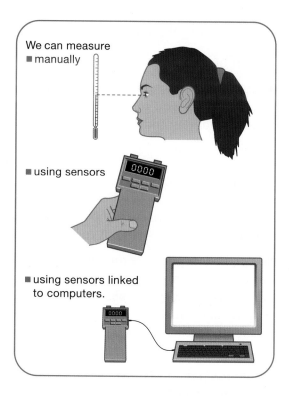

We can measure
■ manually

■ using sensors

■ using sensors linked to computers.

■ Choosing a measuring instrument

The <u>sensitivity</u> of an instrument is the smallest change in a property or value that the instrument detects. You must choose a measuring instrument that is sensitive enough to detect the change you wish to measure. An ordinary room thermometer, for example, is sensitive to temperature changes of about 1 °C. This is not sensitive enough to detect changes in body temperature when you are ill. A clinical thermometer is sensitive to changes of 0.1 °C.

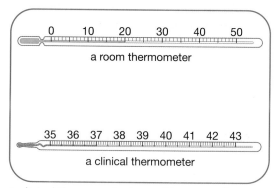

a room thermometer

a clinical thermometer

A clinical thermometer is sensitive to smaller temperature changes than a room thermometer.

■ Errors in measurement

When we measure a quantity, there is always some degree of error or uncertainty. Errors may be due to limitations of the measuring instrument, difficulties in making the measurement, or the different ways experimenters use the instrument. Some causes of errors are

■ zero error (the pointer does not read exactly zero when no measurement is being made)
■ calibration error (the instrument is wrongly adjusted)
■ parallax error (from reading a scale at an angle).

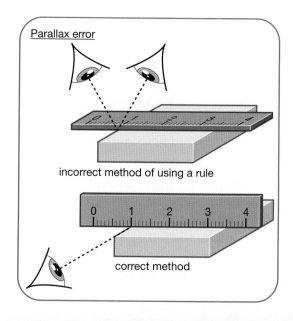

Parallax error

incorrect method of using a rule

correct method

■ Validity of data

When you are planning an investigation, you need to think about whether the data you collect or the measurements you make are going to give you the information that you need. For example, if you want to find out how acidic the rainwater is in your area, you might collect rainwater from puddles or draining from roofs and measure the pH. But dirt and living things can affect pH. So, for your results to be valid, you need to collect the rain in clean containers as it falls.

■ Reliability

The way that you make your measurements affects their reliability. If you and others can obtain the same results in repeats of the experiment, then your results are reliable.

Things that affect reliability include

- the type of instrument you select and use
- whether the instrument was accurate
- whether it was set up correctly
- who took the measurements
- whether or not measurements were repeated to obtain mean values.

Sophie measures the length of a bench with a cheap plastic tape measure. She can read the tape to the nearest millimetre, so her measurement is <u>precise</u>. But the tape has stretched so her result is <u>not accurate</u>.

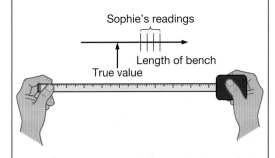

The readings are close together but the mean is not the true value.

Mohan is measuring the bench with a wooden rule which only has centimetre divisions. He must estimate the readings between the divisions. His rule is not as <u>precise</u> as Sophie's tape, but is more <u>accurate</u> because it has not stretched.

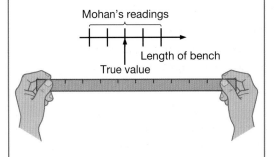

The readings vary, but the mean is close to the true value.

Presenting data

You will often be asked to record data in a table as you carry out an investigation. Then, you may need to present this data in a way that allows you to pick out any patterns most easily.

So, in your coursework and in tests and examinations, you will need to be able to

- design tables for your results and complete them accurately
- present data in several different ways, for example as bar charts and line graphs
- choose the best way of presenting data for different types of datasets.

The best way to present your data depends on the types of variables you are dealing with.

Types of variables

- Independent variable. This is a variable that you decide to alter. In the example on page 295, we varied the temperature.

- Dependent variable. This is the variable that you measure. In this example investigation, we measured and recorded the volume of the dough.

- In this example, both variables are continuous, so you could choose a line graph.

- The independent variable goes on the x-axis.

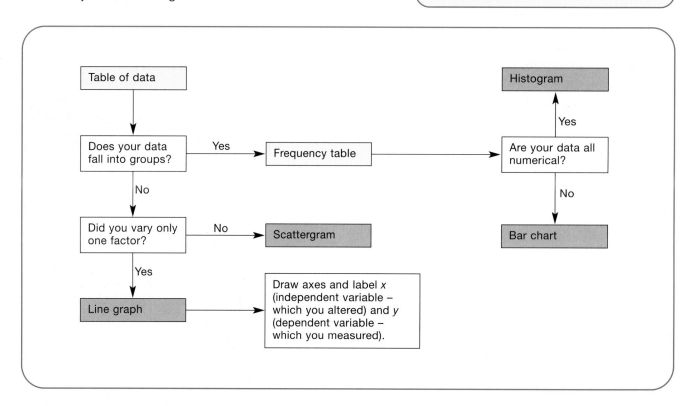

■ Drawing bar charts

You may be asked to draw a bar chart.

As with line graphs, choose sensible scales that allow you to use at least half the page, and label the axes.

Remember

- to look carefully at the scale
- to draw the bars the same thickness and equally spaced out
- to draw the top of each bar with a thin straight line
- to label each bar, or draw a key like this:

resting	
after exercise	

The bar chart shows a person's heart rate before and after exercise.

You may be asked to compare the bars on a bar chart.

You could say that the heart rate is faster after exercise.

A better answer is to say that the heart rate is twice as fast after exercise.

Continuous and categoric variables

Suppose you were investigating the effect of exercise on heart rate.
You could

- investigate the change in heart rate as the exercise rate increased. Both of these variables are continuous so you should present the data as a line graph.
- investigate the heart rate at rest and after 5 minutes of exercise. You then have only two sets or categories of data.
This is a categoric variable.

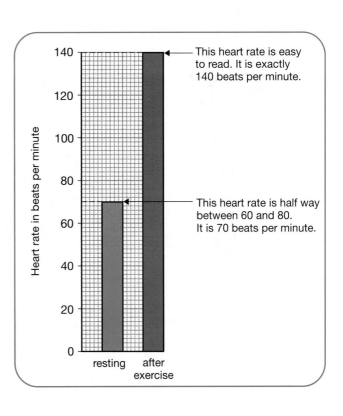

■ Drawing line graphs

- ■ Choose sensible scales for the axes. (You should use more than half of the available squares along each axis.)
- ■ Label the axes (for example, *Time taken for completion of reaction in minutes*).
- ■ Mark all the points neatly and accurately …

… like this   … or like this

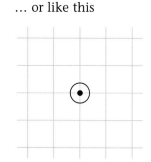

- ■ Use a pencil to draw your line so you can rub it out if you don't get it right first time.

■

If …	Then …
… the points are close to being a straight line or a smooth curve …	… draw the 'best fit' straight line or smooth curve. If there is a point that is obviously wrong, ignore it. Indicate that you did so.
… the theory suggests that the change is smooth …	
… the points are <u>not</u> close to being a straight line or a smooth curve …	… rule short, straight lines between the points. (You would not usually do this in physics, where most of the changes you investigate <u>are</u> smooth.)
… the theory suggests that the change is <u>not</u> smooth …	

■ Anomalous results

If one measurement does not fit the pattern of the others (for example, it is a long way from a straight line on which all the other points lie), this measurement must be checked. If you can show that there was a mistake or a large error in making the measurement, then it can be ignored.
You should make a note on the graph to explain why the point was ignored. If no mistake can be found then the anomalous result should be investigated further – it could be a new discovery!

> **REMEMBER**
>
> You choose a line graph when both variables are <u>continuous</u>.

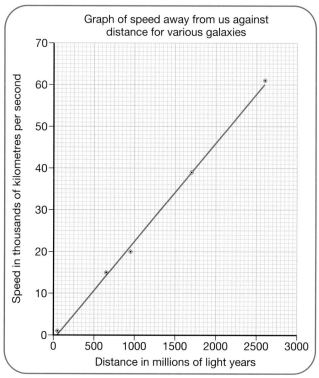

The theory suggests that the change is smooth and the points are close to being in a straight line, so a best fit straight line is drawn through them.

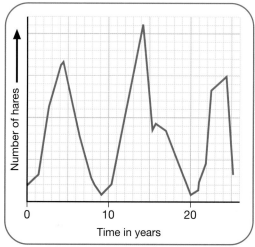

The theory indicates that there are population cycles for hares so the change is not smooth.

■ Interpreting line graphs

When you are reading off values from a graph make sure you do the following.

■ Check the scales on the axes so that you know what each small square on the grid represents.

■ Remember to quote units in your answer. (You can find these on the axis where you read off your answer. You can still quote the correct units even if you don't understand what they mean!)

■ Be as precise and accurate as you can

– when describing trends or patterns (in the example, both reactions are fastest at the start, gradually slow down and eventually stop)

– when specifying key points (in the example, saying that both reactions are complete when 4 g of carbon dioxide have been produced is better than saying that both methods produce the same amount of carbon dioxide)

– when making comparisons (in the example, saying that the reaction is complete after 80 seconds with the small pieces and after 120 seconds with the larger pieces is better than simply saying that the reaction stops sooner with the smaller pieces).

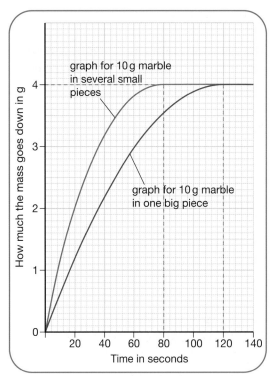

The graphs show the results of an experiment on rates of reaction. Marble reacts with acid and releases carbon dioxide gas. You can measure the rate of reaction by weighing. Carbon dioxide escapes into the air during the reaction, so the mass of what is left goes down.

■ The presentation of units

You will find that the books in this series usually use brackets in the presentation of units within tables and on graph axes. For example, the volume of gas produced at 30 second intervals during a reaction wil be represented in this way:

Time (seconds)	Total volume of gas produced (cm^3)
0	0
30	6

AQA examination papers will usually use the following convention:

Time in seconds	Total volume of gas produced in cm^3
0	0
30	6

In real life, when you see scientific information in tables or graphs either of these ways of presenting information might be used. The important thing is that they mean the same thing.

■ Pie charts

The pie chart shows the average amount of radiation that gets into your body from different sources.

You may be asked to <u>compare</u> the amount of radiation we receive from artificial and from natural sources.

You could say that we receive <u>more</u> radiation from natural than from artificial sources.

A better answer is to say that we receive <u>nearly six times as much</u> radiation from natural sources as we do from artificial sources.

You may be asked to read the data from a pie chart and put it into a table like this.

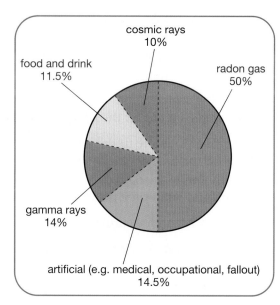

Natural	radon gas	50%
	gamma rays	14%
	food and drink	11.5%
	cosmic rays	10%
Artificial	e.g. medical, occupational, fallout	14.5%

You may be asked to complete a pie chart.

Draw thin, straight lines. Remember to add all the labels, or provide a key.

■ Sankey diagrams

What happens to the energy? The diagram shows what happens to each 100 J of energy in the food a young rabbit eats.

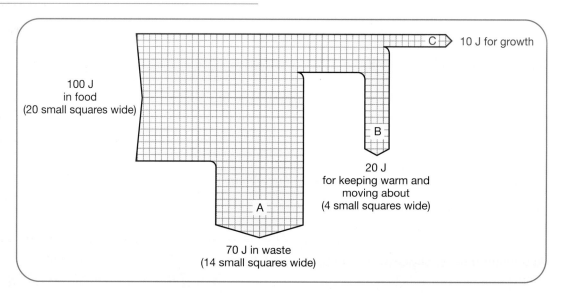

Get plenty of practice handling data in these ways so that you'll

- do well in your coursework
- do the right thing even if you're nervous in an examination.

REMEMBER

A + B + C = energy in the food

70 J + 20 J + 10 J = 100 J (the same as the food)

■ Identifying patterns in data

When you draw conclusions, you are not just describing the data, but looking for patterns. Your conclusions must be limited by the data available.

You have already seen that presenting data in suitable graphs and charts can help you to identify patterns.

Line graphs often show whether or not there is a correlation or link between two factors.

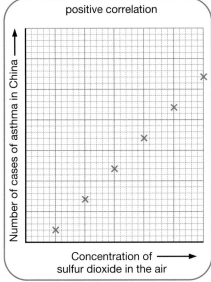

positive correlation

Number of cases of asthma in China →

Concentration of → sulfur dioxide in the air

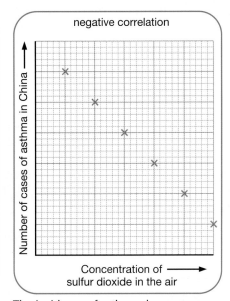

negative correlation

Number of cases of asthma in China →

Concentration of → sulfur dioxide in the air

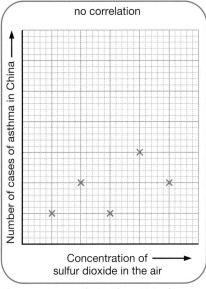

no correlation

Number of cases of asthma in China →

Concentration of → sulfur dioxide in the air

The higher the concentration of sulfur dioxide in the air, the greater the number of cases of asthma. This is a positive correlation. The factor (sulfur dioxide in the air) may or may not be a cause of asthma.

The incidence of asthma decreases as the concentration of sulfur dioxide in the air increases. This is a negative correlation. The factor (sulfur dioxide) may or may not be a cause of the fall in the number of cases of asthma.

There is no correlation between the incidence of asthma and the concentration of sulfur dioxide in the air.

Sulfur dioxide pollution <u>could</u> cause an increase in cases of asthma because sulfur dioxide pollution can cause breathing problems.

<u>But</u> you need to consider other factors too. Other air pollutants such as particles of soot can also affect the breathing system. You need to look at data for that and other factors too.

So you can't say that sulfur dioxide pollution causes an increase in cases of asthma.

If there is a correlation between two factors, then this suggests that one <u>may be</u> a cause of the other. But to say that one <u>causes</u> the other, you need

- further evidence
- some backing from theory to show how the factor could cause the effect.

You can find many examples of data showing links that may or may not be causal. For example some scientists claim that certain food additives cause some children to behave badly. They have found that removing the additives from a child's diet can make them behave better. Others believe that any improvement in behaviour could be due to the extra attention that the child receives when on the diet.

■ Evaluation – including the validity and reliability of evidence

You need to be able to evaluate information in science.

For example, when you evaluate an investigation, you are probably used to thinking about

- the strengths and weaknesses of your plan
- whether the data or information you gather is valid and reliable (see page 297)
- checking for anomalies in data (data that do not fit the pattern) and suggesting reasons for them. It could be that you made an error or that your original model or hypothesis needs revising.
- suggesting improvements for future investigations.

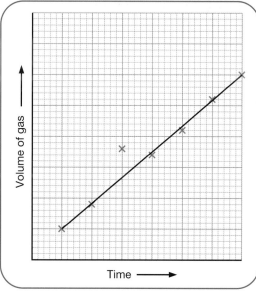

One point doesn't fit the pattern, so it must be checked. It's an anomalous result.

You need to be able to do these things in relation to the work of others too. For example, in Biology, on page 71, you evaluate data from experiments by Banting and Best that led to the discovery of insulin.

> ### How to evaluate information is a skill that you can learn
> You need this skill in your everyday life too.
> For example
>
> - to judge what you read in the newspapers, hear on the radio or see on TV. You need to be able to recognise whether what you are reading is fact or opinion.
> - to judge the ideas of others
> - to have confidence in your own ideas because you have thought about the evidence that supports them.

Vote on change to embryo-selection rules!

Should we invest more money in nanoscience?

Pressure to continue nuclear fusion research

'Give up over-consumption to make the world a fairer place', says leader

Should we tax factories for wasting energy?

Campaigners call for 20 mph speed limits in residential areas

You may have to make decisions about these issues. You'll need to be able to judge the information you are given and to find out more information for yourself.

■ How society judges evidence

As individuals, we have to look at evidence and evaluate it in relation to the decisions we make

- about our own lives
- about the lives of our families
- when we serve on juries
- when we vote.

Drugs companies have a lot of money invested in the drugs they develop. We need to know that the evidence they give is not biased.
So their methods, results and conclusions need careful evaluation. For example, some drugs are prescribed for women and children that have only been tested on men. Scientists are now beginning to realise that this can cause problems. Validity and reliability of evidence are particularly important in drugs trials.

Many people continue to use plastics widely even though they know that plastics take hundreds of years to break down in landfill sites. Plastics are so convenient to use, many people choose to ignore the consequences.

Social factors sometimes influence whether scientific evidence and new theories are accepted.

For example, it sometimes depends on

- what ideas are fashionable at the time
- who put forward the new ideas.

Galileo was put on trial for suggesting that the Earth orbited the Sun, because this went against the accepted religious teaching of the time.

Mendel was a monk and published his work in Brno where he lived. Few people even knew about his work until after his death.

Sometimes people just don't want to accept evidence.

There is no clear evidence of nanoparticles being harmful to humans. But people are likely to be concerned by even the suggestion of a risk, and may wish to avoid them.

People continue to use sunbeds despite health concerns. They may feel that the benefits they gain from them now outweigh any potential long term risks.

So, you need to be aware that decisions aren't always based on evidence alone.

Revising

You are more likely to remember things if you

- review your work regularly. The first time you revise should not be for an examination.
- revise actively rather than just reading through notes. You'll find that it helps to stop your mind wandering. For example, you could make brief notes or a chart of key points, memorise formulae and plan answers to questions. Notes and charts are useful for last-minute revision.

■ Using this book

See if you know which words go into the **What you need to remember** boxes for the pages you are revising.

Try to do this without looking at the text or diagrams on the pages. Then, if there is anything you can't remember, read the text and look at the diagrams to find the answer.

What you need to remember *Copy and complete using the **key words***

Velocity and acceleration

The speed of an object in a particular direction is called its ___velocity___.

The rate at which the velocity of an object changes is called its ___acceleration___.

The units of acceleration are ___metres___ ___per___ ___second___ ___squared___ (m/s²).

Acceleration can be calculated like this: acceleration $= \dfrac{\text{___change___ in velocity}}{\text{___time___ taken}}$

Remember that

- the key words are printed in bold type like this:
  Velocity is speed in a given direction.
- you can check your answers at the back of the book (pages 316 to 332).

You can also use the **What you need to remember** boxes for a last-minute review of the things that you need to <u>know</u>.

But you don't just have to <u>remember</u> the scientific ideas, you also need to be able to <u>use</u> them. You may be asked to do this in a situation you haven't met before.

Tests and examinations

In tests, you will be assessed on

- your knowledge and understanding of
  - science
  - how science works.

- your ability to apply your
  - skills
  - knowledge
  - understanding.

In the <u>centre-assessed unit</u>, you will be assessed on your practical, enquiry and data-handling skills.

In the <u>external assessment tests</u>, the questions are structured and based on

- science knowledge and understanding
- the way science works
- application of knowledge and understanding to new situations.

Answering structured questions

It's easy to tell when you are expected to give a longer answer to a question.

There will be lots of space for your answer and the question paper will indicate that you can score more than one or two marks for your answer. For example:

1 Write down **three** things that plants use to make sugar. (3 marks)

2 Market gardeners sometimes burn paraffin in their greenhouses to increase the temperature and the amount of carbon dioxide.

Describe and explain the effect on the rate of sugar production of
 a increasing the temperature
 b increasing the amount of carbon dioxide. (4 marks)

When answering these questions, don't just write down the first thing you think of and then leave it at that. Don't write down things that you hope might just possibly be relevant, such as temperature affects photosynthesis or plants respire faster when it's warm. That's a sure way to lose marks because, if they're not relevant, it tells the person marking your answer that you don't really understand the question.

For **2b** you could write

If there is sufficient light, increasing the carbon dioxide concentration can increase the rate of sugar production by photosynthesis. This is because carbon dioxide is one of the raw materials for photosynthesis.

Make sure that you use good English and present your answers clearly and neatly.

Calculations

Even if you get the wrong answer to a calculation, you can still get quite a lot of marks.

To gain these marks, you must have gone about the calculation in the right way. But the person marking your answer can only see that you've done this if you write down your working neatly and set it out tidily so it's quite clear what you have done.

It's very important that you gain as many marks from calculations as you can. Physics questions in particular include a lot of calculations. The formulae you are expected to know and/or be able to use in physics are listed on pages 314–315 of this book.

> You should
>
> - write down the formula you are using (in words or symbols)
> - put in the figures for the quantities you know
> - calculate the quantity you have been asked to
> - write down the answer together with the units.

Always set out your class work and homework calculations like this so that you get into good habits.

Then you'll still do calculations in the right way even under the pressure of examinations.

Answering short answer questions involving calculations

Example 1

Calculate the relative formula mass (M_r) of calcium carbonate ($CaCO_3$).

Relative atomic masses:
C = 12; O = 16; Ca = 40.

Relative formula mass

$$= 40 + 12 + (3 \times 16)$$
$$= 40 + 12 + 48$$
$$= 100$$

You gain marks for these steps even if you make a mistake.

Example 2

The current through a 12 V car headlamp bulb is 3 A.
Calculate the resistance of the bulb.

(3 marks)

watts = volts x amps

[or power = p.d. x current]

[or $P = V \times I$]

$= 12 V \times 3 A$

$= 36 W$ (or watts)

Any one correct step gets 1 mark, even if your final answer is wrong.

The correct answer gets 2 marks.

The correct unit gets a mark even if your answer is wrong.

Chemical data

You will be expected to be able to use the data on these pages. In GCSE Science examinations, you will be given the information on a Data Sheet or in the question.

Reactivity series for metals

(Elements that are underlined, although they are non-metals, have been included for comparison.)

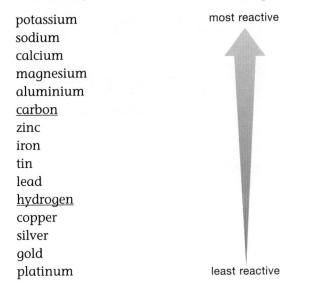

potassium
sodium
calcium
magnesium
aluminium
carbon
zinc
iron
tin
lead
hydrogen
copper
silver
gold
platinum

most reactive

least reactive

Names and formulae of some common ions

Positive ions

hydrogen	H^+
sodium	Na^+
silver	Ag^+
potassium	K^+
lithium	Li^+
ammonium	NH_4^+
barium	Ba^{2+}
calcium	Ca^{2+}
copper(II)	Cu^{2+}
magnesium	Mg^{2+}
zinc	Zn^{2+}
lead	Pb^{2+}
iron(II)	Fe^{2+}
iron(III)	Fe^{3+}
aluminium	Al^{3+}

Negative ions

chloride	Cl^-
bromide	Br^-
fluoride	F^-
iodide	I^-
hydroxide	OH^-
nitrate	NO_3^-
oxide	O^{2-}
sulfide	S^{2-}
sulfate	SO_4^{2-}
carbonate	CO_3^{2-}

How to write a balanced symbol equation

Step 1. Write down the word equation for the reaction

Step 2. Write down the formulae for the reactants and products.

Step 3. Check to see if the equation is balanced. Count the atoms on both sides of the equation.

(You do not need to write this down.)

If the equation is not balanced, you need to go on to Step 4.

Step 4. Balance the equation. Do this by writing a number in front of one or more of the formulae. This number increases the numbers of all of the atoms in the formula.

Step 5. Check that the equation is now balanced.

If it isn't, go back to Step 4.

1 a Copy the word equation and the unbalanced symbol equation for the following reaction:

calcium + water → calcium + hydrogen hydroxide

$$Ca + H_2O \rightarrow Ca(OH)_2 + H_2$$

b Balance the symbol equation.
c Add state symbols to your equation.

2 Write balanced symbol equations for these reactions. Show all the steps.

a potassium + chlorine → potassium chloride
b copper oxide + hydrogen → copper + water

Formulae you need for question 2

chlorine	Cl_2
hydrogen	H_2
potassium chloride	KCl
copper oxide	CuO
water	H_2O

Example: the reaction between sodium metal and water

sodium + water → sodium + hydrogen hydroxide

$$Na + H_2O \rightarrow NaOH + H_2$$

Reactants		Products
1	sodium atoms	1
2	hydrogen atoms	3
1	oxygen atoms	1

The equation is not balanced because the number of hydrogen atoms is not the same on each side.

We can balance the hydrogen atoms by doubling up the water and sodium hydroxide.

$$2Na + 2H_2O \rightarrow 2NaOH + H_2$$

2NaOH means 2 Na atoms, 2 O atoms and 2 H atoms.

This means 4 H atoms and 2 O atoms. So the O atoms also balance (2 on each side).

This 2 is then needed so that there are 2 Na atoms on each side.

Check:

Reactants		Products
2	sodium atoms	2
4	hydrogen atoms	4
2	oxygen atoms	2

The equation now balances. There are the same numbers of each type of atom on each side.

Adding state symbols
When you have balanced an equation, you should then add state symbols. For example:

$$2Na(s) + 2H_2O(l) \rightarrow 2NaOH(aq) + H_2(g)$$

Remember: (s) = solid
(l) = liquid
(g) = gas
(aq) = in solution in water

Working out the formula of an ionic substance

Ionic substances form giant structures. When ions combine to form compounds, the electrical charges must balance. For example, if there are two positive charges, there must also be two negative charges.

Look at the examples in the box.

Na^+ balances Cl^- to give the formula   NaCl

Ca^{2+} balances $\begin{cases} Cl^- \\ Cl^- \end{cases}$ to give the formula $CaCl_2$

Mg^{2+} balances O^{2-} to give the formula   MgO

Mg^{2+} balances $\begin{cases} OH^- \\ OH^- \end{cases}$ to give the formula $Mg(OH)_2$

Some common ions

sodium	Na^+	chloride	Cl^-
potassium	K^+	bromide	Br^-
calcium	Ca^{2+}	hydroxide	OH^-
magnesium	Mg^{2+}	oxide	O^{2-}
aluminium	Al^{3+}	sulfide	S^{2-}

The mole

> **REMEMBER**
>
> The atoms of different elements have different masses.
> We compare the masses of atoms with the mass of the
> ^{12}C isotope. We call this the relative atomic mass or A_r
> for short.

The mass of a molecule is called its relative formula mass.
We call this M_r for short.
If we know the formula of a molecule then it is easy to
work out the relative formula mass.
We look up the relative atomic masses of the elements.
Then we add the masses of all the atoms in the formula.

For example, to work out the relative formula mass of
carbon dioxide (CO_2) we do the following calculation.

M_r = 12 + (2 × 16)

= 12 + 32

= 44

1 Calculate the relative formula mass of

    a magnesium chloride ($MgCl_2$)
    b sodium carbonate (Na_2CO_3).

Chemists often find it useful to use <u>the mole</u> in their
calculations. One mole of a compound is the relative
formula mass in grams.

For example, the relative formula mass of water (H_2O) is
18. One mole of water has a mass of 18 g.

2 Use your answers to question 1 to write down the
    mass of one mole of

    a magnesium chloride
    b sodium carbonate.

3 Calculate the mass of one mole of

    a hydrogen sulfide (H_2S)
    b aluminium bromide ($AlBr_3$).

Element	Symbol	A_r
aluminium	Al	27
bromine	Br	80
carbon	C	12
chlorine	Cl	35.5
hydrogen	H	1
magnesium	Mg	24
nitrogen	N	14
oxygen	O	16
sulfur	S	32

The relative atomic masses of some elements.
You need some of these to answer questions 1
and 3.

Although chemists sometimes joke about the mole
being a small creature who lives underground,
'the chemical mole' is very useful in calculations.

Periodic table

The periodic table of elements

Group

	1	2																3	4	5	6	7	0
																							4 **He** helium 2
	7 **Li** lithium 3	9 **Be** beryllium 4																11 **B** boron 5	12 **C** carbon 6	14 **N** nitrogen 7	16 **O** oxygen 8	19 **F** fluorine 9	20 **Ne** neon 10
	23 **Na** sodium 11	24 **Mg** magnesium 12																27 **Al** aluminium 13	28 **Si** silicon 14	31 **P** phosphorus 15	32 **S** sulfur 16	35.5 **Cl** chlorine 17	40 **Ar** argon 18
	39 **K** potassium 19	40 **Ca** calcium 20	45 **Sc** scandium 21	48 **Ti** titanium 22	51 **V** vanadium 23	52 **Cr** chromium 24	55 **Mn** manganese 25	56 **Fe** iron 26	59 **Co** cobalt 27	59 **Ni** nickel 28	63.5 **Cu** copper 29	65 **Zn** zinc 30	70 **Ga** gallium 31	73 **Ge** germanium 32	75 **As** arsenic 33	79 **Se** selenium 34	80 **Br** bromine 35	84 **Kr** krypton 36
	85 **Rb** rubidium 37	88 **Sr** strontium 38	89 **Y** yttrium 39	91 **Zr** zirconium 40	93 **Nb** niobium 41	96 **Mo** molybdenum 42	[98] **Tc** technetium 43	101 **Ru** ruthenium 44	103 **Rh** rhodium 45	106 **Pd** palladium 46	108 **Ag** silver 47	112 **Cd** cadmium 48	115 **In** indium 49	119 **Sn** tin 50	122 **Sb** antimony 51	128 **Te** tellurium 52	127 **I** iodine 53	131 **Xe** xenon 54
	133 **Cs** caesium 55	137 **Ba** barium 56	139 **La*** lanthanum 57	178 **Hf** hafnium 72	181 **Ta** tantalum 73	184 **W** tungsten 74	186 **Re** rhenium 75	190 **Os** osmium 76	192 **Ir** iridium 77	195 **Pt** platinum 78	197 **Au** gold 79	201 **Hg** mercury 80	204 **Tl** thallium 81	207 **Pb** lead 82	209 **Bi** bismuth 83	[210] **Po** polonium 84	[210] **At** astatine 85	[222] **Rn** radon 86
	[223] **Fr** francium 87	[226] **Ra** radium 88	[227] **Ac*** actinium 89	[261] **Rf** rutherfordium 104	[262] **Db** dubnium 105	[266] **Sg** seaborgium 106	[264] **Bh** bohrium 107	[277] **Hs** hassium 108	[268] **Mt** meitnerium 109	[271] **Ds** darmstadtium 110	[272] **Rg** roentgenium 111							

1 **H** hydrogen 1

Elements with atomic numbers 112–116 have been reported but not fully authenticated.

* The Lanthanides (atomic numbers 58–71) and the Actinides (atomic numbers 90–103) have been omitted.
The mass numbers of **Cu** and **Cl** have not been rounded to the nearest whole number.

Key

relative atomic mass
atomic symbol
name
atomic number

Gases at room temperature

Liquids

Solids

Metals

Alkali metals

Transition metals

Other metals

Non-metals

Halogens

Noble gases

Other non-metals

313

Formulas that you must remember and be able to use

■ Movement and forces

The speed of an object is given by

speed (metres per second, m/s) = $\dfrac{\text{distance travelled (metres, m)}}{\text{time taken (seconds, s)}}$

For an object moving in a straight line with a steady acceleration

acceleration (metres per second squared, m/s^2) = $\dfrac{\text{change in velocity (metres per second, m/s)}}{\text{time taken (seconds, s)}}$

Force, mass and acceleration are related as follows:

force (newtons, N) = mass (kilograms, kg) × acceleration (metres per second^2, m/s^2)

The weight of an object is the force of gravity that acts on it.

weight (newtons, N) = mass (kilograms, kg) × gravitational field strength (newtons per kilogram, N/kg)

When a force moves an object, energy is transferred and work is done. The work done (energy transferred), force and distance are related as follows:

work done (joules, J) = force (newtons, N) × distance moved (metres, m)

The kinetic energy of a moving object is given by

kinetic energy (joules, J) = $\frac{1}{2}$ × mass (kilograms, kg) × speed^2 [(metres per second)^2, (m/s)^2]

The momentum of a moving object is given by

momentum (kilogram metres per second, kg m/s) = mass (kilograms, kg) × velocity (metres per second, m/s)

Force, change in momentum and time for the change to take place are related as follows:

force (newtons, N) = $\dfrac{\text{change in momentum (kilogram metres per second, kg m/s)}}{\text{time for the change (seconds, s)}}$

You can calculate the potential difference across a component as follows:

$$\text{potential difference} = \text{current} \times \text{resistance}$$
$$\text{(volts, V)} \qquad \text{(amps, A)} \qquad \text{(ohms, } \Omega\text{)}$$

The rate of energy transfer by an electrical appliance (its power) is given by

$$\text{power (watts, W)} = \frac{\text{energy transferred (joules, J)}}{\text{time (seconds, s)}}$$

or

$$\text{power} = \text{potential difference (p.d.)} \times \text{current}$$
$$\text{(watts, W)} \qquad \text{(volts, V)} \qquad \text{(amps, A)}$$

The electrical charge that flows depends on current and time as follows:

$$\text{charge} = \text{current} \times \text{time}$$
$$\text{(coulombs, C)} \qquad \text{(amps, A)} \qquad \text{(seconds, s)}$$

Voltage is a measure of the energy transferred when one coulomb of charge flows.

$$\text{energy transferred} = \text{potential difference} \times \text{charge}$$
$$\text{joules, J)} \qquad \text{(volts, V)} \qquad \text{(coulombs, C)}$$

Biology

A1 Cells

1   **What are cells like?**
Most human cells are made up of the same basic parts. Cells have a **nucleus** which controls everything that happens in the cell. It is the cell **membrane** that controls the passage of substances in and out of the cell. Most of the chemical reactions in a cell take place in the **cytoplasm**. For example, most energy release in respiration happens in **mitochondria** and protein synthesis happens in **ribosomes** in the cytoplasm. These and other chemical reactions in cells are controlled by **enzymes**.

You need to be able to use your skills and knowledge to match specialised cells to the jobs that they do in tissues and organs or the whole organism.

2   **How are plants built?**
Plant cells have cell walls to make them **stronger**. They often have permanent spaces called **vacuoles**. These are filled with a liquid called cell **sap**. Some plant cells have **chloroplasts** to absorb the light energy that plants use to make food.

3   **The cell for the job!**
There is nothing new for you to remember in this section.

You need to be able to look at a cell and work out its job like you did in question 11.

A2 Diffusion and osmosis

1   **How substances get into and out of cells**
To get into or out of cells, dissolved substances have to cross **cell membranes**. Particles of a gas or a **dissolved** substance move in all directions. So there is a net movement from a region of **higher** concentration to one of **lower** concentration. We call this **diffusion**. The greater the difference in **concentration**, the higher the rate of diffusion. This is how **oxygen** for respiration gets through cell membranes into cells.

2   **Losing and gaining water**
Water can **diffuse** into or out of a cell when there is a difference in the **concentration** of the solution inside and outside the cell. Water diffuses from a **dilute** solution into a more **concentrated** solution through a partially permeable membrane. We call this process **osmosis**. A **partially permeable** membrane is one that freely lets water molecules through but controls the passage of dissolved substances (**solutes**).

A3 How plants obtain food

1   **Food factories – leaves**
Green plants use **light** energy to make food. This process is called **photosynthesis**. A green substance called **chlorophyll** absorbs the light energy. Chlorophyll is found in the parts of cells called **chloroplasts**. These are mainly in the **leaves** of plants.

2   **What do plants make sugar from?**
Plants make their own food by **photosynthesis**. They use the energy from sunlight to convert carbon dioxide and water into sugar (**glucose**). They release **oxygen** as a by-product.

3   **Limits to plant growth**
The **rate** of photosynthesis can be limited by

■ shortage of **light** or **carbon dioxide**
■ low **temperature**.

These factors interact and it takes a shortage of only one of them to **limit** the rate of photosynthesis.

You need to be able to interpret data on factors affecting the rate of photosynthesis and to consider the advantages and disadvantages of changing the environment in which plants grow.

4   **What else affects plant growth?**
Plant **roots** absorb the mineral ions that plants need for healthy growth including

■ nitrates for making **amino acids**. Amino acids are important for growth because they are used to make **proteins**. Shortage causes **stunted** growth.
■ magnesium for making **chlorophyll**. Leaves are yellow if magnesium ions are **deficient**.

5   **How plants use the food they make**
Plant cells use the **glucose** produced in photosynthesis

■ for **respiration**
■ for making insoluble **starch** for storage.

A4 Energy and biomass in food chains

1 Energy for life

The source of energy for most communities is **radiation** from the Sun. Green plants trap a small amount of this **energy** and store some of it in the form of the **materials** that make up their cells. The higher in the food **chain**, the lower the mass of living material (**biomass**). You can draw this to scale as a **pyramid** of biomass.

You need to be able to draw and to interpret pyramids of biomass.

2 Less biomass, less energy

At each stage in a food chain the amount of **biomass** and energy falls because

- materials and energy are lost in **waste**
- energy for life processes is released in **respiration**. Much of this is transferred to the surroundings as **heat**.

Heat loss from birds and mammals is particularly high because they keep their bodies at a **constant** temperature. This **temperature** is usually higher than that of their surroundings.

3 Managing food supplies

We can improve human food supplies by reducing the **energy** loss from food animals by controlling the amount they can **move** and by keeping them in **warm** surroundings. Another way is to reduce the number of stages in human **food chains**.

You need to be able to weigh up the problems of managing food production and distribution. To solve the problems of competing priorities, we may need to compromise.

A5 Waste and recycling

1 Recycling mineral ions

Living things remove materials such as **mineral** ions from the **environment**. They use them for **growth** and other life processes. These **materials** are returned to the environment when dead organisms and their waste **decay**. They are then **recycled**.
In a stable **community** there is a balance between the materials taken out and those put back into the system.

2 Microorganisms – little rotters!

Dead organisms and **waste** materials decay because **microorganisms** digest them, or break them down. The decay releases **mineral** ions and carbon dioxide, which plants need to grow. Microorganisms digest materials faster in **warm**, moist conditions. Many work better when there is also plenty of **oxygen**.

3 The carbon cycle

Green **plants** take **carbon dioxide** from the air for photosynthesis. They use the **carbon** to make carbohydrates, fats and proteins. When animals eat plants, some of these **compounds** become part of the animals' bodies. Animals called **detritus** feeders and microorganisms called **decomposers** feed on dead organisms and waste materials in **ecosystems**. All these organisms return carbon dioxide to the atmosphere when they **respire**. In the **carbon cycle**, all the carbon is constantly recycled. At the same time, all the **energy** captured by green plants is **transferred**.

A6 Enzymes

1 Why are living things good chemists?

Catalysts increase the rate of chemical reactions. We call biological catalysts **enzymes**. An enzyme is a protein made of long chains of **amino acids** folded up into a special shape. It works only because its shape allows molecules of a particular **reactant** to fit into it exactly. High temperatures destroy this special **shape**. Different enzymes work best at different **pH** values.

2 Energy for life

Enzymes in cells catalyse many processes, including **respiration**, photosynthesis and protein synthesis. Aerobic respiration uses **oxygen**. It is a series of reactions that release energy from glucose (a sugar). Most of these reactions happen inside **mitochondria**. We can summarise these reactions in the **equation**

$$\text{glucose} + \text{oxygen} \longrightarrow \text{carbon dioxide} + \text{water} (+ \text{energy})$$

3 Why do cells need energy?

All living things use the **energy** released in respiration to build up large **molecules** from smaller ones. Plants build up sugar, **nitrates** and other **nutrients** into amino acids. All living things build **amino acids** into proteins. Enzymes in cells **catalyse** all these reactions. Animals use energy to enable muscles to **contract**. In colder surroundings, mammals and **birds** also need energy to maintain a steady body **temperature**.

4 Enzymes digest our food

Some enzymes work **outside** cells. Examples are our **digestive** enzymes. We make them in **specialised** cells in **glands** and in the **lining** of the gut. Most pass into the **gut**, where they meet the large food molecules. They **catalyse** the breakdown of these molecules into smaller molecules.

5 Different enzymes digest different foods

Amylase catalyses the breakdown (digestion) of **starch** into sugars in the mouth and small intestine. It is made in the **salivary** glands and the pancreas. Gland cells in the lining of the small intestine make a carbohydrase that completes the breakdown of starch to glucose. Proteases catalyse the breakdown of **proteins** into amino acids. **Lipases** digest lipids (fats and oils) into fatty acids and glycerol.

6 Digesting proteins and fats

Type of food	Where it is digested	What makes the enzymes
protein	**stomach** and small intestine	stomach, **pancreas** and small intestine
lipid (fats and oils)	**small intestine**	pancreas

Your stomach makes **hydrochloric acid** to provide acid conditions for stomach protease. Your liver makes **bile** and stores it in your gall bladder. In your small intestine, bile neutralises acidity to provide the **alkaline** conditions in which the enzymes there work best.

7 Enzymes from microorganisms

We use enzymes from **microorganisms** at home and in industry. We use many of them **outside** the cells that make them. At home, we use **biological** washing powders to remove biological stains because they contain **proteases** (protein-digesting enzymes) and **lipases** (fat-digesting enzymes).

You may be given similar information about using an enzyme to bring about a chemical reaction. You need to be able to explain the advantages and disadvantages of using the enzyme.

8 Enzymes in the food industry

Job	Enzyme
to break down starch into sugar syrup	**carbohydrases**
to change glucose syrup to a sweeter fructose syrup for use in slimming foods	**isomerase**
to 'pre-digest' the proteins in some baby foods	**proteases**

You may be given similar information about using an enzyme to bring about a chemical reaction. You need to be able to explain the advantages and disadvantages of using the enzyme.

A7 Keeping conditions constant

1 Getting rid of waste

You have to remove waste products from your **blood**. Your cells make **carbon dioxide** waste in respiration. You remove it via your **lungs** when you breathe out. Your liver cells make **urea** when they break down excess **amino acids**. Your kidneys remove this from your blood. They make **urine** that is stored temporarily in your **bladder**.

2 Balancing acts

Humans need to keep their **internal** environment fairly constant. That includes the body **temperature** and the water, **sugar** and ion content of the **blood**. If the water or ion content of the blood is wrong, too much water passes in or out of cells and **damages** them. Water and **ions** get into your body in food and drink.

3 Temperature control

If your **core** body temperature is too high, the blood vessels to the **skin** capillaries **dilate**. More blood flows through the **capillaries** so more heat is lost. Sweat **glands** release more sweat. Evaporation of **sweat** cools your body.

H If your body temperature is too low, the **blood** vessels to the capillaries in the skin **constrict** so that less blood flows through them and less heat is lost. You may shiver. The contraction and relaxation of **muscles** needs energy released in **respiration**. Some of the energy is released as **heat**.

4 Your body's thermostat

The thermoregulatory centre in your **brain** monitors and controls your core body **temperature**. This centre has **receptors** that sense the temperature of the **blood** flowing through your brain. The **thermoregulatory centre** receives information about skin temperature in the form of nerve **impulses** from temperature receptors in your **skin**.

5 Keeping your blood glucose concentration constant

Your blood glucose **concentration** must be kept constant. Your **pancreas** monitors and controls this. If there is too much glucose, your pancreas releases the **hormone** insulin. Insulin allows **liver** cells to take in glucose from the blood. People with **diabetes** cannot make enough **insulin** so the concentration of glucose in their blood can rise too high. Some diabetics need **injections** of insulin and they all have to control their **diet**.

6 More about insulin

Without treatment, **diabetes** is fatal.

You need to be able to evaluate data from experiments by Banting and Best which led to the discovery of insulin.

7 Diabetes now

There is nothing new for you to <u>remember</u> in this section.

You need to be able to evaluate modern methods of treating diabetes.

A8 Genetics

1 How are characteristics inherited?

We find out about **inheritance** patterns from breeding experiments and, in the case of humans, from **family trees**.

You need to be able to explain

- why Mendel suggested that factors were inherited separately
- why the importance of Mendel's discoveries was not recognised until after his death.

You don't need to remember the details of Mendel's work.

2 Body cells and sex cells

H Testes and ovaries contain cells that divide by **meiosis** to form **sex** cells or gametes. These cells make copies of their **chromosomes** then divide twice to make four **gametes**.
Each gamete has a **single** set of chromosomes. So it has a single set of **genetic** information.

3 Making new body cells

Gametes join at **fertilisation** to form a single cell. Its nucleus contains new pairs of **chromosomes**. It divides by **mitosis** over and over again to produce the new individual. Your body has to make new cells to **replace** lost and worn out cells as well as for **growth**. In body cells, the chromosomes are in **pairs**. Some living things produce offspring by asexual reproduction. Their cells are made by mitosis from the **parent** cells. So they are genetically the same as their parent.

4 Growing and changing

Many plant cells keep the ability to **differentiate**. Most animal cells don't. In mature animals, cells **divide** mainly to provide new cells for **repair** and replacement. However, special cells called **stem cells** can differentiate into many different types of cells. Embryos and adult **bone marrow** are sources of stem cells.

5 Why are stem cells useful?

We can clone **stem cells** from embryos and from adults to repair some body tissues.

You need to be able to consider social and ethical issues surrounding the use of embryonic stem cells in medical research and treatments.

6 What makes you male or female?

One of your 23 pairs of chromosomes carries the genes that determine sex. In females, both sex chromosomes are the same; they are both **X**. In males, one sex chromosome is an **X** and the other a **Y**. All the **egg** cells of a woman contain an X chromosome. **Sperm** cells contain an X or a Y chromosome.

X egg cell + Y sperm cell ⟶ a baby **boy**

X egg cell + X sperm cell ⟶ a baby **girl**

7 Some human genes

Just one gene controls some **characteristics**. A gene may have different forms called **alleles**. When **gametes** or sex cells fuse, one of each pair of alleles comes from each **parent**. So sexual reproduction leads to **variation**.

8 **Why are some alleles hidden?**
Some characteristics are controlled by one **gene**.
This gene may have different forms called **alleles**.
If an allele controls the development of a
characteristic when it is on one **chromosome** only,
we call it a **dominant** allele. An allele that doesn't
show up if the dominant allele is present is called a
recessive allele.

You need to be able to construct genetic diagrams like
you did in question 6.

9 **DNA and the genetic code**
Chromosomes are made up of large **molecules** of
deoxyribonucleic acid. We usually call it **DNA**.
A **gene** is a small section of DNA.
Each gene codes for a particular combination of
amino acids that makes a particular **protein**.

10 **DNA fingerprinting**
Apart from **identical** twins, each person has **unique**
DNA. Scientists can use this to **identify** individuals
in a process called DNA **fingerprinting**.

11 **Huntington's disease**
This is a disorder of the **nervous** system. The allele
that causes it is **dominant** so it takes only **one**
parent with the disorder to pass it on.

You need to be able to draw and interpret genetic
diagrams just like you did in question 8.

12 Cystic fibrosis
Some disorders are passed on by genes. We say they
are **inherited**. Cystic fibrosis is a disorder of **cell**
membranes. The cause is a **recessive** allele. So to get
cystic fibrosis you must inherit a faulty allele from
both of your parents. People who have one copy of
the allele are called **carriers**. They don't have the
disorder but they can pass on the faulty **allele**.

You need to be able to construct genetic diagrams
and to predict and explain the results of crosses just
like you have done on these pages.

13 **A genetic disorder in the family!**
Embryos can be screened for the **alleles** that cause
genetic disorders such as Huntington's disease and
cystic fibrosis.

You need to be able to make informed judgements
based on economic, social and ethical issues
concerning embryo screening.

14 **More genetic crosses**
There is nothing new for you to <u>remember</u> in this
section.

You need to be able to predict and explain the results
of crosses for all the possible combinations of
dominant and recessive alleles of the same gene.

Chemistry

A1 Subatomic particles and the structure of substances

1 What are atoms made of?
The centre of an atom is called the **nucleus**.
The nucleus can contain two kinds of particle:

- particles with no charge called **neutrons**
- particles with a positive charge called **protons**.

Every element has its own special **atomic number** (proton number) which is equal to the number of protons. Atoms of the same element always have the **same** number of protons. Atoms of different elements have **different** numbers of protons. Around the nucleus there are particles with a negative charge called **electrons**. In an atom the number of electrons is **equal** to the number of protons. This means that atoms have no overall electrical charge.

2 The periodic table
In the modern periodic table, elements are arranged in order of their **atomic number** (proton number). This tells us the number of protons and also the number of **electrons** in an atom.

3 Families of elements
In atoms, the electrons are arranged in certain **energy levels**. The first level has the **lowest** energy. It can take up to **two** electrons. The second and third energy levels can each take up to **eight** electrons. Elements in the same group have the same number of electrons in their **top** energy level.

You need to be able to show how the electrons are arranged in the first 20 elements of the periodic table.

4 Why elements react to form compounds
When two or more elements are joined together with a chemical bond, they form a **compound**. Atoms form chemical bonds when they **share** electrons, or **give and take** electrons. For an atom to be stable, its **highest energy level** must be full. When an atom gives or takes electrons, it forms an **ion**. Ions have electron arrangements like those in the **noble gases**.

5 Group 1 elements
Another name for the Group 1 elements is the **alkali metals**. All of the elements in this family have similar **chemical properties**. Group 1 elements all have **one** electron in their highest energy level. When they react, they give away this electron. Atoms which lose electrons become **positively charged** ions. Group 1 elements form ions with a **single** positive charge.

6 Group 7 elements
Another name for the Group 7 elements is the **halogens**. All of the elements in this family have similar **chemical properties**. Group 7 elements all have **seven** electrons in their top energy level. When they react, they gain one electron. Atoms which gain electrons become **negatively charged** ions. Group 7 elements form ions with a **single** negative charge.

7 Metals reacting with non-metals
When metals react with non-metals they form **ionic compounds**.

You need to be able to show how the electrons are arranged in the ions for sodium chloride, magnesium oxide and calcium chloride. You can do this in the following forms:

 and $[2,8]^+$ for the sodium ion.

8 How atoms of non-metals can join together
Atoms can join together by **sharing** electrons. The bonds that they form are called **covalent** bonds and are very **strong**.

You need to be able to show the covalent bonds in molecules like water, ammonia, hydrogen, hydrogen chloride, methane and oxygen in the following forms:

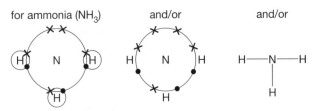

for ammonia (NH₃)   and/or   and/or

9 Giant structures

Many substances form giant structures. Ionic compounds form giant structures of ions. We call these a **lattice**. The ions have **opposite** charges and there are strong **forces of attraction** between them. The forces act in all directions and this is called **ionic bonding**. Some substances with covalent bonds form giant structures, for example **diamond** and **silicon dioxide**. We call these giant structures **macromolecules**.

[H] Metals also form giant structures. Electrons from the top energy level of the atoms are **free** to move. The metal atoms form **positively** charged ions. The free electrons are **negatively** charged. The metal ions and free electrons are held together by strong **electrostatic** attractions.

A2 Structures, properties and uses of substances

1 Simple molecules

Substances that consist of simple molecules can be a **gas**, a **liquid** or a **solid** at room temperature. They all have a low **melting point** and **boiling point**.

[H] This is because there are only **weak** forces **between** the molecules. We say there are weak **intermolecular** forces. When the substance melts or boils, these forces are overcome but the covalent bonds are not affected. Substances that consist of simple molecules do not **conduct electricity** because the molecules do not have an overall **electric charge**.

2 Different bonding – different properties

The ions in compounds like sodium chloride are arranged in a giant **lattice**. There are strong **electrostatic** forces between the oppositely charged ions. These act in all **directions**. Ionic compounds like sodium chloride have very high **melting points** and **boiling points**. When they are dissolved in water or melted, they can **conduct electricity**. This is because their ions are free to **move** about and carry the **current**.

3 Diamond and graphite

The atoms of some substances can share electrons to form giant structures. We call these **macromolecules**. Two examples of this are the two forms of carbon, **diamond** and **graphite**. Both of these substances have high **melting points** because the covalent bonds between their atoms are very **strong**. The table shows how the properties of diamond and graphite are linked to their structure.

Substance	Hard or soft?	How many covalent bonds each carbon atom makes	Type of structure
diamond	**hard**	**four**	**rigid** structure called a **lattice**
graphite	**soft**	**three**	forms **layers** which can slip over each other

You need to be able to relate the properties of substances like diamond and graphite to their uses.

4 More giant structures – metals

The **layers** of atoms in metals are able to **slide** over each other. This is why we can **bend** and **shape** metals.

[H] Metals conduct heat and electricity because their structures contain **delocalised** electrons. The non-metal graphite can also conduct **heat** and **electricity**. This is because one electron from each carbon atom is **delocalised**.

You need to be able to relate the properties of substances to their uses.

5 Which structure?

Another example of a compound with a giant covalent structure is **silicon dioxide**.

You need to be able to use information about the properties of a substance to suggest the type of structure it has.

6 What is nanoscience?

Nanoscience is the study of materials on a very small scale. A **nanometre** is a millionth of a millimetre. **Nanoparticles** are particles which are smaller than 100 nm. They have different **properties** from bigger particles of the same substance. Because nanoparticles are so small, they have a high **surface area to volume ratio**. We can use them to make new **coatings**, for example for glass.

7 More new materials

The properties of nanoparticles may lead to the development of new **computers**, improved **catalysts**, selective **sensors** and **construction materials** which are stronger and lighter.

You need to be able to use information like this to weigh up the advantages and disadvantages of using new materials like nanomaterials and smart materials.

A3 How much can we make and how much do we need to use?

1 Masses of atoms

The symbol $^{23}_{11}$Na tells us that sodium has a **mass number** of 23 and an **atomic number** of 11. The mass number tells us the total number of **protons** and **neutrons** in an atom. We can show the relative masses of protons, neutrons and electrons in the following way.

Name of particle	Mass
electron	very small
proton	1
neutron	1

Atoms of the same element can have different numbers of **neutrons**. These atoms are called **isotopes** of that element.

2 How heavy are atoms?

H We compare the masses of atoms with the mass of the ^{12}C isotope. We call this the **relative** atomic mass, or A_r for short. Many atoms exist as different isotopes so the A_r is an **average** value.

3 Using relative atomic mass

To work out a relative formula mass (M_r for short)

- look up the relative **atomic** masses of the elements
- then **add** together the masses of all the atoms in the formula.

4 Elementary pie

Chemical compounds are made of **elements** (just as an apple pie is made of ingredients). We can work out the **percentage** of an element in a compound using the relative **mass** of the element in the formula and the **relative formula mass** of the compound.

You need to be able to work out the percentage by mass of each element in a compound, just like you have on these pages.

5 Working out the formulae of compounds

H The simplest formula of a compound is called its **empirical formula**.

You need to be able to calculate chemical quantities using empirical formulae.

6 Using chemical equations to calculate reacting masses

H We can work out the masses of reactants and products from **balanced symbol** equations.

You need to be able to work out masses of products and reactants just like you have on these pages.

7 Reactions that go forwards and backwards

In some chemical reactions, the products of the reaction can react to produce the original reactants.

$$A + B \rightleftharpoons C + D$$

We call this kind of reaction a **reversible reaction**.

ammonium chloride (white solid) $\rightleftharpoons$ ammonia + hydrogen chloride (colourless gases)

8 How much do we really make?

Atoms are not gained or lost in a chemical reaction. But when we carry out a chemical reaction we don't always obtain the **mass** of a product we expect. This could be because

- some of the product may **escape** or get **left behind** in a mixture
- the reaction may be **different** from the one we expected
- the reaction is **reversible** and may not go to **completion**.

9 Catching nitrogen to feed plants – the Haber process

The raw materials for the Haber process are **nitrogen** (from the **air**) and **hydrogen** (from **natural gas**). We pass the gases over a catalyst of **iron** at a **high temperature** (about **450 °C**) and a **high pressure** (**200** atmospheres).

H These conditions give us the best **yield** of ammonia. The yield is the amount of **product** we obtain in a reaction.

This equation shows us that the reaction is **reversible**.

nitrogen + hydrogen $\rightleftharpoons$ ammonia

When the ammonia is cooled it turns into a **liquid**. The remaining hydrogen and nitrogen is **recycled**.

10 Reversible reactions and equilibrium

H In a reversible reaction, when the forward reaction occurs at the same **rate** as the reverse reaction we say it has reached **equilibrium**. We can only reach equilibrium in a **closed system**, when products and reactants can't leave the reaction vessel. How much of each reacting substance there is at equilibrium depends on the reaction **conditions**.

11 As much as possible!

The Haber process for producing ammonia is a **continuous** process. This type of process makes reversible reactions more **efficient**.

H The reaction conditions used in the Haber process are chosen because they produce a reasonable **yield** of ammonia **quickly**. The **percentage yield** is the amount of product we make when compared with the amount we should make. We can work it out if we do the following calculation:

$$\frac{\text{percentage}}{\text{yield}} = \frac{\text{amount of product obtained}}{\text{maximum possible amount}} \times 100\%$$

12 Atom economy

We can measure the amount of **starting materials** that end up as useful products. This is the **atom economy**. Using reactions with a high atom economy is important for **sustainable development**. It can also help manufacturers make chemicals more **cheaply**.

You need to be able to calculate the atom economy for industrial processes.
H You need to be able to say whether they meet the aims of sustainable development.

A4 How can we control the rates of chemical reactions?

1 Using heat to speed things up

Chemical reactions go at different speeds or **rates**. Chemical reactions go faster at **higher** temperatures. At low temperatures, chemical reactions **slow down**.

2 Making solutions react faster

When we dissolve a substance in water we make a **solution**. A solution that contains a lot of dissolved substance is a **concentrated** solution. To make a concentrated solution react more slowly, we can **dilute** it. To make gases react faster, we need a **high** pressure.

3 Making solids react faster

A solid can react with a liquid only where they touch. The reaction is on the **surface** of the solid. If we break up the solid, we increase the total **surface area**. This means that smaller pieces react **faster**.

4 Substances that speed up reactions

A substance that speeds up a chemical reaction is called a **catalyst**. The catalyst increases the rate of reaction but is not **used up**. We can use catalysts **over** and **over** again. Each chemical reaction needs its own **special** catalyst. Useful materials like margarine **cost** less to make when we use a catalyst.

5 More about catalysts

There is nothing new for you to remember in this section.

You need to be able to

- weigh up the advantages and disadvantages of using catalysts in industry
- explain why the development of catalysts is important.

6 Investigating rates of reaction

There is nothing new for you to remember in this section.

You need to be able to understand what graphs like the ones on this page are telling you about rates of reactions. The graphs show how much of a product is formed (or how much of a reactant has been used up) over time.

7 What makes chemical reactions happen?

For substances to react:

- their particles must **collide**
- the particles must have enough **energy** when they do this.

The smallest amount of energy they need to react is called the **activation** energy. If you increase the temperature, reactions happen faster. This is because the particles collide more **often** and with more **energy**. Breaking solids into smaller pieces, making solutions more concentrated and increasing the pressure of gases all make reactions **faster**. All these things make the collisions between particles more **frequent**.

8 **Measuring the rate of reaction**
We can find the rate of a chemical reaction if we measure

- the amount of **reactant** used over time or
- the amount of **product** formed over time.

$$\text{rate of reaction} = \frac{\text{amount of reactant used}}{\text{time}}$$

or

$$\text{rate of reaction} = \frac{\text{amount of product formed}}{\text{time}}$$

9 **Particles, solutions and gases**

[H] We can measure the concentration of a solution in **moles per cubic decimetre** or **mol/dm^3**. Equal volumes of solutions with the same **molar concentration** contain the same number of **particles**. Equal volumes of gases at the same **temperature** and **pressure** contain the same number of **particles**.

You can learn more about the mole on page 312.

A5 Do chemical reactions always release energy?

1 **Getting energy out of chemicals**
Some chemical reactions release (transfer) **energy** into their surroundings. The energy they release is often **heat** energy. We say that these reactions are **exothermic**. Some examples of exothermic reactions are **combustion**, **neutralisation** and **oxidation**.

2 **Do chemical reactions always release energy?**
When chemical reactions occur, energy is transferred **to** or **from** the surroundings. When a reaction takes in energy from the surroundings we call it an **endothermic** reaction. Often the **energy** it takes in is heat energy. Examples of endothermic reactions include **thermal decomposition** reactions. In these reactions, **heat** is taken in to split up a compound.

3 **Backwards and forwards**
If a reversible reaction is **exothermic** in one direction it is **endothermic** in the opposite direction. The amount of energy that is transferred is the **same**. When we heat **hydrated** copper sulfate it produces **anhydrous** copper sulfate. We can use the reverse reaction as a **test** for **water**.

[H] We reach equilibrium in a **closed system** when the forward and reverse reactions occur at exactly the same **rate**.

4 **Equilibrium and temperature**

[H] At equilibrium, the relative amounts of the substances in the equilibrium mixture depend on the **conditions** of the reaction. If we raise the temperature, the yield from the endothermic reaction **increases** and the yield from the exothermic reaction **decreases**. If we lower the temperature, the yield from the endothermic reaction **decreases** and the yield from the exothermic reaction **increases**.

You need to be able to describe the effects of changing the temperature on a reaction like the Haber process.

5 **Equilibrium and pressure**

[H] In reactions with gases, if we increase the pressure, the equilibrium **favours** the reaction which **reduces** the number of molecules. We can see the number of molecules in the products and the reactants if we look at the **equation**.

You need to be able to describe the effects of changing the pressure on a reaction like the Haber process.

6 **Using less energy**

[H] Manufacturers have to find the best **temperature**, **pressure** and **rate** of reaction for producing chemicals. We call these the **optimum conditions**. It is important for industries to use as little **energy** as possible and to reduce the amount that is **wasted**. This is because using energy

- is expensive (for **economic** reasons)
- can affect the **environment**.

Using **non-vigorous** conditions for chemical reactions helps to **use** less energy and to **release** less energy into the environment.
This is important for **sustainable development**.

You need to be able to weigh up the conditions that industrial processes use in terms of the energy they require.

7 **Saving steam!**
There is nothing new for you to <u>remember</u> in this section.

You need to be able to weigh up the conditions that industrial processes use in terms of how much energy they use.

A6 How can we use ions in solution?

1 Using electricity to split up compounds
We can use electricity to split up **ionic** compounds into **elements**. We call this **electrolysis**. First we must **melt** the compound or **dissolve** it in water. When we do this the ions are free to **move** about in the liquid or solution. When we pass electricity through an ionic substance

- the positive ions move to the **negative** electrode
- the negative ions move to the **positive** electrode.

2 What happens at the electrodes?
At the negative electrode, positively charged ions **gain** electrons. We call this **reduction**. At the positive electrode, negatively charged ions **lose** electrons. We call this **oxidation**.

3 Which ion?
When we pass electricity through a dissolved substance, the **water** in the solution can split up too. The products formed at the electrodes depend on how **reactive** the elements are.

You need to be able to predict the products of passing electricity through a solution.

4 Half equations
H We can show the reactions that take place during electrolysis using **half equations**, for example

$$2Cl^- \rightarrow Cl_2 + 2e^-$$

It is important to **balance** these.

You need to be able to complete and balance half equations like the ones on this page.

5 Useful substances from salt
The electrolysis of sodium chloride solution produces **hydrogen**, **chlorine** and **sodium hydroxide** solution. These are important reagents for the **chemical industry**.

You need to be able to weigh up the good and bad points of chemical processes, just like you did for the electrolysis of sodium chloride.

6 Purifying copper
We purify copper by a process called **electrolysis**. We use a positive electrode made from the **impure** copper and a negative electrode made from **pure** copper. The solution we use for the process contains copper **ions**.

You need to be able to explain processes using the terms oxidation and reduction, just like you did here for the purification of copper.

7 Making salts that won't dissolve
If a salt won't dissolve we say it is **insoluble**. We can make insoluble salts by mixing certain solutions which form a **precipitate**. Reactions like this are called **precipitation** reactions. We can use them to remove **unwanted** ions from solutions, e.g. for treating **drinking water** and **effluent**.

You need to be able to suggest the ways you could make a named salt. You will learn more of these on pages 202–206.

8 Making salts using acids and alkalis
We can make a **soluble** salt by reacting an acid with an alkali. We use an **indicator** to tell us when the acid and alkali have completely **reacted**. The **solid** salt can be **crystallised** from the salt solution we make. The type of salt we make depends on the acid we use.

- To make a **chloride**, we use hydrochloric acid.
- To make a **sulfate**, we use sulfuric acid.
- To make a **nitrate**, we use nitric acid.

The salt we make also depends on the **metal** in the alkali.

9 Other ways to make soluble salts
We can make a salt from an acid if we react it with a **metal**. Not all metals are suitable because some are too **reactive** while other metals are not reactive enough. We can also use **insoluble bases** to produce salts. A base is a metal **oxide** or **hydroxide**. A base which will dissolve is called an **alkali**. To make a salt from an insoluble base we add it to the acid until no more will **react**. Then we **filter** off the solid that is left over.

10 Making salts that don't contain metals
When we dissolve ammonia in water it produces an **alkaline** solution. We use this to produce **ammonium** salts. Farmers use large amounts of ammonium salts as **fertilisers**.

11 What happens during neutralisation?
Hydrogen ions (H^+) make solutions acidic. **Hydroxide ions** (OH^-) make solutions alkaline. The **pH scale** measures how acidic or alkaline a solution is. When hydroxide ions react with hydrogen ions to produce **water** we call it **neutralisation**. We can show this by the equation

$$H^+(aq) \quad + \quad OH^-(aq) \quad \rightarrow \quad H_2O(l)$$

Physics

A1 How can we describe the way things move?

1 Travelling at speed
The **slope** of a distance–time graph represents **speed**. A horizontal line on a distance–time graph shows that the object is **stationary**.

You need to recall and be able to use the formula

$$\text{speed (metres per second)} = \frac{\text{distance travelled (metres)}}{\text{time taken (seconds)}}$$

2 Velocity and acceleration
The speed of an object in a particular direction is called its **velocity**. The rate at which the velocity of an object changes is called its **acceleration**. The units of acceleration are **metres per second squared** (m/s^2). Acceleration can be calculated like this:

$$\text{acceleration} = \frac{\textbf{change in velocity}}{\textbf{time taken}}$$

3 Velocity–time graphs
The **slope** of a velocity–time graph represents acceleration. The **steeper** the slope the higher the acceleration.

You need to be able to construct velocity–time graphs for a body moving with a constant velocity or a constant acceleration.

4 More about motion graphs
The **area** under a velocity–time graph represents the **distance** travelled.

You need to be able to:
- calculate the speed of a body from the slope of a distance–time graph
- calculate the acceleration of a body from the slope of a velocity–time graph
- calculate the distance travelled by a body from a velocity–time graph.

A2 How do we make things speed up or slow down?

1 Applying forces
When two bodies **interact**, the forces they exert on each other are **equal** and **opposite**. A number of forces acting on a body may be replaced by a **single force** which has the **same effect** on the body as the original forces all acting together. The force is called the **resultant** force.

2 Staying still
If the **resultant** force acting on a stationary body is **zero**, the body will remain **stationary**.

3 Moving at constant speed
Air resistance and water resistance are **friction** forces. They always act in the **opposite** direction to movement. If the **resultant force** acting on a moving body is **zero**, the body will continue to move at the **same speed** and in the **same direction**.

4 Accelerating
If the **resultant** force acting on a stationary body is not zero, the body will **accelerate** in the direction of the resultant force. If the resultant **force** acting on a **moving** body is not zero, the body will accelerate in the **direction** of the resultant force. This may cause the body to **speed up**, **slow down** or **change direction**.

5 Force, mass and acceleration
Force, mass and acceleration are related by the formula

$$\underset{\text{(newtons, N)}}{\textbf{force}} = \underset{\text{(kilograms, kg)}}{\textbf{mass}} \times \underset{\textbf{(metres/second}^2\textbf{, m/s}^2\textbf{)}}{\textbf{acceleration}}$$

6 Stop that car!
The higher your **speed**, the greater the braking **force** needed to stop in a given **distance**.

$$\underset{\text{distance}}{\text{Stopping}} = \underset{\text{distance}}{\textbf{thinking}} + \underset{\text{distance}}{\textbf{braking}}$$

A driver's reaction time can be affected by tiredness, drugs and **alcohol**. A skid is more likely when the roads are **wet** or **icy**, or the tyres are **worn**.

7 It's a drag!

When a car travels at a steady speed, the frictional forces **balance** the **driving force**. The faster a body moves through a **fluid**, the greater the **drag** force which acts on it. A body falling through a fluid initially **accelerates** owing to the force of gravity. Eventually the **resultant** force on the body will be zero and it will fall at its **terminal velocity**.

You need to be able to draw and interpret velocity–time graphs for bodies that reach terminal velocity, including a consideration of the forces acting on the body.

8 Mass and weight

An object always has the same mass. We measure this in **kilograms**. The weight of an object is the force of gravity that acts on it. We measure this in **newtons**. On Earth, the force of gravity is about **10** N/kg. We call this the Earth's **gravitational field strength**.

You need to be able to calculate the weight of a body using the formula

weight　=　mass　×　gravitational field strength
(newtons, N)　(kilograms, kg)　(newtons/kilogram, N/kg)

A3 What happens to movement energy?

1 Doing work

When a force moves an object, **energy** is transferred and **work** is done. You can calculate the amount of work done like this:

work done　=　**force**　×　distance moved
(joules, J)　(newtons, N)　**(metres, m)**

Work done against friction is mainly transferred as **heat**.

2 Giving it energy

Elastic potential energy is the energy stored in an object when work is done on the object to change its **shape**. The **kinetic energy** of a body depends on its **mass** and its **speed**.

You can calculate the kinetic energy of a body with the formula

kinetic energy =　×　**mass**　×　**speed**^{2}
(joules, J)　(kilograms, kg)　(m/s)^2

3 Energy thrills

H There is nothing new for you to <u>remember</u> in this section.

You need to be able to discuss the transformation of kinetic energy to other forms of energy in particular situations.

A4 What is momentum?

1 Momentum

You can calculate the momentum of an object with the formula

momentum　=　**mass**　×　**velocity**
(kilogram metre/　(kilograms, kg)　(metres/second,
second, kg m/s)　　　　　　　　m/s)

Momentum has both **magnitude** and **direction**. A force acting on a body that is moving, or able to move, changes its **momentum**.

H You can calculate the change of momentum with the formula

change in momentum　=　**force**　×　**time**
(kilogram metre/　　(newtons, N)　(second, s)
second, kg m/s)

2 Explosions

Momentum is **conserved** in any explosion provided no **external** forces act on the exploding bodies.

You need to be able to use the conservation of momentum to calculate the mass, velocity or momentum of a body involved in an explosion.

3 Collisions

Momentum is **conserved** in any collision provided no **external** forces act on the colliding bodies.

You need to be able to use the conservation of momentum to calculate the mass, velocity or momentum of a body involved in a collision. You need to be able to use the ideas of momentum to explain safety features.

A5 What is static electricity?

1 **Electricity that can make your hair stand on end**
When you rub two **different** materials together, they become **charged** with electricity. This is called **static** electricity. There are two types of charge, called **positive** (+) and **negative** (–). Charges of the same type **repel** each other. Charges of different types **attract** each other. We say that **like** charges repel and **unlike** charges attract.

2 **Why rubbing things together produces electricity**
When two different materials are rubbed together, **electrons** are rubbed off one material and onto the other. One, or both, of the materials must be an electrical **insulator**. Each electron carries a small, **negative** electrical charge. The material that gains electrons becomes **negatively** charged. The material that loses electrons becomes **positively** charged. These two charges are exactly **equal** in size.

3 **Making use of static electricity**
Electrostatic charges can be useful, for example in a **photocopier** and a **smoke precipitator**.

You need to be able to explain how static electricity is used in the operation of devices such as the photocopier and the smoke precipitator.

4 **Conductors and insulators**
Electrical charges can move easily through some substances, for example **metals**. The rate of flow of electrical charge is called the **current**. We can **discharge** a charged body by connecting it to **earth** with a **conductor**. **Electrons** then flow through the conductor to the earth.

5 **Danger from sparks**
The greater the charge on a body, the greater the **potential difference** between the body and **earth**. If the potential difference becomes high enough, a **spark** may jump across the gap between the body and any **earthed conductor** which is brought near it.

You need to be able to explain why static electricity is dangerous in some situations and how precautions can be taken to ensure that the electrostatic charge is discharged safely.

A6 What does the current through an electrical circuit depend on?

1 **Circuit diagrams**
We use **symbols** to show **components** in circuit diagrams.

You need to know all the circuit symbols in the table at the top of page 256. You need to be able to draw and to interpret circuit diagrams like you have on these pages.

2 **How does current change with voltage?**
A current–**potential-difference** graph shows how the **current** through a **component** varies with the potential difference across it. The current–potential-difference graphs for a resistor, a diode and a filament lamp are as shown.

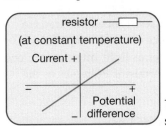

The resistance **stays the same**.

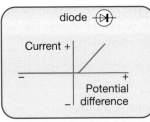

Resistance is low in one direction but **very high** in the other.

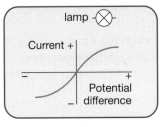

As the filament gets hotter, its resistance **increases**.

3   Measuring resistance

The current through a resistor (at a constant temperature) is **directly proportional** to the **potential difference** across the resistor. Potential difference, current and resistance are related by the formula

potential difference = **current × resistance**

You can find the **resistance** of a component by measuring the current through and the potential difference across the component. The current through a **component** depends on its **resistance**. The greater the resistance, the **smaller** the current for a given **potential difference**.

4   Resistances that change

The resistance of a filament lamp **increases** as the temperature of the **filament** increases. The current through a **diode** flows in one direction only. The diode has a very high **resistance** in the reverse direction. The resistance of a **light dependent resistor** (LDR) decreases as **light intensity** increases. The resistance of a **thermistor** decreases as the **temperature** increases.

5   How many 'batteries' do I need?

To get a bigger voltage, you can connect more than one cell **in series**. This is called a **battery**. The total potential difference is the **sum** of the potential difference of each **cell**.

6   Parallel circuits

For components connected in parallel

■ the potential difference across each component is the **same**
■ the **total** current through the whole circuit is the **sum** of the currents through the **separate** components.

7   Series circuits

For components connected in series

■ the total resistance is the **sum** of the resistance of each component
■ there is the **same** current through each component
■ the **total potential difference** of the supply is **shared** between the components.

8   Using electrical devices

There is nothing new for you to <u>remember</u> in this section. You have been applying ideas that you have met before. You may be asked questions like these in tests and examinations.

You need to be able to apply the principles of basic electrical circuits to practical situations.

A7 What is mains electricity and how can it be used safely?

1   V/a.c./d.c./Hz – what do they all mean?

Cells and batteries supply current which always passes in the same **direction**. This is called **direct current** (**d.c.**). An **alternating** current (**a.c.**) is one which is constantly **changing** direction. Mains electricity is an a.c. supply.

H   In the UK it has a **frequency** of 50 cycles per second (**50 hertz**). The UK mains supply is about 230 **volts**.

You need to be able to interpret oscilloscope pictures for a direct current and an alternating current in the way that you have on these pages.

2   Wiring a three-pin plug

Most electrical appliances are connected to the mains using cable and a **three-pin** plug.

H   The current is supplied through the **live** and **neutral** pins. The neutral pin is at **zero** potential with respect to earth. The live pin alternates between **positive** and **negative** potential with respect to the neutral pin. The **earth** pin is there for safety.
The colour code for the cable wires is: **brown** – live, **blue** – neutral, **green** and **yellow** – earth.

You need to be able to recognise errors in the wiring of a three-pin plug.

3   Some 'do's' and 'don'ts' that could save your life

There is nothing new for you to <u>remember</u> in this section.

You need to be able to spot whenever mains electricity is being used dangerously. You will find more examples on pages 267 and 275.

4 **Why do plugs have fuses?**
   If an electrical fault causes too great a current, the circuit should be switched off by a **fuse** or a **circuit breaker**. When the current exceeds a safe value the fuse **melts**, breaking the circuit. Appliances with metal cases are usually **earthed**. The earth wire and fuse protect the **appliance** and the user.

A8 Electric power

1 **Electric power**
   When a current flows through a resistor, electrical energy is transformed into **heat** energy. The rate at which energy is transformed in a device is called the **power**. Power is measured in watts (**W**) or in kilowatts (**kW**).

   $$\text{power (watts)} = \frac{\textbf{energy transferred (joules)}}{\textbf{time taken (seconds)}}$$

2 **Watts, volts and amps**
   Power, potential difference and current are related by the formula

   power = **potential difference** (p.d.) × **current**
   (watts)   (volts)   (amperes)

   You need to be able to calculate the current through an appliance from its power and the potential difference of the supply and from this determine the size of fuse needed.

3 **Understanding electrical energy**
   Energy transformed, potential difference and charge are related by the formula

   energy transformed = **potential difference** × **charge**

   The amount of electrical charge that flows is related to current and time by the formula

   charge = **current** × **time**

A9 What happens to radioactive substances when they decay?

1 **Inside atoms**
   In an atom the number of **electrons** is equal to the number of **protons** in the nucleus. The atom has no net electrical **charge**. The relative masses and electric charges of protons, neutrons and electrons are:

Particle	Relative mass (mass units)	Relative charge (charge units)
proton	1	+1
neutron	1	0
electron	1/2000	−1

   H You need to be able to explain how the Rutherford and Marsden scattering experiment led to the 'plum pudding' model of the atom being replaced by the nuclear model.

2 **Can atoms change?**
   All atoms of a particular element have the same number of **protons**. Atoms of different **elements** have different numbers of protons. Atoms of the same element which have different numbers of neutrons are called **isotopes**. The total number of protons and neutrons in an atom is called its **mass number**. Atoms may lose or gain electrons to form charged particles called **ions**.

   You need to know the effects of alpha and beta decay on radioactive nuclei.

3 **How much harmful radiation do you get?**
   The bigger the dose of radiation you get, the greater the risk of **cancer**. Our bodies receive radiation all the time from **radioactive** substances in the air, the ground, food, water and building materials. Our bodies also receive **cosmic** radiation from space. All this radiation is called **background** radiation.

A10 What are nuclear fission and nuclear fusion?

1   **What are nuclear fission and nuclear fusion?**
    Nuclear **fission** is the splitting of an atomic nucleus.
    Fission may be caused by a **neutron** entering a
    nucleus of uranium or plutonium. The nucleus
    undergoing fission **splits** into two **smaller** nuclei and
    two or three **neutrons**, and **energy** is released.
    The neutrons may go on to start a **chain reaction**.
    Uranium-235 and **plutonium-239** are fuels used in
    nuclear reactors. Nuclear **fusion** is the joining of two
    atomic nuclei to form a larger one. Nuclear fusion is
    the process by which energy is released in **stars**.

    You need to be able to sketch a labelled diagram to
    illustrate how a chain reaction may occur.

Biology

Some words are used on lots of pages. Only the page numbers of the main examples are shown. You will find the *italic* words in the definitions elsewhere in the Glossary/index.

A

abort, abortion to *terminate* or end a *pregnancy* 99

absorb, absorption when *cells* or blood take in dissolved food or *oxygen* 13, 19, 51, 61

aerobic respiration using *oxygen* to break food down to release energy 46

air sacs gas exchange surfaces at the end of *bronchioles* in the *lungs* 17

allele a form of a gene, e.g. there is an allele for blue eyes 86, 88–89

alveoli small *air sacs* in the *lungs*; one is called an alveolus 60

amino acids carbon compounds that *proteins* are built from 29, 48, 55, 61, 91

amniocentesis a medical procedure where a sample of fetal cells from the *amniotic fluid* surrounding a *fetus* is taken for genetic testing 99

amniotic fluid the fluid surrounding a *fetus* in the *uterus* (*womb*) 99

amylase an *enzyme* that *digests starch*; it changes starch to a sugar called maltose 44, 52, 53

anus the opening at the end of the *digestive system* 51, 55

B

bacteria *microorganisms* made of *cells* with a *chromosome* which is not in a *nucleus*; one is called a bacterium 40, 56

Banting, Frederick (1891–1941) 71

bases the pairs of chemicals that link the two strands of *DNA* molecules; base A always pairs with base T, and base G pairs with base C 90, 91, 92

Best, Charles (1899–1978) 71

bile a substance secreted by the *liver*; it neutralises acid and *emulsifies fats* in the *small intestine* 54, 55

biodegradable made of materials which *microorganisms* can break down or *decay* 39

biomass the material that plants and animals are made of 33, 34

bladder a stretchy bag which stores *urine* 61

blood glucose the glucose in blood 68–69, 70, 72, 73

blood group a group of people whose blood has the same marker proteins; within the group, blood can safely be transferred in a *blood transfusion* 87, 88–89

blood transfusion the transfer of blood from a *donor* into the circulating blood of a *recipient*; the *blood groups* of the donor and recipient must be compatible or the *red blood cells* will clump together 88

body temperature inner or core body temperature; in humans, it is about 37 °C 35, 36, 49, 64, 65, 66, 67

bone marrow a *tissue* which lies in the centre of some bones; it is where blood *cells* are made and is a source of *stem cells* 81, 82

breathe, breathing to take air in and out of the *lungs* 60, 62, 96

bronchi tubes which branch from the *windpipe* into the *bronchioles* in the *lungs*; one is called a bronchus 60

bronchioles tubes which branch from *bronchi* into each *lung* 60

C

capillary a narrow blood vessel with walls only one *cell* thick; the plural is capillaries 10, 17, 65, 67, 102

carbohydrases *enzymes* that *digest carbohydrates* 45, 53, 58

carbohydrates part of our food which we use for energy, e.g. *starch* and sugars 42, 55, 58, 69, 72

differentiate, differentiation when *cells* become *specialised* 80, 81

diffuse, diffusion the spreading of liquids and gases from where the concentration is high to where it is low 16–17, 18, 60

digest, digestion to break down large insoluble molecules into small soluble molecules, e.g. in the *digestive system* 50–51, 52–53, 54–55, 56, 58, 96

digestive enzymes *enzymes* that *digest* or break down large food molecules 51, 52–53, 54–55

digestive glands *glands* that produce digestive juices 51, 96

digestive system all the *organs* which are concerned with the *digestion* of food 9, 55

disease, disorder when some part of a plant or animal isn't working properly 94–95, 96, 97, 98, 101, 102

DNA see *deoxyribonucleic acid*

DNA fingerprinting using some of the patterns of *bases* in *DNA* to identify individuals 92–93

dominant an *allele* that can hide the effect of another (*recessive*) allele 74, 88, 94, 95, 102, 103

donor someone who donates or gives, e.g. donation of blood or body *organs* 81, 88

E

ecosystem all the living and non-living things in an area 42, 43

effector a part of the body which brings about a response, such as a *muscle* or a *gland* 66

egg (cell) the female *gamete* (*sex cell*); also called an ovum 11, 76–77, 83, 84, 85, 100, 101

embryo a plant or animal at an early stage of development, before all its *organs* have started to grow; up to 6–8 weeks in humans 80, 83, 100–101

embryo screening examining a *cell* from each *embryo* in a series of embryos to identify *genetic* disorders 100, 101

embryo selection when *egg cells* are *fertilised* outside the body and only those *embryos* with certain *genes* are selected and *implanted* in the *womb* 101

embryonic stem cells unspecialised *cells* from early *embryos* 80, 82, 83

emulsify to break down *fat* into tiny droplets 55

environment the surroundings or conditions in which a plant or animal lives 16, 39, 62, 86

enzymes *protein* substances made in *cells* which speed up chemical reactions; they are *catalysts* 44–45, 50–51, 56–57, 58–59, 92, 96

ethical describes actions based on a generally accepted set of principles or values as to how we should behave or make decisions 83

excrete, excretion to get rid of *waste* produced in *cells* 61, 70

F

F₁ generation first generation offspring 74

F₂ generation offspring resulting from a cross between two individuals from the *F₁ generation* 74

faeces undigested *waste* which passes out through the *anus* 35, 55, 62

family tree a diagram showing the *inheritance pattern* of a *characteristic* through several generations of a family 75, 95

fat part of our food which we use for energy and for making *cell membranes* 42, 50, 52, 55

fatty acids one of the building blocks of *fats* 50, 52, 55

fertilise, fertilisation when a male *sex cell* joins with a female sex cell to start a new plant or animal; it forms a single *cell* which gets half its *chromosomes* from each parent 76, 85, 86

fertilisers you add these to soil to provide the minerals plants need to grow; some are natural, e.g. manure; others are artificial, e.g. potassium nitrate 25, 27, 41

P

palisade cells *cells* that form a layer just below the upper epidermis of a leaf; they contain more *chloroplasts* than other cells in a leaf   14, 21

pancreas the *organ* which makes pancreatic juice and *insulin*   9, 51, 53, 54, 55, 68, 69, 70, 71

partially permeable membrane a membrane which allows the passage of some substances but not others   18

phloem a plant *tissue* which transports sugars   14, 15

photosynthesis the process in which plants use light energy to make glucose from *carbon dioxide* and water   20–21, 22–23, 24, 42, 43, 47

placenta the *organ* through which a *fetus* takes in food and *oxygen* and gets rid of *waste*   99

platelets fragments of *cells* that are needed for clotting blood   81

polydactyly an *inherited* condition in which there are extra fingers or toes   103

pregnant, pregnancy expecting a baby   99, 100

producer an organism (usually a green plant) which makes its own food   30

protease an *enzyme* that *digests* proteins   45, 52, 54, 56, 59

proteins part of our food which we need for growth and repair; *genes* control the order of the *amino acids* which make up *proteins*   29, 42, 44, 47, 48, 50, 54, 55, 91

protein synthesis making *proteins*   10, 47

Punnett square one way of showing the results of a genetic cross   95

pyramid of biomass a pyramid-shaped diagram showing the decrease in *biomass* as you go up a *food chain*   33, 37

pyramid of numbers a pyramid-shaped diagram showing how the numbers of organisms change as you go up a *food chain*   31, 33

R

receptors sensory *cells* – that is, cells which detect stimuli   66

recessive an *allele* whose effect is hidden if a *dominant* allele is present   74, 88, 95, 96, 102, 103

recipient someone who receives, e.g. an *organ* from an organ *donor* or blood in a *blood transfusion*   88

recycle, recycling when materials are used over and over again   39, 40, 43

red blood cells the *cells* in the blood which carry *oxygen*   10, 19, 78, 81, 88, 102

rejection when the *immune* system starts to destroy a *transplanted organ*   82

relax in the case of a *muscle*, to become longer and thinner; the opposite of *contract*   8, 49, 65

respiration the breakdown of food to release energy in living *cells*   28, 29, 34, 42, 43, 46, 62

ribosomes the structures in a *cell* which make *proteins*   10, 91

root hairs the tiny hairs just behind root tips in a plant; they increase the surface area for *absorption* of water and minerals   18, 19

S

salivary glands *glands* in the mouth which produce a digestive juice called saliva   51, 53

Sankey diagram a diagram that shows energy transfers   35

sex cells *cells* which join to form new plants or animals; also called *gametes*   76, 84, 86, 87, 89

sickle cell disorder an *inherited disorder* of *red blood cells* caused by a *recessive allele*   102–103

small intestine the narrow part of the intestine that lies between the *stomach* and the *large intestine*; it is where *digestion* finishes and *absorption* takes place   9, 51, 53, 54, 55

Chemistry

Some words are used on lots of pages. Only the page numbers of the main examples are shown. You will find the *italic* words in the definitions elsewhere in the Glossary/index.

chlorine an *element* in *Group 7* of the *periodic table* – the *halogens* 114–115, 116–118, 119, 125, 139, 195

closed system in a closed system, both *reactants* and *products* are prevented from leaving the *reaction* vessel in an *equilibrium* reaction, e.g. *ammonia* production 153, 181

combustion another word for *burning* 176

completion when all of the *reactants* turn to *products* in a *reversible reaction* 149

compound a substance made from *atoms* of different *elements* joined together by *covalent* or *ionic bonds* 140, 142–145

concentrated, concentration a concentrated *solution* is a strong solution containing a lot of dissolved substance 160, 171, 174–175

conditions the conditions of a *chemical reaction* are the *temperature* and *pressure* at which it takes place 153, 182, 186

conductor a substance that allows electricity or thermal (heat) energy to pass through it easily 121, 129

copper a useful *metal* because it is a good *conductor* and not very *reactive* 190, 192, 194, 198–199

copper sulfate we use a *solution* of copper sulfate when we purify *copper* by *electrolysis*; we can also use it as a test for *water* – when a substance containing water is added to anhydrous copper sulfate, it changes colour from white to blue 180, 198

correlation a link between two factors 189

corrosive a corrosive substance, for example an *acid*, can dissolve or eat away other materials 151, 197

covalent bond the type of chemical bond that forms between *atoms* because they share one or more pairs of *electrons* 119, 126–127

crystallise, crystallisation the method we use to produce a *solid salt* from a *solution* of that salt 202

D

delocalised electrons *electrons* from the highest *energy levels* of *atoms*; they are free to move through the whole structure of a material; also called free electrons 128–129

diamond a very *hard* form of the *element carbon* 120, 126

dilute, dilution a dilute *solution* is a weak solution containing very little dissolved substance 160, 171

E

electrodes these supply an electric current to a *molten* or dissolved *ionic compound* so that *electrolysis* can occur; the *products* of the electrolysis form at the electrodes 129, 191, 192–196, 198, 199

electrolysis the process of splitting up a *molten* or dissolved *ionic compound* by passing an electric current through it 191–199

electron arrangement the arrangement of the *electrons* in *atoms* into different *energy levels* (or shells) 109, 113

electrons *particles* with a negative electrical charge and very little *mass* that surround the *nucleus* of an *atom* 104, 108–111, 121, 128–129, 192–193, 196, 199

electrostatic attractions forces of attraction between *particles* with opposite charges 121

element a substance that is made of only one type of *atom* 105–108

empirical formula the simplest *formula* for a *compound* 144–145

endothermic reaction a *chemical reaction* that takes in energy from its surroundings, often as thermal (heat) energy 178, 181, 182, 183

energy level the *electrons* in an *atom* are arranged around the *nucleus* in energy levels; the top energy level is the one on the outside of the atom 108–111, 118

environment the surroundings or conditions in which plants and animals live 157, 186–187

enzymes *catalysts* that are found in living cells 167

equilibrium the point in a *reversible reaction* when the *rate of reaction* of the forward *reaction* (*reactants → products*) exactly balances the rate of the reverse reaction (products → reactants); usually represented by ⇌   152–153, 182–185

exothermic reaction a *chemical reaction* that transfers energy to the surroundings, often as thermal (heat) energy   176–177, 181, 182, 183

F

fertilisers substances put into soil to make crops grow better   150, 151, 206

formula the *symbols* and numbers that tell you the number of *atoms* of each *element* in a *compound*   117, 141, 144–145

free electrons see *delocalised electrons*

fuels substances that are *burned* to release energy   176

G

gases substances that spread out to fill all the space available   161, 165, 168–169, 171, 175, 184–185

giant structures structures which consist of a large, usually three-dimensional lattice of *atoms* or *ions* held together by *covalent* or *ionic bonds*   120–121

graphite a form of *carbon* that is a *conductor* of electricity   126–127, 129

group a vertical column in the *periodic table*; *elements* in the same group have the same number of *electrons* in their highest *energy levels*   106, 107

Group 0 elements also known as the *noble gases*   107, 111

Group 1 elements also known as the *alkali metals*   107, 112–113

Group 7 elements also known as the *halogens*   107, 114–115

H

Haber, Fritz (1868–1934)   150

Haber process a process for making *ammonia* from *hydrogen* and *nitrogen*   150–154, 181–185, 186, 187

half equations these show what happens at each *electrode* during *electrolysis*   196

halogens *reactive* non-metal *elements* in *Group 7* of the *periodic table*, e.g. *chlorine* and *bromine*   107, 114–115, 195

hard a hard material is difficult to scratch, e.g. *diamond* is a very hard form of *carbon*   126, 130

hydrochloric acid an *acid* that is used to make *salts* called *chlorides*   162, 172–173, 203, 204, 205

hydrogen a *gas* that *burns* to produce *water*; its *atoms* are the smallest of all   105, 106, 108, 118, 119, 139, 194

hydrogen ions these *ions* make *solutions acidic*; we write them as $H^+(aq)$ 207

hydroxide ions these *ions* make *solutions alkaline*; we write them as $OH^-(aq)$ 207

I

ibuprofen a drug which is widely used to relieve pain and inflammation   156–157, 167

indicators substances whose colour depends on the *pH* of the *solution* they are in   202, 207

insoluble not able to dissolve; the opposite of *soluble*   200, 205

intermolecular forces forces between *molecules*   123

iodine an *element* in *Group 7* of the *periodic table* – the *halogens*   114, 122, 195

ionic bond the type of chemical bond that forms between positively and negatively charged *ions*   120, 190

ionic compounds *compounds* made from *ions*   117, 124–125, 190, 194–195

ions *atoms* that have gained or lost *electrons* and so have either a negative or a positive electrical charge   110–111, 113, 115, 121, 192, 201, 207

Physics

Some words are used on lots of pages. Only the page numbers of the main examples are shown. You will find the *italic* words in the definitions elsewhere in the Glossary/index.

A

A short for *ampere*   255

a.c. short for *alternating current*   273

accelerate, acceleration the rate at which the *speed* or *velocity* of a moving object increases; it can be calculated from the *gradient* of a *velocity–time graph*   210–211, 214, 222–225

air resistance the *drag* (*friction*) *force* on an object moving through air   220, 228–229

alpha (α) one of the types of *radiation* emitted when the *nucleus* of a radio-isotope *decays*; it consists of *particles*, each of which is the nucleus of a *helium atom*   287, 289

alternating current an electric *current* that constantly changes direction with a particular *frequency*; *a.c.* for short   273

ammeter a meter that is used to measure electric *currents*   255, 256, 258

ampere the size of an electric *current* is measured in units called amperes; *A* or amp for short   255

atoms all substances are made of atoms; atoms have a *nucleus* that is made up of *protons* and *neutrons* and that is surrounded by *electrons*   286–289

attract, attraction the action of a *force* that pulls things together, e.g. magnets or opposite electrical *charges*   216, 244–245, 249

B

background radiation the *radiation* from *radioactive* sources that is around us all the time   290

battery two or more electrical *cells* joined together; often wrongly used to refer to a single cell   254, 256, 264–265, 285

beta (β) one of the types of *radiation* emitted when the *nucleus* of a radio-isotope *decays*; it consists of *particles* called *electrons*   289

braking distance the distance a vehicle travels during the time in which a *braking force* acts to bring it to rest   227

braking force the *force* that slows down a vehicle, i.e. makes it *decelerate*   226

C

C short for *coulomb*   284

cable grip the part of an electrical *three-pin plug* that takes the strain if the cable is pulled   275

calibrate, calibration to give values to the scale of a measuring instrument or device, e.g. a *thermistor* must be calibrated so that temperature can be found by measuring its *resistance*   270

carbon the chemical element with *proton number* 6   288

cell a cell uses chemicals to produce a *potential difference*; when it is connected to a complete *circuit*, it causes a *current* to flow; two or more cells connected together form a *battery*   256, 264–265, 285

chain reaction a reaction that continues by itself once it has been started, e.g. *nuclear fission*   292

charge to give something a net electrical charge; electrical charge can be *positive* or *negative charge*; electric *currents* are caused by moving charges; charge is measured in units called *coulombs*   244–247, 250, 252, 284

charged particles *particles* that possess an electrical *charge*   286–287

circuit an arrangement of *components* connected by conducting wires in such a way that a *current* can flow through them   256–257, 258, 266–269

circuit breaker a device that protects an electric *circuit* by switching off a *current* if it is too big; it is then reset   279

circuit diagram a diagram of a *circuit* in which the *components* are shown by *circuit symbols* 256–257

circuit symbols a way of showing electrical *components*; they make it easy to draw *circuit diagrams* 256

component a part designed to do a certain job in an electrical *circuit*, e.g. a *filament lamp* or a *switch* 256

conduction
1 electrical – the flow of an electric *current* through a substance 250
2 thermal – the transfer of *thermal energy* (heat) from the hotter parts of a substance to colder parts without the substance itself moving

conductor a substance which readily allows electricity or *thermal energy* (heat) to pass through it (*conduction*); metals are good conductors 250–251

copper a reddish metal that is a good *conductor* and is easily made into wires 250, 275

cosmic radiation harmful *radiation* that comes from space 290

coulomb the unit of electrical *charge*; the amount of charge that flows when a *current* of 1 *ampere* flows for 1 second; *C* for short 284

current a flow of electrical *charge*; current is measured in units called *amperes* 250–251, 254–255, 258–259, 261, 267, 268, 272–273, 278, 283

current–potential-difference graph a graph that shows how the *current* through a *component* depends on the *potential difference* across the component 258–259

current rating (for a *fuse*) the value of the *current* at which the fuse is designed to break a *circuit* by melting 283

curved paths paths that are not straight lines but curved, e.g. like an arc of a circle 223

cycle one complete wave of an *alternating current*; the number of cycles each second is the *frequency* 273

D

d.c. short for *direct current* 272

decay what happens to the unstable *nucleus* of a radio-isotope *atom* when it emits *radiation* 289

decelerate, deceleration the rate at which the *speed* or *velocity* of a moving object decreases; the opposite of *acceleration* 212, 222

diode an electrical *component* that lets a *current* pass through it in one direction only 256, 259, 262

direct current an electric *current* that always flows in the same direction; *d.c.* for short 272

directly proportional describes two quantities that are linked so that a change in one produces a proportional change in the other, e.g. if one quantity doubles, so does the other 260

discharge to reduce the *charge* on an object to zero 251, 285

distance–time graph a graph of the distance moved by an object plotted against time; the *gradient* of the graph represents *speed* 208–209, 214

drag a *friction force* in a *fluid*, e.g. air resistance or water resistance 228

driving force the *force* that propels a vehicle to make it *accelerate* and/or to overcome *friction* 228

E

earth
1 to connect something to the Earth with an electrical *conductor* 251, 278
2 one of the three wires in a *three-pin plug*; in the flex connected to electrical appliances, the earth (E) wire is covered with green and yellow plastic 274

elastic potential energy the energy that is stored in things which are stretched or squashed 234, 236

electrons tiny *particles* with a *negative charge* (–1) and very little *mass*; in an *atom*, electrons move around the *nucleus*; they move when a *current* flows through a solid substance (usually a metal) 246–247, 250, 251, 286, 287, 289

electrostatic generator a machine that generates *static electric charge* on objects   245, 252

F

filament lamp a lamp that emits light because a metal filament becomes very hot when an electric *current* passes through it   256, 259, 262, 280

fluids a general term for liquids and gases; states of matter that can flow   228

force any push or pull that changes, or tends to change, the motion of an object; force is measured in units called *newtons*   216–225, 226, 228, 243

frequency the number of complete waves or vibrations each second; frequency is measured in units called *hertz* or *cycles* per second   273

friction a *force* which acts on an object in the opposite direction to the direction it is moving (or tending to move)   220–221, 226, 233

fuse a fuse protects an electrical *circuit* by melting if the *current* is too big, so breaking the circuit; the fuse then has to be replaced   256, 278–279, 283

G

Geiger, Hans (1882–1945)   287

gradient the slope of a graph; on a *distance–time graph*, the gradient represents *speed*; on a *velocity–time graph*, the gradient represents *acceleration*   214

gravitational field strength the *force* of *gravity* per unit *mass*; the gravitational field strength at the Earth's surface is approximately $10\,N/kg$ 231

gravitational potential energy the energy that is transferred either to an object when it is lifted against the *force* of *gravity* or from an object as it falls because of gravity   233, 234, 236

gravity the *force* of *attraction* between two objects because of their *mass*; for this force to be big enough to be noticeable, at least one of the bodies must have a very large mass   216, 230–231, 233

H

helium the chemical element with *proton number* 2   287, 288, 293

hertz the unit of *frequency*; the number of complete vibrations, oscillations or *cycles* per second; *Hz* for short   273

hydrogen the chemical element with *proton number* 1   293

Hz short for *hertz*   273

I

in parallel describes an arrangement of two *components* in a *circuit* such that the *current* divides to flow partly through one component and partly through the other   254, 266–267

in series describes an arrangement of two *components* in a *circuit* such that the *current* flows through one component after the other   255, 264, 268–269

insulation a material which is a poor *conductor* (has a low conductivity); a layer of *insulator* is placed around an electrical conductor to prevent shocks and short circuits   274

insulator a substance which does not allow electricity or *thermal energy* (heat) to pass through it by *conduction*   246, 250

ions *atoms* or molecules that have acquired an electrical *charge* by gaining or losing one or more *electrons*   250, 289

ionise, ionisation to produce an *ion* by causing an *atom* or a molecule to gain or lose *electrons*   289

isotopes *atoms* of the same element that have different numbers of *neutrons* in their *nucleus*   288

J

J short for *joule*   232

joule energy or *work* is measured in joules; 1 joule is the work done when a force of 1 *newton* moves through a distance of 1 metre; *J* for short   232

K

kilowatt *power* is measured in units called *watts*; 1 kilowatt is 1000 watts; *kW* for short   280

kinetic energy the energy an object has because it is moving   234–235, 236

kW short for *kilowatt*   280

L

light dependent resistor (LDR) an electrical *component* whose *resistance* decreases as the intensity of the light that falls on it increases   263

live one of the two wires in the *mains supply* that carries the *current*; it has a varying *potential difference* relative to the *neutral* and *earth* wires; in the flex connected to electrical appliances, the live (L) wire is covered with brown plastic   274, 278

M

mains supply the electricity that is supplied to our homes   267, 272, 274, 276–277

Marsden, Ernest (1889–1970)   287

mass the amount of matter in an object; mass is measured in units called kilograms (kg)   224–225, 230–231, 288

mass number the total number of *protons* and *neutrons* in a *nucleus*   288, 289

momentum the *mass* of an object multiplied by its *velocity*   238–243

N

N short for *newton*   230

negative charge the electrical *charge* on *electrons* and on objects that have gained electrons   245, 246–247, 286, 289

neutral one of the two wires in the *mains supply* that carries the *current*; it has hardly any *potential difference* relative to the *earth* wire; in the flex connected to electrical appliances, the neutral (N) wire is covered with blue plastic   274

neutron one of the types of *particle* found in the *nucleus* of *atoms*; it has the same *mass* as a *proton* but it has no electrical *charge*   286, 288–289, 292–293

newton *forces* are measured in units called newtons; a force of 1 newton will *accelerate* a *mass* of 1 kilogram at a rate of 1 metre per second squared; *N* for short   230

nuclear fission the deliberate splitting of an unstable radio-isotope *atom* by bombarding it with *neutrons*; *thermal energy* (heat) is released   292

nuclear fusion the nuclear reaction that occurs in the Sun and other stars when small *atomic nuclei* join together (fuse) to form larger ones; *thermal energy* (heat) is released   293

nuclear reactor the central part of a nuclear power station in which the nuclear fuel undergoes *nuclear fission*   292

nucleus the central part of an *atom*; it is made from *protons* and *neutrons*; the plural is nuclei   286, 287, 289, 292–293

O

ohm the unit of electrical *resistance*; if a *potential difference* of 1 *volt* produces a *current* of 1 *ampere*, the resistance is 1 ohm; Ω for short   260

oscilloscope a device that shows a varying *voltage* as a graph on a screen, e.g. voltage either from an *a.c.* supply or produced by a microphone from a sound wave   272, 273

P

parallel circuit a *circuit* where *components* are connected *in parallel*; an electric *current* flows through each component separately   257, 266–267

particle a tiny portion of matter   286–287, 289

p.d. short for *potential difference*   282

period the time for one *cycle* of an *alternating current*   273

Acknowledgements

We are grateful to the following for permission to reproduce photographs:

Cover image, l, r, Digital Vision, m Alfred Pasieka / SPL; 8t, B. Runk / S. Schoenberger / Grant Heilman Photography; 8b, Colorsport / Andrew Cowie; 12t, Dr Jeremy Burgess / SPL; 12b, 56, 69, 76, 84, Biophoto Associates; 16, Astrid & Hanns-Frieder Michler / SPL; 25, Garden Picture Library / Michael Howes; 27t, b, Holt Studios International Ltd / Alamy; 36t, Jay Freis / Imagebank; 36m, Natalie Fobes / Corbis; 36b, Vincent MacNamara / Alamy; 38t, Geoff DorÇ / Bruce Coleman Ltd; 38m, Dr Kari Lounatmaa / SPL; 38b, David Scharf / SPL; 40, Adrian Davies / Alamy; 44, 134b, Alfred Pasieka / SPL; 48, Professors P. Motta & T. Naguro / SPL; 62, Michael Wyndham Picture Collection; 63, Colorsport; 70, Cristina Pedrazzini / SPL; 71, Astrid Kage / SPL; 72, LWA-Stephen Welstead / Corbis; 73, Mark Sykes / SPL; 74, 107, SPL; 79, Science Pictures Limited / SPL; 80t, Dr Yorgos Nikas / SPL; 80m, J. C. Revy, Ism / SPL; 80b, Phototake Inc. / Alamy; 88t, Ed Reschke / Still Pictures; 88b, H. Rogers / Trip; 90, Science Source / SPL; 92, Philippe Psaila / SPL; 93, Michael Gilbert / SPL; 96, Cystic Fibrosis Trust; 100, Owen Franken / Corbis; 102t, Dr Gopal Murti / SPL; 102b, Omikron / SPL; 112, 114ml, mr, b, 119l, r, 130, 158r, 162 (all), 165, 168t, b, 176bl, br, 178t, 180t, b, 198t, b, 250, 279l, r, 283t, b, Andrew Lambert; 114t, Sciencephotos / Alamy; 120, Geoscience Features Picture Library; 126t, Lawrence Lawry / SPL; 126b, Andrew McClenaghan / SPL; 128, WR Publishing / Alamy; 131t, David Taylor / SPL; 131m, James L. Amos / Corbis; 131b, Eye Of Science / SPL; 132t, Susumu Nishinaga / SPL; 132b, BSIP, Theobald / SPL; 133, The Zoological Society of London; 134t, Tek Image / SPL; 135, J. Bernholc et al, North Carolina State University / SPL; 137, The Natural History Museum, London; 150, Mary Evans Picture Library; 151, Nigel Cattlin / Holt Studios International; 156, Charles Bach / SPL; 158l, Chinth Gryniewicz / Ecoscene; 158m, Michael Brooke; 166, Clive Freeman, The Royal Institution / SPL; 167, Dr Mark J. Winter / SPL; 176t, Graham Portlock; 177, Magrath Photography / SPL; 178b, 200, Andrew Lambert Photography / SPL; 186, Gabe Palmer / Alamy; 187, Time Life Pictures / Getty Images; 188t, m, b, AH Marks Ltd; 188tl, Agence Images / Alamy; 188tm, Martyn F. Chillmaid / SPL; 188tr, Photofusion Picture Library / Alamy; 201, Aflo Foto Agency / Alamy; 206, Geogphotos / Alamy; 208, Duomo / Corbis; 210, Sutton Motorsport Images; 213, 230, Corbis; 221t, Smiley N. Pool / Sports_NS / Dallas Morning News / Corbis; 221b, NASA / SPL; 226, Sutton Motorsport Images; 227, Eye Candy Images / Alamy; 228, Takeshi Takahara / SPL; 234t, Miles / zefa / Corbis; 234m, Dimitri Iundt / Corbis; 234b, Tony Wayrynen / NewSport / Corbis; 243tl, Rick Gayle / Corbis; 243tr, David Woods / Corbis; 243b, Tim Wright / Corbis; 251l, Kevin T. Gilbert / Corbis; 251r, James Marshall / Corbis; 253, Photograph courtesy of IBM UK Labs, Hursley; 280, Todd Gipstein / Corbis; 285t, David Glover; 285b, Vanessa Miles; 293, Ron Watts / Corbis.

Abbreviations: SPL, Science Photo Library.
Letters used with page numbers: b, bottom of the page; l, left-hand side of the page; m, middle of the page; r, right-hand side of the page; t, top of the page.

Picture research: Vanessa Miles